# THE
# SECRET
# SERVICE

# THE SECRET SERVICE

## THE HIDDEN HISTORY
## OF AN
## ENIGMATIC AGENCY

PHILIP H. MELANSON, PH.D. WITH PETER F. STEVENS

CARROLL & GRAF PUBLISHERS
NEW YORK

THE SECRET SERVICE
*THE HIDDEN HISTORY OF AN ENIGMATIC AGENCY*

Carroll & Graf Publishers
An Imprint of Avalon Publishing Group Inc.
161 William St., 16th Floor
New York, NY 10038

First Carroll & Graf cloth edition 2002
First Carroll & Graf trade paperback edition 2003

Library of Congress Cataloging-in-Publication Data is available.

ISBN: 0-7867-1251-1

Printed in the United States of America
Distributed by Publishers Group West

# CONTENTS

## PART ONE—THE EVOLUTION OF THE MISSION

## PART TWO—ON THE JOB

# THE
# SECRET
# SERVICE

# PART ONE

# THE EVOLUTION OF THE MISSION

## CHAPTER 1

# "DEATH TO TRAITORS"

*It should not be concluded that important events in the evolution of governmental programs take place prior to the time when the birth of a new agency is legitimatized by legislative enactment. On the contrary, existing agencies are undergoing a continual process of adaptation and change that may so transform them over a span of years as to make them into almost new organizations.*

*—Herbert A. Simon*

On July 5, 1865, in Washington, D.C., a tall, wiry man raised his right hand. Clean shaven in contrast to most men of the day, with thick, neatly parted brown hair, square-jawed William P. Wood, the former keeper of the city's infamous Old Capitol Prison, was sworn in by U.S. Secretary of the Treasury Hugh McCulloch as the head of a new agency. McCulloch entrusted Wood with a daunting mission: "Your main objective is to restore public confidence in the money of the country"—that is, to go after counterfeiters.

With those words, the U.S. Secret Service was officially born. However, nowhere in the fledgling agency's original mandate was the notion of protecting the president from harm. Protection of the nation's money supply was the mandate of the day for Wood and his men.

From its creation in the summer of 1865 until the present, the Secret Service was to protect something that the U.S. system may value even more than the lives of its political leaders—money. The presidential protection mission emerged much later in the agency's history and was a congressional afterthought. For Wood and his first band of agents, presidential protection was never a concern.

The United States faced an immense crisis as Wood assumed his new post. Counterfeiting, endemic throughout the just-ended Civil War, still bedeviled the federal government and posed a serious threat to the nation's banking system. By the time that Robert E. Lee had surrendered the Rebel

Army of Northern Virginia to Ulysses S. Grant on April 9, 1865, between one-third and one-half of all U.S. currency in circulation was counterfeit. Some sixteen hundred state banks designed and printed their own money at the start of the war, 1861, and with several thousand varieties of genuine currency flooding the nation, counterfeiters had a field day. All the notes were issued individually by each state. Criminals used bribery or influence to open a bank and print money, so counterfeiters grabbed the opportunity and hired printers to produce currency with a bank's name printed on it. With all the assorted notes in circulation, shopkeepers had difficulty determining the difference between bogus bills and genuine banknotes. Meanwhile, people hoarded coins, believing they were the only safe currency. Banks, in turn, had to print smaller-size bills (fractional currency): 3 cents, 5 cents, 10 cents, and 50 cents. There were simply too many varieties of currency; even the crudest "bogus bills" passed muster in banks and shops alike.

Congress responded by setting up a national currency system with the Legal Tender Act in 1862, authorizing the issuance of U.S. legal tender notes—a set of bills ranging in denomination from one dollar to one thousand dollars and soon dubbed "greenbacks." Congress hoped that refined printing techniques and the use of green ink on the reverse side of the notes would eliminate the counterfeiting problem. However, even though the new system made it easier to detect counterfeit money, the nation's coney men (as counterfeiters were known) proved up to the task of churning out well-crafted bogus greenbacks.

State and local enforcement of the new system proved ineffective, and counterfeiting continuing to rise. The new national system needed national-level enforcement in order to succeed. From states throughout the Union, governors and bankers appealed to Washington for help in stemming the flood of bogus bills.

Two false starts would result in the official creation of the Secret Service. The Treasury Department's pursuit of counterfeiters throughout the Civil War would carve one trail to the future agency, with William Wood ranking among a host of often ruthless federal characters who had tracked down an array of equally ruthless and colorful counterfeiters, as the Union and the Confederacy waged five years of battle.

The second false start emerged early in the conflict. Scottish immigrant Allan Pinkerton, a tough, savvy investigator who had founded the first financially successful private detective agency in the United Stated and who turned handsome profits from solving crimes, was working on a criminal case in Baltimore in 1861 when he claimed to have "inadvertently" discovered a plot to assassinate President-elect Abraham Lincoln. Pinkerton reported the plot to Lincoln, who quickly changed his itinerary and avoided harm. Impressed with Pinkerton's skills at intelligence gathering and intrigued by his reputation as a sleuth, Lincoln and Gen. George B. McClellan held a series of meetings with the detective; the transplanted Scotsman persuaded them that he could create and run a spy agency, dispatching agents to penetrate the Confederate armies and government, gather intelligence, and plant disinformation. Pinkerton called his spy network the Secret Service.

The venture soon fell apart for Pinkerton, whose star fell with that of his chief patron, McClellan, the grandiloquently nicknamed "Little Napoleon." When Lincoln sacked McClellan as commander of the Army of the Potomac for his ""unwillingness to fight," Pinkerton was soon removed from his post, too. Still, an organization called the Secret Service had been informally established and was functioning as an intelligence agency.

After several months of confusion following Pinkerton's departure, Lafayette C. Baker took over as head of the fledgling organization. Baker, who had participated in a vigilante movement aimed at Irish immigrants in San Francisco in 1856, had later risen to the rank of brigadier general in the Federal Army by virtue of his daring espionage work against the Confederacy.

Soon the swashbuckling Baker was running the Secret Service as if it, too, were a vigilante organization. His agents became notorious for disregarding constitutional rights, making arrests without due process, and conducting searches without warrants. According to biographer Jacob Mogelever, Baker's "name struck terror in the hearts of the embattled, divided countrymen. He was red-bearded, ferret-eyed . . . the man who [unofficially] created the Secret Service, a frightening, oppressive organization under his drumming, doodling fingers. . . . Woe to spies, contraband smugglers, thieving contractors, bounty jumpers, streetwalkers and madams, Copperheads and deserters! Woe to the civil rights of every American!"

He was the man who wore a gleaming badge with the chilling motto: Death to Traitors. Secretary of War Edwin McMasters Stanton accorded

Baker vast power and funding to pursue counterfeiters, Confederate spies, and virtually anyone Baker deemed disloyal to the Union. From his headquarters, a two-story brick building at 217 Pennsylvania Avenue, Baker dispatched agents from his detective bureau throughout the war-ravaged nation. He filled the grim stone cells of the Old Capitol Prison and its Carroll Annex with forgers and other lawbreakers. His heavy-handed tactics notwithstanding, Baker was also an innovator, creating America's first police criminal dossier and criminal photo file. Still, his trademark became his curtained vans, rattling to the jail filled with prisoners who faced brutal interrogation.

Typical of the men Baker's unofficial Secret Service and the sanctioned agency to come in July 1865 faced in the early greenbacks era was a master counterfeiter named Peter McCartney, whose "association" with the agency began in 1864. In the summer of that year, a train roared eastward from Indianapolis to Washington, D.C., at 35 miles per hour. Peter McCartney, shackles rattling on both his arms and legs, waited for his guards to get careless. Suddenly he bolted to the rear platform of the train and jumped into the darkness. The locomotive screeched to a halt, and Baker's men, expecting to find their prisoner's shattered body, combed vainly along the tracks. McCartney had vanished; one of the nation's most skilled counterfeiters was on the loose.

After his escape, McCartney, dubbed the "King of the Coney Men," headed back to Indianapolis, the city where his landmark counterfeiting exploits had necessitated the dispatch of U.S. Treasury agents to pursue the master forger.

As in so many states in the Union, counterfeiters infested Indiana from 1862 to 1864, the height of the Civil War. Shortly after the federal government's 1862 issue of greenback bills, counterfeit versions were appearing in banks, stores, and anywhere else money changed hands. Throughout the Union a "startling increase of counterfeiting" had conjured, according to the front page of the July 30, 1862, edition of the *New York Times,* "a national evil demanding a national remedy" from the monetary depredations of master counterfeiters such as Midwesterner McCartney and the infamous New York cabal of Thomas Ballard, Joshua D. Miner, and Henry C. Cole.

Thomas Peter McCartney was born in Illinois in 1824. A quiet, extremely intelligent boy, his ordinary life on his family's farm veered into a criminal course when, as a teen, he went to work for a renowned criminal dynasty of the pre-Civil War Midwest, the Johnson family of Lawrence, Indiana.

Virtually the entire Johnson clan—grandfathers, fathers, sons, mothers, and daughters—was involved in the production of counterfeit bank drafts and phony banknotes. William Johnson, the family's finest engraver, taught young McCartney printing, engraving, and all the other arts of the coney man's trade. The youth soon displayed an astounding eye for detail and a deft drawing hand, and his mentor, recognizing the pupil's illicit talent, introduced the youth to other counterfeiters.

McCartney ran his first scam in the early 1840s, during a trip to visit relatives in northern Illinois. After selling a load of produce for a farmer who employed him, McCartney took his cut of the money and scraped off the $1 denominations marked on the bills. Then, using the numbers from the torn, worthless bills he had collected, he carefully glued higher numerals to the good bill. "Why should anyone make one-dollar bills when it was just as easy to make fives or tens?" McCartney later asked as a means of describing his gambit. His bogus bills ready, the youthful forger drove his rig to Indianapolis, entered a small grocery store, placed a few items on the counter, and handed the storekeeper a phony $10 bill. The grocer, scrutinizing the bill, said, "I don't know about that." McCartney later wrote that he was preparing to flee if his mark discovered the phony numerals on the banknote. Moments later, however, the counterfeiter left the store with change for the phony ten in his pocket. The grocer had not suspected a forgery, he had only wondered if he had change in the till for the ten-dollar note.

Soon afterward, McCartney struck out on his own to launch a career in counterfeiting while maintaining ties to the Johnson family. He studied with a noted Midwestern engraver named Ackerman and, during his tutelage with the Prussian-immigrant craftsman, found time to fall in love with his teacher's daughter, tall, lovely Martha Ackerman. By 1852, twenty-eight-year-old Pete McCartney was a handsome, muscular man with thick, dark hair, hazel eyes, and, most important for a coney man, an abundance of geniality and charm. He married Martha that year and began scrambling up the forger's career ladder.

McCartney burst onto the counterfeiting scene of the Midwest during the 1850s, his phony banknotes brilliantly engraved and easily circulated, his bogus bill plates and coin dies virtually matchless. The quality of his work led to partnerships with the most successful and infamous coney men of the Midwest, and he amassed a small fortune in genuine money for his wife and himself.

As the Civil War loomed, McCartney realized that Indianapolis, teeming with new industry since the arrival of the railroad, would be a major military center, and the city's wartime economy would be a fertile site for passing counterfeit bills. As chronicled in Secret Service files, McCartney employed many of the era's most advanced counterfeiting techniques. He set himself apart from the coney men's rank and file with his masterful engraving touch, not to mention a nineteenth-century coney man's most valuable asset: nerve.

Once the Civil War began, McCartney wasted little time in applying his formidable skills across Indiana's economic landscape. With the Johnsons, he concocted a plot to flood Indiana with bogus bills in the nation's first organized greenbacks scheme. Because wartime inflation ranged from 30 to 150 percent and legal bills were plentiful, McCartney experienced little trouble in moving his merchandise by using unwitting bank clerks and shopkeepers. As other Indiana men left their farms, their businesses, and their families to don uniforms and march off to distant battlefields, Pete McCartney prowled Indianapolis, passing phony greenbacks and reaping illicit profits in his guise as a legitimate businessman. The war was making McCartney and his partners rich.

Flushed with success, the Johnsons decided to cut McCartney out of the scheme. When he discovered his ruthless partners' intention, McCartney broke into their offices, stole their counterfeit plate, made an electrotype copy of it, and returned it before the Johnsons suspected anything. Although one historian writes that the plate was for bogus $10 bills, it was more than likely a $20 plate as William Wood later called McCartney a counterfeiter of $20 bills; the electrotype copy was a vast improvement over the Johnsons' plate.

By 1864 the Treasury Department was investigating the rash of counterfeiting in Indianapolis, and the search, reportedly under the direction of William P. Wood, then a shrewd agent on the rise in law-enforcement circles, soon targeted the Johnsons and McCartney. The latter, running his operation out of several rooms in the city, was still attempting to mask his illicit deeds beneath the veneer of a respectable businessman, even buying various bits of property throughout Indianapolis. He also navigated the murky course of counterfeiting by using a number of aliases, including the name Professor Joseph Wood (whether he did so as a jab at his chief foe, William P. Wood, is unknown).

The Treasury Department noted that McCartney and the Johnsons controlled the region's counterfeiting trade. According to the dense Secret Service file on McCartney, he was

> an expert engraver, printer, and photographer . . . and in connection with other notorious counterfeiters . . . issued most of the well-executed counterfeits. . . . In fact, McCartney put the finishing touches and fine work to the majority of plates which were made West of the Allegheny Mountains. McCartney was for some time connected with the notorious gang of thieves, highway men, and counterfeiters (the Johnsons) in the vicinity of Seymour, Indiana.

By the summer of 1864, McCartney and the Johnsons had circulated more than $100,000—a staggering sum for the era—in phony greenbacks. Finally Baker's men, by tracking McCartney's "business" dealings at banks and the post office, were closing in and casting the arrest of McCartney as the key to shattering the greenbacks gang. Wood wrote in July 1865 that McCartney was "connected" with the Johnsons and held a share in a counterfeit $20 U.S. Treasury plate made by them. The agent believed McCartney was "a desperate and notorious villain" who, "if caught and cornered will blow on the gang and . . . give much information." Wood never elaborated on his confidence that McCartney could be induced to turn on his partners. In the cutthroat world of coney men, however, such behavior was not uncommon.

Agents pounced on McCartney and the Johnsons in a double-pronged raid. In the summer of 1864, they seized the Johnsons at Lawrence and McCartney at the Indianapolis post office. The swaggering, handsome counterfeiter who had passed so many bills in that very post office was dragged away in chains. Curiously, agents did not search any of McCartney's Indianapolis rooms, where he had stored his electrotype plate.

Under heavy guard McCartney's and the Johnsons' captors whisked the forgers aboard a Penn-Central train bound for the Old Capitol Prison in

Washington, D.C., where captured Confederate spies and other criminals deemed a threat to the Union languished in filthy cells. As the train chugged eastward, McCartney and his ex-partners, who were still unaware that McCartney had duplicated and bettered the $20 plate, had plenty of time to dwell upon their plight and scheme how to avoid justice.

"I didn't want to go to Washington," McCartney later wrote. "I didn't like the look of that arrangement. I could manage the boys out West. I had managed them frequently. It cost me a heap of money. . . . In Washington, I thought it was different. And besides, I hadn't just then a pile of money ready by me. So I watched the guard and made up my mind I'd rather not go to Washington. And I didn't."

Wood recorded what happened next: "McCartney jumped from the rear platform of a train of cars on the Penn Central Railroad while they were going at the rate of 35 miles an hour and effected his escape from the officers who had him in charge for counterfeiting."

"I was hurt, of course," McCartney would recall. "But I fled to the woods, waited till all was quiet and the train had gone, struggled along for hours, skulked and secreted myself, and with a stone finally smashed their shackles from my limbs. I suffered for want of food and from the bruises I got, but finally found daylight and got among friends, once more in safety."

The Johnsons also conceived a way to elude prosecution, although a less thrilling one than McCartney's daredevil feat. His erstwhile partners in crime cut a deal: they surrendered their counterfeit plate to Wood and "blew out" other forgers in the region, escaping trial and eliminating several of their criminal rivals in the bargain.

Although the agents had shattered the Indianapolis greenback gang, McCartney's elusiveness would torment the Secret Service well after its official establishment on July 5, 1865. The Civil War ended on April 9, 1865, but the threat of McCartney and a host of other counterfeiters remained.

On the afternoon of April 14, 1865, with Baker still in charge of the anti-counterfeiting campaign, Abraham Lincoln met with Secretary of the Treasury William P. McCullough, who described the ongoing severity of the counterfeiting problem to the president. McCullough suggested; "We should have a regular permanent force whose job it will be to put these counterfeiters out of business." Lincoln agreed. It was the last meeting McCulloch ever had with Lincoln.

John Wilkes Booth assassinated the president at Ford's Theatre that night, and in the weeks that followed, the formation of the official Secret Service was delayed by political chaos and intrigue that climaxed in the dismantlement of Baker's apparatus by Lincoln's successor, Andrew Johnson. Johnson had discovered that Director Baker had established his own espionage network inside the Johnson White House. Outraged, Johnson stripped Baker of his post and shut down the agency. During Johnson's impeachment trial in 1868, Baker returned to render testimony against his foe—and was accused of forging letters to incriminate the beleaguered president.

Although Baker proved instrumental in tracking down John Wilkes Booth and the other suspected conspirators in Lincoln's assassination, his days as head of the unofficial and controversial Secret Service were over. It had not even counted in Baker's favor that he was the only federal operative who could claim "hands-on" experience in unleashing agents against the nation's coney men. In the summer of 1864 Baker was discharged, even though he had carried out a wide-ranging and successful raid against Midwestern counterfeiters. As historian David Johnson notes, "He [Baker] emerged from the adventure as one of the few federal agents with practical experience in coping with counterfeiters on a national scale." The success of the sweep notwithstanding, Baker's forays against counterfeiters in the following year had waned, and he was expendable and suspicious in the view of the federal government.

Treasury Secretary McCulloch, with President Johnson's support, pushed aside Baker while creating the federal anticounterfeiting agency that the secretary and Lincoln had discussed on the final afternoon of the president's life. On July 5, 1865, McCulloch appointed Wood to head the Secret Service Division of the Treasury Department. This time it was not created to spy but to save the U.S. currency system from collapse.

A squad of ten "operatives" was sworn in collectively along with Wood. In the following months, the Service hired additional operatives, including a clandestine band of hirelings with an intimate knowledge of the forger's art: they were several master forgers who had done hard time.

Director William P. Wood soon proved a formidable nemesis of the nation's chief counterfeiters. Historians Walter S. Bowen and Harry Edward Neal observed:

William P. Wood, a man without fear, without a complete stock of scruples, and sometimes without good judgment, had shot and slashed his way through the Mexican War as the head of a column of guerrilla marauders who christened him with a nickname that stuck to the war's end—The Daredevil Leader of Company C. . . .

He was tall, stocky, with a granite face and piercing eyes, a mop of dark brown hair parted on the left, and he had a deep, furry voice.

As with Baker, Wood had firsthand experience in chasing and capturing counterfeiters. Wood had been temporarily attached to the Treasury Department during the Civil War and helped track Pete McCartney, among others. When tapped to head the fledgling Secret Service, Wood had to resign from the War Department to assume his new duties.

Business was brisk for Wood and his agents. During its first four years of operation, 1865–1869, the Service's so-called "operatives" stalked and nabbed over two hundred counterfeiters. The director demanded much from himself and his men—ex-soldiers, police officers, or detectives—as he established the agency's headquarters, in Washington, D.C., and set up field offices in eleven cities across the United States. Wood demanded that every operative was on call to the Secret Service twenty-four hours a day, ready to rush to any location at any time. Paid once a month on a daily scale, operatives were required to itemize all their expenses for everything from travel to personal needs. There were no days off, and any "vacation" time was unpaid. Wood required that each operative maintain peak physical fitness and swear utter, unquestioning obedience to his directives. In short, the early operatives' jobs were their lives.

Their job was to capture and punish the coney men, and they matched wits and nerve with a small legion of canny forgers in a real-life and dangerous game of cat-and-mouse. Such a foe was William E. Brockway, called by some "The King of the Counterfeiters." He was christened William E. Spencer but was adopted by the Brockway family while an infant. In the 1850s he apprenticed as a printer and engraver, and like Pete McCartney, turned a deft hand to forgery. Brockway's first illicit creation was a copy of official bank plates in a lead impression. Soon he expanded his efforts into setting up full-fledged counterfeiting plants, teaching his own criminal apprentices enough tricks of the trade to churn out realistic notes, though he never revealed all his secrets.

Always one step ahead of Baker's agents during the Civil War, even when they stormed into several of his plants in the summer of 1864, Brockway launched his most ambitious scheme—"The $1,000 Bond Caper"—at about the time that William P. Wood became the Secret Service's first director.

In a stunning example of the counterfeiter's art, Brockway crafted $1,000 U.S. Treasury bonds so authentic that the Treasury itself redeemed some $75,000 worth of them, a staggering sum for the era. Secretary McCulloch ordered Wood to examine the bonds, and he immediately recognized the near-perfect notes as the work of Brockway. The director had become well versed in the subtle ways that master counterfeiters such as Brockway and McCartney left faint "signatures," for example, slight flourishes in lettering.

When McCulloch announced that the Treasury Department was offering a $20,000 reward for the capture of Brockway, Wood asked if he could collect the money if he caught the counterfeiter even though he was a federal employee. McCulloch assented.

Driven by both professional pride and the thought of the reward, Wood tracked every lead. One trail led to Philadelphia, where an enigmatic, well-heeled man named William E. Spencer and his "wife" lived; after questioning neighbors and searching the Spencers' brownstone, Wood suspected that Spencer was, in fact, Brockway. He was alarmed to learn that the missing couple was in New York to book passage for a "European vacation."

Wood rushed to New York and seized Spencer, who confessed his true identity. When Brockway, hoping to shave years off his looming prison sentence, revealed the location of his stash of $1,000 Treasury notes and plates, Wood thought he had not only his man, but also the $20,000 reward. When he showed up at McCulloch's office to collect, Wood received the secretary's congratulations, $5,000, and the official's regrets that the department could not afford to pay the remaining $15,000. Shortly afterward, on May 5, 1869, Wood handed in his resignation as the first director of the Secret Service.

After serving a stint in jail, Brockway gained his release in 1885. He resumed his illicit trade until 1890, frequently shuttling in and out of prisons throughout the eastern United States. Finally, after receiving parole in 1904, the "King of the Counterfeiters" put down his engraving tools for good; he lived out his days as a law-abiding sort and passed away in December 1920 at the age of ninety-eight.

In 1869 Hiram C. Whitley was sworn in by new secretary of the treasury, George S. Boutwell, as the successor to Wood. The second director of the Secret Service was a man whose very appearance could intimidate most miscreants. According to one biographer, "Anyone who saw Whitley would never forget him. Still in his forties, he stood 6 feet 10 inches tall. He had deep furrows in his forehead, a black mustache and neatly trimmed beard, and ice-blue eyes as steady and penetrating as those of an eagle."

In lobbying for the post, Whitley had not been shy about how much he craved the directorship. He wrote, "I'd rather be Chief of the Secret Service than President of the United States."

Whitley brought a distinguished military and law-enforcement background to the job. He had risen to the rank of lieutenant colonel in the Union Army, earning a decoration for distinguished service. Since the war's end, he had worked as a tough and resourceful detective in the Internal Revenue Bureau; his chief mission was ferreting out and arresting moonshiners in Kansas and Illinois. He had been appointed assistant tax assessor in Lynchburg, Virginia, shortly before Wood resigned from the Secret Service.

Within weeks of taking the directorship, Whitley unveiled dramatic changes and shake-ups in every aspect of the agency. He would deservedly be credited with transforming the organization into a centralized, professionalized law-enforcement unit—the embryonic stages of a modern bureaucratic agency.

One of his first changes approved by the federal government was to move Secret Service Headquarters to New York City, the unofficial capital of the nation's counterfeiters. "In a small, black, leather-covered trunk," the agency's records were packed up and shipped to the new headquarters at 63 Bleecker Street. Whitley left behind a small team of clerks to handle things in Washington.

The meager records Whitley ferried to New York would soon swell with a series of sweeping administrative measures he devised. Convinced of the need for a permanent and ever-expanding record of every counterfeiter the agency uncovered, he instituted a cataloging system of each forger's name, age, aliases, physical description, dates of arrests and releases, criminal methods, and counterfeiting specialties ranging from engraver and printer to dealer and "passer." Each file contained photos of the counterfeiter or his cohorts.

One of the earliest and lengthiest criminal dossiers was that of Wood's old foe Pete McCartney; the record chronicled McCartney's skill, elusiveness, and even the grudging respect that agents accorded him. Whitley had firsthand experience with the roguish, savvy McCartney. As Whitley knew well, McCartney not only made high-quality bogus bills, but also he continually broke out of jail. Once, when interviewed by Secret Service Chief Whitley in a St. Louis jail, McCartney asked where the chief was staying that evening. He then broke out of the cell so he could visit the chief. Whitley was surprised to see McCartney show up in his hotel room at 10:00 P.M. Whitley returned him to jail without a great deal of resistance. McCartney kept operatives busy from the 1860s until 1875, when he was finally put in jail for twelve years.

Whitley set up new rules, guidelines, and procedures for the agents dispatched to hunt down the McCartneys and Brockways. In Whitley's agency, merit—not favoritism—led to promotion. To better handle the growing administrative load, Whitley created the position of assistant chief, and hired additional clerks and accountants so that he would have more time to oversee his men in the field.

Whitley continued Wood's practice of demanding that field agents submit weekly reports to the director. But unlike his predecessor, Whitley ordered that agents' longhand reports account for their actions and expenses every hour of every day. In a typical 1870s report, an agent wrote: "I got up at 5:30 A.M., ate my breakfast, left home at 7:00, arrived at the office at 8:00. At 8:30 I went the First National Bank . . . I returned home at 10:00 P.M., and at 11:30 I went to bed."

Often, agents worked twelve to sixteen hours per day, their duties ranging from tedious surveillance to sudden raids. There was still no such thing as overtime pay, and one of the most unpopular of Whitley's edicts was his abolition of the $25 bounty Wood had paid his operatives for each conviction of a counterfeiter.

Whitley had only twenty agents scattered among eleven field offices, but his men were allowed to hire clerks and detectives and to set up networks of spies and informers to root out counterfeiters and forgers. Each office sent detailed reports of its activities and expenses to 63 Bleecker Street.

In the opening months of Whitley's landmark tenure, agents operated, in the parlance of the day, "on their faces"—none carried badges. The government would pay only for the handcuffs agents carried, but not for weapons; agents bought their own revolvers, billyclubs, and blades. Although a handful of agents carried letters written on Treasury Department stationery, identifying them as Secret Service agents, these documents hardly proved worth the price of printing, as bankers and other counterfeiting victims proved unwilling to talk with some stranger wielding a piece of paper. The notion that an agent in pursuit of a forger could pull out a piece of government letterhead and instantly compel the man or woman to surrender was laughable.

A crack counterfeiter devised a scheme that ended the era of the paper credentials for good in June 1871. A supreme con man named Ira W. Raymond walked into the San Francisco office of the Secret Service and introduced himself to Agent in Charge Henry F. Finnegass as the new administrator of Secret Service Affairs in the California District. The stranger, asserting that he also represented the Department of State in California, handed Finnegass official documents emblazoned with the signatures of the heads of the U.S. State and Treasury Departments. Then, Raymond, dressed in a well-tailored suit and brimming with authority, said he would return the next day at which time he expected Finnegass to turn over the keys to the office vault, which was packed with seized counterfeit greenbacks and fraudulent Treasury notes, as well as genuine cash for office expenses.

As polished and convincing as Raymond was, Finnegass dashed off a telegram to Whitley and asked him to verify the man's authority. Whitley's urgent reply soon arrived—Raymond was a fraud, as were his "official" documents.

Finnegass and local police burst into Raymond's hotel room and arrested him. A search of his valise turned up a trove of forged papers and letters, including his "Treasury credentials." As the Secret Service investigation of the man deepened, agents discovered that he had written letters to the secretary of state and the secretary of the treasury about mundane subjects and had received brief longhand replies on official Treasury stationery. Dampening the letters with a chemical wash, Raymond removed the handwriting—except for the signatures. Once the papers dried, he inserted the news of his "appointment." Raymond, literally caught red-handed, pled guilty and was hauled off to the California State Prison.

In the aftermath of the Raymond case, Chief Whitley decreed that each agent must carry a badge and printed credentials to head off any more attempted impersonations. The director and his staff looked at a number of designs before settling on a distinctive emblem for agents. The official badge, unveiled on August 5, 1873, was a five-point silver star; each point was engraved with a lacework design and emblazoned with the title "U.S. SECRET SERVICE." Along with the new badge, agents were issued an accompanying message from the director: "It has been deemed best that the cost price, $25, should be deposited by each officer (which amount will be deducted from your account for the current month), to be returned upon your retirement from the Service."

Agents' first printed credentials and commissions, designed by the Bureau of Engraving and Printing, were issued on March 17, 1875.

Under Whitley's innovative and military-style stewardship, the Secret Service field offices developed working relationships with local police departments, a model that the FBI would embrace in the next century. Whitley also fired many of Wood's heavy-fisted operatives and broke ties with some, but not all, of the convicted counterfeiters his predecessor had employed as informers. He sought men with military experience from law-abiding, middle-class backgrounds. Two of his hires, Agents Applegate and Lonergan, reflected the new director's aim to cleanse the Secret Service of all unsavory characters, whether convicted criminals or ex-detectives and police officers as violent as the men they pursued. Bowen and Neal asserted:

> Individuals such as Applegate and Lonergan had not had their personal codes of conduct molded by the values of the under-world. Instead, their ethical standards derived from the more sta-ble world of legitimate business people and professionals. To them, criminals were not personal acquaintances but enemies of the social order. Such operatives were more inclined to consort with criminals out of a sense of duty rather than from personal preference. This situation encouraged an "us versus them" atti-tude, which was useful in fulfilling the Service's mission.

Whitley's Service recruited respectable men who not only were tough, capable, and honorable, but also willing to follow a chain of command. Many of Woods's men had fit the "loose cannon" label by using tactics whereby the "rough handling" of suspects mirrored the precinct-house confessions that urban detectives used.

In Whitley's plan, centralized control of operatives would breed more efficiency and remove any taint from close ties to the criminals themselves. He and Woods were alike in one key respect: they expected and demanded that their dictates be obeyed.

From 1869 to 1874, Whitley's agents were recruited from respectable walks of life, comprising about 12 percent of the Service. Still, the reality that he needed men who knew how to wade into the murky realms of counterfeiters compelled him to keep on a contingent of Wood's rugged operatives who had been police officers or detectives. Yielding further to reality, Whitley also retained a band of informers with criminal records. They comprised up to 27 percent of the Secret Service's ranks but were steadily trimmed as his recruiting strategy evolved.

Whitley also worked to instill an esprit de corps through guidelines and procedures he added to a revised handbook for operatives in 1873. *The Circular of Instructions* still contained Wood's strictures for agents to avoid "any appearance of impropriety or disgraceful behavior." Whitley weighed in with an assessment of the agency's very reason for being. Its mission:

> The detection of crime, when entered upon with an honest purpose to discover the haunts of criminals and protect society from their depredations by bringing them to justice, is held to be an honorable calling and worthy of the commendation of all good men.

Whitley elaborated, "There is no branch of the Government service where so many qualifications are necessary, and none in which the field of operations is so varied." Stressing the qualities agents needed, he wrote, "To meet and thwart [crime] requires the most subtle ingenuity, incessant vigilance, and unflagging energy upon the part of officers of the law."

Allowing that agents would be compelled to act sometimes in ways they found questionable, he assured them that they were acting for society's "greater good":

Having detected the criminal it may be found expedient in the interest of public justice to use him against other offenders of the law of greater magnitude than himself. I am aware that such a measure is open to some objection, but in certain classes of crime, especially that of counterfeiting, experience has demonstrated that a confederate may be used with very great moral and legal effect.

In 1867, while Wood was still at the helm of the Secret Service, Congress had expanded the agency's mission to include "detecting persons perpetrating frauds against the government." Wood had stuck more or less to battling counterfeiters and their associates, but under Whitley's hand, the Service began to branch out into other types of investigation, among them swindling, fraud involving veteran's pensions, revenue, and the New York Customs House, smuggling, mail robberies, and illegal voting schemes. As the congressional mandate "to detect persons perpetrating frauds" against the federal government led the Secret Service into a widening array of cases, Whitley told his agents that the act's "ramifications [for the Secret Service] . . . extend everywhere throughout the country, its officers taking cognizance, not only of counterfeiting and other frauds upon the Treasury, but of all crimes coming within the jurisdiction of the Department of Justice."

Post-Civil War "ramifications" reached Whitley's desk at 63 Bleecker from below the Mason-Dixon Line, in Pulaski, Tennessee. An assault upon civil liberties was materializing in the guise of white-robed, hooded men calling themselves the Ku Klux Klan, who terrorized and assaulted blacks, as well as lynched them. Bowen and Neal wrote:

> The South was straining to recover from its desolation, and was hindered by a growing "society" that called itself the Ku Klux Klan. It began about 1866 in Pulaski, Tennessee, as a loosely organized social group of young men who dressed in long white robes with white hoods that had openings for eyes, nose, and mouth, the openings ringed in red flannel. Horns jutted out from the front of the headpiece. A "nose" was 6 or 8 inches long, and a huge red tongue lolled out of the mouth, so arranged that it could be wagged about by the wearer's real tongue. Under this

fake tongue was an opening to a leather pouch, so that when the robed figures demanded a drink of water he could pour a whole bucketful through the mouth opening into the hidden pouch.

At first the Klan engaged in rather harmless mischief, but soon learned that its hooded costumes struck terror into the hearts of the superstitious Southern Negro, and the one-time pranksters gradually became menaces who sought to "discipline" the freedmen. Disgruntled Southerners saw in the Klan a chance to strike back at the North and at former slaves. Victims were threatened, beaten, or driven out of town. Many were maimed, several were lynched, with little or no reason.

On December 5, 1870, Congress sent a resolution to President Grant condemning the KKK, and in early 1871 Grant's attorney general ordered Whitley to dispatch eight Secret Service operatives to investigate the Klan in North and South Carolina, Alabama, Florida, and Georgia, as well as Tennessee. Over the next three years, the Secret Service shadowed Klan leaders, discovered their meeting places, and pounced throughout the rural South, arresting and prosecuting nearly one thousand persons involved in Klan activities; many were handed sentences of up to ten years.

The ranks of the Klan dwindled from the convictions and from fear of Whitley's relentless agents, who forced local lawmen with Klan sympathies to collaborate with the government or face jail time of their own. Within three years, Klan recruitment and activities were moribund, and the agents were reassigned. Never again would the Secret Service be ordered to battle the Klan; years later, the white-robed, hooded marauders would unleash hatred and violence that the FBI and the Department of Justice, not the Secret Service, would face.

Even with the demands of the Secret Service's campaign against Klan terror stretching Whitley's resources, the agency continued to harass and round up a small army of counterfeiters. Whitley was mailed a counterfeiting plate from an anonymous coney man who enclosed a note reading, "the sender, seeing that his confederates were little by little all arrested by offices of the Division, gives up the plate—having resolved to quit the business forever." Other counterfeiters, however, sprang up to replace any cowed or captured by Whitley's Secret Service agents.

Whitley came under congressional fire in 1874 when his name was mentioned in a murky and controversial investigation of the District of Columbia's Board of Public Works. Amid charges that local officials were skimming federal funds, bilking the taxpayers, and awarding public-works projects to a handful of favored contractors, a set of incriminating account books in the case was stolen from the office safe of U.S. Attorney Richard Harrington; desperate officials caught up in Harrington's investigation, likely hoping to cut a deal with the prosecutor, alleged that Chief Whitley had given them the name of the burglar who broke into Harrington's safe.

Not even a shred of evidence actually implicated Whitley, but the secretary of the treasury insisted that the director step down for the good of the agency. On September 2, 1874, Whitley resigned. Some of the most difficult years in the history of the Service lay ahead.

The next three directors—Elmer Washburn, former chief of police of Chicago and ex-warden of Joliet Penitentiary; James J. Brooks, the first Secret Service agent to rise from the ranks to the helm; and John S. Bell, former chief of police of Newark, New Jersey—faced budget cuts and a shrinking role in law enforcement from 1874–1890. As the agency fell into political disfavor in the wake of Whitley's forced departure, the solicitor general's office launched an investigation of the Secret Service on Washburn's watch.

The final report of the investigation recommended that the Service be totally reconstructed and that most of its investigative work be turned over to federal marshals and the U.S. attorney's office. The number of Secret Service operatives was cut in half (from twenty to ten), which was barely enough to provide one operative for each field office.

Despite the fact that Whitley had left under a cloud, the solicitor of the treasury's investigation of the Secret Service did not dent the agency's reputation. Although the number of agents was reduced, Congress agreed that "the loyalty and efficiency of the agents should be rewarded by increases in pay." To the relief of Director Washburn, the investigators' contention that much of the Secret Service's field work be handed to U.S. attorneys and U.S. marshals was dismissed by the Treasury Department, which did not want to further gut the agency's anticounterfeiting campaigns.

In a move to keep the agency close to the Treasury's and Congress's scrutiny, Secret Service headquarters was reestablished in Washington. Washburn, a hardnosed ex-Union Army officer with flowing sideburns and mustache, set up shop on the top floor of the Treasury Building. A biographer wrote,

> Washburn occupied a high-backed padded swivel chair at an ornate walnut desk. Along one wall were two large safes filled with counterfeit money and other captured contraband. A massive sofa, a wardrobe, and a few small tables matched the heavy pattern of the desk. Hanging from another wall were some of the grotesque hoods and robes of the Ku Klux Klan, symbols of the successful investigation in the South. Near a wood-burning fireplace were rows of "WANTED" posters describing various fugitives from justice.

The trophies from the glory days of the agency's crusade against the Klan belied the diminished role of the Secret Service. From Whitley's departure to 1910, the agency's manpower never numbered more than forty-seven operatives and chief operatives; the average number was only twenty-five. Agents' pay of $4 to $7 a day did furnish a comfortable annual income that placed Secret Service men well within the middle class of the era. By 1890, agents also received a small number of paid vacation days.

Still, the years from 1874-1890 were a difficult period for the agency. Stripped of its investigative mission and its personnel by a hostile Treasury Department and an empire-building U.S. attorney's office looking to control federal investigations, the Service floundered during the presidential administrations of Ulysses S. Grant, Rutherford B. Hayes, James A. Garfield, Chester A. Arthur, Grover Cleveland, and Benjamin Harrison.

By 1880, fifteen years after its creation, the Secret Service had no public support or clientele and no political support in Congress. That year, Congress cut the Service's budget from $100,000 to $60,000. Moreover, Congress added a rider to the budget appropriation that restricted the Service to performing only one mission—investigating counterfeiting and forging. Congress had become distrustful of the organization. The Service further suffered because of the reputations of several of its operatives who allegedly beat suspects and threatened reluctant informers. In just fifteen years, the Secret Service had come full circle; its expanded investigative and law-enforcement missions had been cut back to its original, narrow mission of protecting the nation's money supply.

Even that narrowed mandate did not stop several high-profile cases from coming the Service's way. One of the most bizarre episodes in the agency's annals unfolded in 1876, when Director James J. Brooks received intelligence that the gang of notorious Midwestern counterfeiter Ben Boyd, recently jailed, planned to steal the body of slain President Abraham Lincoln from its grave and ransom it for the release of Boyd. At the suggestion of the president's son, Robert Lincoln, the case was assigned to former Secret Service Chief Washburn, who worked with a team of agents and famed detective Allan Pinkerton to hunt down Boyd's minions. The alliance of past and present agency luminaries arrested several of the plotters and saved the federal government from an immense public-relations debacle.

The agency's shoestring budget and limited manpower notwithstanding, the Secret Service scored countless high-profile successes in the incessant pursuit of counterfeiters and forgers. When it came to protecting the nation's currency, not even "toy money" escaped the attention of the Service. In August 1881, Agent Andrew Drummond, a burly, handlebar-mustached agent who had been one of Whitley's middle-class hires and would serve as director from 1891-1894, decided that several toy-money manufacturers who sold their product to toy stores from coast to coast were crafting bills that looked too genuine. They *were* too realistic—people were easily passing them as the real thing in banks and stores.

For several months, Drummond put together a list of toy moneymakers with the help of a Manhattan toy dealer. Then, in November 1881, he walked into the offices of each outfit, flashing his five-point badge and producing his printed credentials to surprised manufacturers. He carted away each factory's toy-money supplies and equipment.

Drummond's next step was to write to district attorneys across the country and compel them to seize play money produced by local manufacturers. All surrendered their supplies. The climax of Drummond's campaign arrived when R. H. Macy personally delivered 160 boxes of toy money to Drummond at the agency's New York field office. Drummond immediately destroyed the "stash." Tersely, Drummond asserted, "The Securities and Coins of all countries should be held sacred, that people, especially manufacturers, should not seek to transform them into curiosities."

By the early1890s, the Secret Service had proven its mettle again and again in the war against counterfeiting, a fact not lost on Congress. Things had begun to turn around on Capitol Hill for the Service, whose annual appropriations for the agency were on the rise and whose duties were broadened a bit to include the investigation of fraudulent pension claims and the management of national banks. Nobody, however, had yet authorized the Secret Service to provide protective services to the president.

A Secret Service agent had been standing near the waiting room of the Baltimore and Potomac Railroad Station in Washington D.C., on July 2, 1881, and in his daily report, he recorded that he had observed some commotion of unknown origin at the station and witnessed police taking a man into custody. The man turned out to be Charles Guiteau, who had just pumped two shots at point-blank range into the arm and back of President James A. Garfield. The president succumbed to his wounds on September 20, 1881.

In the spring of 1894, for the first time in the agency's history, Chief William P. Hazen assigned two of his men to the White House to help protect President Grover Cleveland. Hazen had no official authority to do so, but he justified his action because a pair of operatives in Colorado had been investigating "suspicious persons who might be Western gamblers, Anarchists, or cranks" who were issuing threats against President Cleveland. Consequently, when the Secret Service detailed operatives to the White House for the first time in the spring of 1894, the agency was exceeding its mandate. Its assumption of protective functions, however, grew directly out of its authorized activities. Hazen even transferred the two agents from Colorado to the White House itself without informing Congress.

That summer, Mrs. Cleveland was at the presidential couple's retreat along Buzzard's Bay, Massachusetts, with their children, and was warned of a plot to kidnap the family from the site. Without a word to the president, the alarmed First Lady contacted Hazen and implored him to post three Secret Service agents at the summer home. Hazen complied without a word to the president or to legislators.

When the president arrived at Buzzard's Bay later in the summer to find a trio of agents on the scene, he consented to the arrangement. The same detail would guard the family the following summer, in 1895, and the Cleveland administration concealed this unauthorized use of the Secret Service for presidential protection.

Hazen and the Clevelands had set a clandestine precedent, one that would erupt into a public contretemps within a few years. Without approval from Congress or even the Treasury Department, the Secret

Service had stepped into the realm of presidential protection—far beyond the agency's mandate.

Until Hazen assigned a pair of agents to the White House and three more to the Cleveland's summer home, who protected presidents? Often no one; sometimes, they protected themselves. Andrew Jackson was foremost among the self-protectors; he was well suited by temperament and experience to fend for himself. In 1835, while he exited the Capitol Rotunda after attending a funeral service for a congressman, the unguarded president was approached by a man named Richard Lawrence, who drew a small pistol and fired at the president from only thirteen feet away. The cap went off with a loud report, but the powder failed to ignite and the gun misfired. Jackson swung back his walking cane and rushed at his assailant. As "Old Hickory" bore down on him, Lawrence dropped the first gun and pulled out a second. He leveled the pistol at Jackson's chest and fired at point-blank range—the second weapon also misfired, and a crowd swarmed Lawrence and seized him.

Earlier in Jackson's presidency, a former Naval officer, who had been drummed out of the service for allegedly misappropriating funds, walked into the White House and up to Jackson and struck the president in the face. Jackson grabbed his trusty cane and chased the intruder out of the mansion.

In April 1865, President Lincoln walked unescorted through the fallen Confederate capital, Richmond, to inspect the aftermath of the fierce fighting. Throughout the conflict, he had taken numerous walks and coach rides without any bodyguard whatsoever. In fact, the first twenty-five of the U.S. presidents had no formal protection at all.

As the twentieth century loomed, all that was about to change. For the Secret Service, *everything* was about to change.

CHAPTER 2

# "THE WORK OF PROTECTING ME HAS AT LAST BECOME LEGAL"

*—President Harry Truman, July 16, 1951*

W hen the Secret Service had assumed protective duties of President Cleveland and his family, Director Hazen had agreed to the technically illegal measure because the Service was the only federal law-enforcement agency of any real note. Hazen's pair of operatives in Colorado had unearthed evidence of a plot against Cleveland's life, which was the reason Hazen risked his own career to assign a pair of agents to the White House to keep an eye out for suspicious "Western characters." To mask their duty somewhat, he dubbed them "special policemen."

Hazen continued the practice when President William McKinley (1897–1901) succeeded Cleveland in the Oval Office. The Secret Service's protective duties became more pronounced, and several agents were always at or near the president's side in public. Then, in 1898, the organization suffered a setback when a routine investigation by the office of the secretary of the treasury "discovered" what was regarded as a blatant misuse of the Service's budget for an activity for which it had no authority—the protection of a president's private home. Legislators and other officials railed against Hazen at the belated revelations that on several occasions two or three Secret Service "operatives" had been assigned to guard Presidents Cleveland's and McKinley's residences. Because the Service had no formal protective mission at all and the guarding of a president's home was perceived as reeking of monarchy, William P. Hazen was demoted to field operative due to his "shocking administrative mismanagement." That his decisions might well have saved a president's life mattered little to the scandalmongers. John E. Wilkie, a polished civil servant and former *Chicago Tribune* journalist, as well as a friend of McKinley, was named to replace the deposed Hazen. A man whose wire glasses, neat mustache, and natty appearance radiated confidence, Wilkie was known as a man with keen "investigative insights."

On February 16, 1898, the Secret Service was thrown from its organizational and political limbo by the news that the Spanish had "blown up" the battleship U.S.S. *Maine* in Havana Harbor. Congress declared war on April 21, 1898.

The onset of the Spanish-American War led Congress to authorize the very policy that had led to Hazen's dismissal from his position as director of the Secret Service. In the first legal use of the Secret Service for presidential protection, a detail of four agents, operating under a special emergency war fund, was assigned to the Executive Mansion to guard McKinley around the clock. They were stationed on the first and second floors of the Mansion and on the White House grounds.

As in the Civil War, the Secret Service was pressed back into another controversial duty—counterespionage. Wilkie's men served as the primary intelligence-gathering network for President McKinley's War Department, displacing—once again—the Pinkerton Detective Agency, founded by the man who had led the unofficial Secret Service during its first and short-lived incarnation under General McClellan's auspices.

By 1898 Allan Pinkerton's two sons ran the family business, which had become America's leading private detective agency. The Pinkertons' staunch antianarchism, as well as the size of the agency, made the firm the leading candidate to receive a contract for espionage missions during the Spanish-American War. Ultimately, however, the Pinkerton firm's checkered reputation, which included charges of falsifying evidence and bungling criminal cases, led the McKinley administration to reject the idea of contracting with the Pinkerton Agency. The government turned to Wilkie and the Secret Service to work closely with the Departments of State and War in counterintelligence missions throughout the war with Spain.

The Service's espionage mission evolved not only because of the tarnished Pinkertons, but also because of the close relationship between Secret Service Director John E. Wilkie and President McKinley. In an unprecedented development, Wilkie was brought in to confer with the president's inner circle of wartime advisors, paving the way for the Secret Service to become the foremost U.S. spy agency of the time.

The Service's work during the Spanish-American War primarily involved the gathering of military rather than political intelligence concerning Spain. Wilkie's operatives also conducted counterespionage activities against Spanish agents and engaged in counterinsurgency against Spanish agents and sympathizers. Across the United States, the Service netted spies attempting to destabilize the United States by fomenting political unrest within its borders and by raising money for the Spanish cause.

From the top floor of the Treasury Department, Wilkie ran a far-flung network of operatives that extended to Cuba and tailed Spanish agents in Washington, D.C., New York, Florida, Louisiana, and Washington state. In one case, the Secret Service intercepted a letter written by an American citizen to a Spanish diplomat describing U.S. coastal defenses and suggesting how to circumvent them. In the agency's most famous case during the war, the Service exposed Ramon Carranza, a former attaché of the Spanish embassy, as the ringleader of an enemy espionage network in the United States.

Overall, the Secret Service performed its espionage duties fairly well, proving more adept at counterintelligence work than at producing effective intelligence. In the latter area, it was criticized for centralizing, or "hoarding," information without properly analyzing it or dispensing it to the War Department. Still, by the end of the war, Secret Service Director Wilkie had built the organization into what historian Jefferys-Jones Rhodri describes as "the pivotal intelligence agency of its day."

At this point in its history, the Secret Service could have evolved to become something like the latter-day FBI or the CIA, or even a combination of both, performing both domestic and foreign intelligence roles. Instead, it was sidetracked and reshaped by a variety of factors, including political intrigue and bureaucratic rivalries. The key factor, however, proved the emergence of a new mission that was to become the organization's hallmark—presidential protection. Perhaps the disgraced Hazen could take some small solace in his foresight.

The emergency war fund for Secret Service protection of McKinley expired with America's victory over Spain, so that his friend Director Wilkie no longer had an official mandate to guard the president. However, because

McKinley was receiving a great many death threats from homegrown anarchists whose counterparts in Europe had gunned down or blown up various European nobles and politicians, the Secret Service Chief acted as his predecessor, Hazen, had—Wilkie ignored his lack of statutory authority and continued to post operatives at the White House. He also sent agents to accompany McKinley on his travels outside the White House.

On September 6, 1901, in Buffalo, New York, President McKinley was standing in a receiving line at the Pan American Exposition. A throng pressed close to the president as three Secret Service operatives flanked him, with eighteen Exposition policemen, eleven members of the Coast Guard, and four Buffalo city detectives close at hand. When the president of the Exposition requested a spot directly alongside McKinley, one of the Secret Service operatives, stationed there in large part to help keep the reception line moving and prevent the crowds from overwhelming the chief executive, assented and took up a new position a few feet from McKinley.

Leon Czolgosz, a nondescript man of medium build, dressed in a black suit, jostled his way toward the president amid a knot of well-wishers. The man worked his way within two feet of McKinley and halted where the agent had stood just minutes earlier—it was a clear angle at the president. Then, Czolgosz raised his right arm and thrust his hand, covered by what looked like a cast or a white bandage, toward McKinley. Suddenly two cracks echoed in the hall and a small sheet of flame flashed from the "bandage." Bullets slammed into McKinley's chest and stomach.

Shrieks burst from bystanders as two Secret Service men and a civilian tackled Czolgosz, ripping the pistol from his fingers.

At 2:15 A.M. on September 14, 1901, McKinley died from an infection in one of his wounds; many medical experts would later charge that his death was the result of negligence. McKinley's doctors should have realized that the wound was festering. Forty-two-year-old Vice President Theodore Roosevelt was immediately sworn in as the youngest chief executive in the nation's history.

Although Wilkie still had no official power to guard the president, no one questioned him when the Secret Service assumed full-time responsibility for President Roosevelt's safety. At all times of the day and night, two or more operatives in street clothes were stationed at the White House; First Lady Mrs. Edith Roosevelt, without her husband's knowledge, often requested additional protection from the Service for her husband. Wilkie always complied. Wherever Roosevelt traveled, agents stood close at hand, unofficially, of course. Meanwhile, Wilkie and his men stepped up intelligence gathering about potential assassination plots and individual threats to the president.

Following the assassination of President McKinley in 1901, Congress groped to devise a presidential-protection measure. No fewer than seventeen bills were introduced; none passed. One unsuccessful resolution called for a constitutional amendment that would declare presidential assassination an act of treason. A bill making it a federal crime to assault a president died in committee. Yet another measure that initially had broad support would have given formal responsibility for presidential protection to the U.S. Army. The proposal would have allowed the secretary of war "to select and detail from the Regular Army a sufficient number of officers and men to guard and protect the person of the President of the United States without any unnecessary display." Additionally, the secretary of war would have been granted the power "to make special rules and regulations as to dress, arms, and equipment . . . of said guard." The popular idea was to create a plainclothes, secret service within the Army.

As debate over the proposed bill raged in the Senate, many senators began to shy away from the notion of turning presidential security over to the Army. A growing number soon argued that a "Presidential Guard" smacked of a monarchy or a dictatorship. Senator Mallory contended:

> I would object on general principles that it is antagonistic to our traditions, to our habits of thought, and to our customs that the President should surround himself with a body of Janizarries or a sort of Praetorian guard, and never go anywhere unless he is accompanied by men in uniform and men with sabers as is done by the monarchs of the continent of Europe.

In a stinging swipe at the Secret Service, a group of senators arguing the Army's case retorted that trained soldiers would make far more effective guards than the agents who had failed to save McKinley in Buffalo.

The House Judiciary Committee, however, countered that the so-called "Army bill" would give the secretary of war far too much power:

> The Secretary of War may detail every man and officer in the

Regular Army, under the pretense of protecting the President, dress them to suit his fancy, and send them abroad among the people to act under secret orders. When such laws begin to operate in the Republic the liberties of the people will take wings and fly away.

Lost in the din of arguments and debates was the fact that the president was the commander in chief of the nation's armed forces, so an Army bodyguard might not have been so radical an idea. But perception buried the measure.

Making a case for the Secret Service, the committee further added "that the President should instead be protected by a secret-service force . . . act[ing] under orders from the Secretary of the Treasury."

The proposed bill never made it to a congressional vote, taking a place in the litany of failed presidential protection measures.

From the earliest days of the republic, Congress and the people had recoiled at an idea of presidential protection that even hinted at "royalism." Legislators' unwillingness to fund more than nominal protection at best was seemingly less rooted in stinginess or even politics than upon roseate but increasingly unrealistic notions of the president as a citizen—not a potentate—first and foremost. So, too, did Jefferson's vision of the "People's House" color politicians' opinions.

While Congress groped for some constitutional or legal formula, President Theodore Roosevelt remained officially unprotected. Wilkie did receive some "after-the-fact" support with the secretary of the treasury's directive that the Secret Service provide Roosevelt protection even without legal authorization. Ever full of both bravery and bluster, "The Hero of San Juan Hill" claimed to loose little sleep fretting over the fate of the protective mandate in the congressional morass. He wrote to his friend Senator Henry Cabot Lodge: "Of course they [the Secret Service] would not be the least use in preventing any assault upon my life. I do not believe there is any danger of such an assault." In 1912, Roosevelt would be proven wrong.

Since the Congress had not appropriated any money for Secret Service protection, the Service was forced to absorb the cost, thus reducing the funds available for pursuing counterfeiters. Predictably, the formation of a presidential protection detail without a legal mandate drew sharp criticism from Roosevelt's foes in Congress, which also discovered other instances in which Secret Service agents had been used for work in various Cabinet departments. Congress formally prohibited Secret Service agents from performing any duties except these specified within the Treasury Department. The White House detail was now utterly illegal, and some legislators actually tried to prevent the Service from providing protection to the president. Meanwhile, most of Congress still floundered in its search for acceptable protective legislation. As always, the image of a Praetorian Guard—whether Secret Service agents or soldiers—disturbed many legislators who had no desire to see another president killed but apparently believed that an open residency trumped security.

Finally, five years after the assassination of President McKinley, Congress passed a single line of legislation inserted into The Sundry Civil Expenses Act of 1907 (actually passed in 1906) that legalized the use of appropriated funds "for the protection of the person of the President of the United States."

Still, assault on a president was not a federal crime.

Law thus caught up to reality, as the Secret Service finally received direct express funding to perform the presidential security functions it had in fact assumed twelve years earlier and sporadically before that. The Secret Service has continued to protect the "person of the president" ever since. Immediately following its official designation as the agency responsible for protecting the president, the Secret Service usually assigned two agents to serve as presidential bodyguards. When the president took extended vacations, the detail increased to eight to allow around-the-clock protection. Still, the public perception, as the *Philadelphia Telegram* opined, was that the Secret Service's dual duties still tilted toward the war against counterfeiting: "The professional criminal never willingly falls in the way of the Secret Service. The chase is as relentless as death, and only death or capture ends it."

Just when the Service obtained authorization for a protective mission, as well as its traditional anticounterfeiting duties, it ran afoul of the Congress, which took punitive action. In 1907 there was a scandal involving false homestead claims that were being used to defraud the federal government of valuable western timberland. Secret Service agents had been loaned to the Justice Department to investigate the case, and in one of the cases, agents traced the conspiracy-to-defraud to an Oregon senator and congressman, who were prosecuted. Their livid colleagues retaliated against the Secret Service by tacking on a rider to the 1909 appropriations bill, making it impossible for Secret Service agents to be paid by funds from any other government agency, as the Justice Department had done during the investigation of the western land fraud.

Although President Theodore Roosevelt might have blustered that he did not need Secret Service protection, he erupted at the congressional action, which denied federal agencies the use of the government's best law-enforcement agents. He harangued the legislators:

> The chief argument in favor of this provision was that the Congressmen did not want to be investigated by the Secret Service men. . . . I do not believe that it is in the public interest to protect criminals in any branch of the public service.

Just before he left office in January 1909, Roosevelt infuriated Congress by using his executive authority to transfer permanently eight Secret Service agents to the Justice Department so that it could continue criminal investigations. In the long run, this had a much greater impact upon the evolution of the Secret Service than did the political fallout from the homestead scandal, for these eight agents became the nucleus for the formation of the FBI, which was founded in 1908.

The political furor caused by the Service's land-fraud investigation, which had ensnared two congressmen, overshadowed another episode out West. It was not in the protection of a president that the Secret Service lost its first agent in the line of duty, or at the hands of counterfeiters. It was at the hands of corporate swindlers.

Agents Joseph A. Walker and Thomas Callaghan, miner and prospector Tom Harper, and John E. Chapson of the Department of the Interior were dispatched to investigate the Porter Fuel Company in Colorado. The business's owners were allegedly filing false claims for homes and the cultivation of land, and the company was amassing vast tracts of rich timberland and coal veins for the partners' own use and profits.

On November 3, 1907, the four government men were checking out a large homestead claim and discovered a gaping hole in the ground. With Walker, who suffered from asthma and was concerned he would not have sufficient air if he entered the shaft, standing guard at the hole's rim, the other three laid a thick railroad tie across the top of the hole and looped a rope over it. Then they slid down the rope to the bottom of the shaft and straight into a cavernous and surreptitious coal mine—on a homestead grant that just happened to belong to William R. Mason, superintendent of the Porter Fuel Company.

As Agents Callaghan, Harper, and Chapson crawled deeper into the mine, shots echoed from the top of the shaft, and they rushed back to the opening. Someone had tossed the rope into the hole—the three men were seemingly trapped.

For hours, Harper, tried to claw his way up the walls with the rope in tow. He finally reached the top, looped the rope across the tie again, and hauled the others out. A few yards from the hole, Walker was sprawled on his back, dead from multiple gunshot wounds.

Callaghan dashed toward the town of Durango to notify the authorities and came across a pair of men in a buggy, one cradling a shotgun. Having surprised them and pulled out his revolver, Callaghan forced them to Durango and ordered the local sheriff to lock them up. The agent had no doubt that they were the men who had gunned down Walker and had left Callaghan, Harper, and Chapson to die in the mine. Callaghan also suspected that the pair were assassins hired by the Porter Fuel Company.

After questioning them, Callaghan arrested them and assumed they would face trial. They did, but were acquitted. According to Callaghan's later comments, "the region didn't have positive feelings about government agents then, and one person who could have helped the case against the defendants refused to testify." Within a year of their acquittal, both suspected killers of Agent Walker committed suicide.

The congressional mandate that had authorized the Secret Service to investigate a wide range of "fraud against the federal government" proved the main reason that agents plunged into such cases such as in Colorado. An underlying reason was that the nation did not have a federal law-enforcement agent, except for the Secret Service, set up with field offices across the United States. Beyond local police departments and U.S. marshals, a law-enforcement vacuum existed, and the Service often stepped into the gap simply because there was no one else that could.

Typical of the crimes that the agency was called upon to investigate before the creation of the FBI was illegal immigration. Ordered to enforce laws dictating exactly how many immigrants from each country could come to the United States, the Secret Service was tipped off that a cadre of businessmen in San Francisco were smuggling Chinese men, women, and children into America. Although the businessmen duped the illegals into thinking that good jobs awaited them, in reality, the men were used as slave labor, and the women were forced into brothels.

In 1907, the Secret Service sent Agent Don Wilkie undercover to Chinatown. Having grown a long, unkempt beard and wearing a suit that he slept in, Wilkie looked every inch a vagrant. He established himself as part of the local "scenery" and talked his way into two jobs. The first job was in a Chinese grocery store where he stocked shelves with vegetables and meat; More important, he landed a job as a lookout in an opium den.

Although Wilkie was white, down-and-out men and women of all races sought solace of a sort in the opium "palaces," so no one paid special attention to the agent. Similarly, no one suspected him as he shadowed people he came to suspect were smugglers of human beings. When he discovered that a large group of Chinese immigrants were about to be loaded onto a boat and taken as slave labor to some unspecified work site in California, he was waiting with local police to seize the smugglers.

Like most agents of the day, Wilkie worked alone when he was undercover. When he was ready to make an arrest, he would head to a Secret Service field office for backup or, if none were available, to local police departments. He also communicated by telegrams with field offices and headquarters, in Washington. But, in reality, he operated alone most of the time.

Wilkie's next assignment was Laredo, Texas, where local authorities had received a tip that Chinese immigrants were being carted into the country on trains steaming north from Mexico. On one all-too-typical night for the agent, he stopped and boarded a train to find seven Chinese stowaways in the engine's water tank. Three had drowned.

During the decade following congressional authorization of presidential protection, in 1906 the law-enforcement missions of the Service began to wane, and the dual mission of chasing counterfeiters and protecting presidents expanded. In 1908 the Service began to protect presidents-elect when it assumed the responsibility for guarding William Howard Taft after his victory. Congress gave the Service a more extensive protective mission in 1913, as the 1906 authorization had granted only temporary authority, but even this new authority had to be renewed annually until 1951, when Congress finally made it permanent.

# THE SECRET SERVICE

In 1912, when Teddy Roosevelt was campaigning once again for the presidency, he learned firsthand just how necessary protection could be for candidates and presidents alike. As a candidate, Roosevelt was not a Secret Service protectee.

He exited a hotel in Milwaukee en route to give a speech when a man named John N. Shrank appeared six feet in front of him, leveled a pistol at the candidate's chest, and fired. The bullet slammed into the former president's metal glasses case and then was slowed by the fifty-page speech that Roosevelt had double-folded in his breast pocket. Still, the bullet penetrated several inches into Roosevelt's chest, fracturing his rib.

Stunned for a few moments, Roosevelt peered down at his wound. Then the former Rough Rider, "The Hero of San Juan Hill," coughed into his hand; when no blood came up, he insisted on delivering the speech.

The Bavarian-born Shrank claimed that President McKinley's ghost had inspired him to prevent Roosevelt from serving another term as president. Five court-appointed psychiatrists determined that Shrank was insane, and he was institutionalized for the remainder of his life. For the first time, some members of Congress mulled over the possibility of the Secret Service offering protection to presidential candidates. But that measure would take a long time to win acceptance.

Even a burgeoning protective mission did not prevent the Service from wading back into actions that had long preceded protection: espionage. As it had done during the Civil War and the Spanish-American War, the agency resumed its traditional intelligence duties in World War I, this time working closely with the State Department in both intelligence gathering and counterespionage. On May 14, 1915, long before the United States declared war on Germany in April 1917, President Woodrow Wilson ordered the secretary of the treasury, once again, to have the Secret Service investigate espionage in the United States.

When the United States did enter the conflict, the man at the helm of the intelligence mission was Secret Service Director William J. Flynn, a broadshouldered, square-jawed man who had started his career as a street cop in the New York City Police Department. A crack sleuth, Flynn rose from the blue-clad ranks to chief of detectives. His reputation was that of a policeman who knew every inch of the city, including the haunts of murderers, counterfeiters, and other miscreants.

In the late 1890s, Flynn joined the Secret Service, the agency's brass were impressed by his track record of catching counterfeiters; he was selected from the more than 3,000 policeman and detectives on the Secret Service's waiting list. Flynn spent the next fifteen years working mainly in the New York field office, racking up scores of arrests and smashing several counterfeiting rings.

When Secret Service Chief John E. Wilkie resigned in 1911 to take a higher-paying post as the president of a public utility company, the Treasury Department interviewed a number of possible successors from inside and outside the agency. William Flynn was one of the candidates.

With anticounterfeiting rather than presidential protection still the Secret Service's main mission, Flynn's success in busting the nation's coney men put him on the agency's short list for the top spot. He was officially appointed as the agency's ninth chief in 1912. Flynn would soon prove that he not only possessed a knack for rooting out counterfeiters, but also a talent for counterespionage.

Authorized to infiltrate and gut a German sabotage network that was plotting against France, England, and the United States, Flynn set up an eleven-man counterespionage unit in New York City. The federal government was concerned about German violations of U.S. neutrality, particularly sabotage against American factories that manufactured supplies for Great Britain, France, and Russia.

The eleven-man unit's most celebrated case occurred in 1917 and involved the infamous briefcase of Dr. Heinrich Albert. Tipped off in New York that a ring of German spies and sympathizers were crafting an unspecified plot against the United States, Secret Service operative Frank Burke and a team of fellow agents began to track the publisher of the pro-German newspaper *The Fatherland* and discovered that he was regularly meeting with Dr. Alpert, a man of aristocratic mien and Old World polish.

One morning, Burke tailed the publisher onto a New York trolley and, remaining at an inconspicuous distance on the crowded car, waited. A man in an expensive coat sidled up to the publisher. As the pair began to chat, Burke instantly recognized Dr. Albert. The agent moved closer to the men.

As the trolley came to a stop, Albert stepped off the trolley and suddenly turned back panic-stricken toward the car. He had left behind his brown-leather briefcase.

Seconds later Albert saw Burke burst from another exit on the trolley and dash down the street. The German saw the briefcase in the agent's hand and chased Burke, but the agent soon vanished into the crowds.

An advertisement running in the New York newspapers two days later offered a detailed description of the briefcase and a $20 reward. It was too late for Albert. Back at the agency's field office, Burke and his colleagues opened the doctor's briefcase and found an astonishing array of documents and letters in it. The agents had seized proof of intricate, organized plots to undermine America.

They learned that Dr. Albert was the chief money man for Germany's spy and sabotage network in the United States; his meticulous account books revealed that he had more than $27 million to spend financing this espionage in America. Among the many plots that Albert and his network planned were longshoremen's strikes, a bombing campaign against munitions plants and other factories manufacturing war supplies, and a propaganda campaign through which German sympathizers intended to affect American public opinion through the spy ring's purchase of newspaper, magazine, and book publishing companies.

Those machinations were almost mild compared with the other plots over which Burke and other agents now pored. Albert planned to gain a monopoly on the supply of liquid chlorine used for poison gas, purchase an American airplane company and its precious patents, organize a protectionist labor movement to choke off the supply of cotton imported from Britain, and work with America's antiwar politicians and labor leaders to force an embargo on all munitions shipments to Britain and France. In perhaps the most shocking discovery from the briefcase, the Secret Service learned of the doctor's scheme for a German invasion of America. Albert and his co-conspirators in American and Berlin had crafted a plan in which the German Navy would land eighty-five thousand battle-hardened troops along the New Jersey coast and seal New York City off until it surrendered because of starvation.

The combination of Albert's carelessness and Agent Burke's quick thinking had yielded an intelligence bonanza. As the agency and the police swooped down on Albert and his cohorts and imprisoned them, newspapers nationwide lauded the Secret Service's counterespionage coup, a success in which both luck and dogged detective work had figured.

Even as Burke and other operatives ferreted out the kaiser's spies and agents, the Secret Service continued to chase and arrest counterfeiters and forgers. As always in wartime, counterfeiters stepped up production of bogus greenbacks and coins, which were rendered with dies and molds of varying quality; in 1917 alone, agents chalked up 1,038 counterfeiting convictions and seized $283,706 in phony bills and coins. They also investigated the counterfeiting of internal revenue stamps used for liquor and pursued investigations of federal pension fraud. As many historians of counterfeiting have noted, governments of nations at war have to devote so many law-enforcement resources to domestic defense that counterfeiters feel there are fewer police and agents watching them. At least early in a conflict, passing bogus money has proven historically easier than in times of peace.

The onset of World War I brought other unprecedented duties to the Secret Service. When President Wilson created the U.S. Food Administration to prevent food hoarding and illegal food monopolies, agents were requested to investigate any such violations. Additionally, the Service acted as an arm of the War Trade Board in investigating war profiteering by businessmen and corporations who sold food and other commodities to Germany.

Despite the agency's myriad wartime intelligence gathering, counter-espionage, and investigations of profiteers, the Service's missions were about to give way to traditional anticounterfeiting campaigns and to an enhanced focus upon presidential protection. However, several controversial investigative episodes in the 1920s still loomed for the agency.

In 1917, disturbing letters began to pour into the Wilson White House; German sympathizers, antiwar activists, and a legion of assorted cranks were routinely venting their anger on the president. That year congress passed a law making it a crime to threaten a president by mail or any other means. This first "threat statute" expanded the Service's protective roles, including investigations of letter writers. Also in 1917, Congress authorized the Service for the first time to protect the president's immediate family, and the White House detail more than doubled, from two to five agents, still a shockingly small number by today's standards.

In 1922 the Secret Service became embroiled in an even greater public-service scandal than the agency's investigation of the 1907 homestead-fraud case that had led to the death of Agent Walker and netted two corrupt congressmen. This time, the scandal's trail led to the White House itself and to the administration of President Warren G. Harding. The case became known as "Teapot Dome."

Harding's secretary of the interior, Albert Fall, had illegally leased the federally owned Teapot Dome oil fields to a private oil company; the lease was awarded secretly—with no competitive bidding as required by law. Congress, which had taken action to sharply curtail the Secret Service's ability to carry out such investigations when congressmen were the targets, showed no such reluctance about authorizing the Secret Service to investigate the Harding White House.

On April 15, 1922, Wyoming Democratic Senator John Kendrick introduced a resolution that set in motion one of the most significant investigations in Senate—and Secret Service—history. He was reacting to an explosive *Wall Street Journal* story of the previous day. The newspaper revealed an unprecedented secret arrangement in which the secretary of the interior, without competitive bidding, had leased the U.S. naval petroleum reserve at Wyoming's Teapot Dome fields to a private oil company. Wisconsin Republican Senator Robert La Follette authorized the Senate Committee on Public Lands to investigate the matter. Within days, someone ransacked his Russell Building office.

The committee's leadership allowed the panel's most junior minority member, Montana Democrat Thomas Walsh, to lead the investigation. He assigned not only a team of prosecutors and clerks to the case, but also four Secret Service agents, who were ordered to investigate a single question: "How did Interior Secretary Albert Fall get so rich so quickly?"

Heading the Secret Service investigation of Fall was the agency's tenth chief, William H. Moran, who had been appointed in 1918 after Chief Flynn stepped down to open the Flynn Detective Agency. Unlike Flynn, Moran had not started out as a street cop, but as a Secret Service clerk. A Hyattsville, Maryland, native, Moran had struck up a relationship with former Secret Service Chief James J. Brooks (1876–1888). Both men attending the same church, and Moran's intelligence and ambition caught his boss's attention.

From an administrative and managerial viewpoint, Moran learned every facet of the agency's day-to-day operation, and his colleagues said that "he ate, drank, and slept Secret Service."

From the moment Moran assumed his new post, at the agency's helm, he would face unprecedented new challenges for the Secret Service: official protection of presidential family members, which began in 1917; the creation of the White House Police in 1922; and new standardization of the nation's currency. But it was the Teapot Dome Scandal that would thrust Moran and his men into the political arena in a way that went far beyond the Secret Service's anticounterfeiting and evolving protective missions.

Moran's agents, along with federal prosecutors, probed President Harding's 1921 executive order that transferred the control of naval oil reserves at Teapot Dome, Wyoming, and Elk Hills, California, from the Navy Department to the Department of the Interior. The oil reserves had been set aside for the Navy by Woodrow Wilson during World War I, but in 1922, Secretary Fall leased the rich fields to Harry F. Sinclair, owner of the Mammoth Oil Company, and the field at Elk Hills, California, to Edward L. Doheny, chairman of the Pan American Petroleum Company.

As the Secret Service began questioning Department of Interior officials throughout 1922–1923, the agents unearthed a series of transactions that tainted the administration and the very president that other agents were sworn to protect. In 1921, Doheny had lent Secretary Fall $100,000 interest-free, and when Fall "retired" as secretary of the interior in March 1923, Sinclair also "loaned" him a large amount of money. The investigation led to Fall's indictment for conspiracy and for accepting bribes. He was convicted of the latter, earning the dubious distinction of becoming the first former cabinet officer to go to prison. The Secret Service proved instrumental in sending one of the president's men to jail.

That the agency had become the investigative arm of those prosecuting Harding's administration enraged the president and his allies and unnerved many politicians who were squeamish at the reality that agents could be spying on the president even as they were protecting him. Although no one dared assail the Service as an organization in the wake of its successful role—too successful for many—in Teapot Dome, a move to make sure that agents would never again double as "snoops" in the White House or in Congress soon began taking shape.

In 1922 Harding had moved to tighten secrecy in the White House by executing something of a coup d'état against the White House police unit, which had been assigned by the Washington, D.C., Police Department. Fearing the presence of a large police contingent over which he had no control concerning personnel or activities, Harding persuaded Congress to create a new police organization called the White House Police Force. This new unit was no longer under the control of the Washington police; instead, the contingent was under the direct authority of the president. Naturally,

Harding assigned command of the new police force under the command of one of his most trusted military aides. Personnel for the new unit were "handpicked" by the Harding administration from Washington, D.C., police and the U.S. Parks Department.

To the dismay of the Secret Service, Harding also undercut their protective mission in a way that Congress would shy away from until the later presidency of Bill Clinton. Harding, a notorious womanizer, routinely brought his mistress into his office for romps as agents stood stoically outside his office door. One of his more famous White House trysts took place in a closet.

In 1930 a flagrant security breach at the White House so angered President Herbert Hoover that he turned to the Secret Service to take full control of his protection at the presidential mansion. A well-dressed, genial intruder who turned out to be a curious and harmless citizen ambled past police guards one evening and straight into the Hoovers' dining room. The president summoned the head of the Secret Service detail and demanded an explanation. Hoover was told that the problem was simple but potentially lethal: the Service had no official control over the police force whatsoever, courtesy of Harding.

Hoover soon remedied the situation. With congressional approval, the Service was placed in charge of the White House police, which would eventually become the Secret Service uniformed division. Now, the agency had achieved complete control over White House protection.

In the decade after Harding's corrupt tenure, the Secret Service faced a host of formidable challenges to its protective, investigative, and intelligence roles. No longer was the agency in the unique position of being the only general federal law-enforcement body it had been for so many decades. Nor was it any longer the most respected and skilled among the agencies. The FBI had grown rapidly during the 1920s and by the mid-1930s it had become the most famous, best-equipped, and largest federal law enforcement agency. This was largely due to the political skills of its ambitious director, J. Edgar Hoover, who took over the Bureau in 1924 at the age of twenty-nine.

With the Bureau's ascendance and congressional restrictions on the Secret Service's investigative role, the FBI had become the federal government's investigative agency of choice. Moreover, Hoover's Bureau even made forays into the Service's protective-mission turf. In 1929, there was no Congressional authorization to protect vice presidents. But there had been no formal authority to protect presidents–elect when the Service simply assumed the responsibility in 1908. When Herbert Hoover's vice president, Charles Curtis, wanted protection, it was the FBI who provided it from 1929 to 1933.

To improve coordination among the security forces and prevent the recurrence of such a breach as the man who had walked up to Hoover while he was dining in the White House, Hoover acted immediately to place the White House Police under the control and supervision of the chief of the Secret Services. On July 1, 1930, Congress passed legislation to this effect. For the first time, the Secret Service was now responsible for every aspect of White House security, and the statute merging the White House Police into the Secret Service also increased the size of the police force to forty-eight.

In Miami on February 15, 1933, the Secret Service came face to face with another gunman seeking to slay a president—in this case President-elect Franklin D. Roosevelt. Roosevelt, who had been on a vacation cruise before his March inauguration, went to Bayside Park to meet a crowd of citizens and Democratic leaders and deliver a speech from a podium to which he was guided by agents. This was done in a way that masked his partial paralysis. After he gave his speech and was escorted by his agents to an open limousine, he spied Anton Cermak, the mayor of Chicago, and beckoned him to come up to the car as it slowly cruised among the waving and cheering throng. A short, stocky man slipped to the front of the crowd and toward an empty chair near the podium.

The man, Giuseppe Zangara, had arrived one-and-a-half hours before the speech but was unable to get a front row seat. Wracked by stomach pains, the deranged man believed that his agony would abate only if he killed Roosevelt.

As Roosevelt's limo began to roll away from the reviewing stand, Zangara clambered onto a spectator's vacated chair. Then, as Roosevelt leaned forward to shake Cermak's hand, gunshots sprayed the open car. None of the shots struck the intended target—Roosevelt—but Cermak crumpled forward into the car, mortally wounded. Secret Service Agent Robert Clark was hit, as were four other people.

While police officers slammed Zangara to the pavement and disarmed him, Secret Service agents tried to whisk the limo away from the scene, but

Roosevelt ordered them to place the doomed Cermak in the car and speed to a hospital. The mayor died there a short time later.

Zangara, professing a hatred of "the capitalists," was adjudged sane despite his belief that Roosevelt's death would end his stomach pains. The would-be assassin was convicted and electrocuted within a month of the tragedy.

After the attempted assassination of Roosevelt, Congress debated a bill making it a federal crime to assassinate the president, vice president, president-elect, vice president–elect and the candidates for president and vice president. The bill died in committee. Although these issues came before Congress again, it would not be until 1965, after the assassination of President John F. Kennedy, that the House and Senate passed legislation making this offense a federal crime.

Protecting Roosevelt, who received a flood of hate mail and written death threats during the 1930s, led to heightened vigilance by the Secret Service. His security was augmented by the expansion of the White House police force to sixty officers in 1935, a measure that was also a response to a tripling of executive office space in the West Wing.

The presidential protection mission of the Secret Service was increasing, while in 1938, the Secret Service was finally frozen out of the intelligence business. After President Roosevelt called for a review of the nation's espionage agencies, his administration developed a plan granting exclusive control over domestic intelligence to a troika of agencies—the FBI, the Military Intelligence Department (MID), and ONI (Office of Naval Intelligence). Roosevelt sent all federal agencies a confidential directive instructing that the troika would have exclusive responsibility over "the investigation of all espionage, counterespionage, and sabotage matters." The Secret Service was out. Its long history of chasing spies and saboteurs during three wars—the Civil War, the Spanish-American War, and World War I—was at an end.

Having lost its last vestiges of an intelligence role, the Service was also confronted with a challenge to its protective role from the empire-building J. Edgar Hoover, who had a close working relationship with FDR. According to Frank Donner, Hoover was encouraged by Roosevelt "to run the Bureau as an adjunct of the White House." Roosevelt came to view the FBI "as his eyes and ears" and used Hoover's men to spy on presidential aides and to plug press leaks in the White House by using wiretaps.

Most alarming to the Secret Service was that FBI agents became a second protective detail in the Roosevelt White House; their ostensible role supposedly was "to supplement the Secret Service's more routine duties." With this seemingly modest opening, Hoover's Bureau was positioned to eventually displace the Service in presidential protection in the same way as the "G-Men" had in espionage. One man stood in his way.

Director William Moran, so fiercely devoted to the Secret Service's unique identity and mission, bucked Hoover at every juncture. Although Hoover was finding some success in wooing Franklin D. Roosevelt to the idea of FBI presidential protection, Moran proved a formidable foe for the FBI chief. Moran had both the president's trust and his ear. Twice, the aging Secret Service director had wanted to retire, but Roosevelt talked him out of it both times. Hoover, unable to cut out Moran and gain anything more than ancillary protection of the president, decided to bide his time until Moran did finally retire in 1937.

Hoover's next move to wrest presidential protection away from the Secret Service unfolded in 1940. With the backing of many senators and congressmen who viewed the FBI and Hoover as the nation's highest-profile law-enforcement agency, Hoover plotted a new gambit to gain control over his chief competitor, the Secret Service.

The FBI chief threatened the Secret Service with organizational disaster through his proposal to transfer the Service from the Treasury Department, where the agency had been since its inception, to the Justice Department— the home of the FBI. There, the Service would, no doubt, have been even further eclipsed by the Bureau, if not gobbled up by it.

The man faced with blunting Hoover's challenge was Secret Service Chief Frank J. Wilson (1937–1946). At first gaze, the balding, bespectacled Wilson looked like a businessman or an accountant; in fact, he had started out as an Internal Revenue Service agent who had specialized in tax investigations and made a behind-the-scenes-name for himself as one of the investigators who brought down Al Capone for tax evasion in 1931.

During the Lindbergh baby kidnapping case in 1936, Wilson, now with the Secret Service, had scrutinized each serial number from the greenbacks given to the kidnapper as ransom and traced a number of the bills to German immigrant Bruno Hauptmann. Wilson's work led to Hauptmann's arrest, his still-controversial trial, and execution in New Jersey's electric chair for the infant's murder.

# THE SECRET SERVICE

To Hoover's frustration, Wilson convinced Roosevelt and enough legislators that placing the Secret Service in the Department of Justice would hamstring its anticounterfeiting duties, which was logically the mission of the Treasury Department. Wilson also persuaded the president that the FBI and the Justice Department would have to pull valuable anticrime personnel from the field in order to have a supporting role in presidential protection. Again, a Secret Service chief's arguments had thwarted the ambitious Hoover.

Although its espionage role had ended and its general investigative role had declined drastically, the Secret Service went on to expand its duties in the missions left to it—protection and combating counterfeiting and forgery. The onset of World War II was about to barrage the agency with new challenges on both those fronts, as well as with some new duties.

Even before December 7, 1941, when the Japanese struck Pearl Harbor, the looming reality that the United States would be dragged into the conflict fueled significant changes in White House security arrangements. In 1940, warfare around the globe induced Congress to expand the White House Police Force to eighty officers. Congress authorized funds to increase the size of the White House protective detail to 140 in 1942, with the nation fully engaged in the war, but the increase was approved only on a temporary basis. Because many Metropolitan Police and Park Police were being conscripted into the armed forces, Congress also eliminated the requirement that all White House Police Officers be drawn from these two entities.

With the advent of war, the military assumed a major role in protecting the White House complex. Sentry boxes were constructed at regular intervals both inside and outside the fence around the grounds and were staffed by a special detachment of Military Police. Sentries toting machine guns stood atop the roof of the Executive Mansion. Several years later, when it became clear that the Allies were winning the war, President Roosevelt ordered that these military guards be assigned elsewhere.

Throughout the war, protecting President Roosevelt and then President Truman took on even more urgency. Escape routes from the White House and Washington, D.C., were put in place to rush the presidents and family to safety should the need arise.

Because Franklin Roosevelt traveled more than any previous president and continued to do so despite the danger during the war, the Secret

Service tightly managed his security. The agency forbid newspapers from publishing the president's schedule and travel stops in advance; at Roosevelt's travels to worldwide conferences, agents took precautions against such possibilities as enemy air raids, submarines attacks, mines, snipers, and paratrooper assaults. In North Africa, agents employed a ruse to guard against any Axis assassins along Roosevelt's motorcade route: Agents in the lead vehicle would point to the sky to distract spectators, and other agents "accidentally" fell out of a Jeep as the president's vehicle sped by. The ruses appear bizarre, but are perhaps understandable given that the Service was trying to protect Roosevelt in bonafide war zones where enemies could conceivably strike from land, sea, or air.

Not only did the Secret Service have to ensure the president's safety during the war, but also that of visiting foreign dignitaries. A detail of agents was assigned early in the war to Norway's Crown Princess Martha and her children, who had fled to America from Nazi aggression in their country. As the conflict dragged on, agents also protected such visitors as Prime Minister Winston Churchill of Great Britain, Madame Chiang Kai-shek of China, and Queen Wilhelmina of the Netherlands.

Fears of Axis saboteurs and agents prodded the administration and Congress to hand the Secret Service a new mission after all: The agency once entrusted with protecting America's secrets during wartime was now charged with protecting the nation's national treasures, such as the original Declaration of Independence, the Constitution, the Gutenberg Bible, Lincoln's Second Inaugural Address, and the Lincoln Cathedral Copy of the Magna Carta. Shortly after the attack on Pearl Harbor, agents carried them out of Washington, D.C., to vaults at Fort Knox, Kentucky, where they were locked up and guarded by the Service until the end of the war. After Japan finally surrendered on September 2, 1945, agents returned the priceless relics to the Library of Congress in Washington, D.C.

The agency not only took on such new tasks as safeguarding national treasures, but also resumed some of the duties it had been assigned in World War I. Once again, counterfeiters and con artists devised ways to turn the nation's homefront patriotism into illicit profits, especially through schemes targeting the nationwide rationing of food and supplies. Counterfeit stamps for meat, butter, sugar, and gasoline flooded America during World War II, along with bogus U.S. Savings Stamps and Bonds. Typical of the Secret Service's relentless investigations against counterfeiters was a raid that netted 210,000 stamps with a value of $52,500; from the bench at the trial of several of the plot's architects, the judge derided them as "despicable traitorous chiselers."

Another scheme the agency battled throughout the war was the theft and forgery of government checks and war bonds. Operatives arrested scores of people churning out fake bonds.

Throughout the Secret Service's wartime chase of counterfeiters, the agency scored an anticrime coup with the "Know Your Money" campaign. Agents used posters, flyers, and radio spots to show the public how to detect the differences between genuine and "funny" money. So effective was the campaign that counterfeit money, whose supply had always swelled during the nation's wars, ebbed from the yearly wartime average of $1 million to $50,000 in circulation.

During World War II, the Secret Service was also used to seize the files of hundreds of Japanese business firms, protect Japanese property confiscated in America, and conduct background investigations on Japanese aliens. The Service's effectiveness in thwarting counterfeiters extended to Europe during World War II, where Axis agents were counterfeiting greenbacks and trying to pass them to their operatives in the United States. The Service's success in cracking Axis counterfeiting rings was largely because the agency had never lost sight of its traditional mission to protect the nation's currency. In the mid-1930s, even as organizational threats from the FBI were parried, the Secret Service cracked many high-profile counterfeiting cases, including the pursuit and capture of one of the world's foremost "coney men," the cunning "Count" Victor Lustig. A native of Vienna, Lustig, a dapper figure with a neatly trimmed mustache and courtly manners, successfully masqueraded as a nobleman—along with more than thirty other "identities"—and amassed a fortune as a confidence man.

Lustig, fluent in an array of languages, bedeviled police and detectives throughout Europe and the United States from 1917–1935; his reputation as a thief, embezzler, con man, and passer of counterfeit bills and securities continued to soar. One of his greatest cons was *twice* "selling" the Eiffel Tower to gulled scrap-metal magnates. Forty-two law-enforcement agencies worldwide were pursuing Lustig by the early 1930s, but the elusive Austrian was always one step ahead of his trackers.

Playing upon the greed of others, Lustig persuaded scores of wealthy people to invest in his "money-making machine," a box that allegedly reproduced any currency. As the Secret Service noted, "he demonstrated his fake box using two currency notes of the same denomination as bait." His eager victims saw only the one note being placed in the machine and were tremendously impressed when the 'Count' turned a crank and a duplicated note came out. Eager to get richer, many of his customers paid heavily for Lustig's money machine. He provided them with the machine, collected his payment, and left before the customers realized that they had been swindled.

In early 1934, Lustig branched out into a new venture that brought him into a contest of wits with the Secret Service. He formed a partnership with William Watts, a gifted photoengraver, to counterfeit greenbacks and flood them throughout America. When Watts crafted over a million dollars in forged bills, Lustig, under the alias of "Robert Miller," boarded a passenger ship bound from London to New York City; he had already set up a distribution network in America to circulate the bogus bills in the nation's banks.

Alarmed bankers in New York City alerted the Secret Service that over $100,000 per month of near-perfect counterfeit currency was flowing through the windows of unwitting tellers by mid-1934. Agents began to investigate and discovered that "Robert Miller" and William Watts were in the city. After tailing the duo for several weeks, agents from the New York field office pounced, arresting the two men and seizing stacks of counterfeit bills. Count Lustig's days as the "crown price of 20th-century counterfeiters" were over.

Four years later, in 1938, one of the Secret Service's many counterfeiting investigations took a shocking twist. In August, agents, believing that they were on a run-of-the-mill bogus money mission, waded into one of the largest mass-murder cases in the nation's annals. The grim saga unfolded when Agent Stanley Phillips, investigating undercover, met Herman Petrillo, a balding, inconspicuous-looking food distributor and insurance man who had been passing piles of counterfeit greenbacks in and around Philadelphia. Phillips, posing as a con man interested in buying a stack of Petrillo's counterfeit money and passing it into circulation at a large profit, was surprised by another offer from Petrillo. He offered to pay Phillips $500, considered a tidy sum in the Great Depression, to murder a man, so that his wife could collect on his life insurance policy.

The cool-headed agent kept his "poker face" as Petrillo outlined the murder-for-hire scheme. Phillips "agreed" to join in, all the while pumping

Petrillo for more information. What Phillips learned was shocking: Petrillo was one of the ringleaders of a gang that was poisoning men and women to cash in on their insurance policies. Petrillo did not wait for Phillips to kill the man for him; instead, one of the gang poisoned him with arsenic. The man later died in a hospital.

When the Secret Service pounced on the murder-for-hire ring, they arrested seventeen men and seventeen women for the murder of twenty-one people in Pennsylvania, New Jersey, New York, and Delaware. Agents suspected that many more had been killed. Petrillo and his accomplices had used arsenic as their favorite tool for murder. Victims had been fed poisoned food or medicine, enduring a slow, agonizing death that doctors mistakenly attributed to heart disease or acute indigestion. However, it was not their only method; others proved equally savage. Victims were cracked over the head with a blackjack and tossed into the ocean or a river to simulate "accidental drownings." In one case, a victim had been deliberately run over by a car and appeared to have been killed as a result of a hit-and-run accident.

As the result of the Secret Service's investigation, Petrillo and three other killers were strapped into the electric chair. Twenty-six of their accomplices were sentenced to prison. The nation's newspapers lauded the role of the agency in obtaining the evidence that shattered the band of mass murderers.

The Service did not bring local police into the case until the very end, in part because the episode had started as a counterfeiting investigation and in part because agents feared that a local law officer might tip off the suspects. Chief Wilson allowed his field agents a great deal of latitude in how much and how soon they chose to involve local and regional police in cases.

By the end of World War II, the Secret Service's primary missions of anticounterfeiting and presidential protection generally precluded their involvement in cases such as the investigation of the murder-for-hire ring. As returning servicemen swelled the ranks of the Metropolitan Police and Park Police by 1947, Congress, with an eye toward the status quo of White House protection, restored the requirement that White House policemen be recruited from these two entities. The temporary wartime enlargements of the White House Police Force ended, and Congress ceased appropriating funds for additional officers. Simultaneously, however, Congress increased the numerical limit on the permanent force from eighty to one hundred and ten.

One thing that did not change, however, was J. Edgar Hoover's ambition to supplant the Secret Service with FBI agents as the presidential security detail. In the fall of 1947, President Harry Truman, who did not relish the idea of Hoover watching the president's back, wrote his wife, Bess, a letter hinting that the protective power struggle between Hoover and the Secret Service had taken an unnerving turn:

> Dear Bess,
>
> I am sure glad the Secret Service is doing a better job. I was worried about that situation. Edgar Hoover would give his right eye to take over, and all Congressmen and Senators are afraid of him. I'm not and he knows it. If I can prevent it, there'll be no NKVD or Gestapo in this country. Edgar Hoover's organization would make a good start towards a citizen spy system. Not for me.
>
> Lots of love,
> Harry

Hoover's last gasp effort at supplanting the Service's protective mission was during Lyndon B. Johnson's presidency. When the president left office, as journalist Anthony Summers describes, "a depressed Lyndon Johnson worried—again—about his personal safety." The president reportedly told an administrative aide: "Tell Edgar Hoover that I have taken care of him since the beginning of my administration and now I am leaving. I expect him to take care of me. . . . There will be any number of crackpots trying to get after me after January 20, 1969 [when he'd be leaving office]." Johnson held this fear despite the law providing Secret Service protection to former presidents. Perhaps the assassination of his predecessor in Dallas contributed to this apprehension.

Truman's preference for the Secret Service over Hoover's G-men was cemented on November 1, 1950, when the president was residing at Blair House because of extensive renovations underway at the Executive Mansion. At 2:30 P.M. that day, Truman was napping in a second-floor bedroom at his temporary quarters, directly across Pennsylvania Avenue from the White House.

A pair of Puerto Ricans, Griselio Torresola and Oscar Collazo, strode toward Blair House from the west, both men attracting little attention from passersby. Earlier that day, the pair had strolled past the house, scrutinizing the mansion's security posts and possible points of entry. Concealing pistols, Torresola and Collazo intended to assassinate Truman in a blow for Puerto Rican nationalism.

Around 2:00 P.M., they walked to 15th Street and chose to separate and approach the house from different directions. Torresola walked toward the mansion from the west, Collazo from the east; the pair planned to arrive simultaneously, storm the president's security detail, and shoot their way into Blair House.

As the two men converged on Blair House, Private Leslie Coffelt, of the Secret Service White House Police, was manning the west security booth, and Private Joseph Davidson was in the east booth with Special Agent Floyd Boring. Standing on the first step of Blair House's front door and under a canopy was Washington Police Officer Donald Birdzell.

Collazo walked within eight feet of Birdzell. The assassin pulled his automatic pistol on the officer, who had his back turned to the attackers as he talked with Agent Boring, and fired. The gun clicked—nothing happened for an instant. Then the pistol cracked and a round tore into Birdzell's right knee. Immediately Boring and Davidson drew their pistols and opened up on Collazo, as did Special Agent Vince Mroz a moment later. Inside Blair House, Agent Stewart Stout heard the shots, rushed to a gun cabinet, retrieved a Thompson submachine gun, and stood in the hallway guarding the stairs and elevator to the second floor, where Truman was trying to nap. His wife, Bess, was not in Washington.

At the same time, Torresola halted in front of the west booth, whipped out his Luger, and pumped rounds into Coffelt's abdomen and left side. Coffelt slumped to the floor of the sentry box. Then Torresola leveled his Luger at White House Police Officer Joseph Downs, dropped him with three shots, and hurdled a hedge to get to Collazo and up the steps.

Seconds later Torresola also snapped off a shot at Birdzell, who had crawled onto Pennsylvania Avenue to try and pull Collazo away from Blair House. As Birdzell squeezed off a round at Torresola and missed, the attacker's shot ripped into the officer's left knee. Suddenly the dying Coffelt lurched to his feet, propped himself against the booth, pointed his revolver at Torresola's head, and fired. The bullet slammed into Torresola's ear and he pitched forward, dead before he hit the ground.

The other officers and agents blasted away at Collazo, bullets whistling through his hat and nicking one of his ears and his nose. Finally he crumpled as a shot slammed into his chest. In all, the would-be assassins and the agents and officers had exchanged twenty-seven shots.

Coffelt died three hours and forty minutes later during surgery. President Truman later remarked, "The one [officer] who was killed was just cold bloodily murdered before he could do anything." The other White House police officers recovered from their injuries.

The assassins never had a chance of reaching the president. Inside the mansion, Stout and other agents would have cut down the assailants even if they had miraculously shot their way past the front door. The protection perimeters had been tested and were proven to be effective; the Secret Service and the White House Police proved their valor and their efficiency in protecting the president.

In the annals of the Secret Service's protective mission, the wild scene outside Blair House was the agency's most savage gun battle, an assassination attempt purely political and nationalistic in purpose and so different from the "lone nuts" who had gunned down Presidents Garfield and McKinley. Collazo and Torresola had hoped to kill the president as a means by which to shock the American public and thereby draw attention to the cause of Puerto Rican nationalism—even though President Truman had already sent Congress a special message recommending that Puerto Rico's status be changed to one of four options, including outright independence. In spite of Truman's expressed sympathy for Puerto Rican self-determination, he was selected as a target because of the shock and visibility the would-be assassins hoped to create.

Collazo was sentenced to death after he refused to allow his lawyers to plead insanity and after the defense failed to convince the jury that Collazo, who was armed, had planned only to demonstrate in front of Blair House and that his deceased accomplice, Torresola, had started the shooting. President Truman commuted the sentence to life in prison. In 1979, Collazo was returned to Puerto Rico, where he lived until his death in 1994.

In the fallout from the foiled assassination attempt, American newspapers exposed the fact that the Secret Service lacked permanent authority for its protective and criminal investigative missions. The agency's only legal authority to carry out its protective duties and responsibilities came from Congress's annual Treasury Appropriation Act, and any congressman or senator could delay Secret Service appropriations by simply objecting to them. With voters demanding that presidents be better protected in the wake of the Blair House gun battle, the House of Representatives unanimously passed House Resolution 2395 on May 21, 1951. When the bill arrived at the White House on July 16, 1951, President Truman signed it and quipped, "Well it is wonderful to know that the work of protecting me has at last become legal." The measure permanently authorized the protection of the president, his immediate family, the president-elect, and the vice president, at his request. The legislative branch of the U.S. government had finally, years after the birth of the republic, affirmed the need of the executive branch for security protection. Thankfully, in 1950 they had already approved an increase to the White House Uniformed Officer detail to 133 officers to accommodate a switch to a shorter workweek. The legislative branch of the U.S. government had finally affirmed the need of protection for the executive branch 162 years after Geroge Washington was sworn in as the nation's first president.

There were no direct assaults on presidents from November 1, 1950, to November 22, 1963. In 1952, again in the wake of the attempt on President Truman's life at Blair House, Congress again expanded the maximum size of the protective force, to 170 uniformed officers, as well as a Secret Service detail.

Americans had glimpsed the valor of Secret Service agents in newsreel footage taken just after the assassination attempt in 1950. That same year, they saw the agency portrayed in a far less risky episode on the big screen. Secret Service Case Number 880 was the inspiration for the movie *Mister 880,* the biopic of a counterfeiter who had matched wits with agents for a decade. Starring Burt Lancaster as the agent who finally nabs the enigmatic counterfeiter, the film cast the grandfatherly Edmund Gwen as the coney man who had crafted and circulated phony $1 bills to make ends meet.

In truth, Case 880 began when counterfeit $1 bills started showing up in New York City in late 1938. The bills were not flooding banks and businesses—just a few of the greenbacks would turn up each week, and the strange pattern continued for ten years. With few people able to remember who—it could have been virtually anyone—might have given them a $1 bill, the lowest denomination, the Secret Service had little chance to come up with the culprit.

That all changed on January 13, 1948, when four boys were playing around a trash heap behind an apartment building on Ninety-sixth Street in

New York. Gleaming amid the garbage were several brass plates with an impression of a $1 bill and several counterfeit $1 notes. The boys alerted the police, who, in turn, summoned the Secret Service.

Agents taking possession of the plates learned that a fire had broken out on December 4, 1947, in the apartment of Emerich Juettner, a junk dealer who lived near the site of the boys' find. When firemen had gone into the apartment to quell the blaze, they had tossed heaps of papers and trash into the vacant alley outside the building. Snow had covered the trash heap for some two weeks after the fire.

On January 14, 1948, Juettner was arrested. At seventy-two years of age, Juettner had not counterfeited to make a fortune; like the character in the movie, he turned out bills only when he needed to make ends meet. He had kept a detailed map of New York throughout his decade of counterfeiting so that he could track where he passed his bogus bills and not stick any stores for more than $1.

When Juettner pleaded guilty, the judge lectured him on the seriousness of the crime against not only the government, but also the people of this country, and sentenced him to nine months in jail, along with a fine of $1. The Secret Service made no argument that the judge hand down a harsher sentence.

In 1951, according to agency figures, the Service "seized $1.44 million in counterfeit notes, completed almost 50,000 investigations, worked 95,000 hours in uncompensated overtime, and had a 98 percent conviction rate for cases that went to trial, all accomplished by 250 agents." Still, the mission that they would become most identified with—presidential protection—was at last taking center-stage. The dual mission—anticounterfeiting and protection—was becoming clearly defined. Yet when it came to legislators increasing the budget for the protective mission, parsimony still reigned, and the tightfisted approach seemed less egalitarian than partisan.

Dwight D. Eisenhower won the presidency in 1952, and with his victory came a potential security nightmare for the Secret Service. Ike had vowed to the nation that if elected, he would fly to Korea to see firsthand how he might end the war there. Three weeks after his election, he left for the war-ravaged country on a secret six-day trip; the Secret Service's mission was to keep him safe—in a war zone. They did, but not without several "close shaves." President-elect Eisenhower traveled to the front lines to positions that (were overrun) by the Chinese and North Koreans scant hours after he left. Snipers posed a constant threat. But by working closely with military intelligence and scouting out sites as best they could before Ike arrived, the agents returned the president-elect safely home. I bet he didn't take helicopters.

On May 13, 1958, Eisenhower's vice president, Richard Nixon, and his wife, Pat, arrived in Caracas, Venezuela, during a goodwill tour of South America, and barely escaped with their lives. That they did remains a testament to the quick wit and courage of the couple's Secret Service detail.

At the Caracas airport, a horde of demonstrators jeered, shouted, blew whistles that added to the din, and waved placards haranguing the United States as Venezuelan officials tried to welcome the Nixons in an official ceremony on the tarmac. Then stones and bottles rained down on the couple. Secret Service agents formed a tight ring around the pair and quickly escorted them to a bulletproof limousine; protestors closed in and spit at the Nixons as they climbed inside the car.

As the motorcade wound at a near crawl into the city, several makeshift roadblocks forced the procession to stop. Swinging pipes and clubs, a screaming crowd swarmed the Nixons' car and swung the weapons against the windows and roof and at the Secret Service agents flanking the limo. Inside the vehicle, several agents shielded the Nixons.

The Caracas police did nothing to hold back the mob. Spat on, kicked, and punched, the Secret Service men did not draw their weapons; instead, the agents used their palms—not even closed fists—to stop protestors from ripping open the limo doors and assaulting the vice president and his wife.

A shell casing slammed against an agent's head. Though bleeding and dazed, he did not give an inch, pushing back demonstrators with his open palms.

The crowd pressed all around the limo and started to rock it, trying to tip it over and set it on fire. Inside the car, agents finally drew their guns. They did not have to use them as help in the form of a flatbed truck packed with reporters rumbled into the crowd and cleared a path for the limo to slowly follow.

All ceremonies for the Nixons were canceled. Agents later discovered that in a building next to the site of a wreath-laying ceremony in which the Nixons would have participated, anti-American rioters had stored a cache of Molotov cocktails. The vice presidential couple left hurriedly the following day.

Having no doubt that the coolness and professionalism of the Secret Service had saved his and his wife's lives in Caracas, Richard Nixon wrote a letter to Secretary of the Treasury Robert B. Anderson. Recommending that each agent from the Caracas team receive the Exceptional Civilian Award and a citation for heroism, Nixon noted:

> In Caracas, at a time when local police protection was virtually nonexistent, they [agents] moved back an armed mob with their bare hands, then broke the roadblock and freed the motorcade so that it could proceed out of danger. There is no doubt in my mind but that, had one of them failed to exercise that rare combination of restraint and courage in an exemplary degree, bloodshed might have resulted which could have led to almost frightening international repercussions.

When Nixon penned those well-deserved accolades for the agents, the image of the Secret Service as a highly efficient organization of somber, fearless men wearing sunglasses and ready to spring into action at any hint of trouble for a president or vice president colored Americans' collective view. In truth, the image did not—and does not—tell the whole story.

## CHAPTER 3

# LOSING LANCER— THE JFK ASSASSINATION

*Jim Rowley [Secret Service Director] is most efficient. He has never lost a president.*
*—President John F. Kennedy, November 1963*

I n 1982 author Philip H. Melanson initiated a Freedom of Information Act request with the Secret Service for additional documents relating to the John F. Kennedy assassination, documents that he believed might not be contained in Warren Commission files available to researchers at the National Archives in Washington, D.C., as Commission File Number 22, "Records Relating to the Protection of the President." The Secret Service responded that in 1979, it had turned over to the National Archives *all* remaining documents pertaining to the Kennedy assassination. The author then queried Mr. Marion Johnson, the chief archivist in charge of the Warren Commission records, about whether the 1979 material was contained in the Commission files that the author had already reviewed. It was not.

Because of a shortage of staff, the six boxes of "new" material remained unprocessed: the documents had not been cataloged and security clearance sought. Within two weeks of Melanson's query, the additional material had been processed. He traveled to Washington, D.C., to review it and uncovered more data relating to the Service's duties and performance in November 1963.

The struggle to obtain full disclosure of the records was grueling. The American people needed to know what went wrong, yet had never received the complete truth. The Treasury Department lobbied quickly and hard in the aftermath of the Kennedy assassination to restrict press and public access to analyses of Secret Service methods, fearing not only that public exposure of protective procedures would increase the risk of future assassinations, but also, perhaps, that such scrutiny would reveal, in some cases, the disastrous gaffes of agents in Dallas.

From the start of the postassassination fallout, Treasury Department lawyers working on behalf of the Secret Service sought to place legal roadblocks in the path of evolving investigation of the Warren Commission. The agency hoped to blunt any congressional attempt to examine the agency's protective methods. The Commission, however, responded that it was "unwilling to agree in advance to any limitation upon its prerogative of suggesting any change in arrangements for presidential protection which it may consider desirable." Still, in a nod to the agency, Commission lawyers did promise the Treasury Department to respect Secret Service appeals to restrict public access to information detailing protective methods. Further acceding to the agency's campaign to block revelations about agents' flawed performances and reactions in Dallas, the Warren Commission attempt to seal its records for a generation failed; the effort fell apart with the passage of the Freedom of Information Act in 1966. More and more documents have been released as the years passed.

The Secret Service documents in the Warren Commission files provide a clear picture of the organization's protective efforts for the president's trip to Dallas. Though the record indicates that the Service's performance was constrained by the political priorities of the president and the White House staff and by the mistakes made by local law-enforcement units, it also reveals significant failure of performance—failure for which the Secret Service itself bore full responsibility.

On November 22, 1963, when the first bullet tore into "Lancer's" upper body and the final shot slammed into his head, everything changed—for the nation and the Secret Service. The agency had lost Lancer, President John F. Kennedy.

The Secret Service immediately began a pattern of lies about its fatal missteps in Dallas that day and the days preceding it. The agency was experiencing the worst crisis it had ever faced.

At least two agents lied to the Warren Commission. Even worse, as they created the fiction about how thorough they had been, they implicitly pinned the blame on the fallen president himself, hinting that Kennedy's recklessness or fatalism—not anything the agents had done in Dallas—

ignited a tragic sequence of events. Kennedy's critics still chant the mantra that the president brought it on himself. These outright lies and half-truths cannot absolve the Secret Service for losing the life of a president for the first time in its history.

Within hours of the assassination, Agent Roy Kellerman, who had sat in the front seat of Kennedy's limousine, assured the FBI: "The precautions employed in Dallas were the most stringent and thorough ever employed . . . for the visit of a president to an American city."

He did not relate how he had frozen for those six or seven seconds after the first shot—a time span that allowed the "kill shot" to the president's head.

Agent William Greer, the driver of Kennedy's car, neglected to admit how he had failed to hit the gas after the first shot or swerve the vehicle to throw off the unseen sniper's aim. The limo continued rolling at a snail's pace down Dealy Plaza. Worse, he actually slowed down almost to a complete stop.

As Greer followed the established procedures and waited for a command from Kellerman, the president was a proverbial sitting duck. The agents had those six or seven seconds to do *something, anything,* before the president's head was nearly blown off. They did nothing and covered up their actions— or lack of them—to the Warren Commission and others.

The Service's advance team in Dallas chose a flawed motorcade route and failed to check out such potential sniper perches as the Texas Book Depository and to secure an overpass. For years, the fiction that Kennedy had refused to allow agents to place a bulletproof bubbletop on the limousine persisted. The top was not actually bulletproof.

On November 21–22, the night before the assassination, nine of Kennedy's agents who were "on call" were out drinking. The next day, several of the agents failed to notice that the motorcycle formation surrounding Kennedy's limo was all wrong.

Because of poor coordination among the Secret Service, the FBI, and the Dallas Police, agents had no idea that a band of Cuban dissidents called Alpha-66 had threatened Kennedy's life. Not until the day after the assassination did Dallas police tell the Secret Service that they had been watching Oswald and that he had met with another group of Cubans; unlike Alpha-66, they were pro-Castro.

There was much to conceal in the performance of some of the Secret

Service detail in Dallas, and a great deal that sank far below agency standards. Even today, many people believe that Kennedy, not the agency, bears full blame for the tragedy. But the truth is that from the moment the president's advance security men planned his Dallas trip, mistakes were made.

As the perception of Kennedy's own "recklessness" took hold publicly, it has become historically fashionable to blame him for his own death, or for at least contributing to it by flaunting security. In 1979, the U. S. House of Representatives Select Committee on Assassinations asserted:

> President Kennedy posed a problem for the Secret Service from the start. . . . His personal style was known to cause agents assigned to him deep concern. He traveled more frequently than any of his predecessors, and he relished contact with crowds of well-wishers. He scoffed at many of the measures designed to protect him and treated danger philosophically.

Such language makes it appear as if the committee thought he almost had it coming because he was brash and "reckless." From that contention, many of Kennedy's critics contend that his reckless style resulted in there being no bubble top on his limo in Dallas, no agents on his running boards, no flanking motorcycles. The Secret Service has done little to contest these bromides, allowing much of the blame to fall squarely on the slain president. Rarely mentioned is the fact that the cycles and running boards would only have protective relevance if a shot came from the grassy knoll, which many conspiracy theories and the House Committee's own acoustical evidence identify as the site of a "shooter." By the official version, subscribed to by the Secret Service, Lee Harvey Oswald fired from the sixth floor of the book depository, and the downward trajectory could not have been effected by anything but the bubble top, which was not even bulletproof, and would have been like shooting the president through a window. None of this absolves the Service of losing the president.

For starters, the motorcade route should never have included a dog-leg turn that would slow the limo and relegate it to the pace of a sitting duck. Kennedy didn't take agents out drinking the night before. Greer and Kellerman had nearly seven seconds to take action, before the president's head was blown off as he sat in a near-stationary position: a swerve, a rapid acceleration, a leap into the backseat, instead of breaking and looking back twice (Greer) after hearing the "firecracker." Neither Kennedy nor his aides were the ones who made the follow-up car lag so far behind that it was practically out of play. The president's wounds were survivable until the final head shot. Bill Greer never took evasive action at the limo's wheel.

Consider that no agents were fired for drinking or for bad judgment. Some of the agents, though not Winston G. Lawson, lied to the Warren Commission. They lied to the Commission about how thorough they were, and implicitly placed the blame on Kennedy for his own assassination. It has become mainstream fashionable among people who know little or nothing about presidential protection to harangue the "reckless" Kennedy. For the Secret Service, this take among so many people has served the purpose of throwing a smokescreen around what really happened in Dallas on November 22, 1963.

The assassination of John F. Kennedy traumatized the nation, and for the Secret Service, the assassination brought a maelstrom of questions from the press and from legislators all demanding answers to one crucial question: The U.S. Secret Service had failed at its most important assignment—to protect the life of the president. How could this have happened?

Prior to November 22, 1963, the Secret Service had never lost a president. It did not have legal responsibility for presidential protection when President McKinley was killed in 1901, the last president to be assassinated prior to Kennedy.

In no dispute is the fact that President Kennedy's trip to Texas was purely political in purpose. The state's Democratic Party was bitterly divided, and the president's policies on a range of issues from Cuba to Civil Rights to the oil depletion allowance had infuriated Texans. With Kennedy having barely won the state's sizable chunk of electoral votes in 1960, even with Lyndon Baines Johnson on the ticket, many Texans' contempt for his administration signaled a real chance that Texas might vote Republican in 1964. Kennedy's two-day trip, designed for political repair, had the president in San Antonio on November 21, in Fort Worth on the morning of November 22, then flying to Dallas for a lunch-hour motorcade and a luncheon at the Trade Mart with Dallas business and civic elites. In a reflection of just how important the White House considered the need to shore up Texans' support, Vice President Johnson, the star of the state's political roster, would accompany Kennedy on the trip.

Secret Service documents reveal again and again the dominance of politics over protection in planning for the trip. In a disturbing development for the agency, the president's protectors were not informed about the trip by the White House until political planning and publicity were well underway. The idea of a presidential visit to Texas had been discussed by President Kennedy, Vice President Johnson, and Texas Governor John Connally in a Texas hotel room on June 5, 1963, long before the Service had any inkling of the plan. On September 13, 1963, the White House confirmed the trip, and the Dallas newspapers announced it as a fact, although the dates and itinerary were not actually settled.

On October 4, John Connally visited the White House to work out the basic agenda for a motorcade and luncheon. He also held a press conference in Dallas to announce the visit. Finally, three days later, on November 4, the Secret Service was first informed by the White House staff that the president would be going to Dallas; the Agency finally learned that the logistics of the trip had been planned long before they were apprised of the plan.

The head of the Secret Service's Dallas field office, Agent Forrest Sorrells, was directed on November 4, 1963, by the head of the White House protective detail, Gerald A. Behn, to check out possible luncheon sites. The two venues considered best were the Trade Mart and the Women's Building. The Secret Service preferred the Women's Building because it had fewer entrances and appeared better suited to security; some of the White House staff preferred it also because it could hold four thousand people, far more than the Trade Mart. However, the president and his inner circle had already selected the Trade Mart, a symbol to Texans of their state's burgeoning economic status, dropping the news on the Secret Service at the last minute.

Governor Connally was given primary responsibility for arranging the political agenda to refurbish the president's image within the Dallas business elite. As far as Dallas political and commercial movers and shakers were concerned, the Trade Mart's recently completed, ornate symbol of their burgeoning status as Texas's finest was the only location that made sense, given the political purpose of the luncheon.

The Secret Service's preference, the Women's Building, contained low ceilings with beams that hung even lower, giving it a claustrophobic ambience; it also featured ugly "exposed conduits." Most important, the building did not have adequate food-handling facilities for a catered luncheon.

When Governor Connally heard that the luncheon might not be held at the Trade Mart if the Secret Service had its way, he threatened to boycott the entire trip. As the host politician, whose political image was on the line, Connally was not about to oversee a presidential luncheon held at an inferior facility; such a venue would make him appear "small-time"—political suicide for an ambitious Texas politician. The Secret Service had been sent on a fool's errand when told to look for a luncheon site that could be best secured; politically, there was only one site—the Trade Mart.

From the initial planning of the trip, many politicians and aides were concerned about the president's safety in Texas. The week before Kennedy's visit, United Nations Ambassador Adlai Stevenson had come to Dallas to speak to the local United Nations Association. He was confronted by demonstrators who cursed him, spat upon him, and shoved to get at him. One picketer slammed his sign against the ambassador's head. The shaken Stevenson called Kennedy advisor Arthur Schlesinger Jr. and urged that the president not go to Dallas. Similarly worried, Democratic Senator J. William Fulbright warned the president: "Dallas is a very dangerous place. I wouldn't go there. Don't you go."

Kennedy and his staff thought otherwise. He and Vice President Lyndon B. Johnson, a Texan, had barely carried the state in their narrow victory in the 1960 election, and many campaign strategists concurred that Kennedy would have an even harder time keeping Texas in the democratic camp in the 1964 election unless the president somehow shored up support there. In the midterm elections, the Democrats had lost seats. Now, in 1963, Kennedy's pro–Civil Rights stance and the Bay of Pigs fiasco had turned many conservative Texas Democrats against him. Needing to woo them back, he was committed to the November 1963 trip to the state.

A man who had survived war and had lost a brother and sister in plane crashes, Kennedy was too fatalistic to worry about protection, and as far as the Secret Service was concerned, this was just another trip, not one uniquely fraught with danger. With the seemingly minor exception of trying to identify the demonstrators who had attacked Stevenson, the Secret Service simply followed its standard protective routine, which it perceived as providing adequate protection. Moreover, the man they were protecting loathed tight security if he believed that a threat was not real. Still, in contrast to his purported "recklessness," Kennedy had acceded to tight protection during a previous motorcade, allowing his limousine to be flanked by police motorcycles because of a specific threat to his safety discovered in advance by the Service. Such examples notwithstanding, the House Select Committee on Assassinations generally described Kennedy as "almost recklessly disregarding of Secret Service protection," a distortion that the Service would not hesitate to invoke on numerous occasions over the years as a contributing factor or even the chief reason for the tragedy in Dallas.

Kennedy used the motorcade as a primary political tool as he had during the 1960 presidential campaign. According to White House aide O'Donnell, motorcades were used to provide "extended public exposure." Having agents on the running boards or having the president ride under the transparent bubble top reduced that exposure and hindered his ability to project a dashing, charismatic public face. Retired Agent Winston G. Lawson, part of the advance detail for the Dallas trip, says, "Political priorities have always been a problem, 99% of the time. . . . There's always gonna be a political side versus a Secret Service side."

As with the other details of the trip, the selection of a motorcade route was, in great measure, politically determined. According to O'Donnell, the Secret Service was so generally attuned to White House political priorities that "it would be automatic" for the Service to arrange a route that, in the time allotted by the president, would take him "through an area which exposes him to the greatest number of people."

On November 14, 1963, Agents Sorrells, of the Dallas field office, and Winston G. Lawson, from the White House detail, were riding over the proposed routes when they were informed by a member of the Democratic National Committee that the luncheon would definitely be held at the Trade Mart. Given the Love Field Landing and a downtown motorcade, the Trade Mart luncheon site dictated most of the motorcade route, which would logically wind through Dealy Plaza and in front of the Texas School Book Depository.

The Dallas *Times Herald* announced the general route two days later, stating that it "apparently will loop through the downtown area probably on Main Street en route from Dallas Love Field." On November 19, 1963, the precise route was published by the Dallas newspapers—three days before the president's visit.

There was no attempt to exercise any secrecy regarding the president's itinerary or the motorcade route. The closest thing to secrecy seems to have been the way in which the politically determined plans concerning the trip were made known to the Secret Service at the last possible minute. Of course, publicity was an absolute necessity if the motorcade was to be a political success, for if the people of Dallas did not turn out in throngs along the motorcade route, the media might label the president's trip a failure. A well-advertised route was essential if people were to make plans to see the president on their Friday afternoon lunch hour.

As was usual for the Secret Service, it met with local law-enforcement authorities in advance of the trip in order to obtain their help in placing protection. On November 18, 1963, Agents Lawson and Sorrells and two representatives of the Dallas Police Department drove over the motorcade route, taking notes on crowd control, traffic patterns, the location of intersections, overpasses, and railroad crossings. They discussed how to seal off the motorcade route from other traffic so that there would be no snarls and drew up plans to assign police to each of the overpasses along the route to keep spectators off of them and to protect the president's open limousine from being hit by any falling objects. At all railroad crossings, police officers would control the switching mechanisms.

Secret Service agents and police checked out both Love Field, to which the president would make a short flight from Fort Worth, and the few miles to the Trade Mart. Agents decided to set up rope barriers flanked by police and designed to keep the crowd at a safe distance. A police officer would be assigned to guard the only stairway leading to the Trade Mart roof to prevent anyone from perching up there while the president was entering or leaving. At the building across the street, a Trade Mart security guard would man the roof.

Security guards would guard the Trade Mart overnight and would be joined by Secret Service agents on the morning of the luncheon. No freight deliveries would be allowed while the president was there, and all entrances except the main one were closed. Only individuals with appropriate credentials would be allowed to enter.

Designing security arrangements for the Trade Mart luncheon was the most complex of the advance protective tasks for the Secret Service. Lists of employees who worked for the Trade Mart and for the catering firm that would service lunch were obtained and cross-checked against the Service's protective-research files in Washington. Agents discovered no problem employees.

Various identification badges, a different one for each role, were manufactured and issued: one denoted the local press, one was for the White House press, and others were for the airport reception committee, waiters, and plainclothes police. Dallas police were shown and given samples of the color-coded lapel pins worn by the Secret Service, White House staff, and White House communications personnel. At Love Field, the Service arranged for the landing and taxi routes for Air Force One; Air Force personnel were called upon to secure the routes.

Strangely, this meticulous advance work did not include checking the triple overpass that crossed Elm Street just after the soon-to-be infamous grassy knoll. No one cleared the area of spectators or guarded it with police—as it should have been—when the presidential limousine headed directly at and under it. Though no hard evidence proves that a shot came from the overpass area, agents' failure to secure the area prior to the president's arrival was yet another glaring security glitch, as was the failure to secure the area on top of the grassy knoll, hidden from the motorcade's view by a stockade fence. This potential danger spot commanded a close-up, unobstructed view of the president's limousine as it passed in the middle lane of one-way Elm Street.

The parking lot and railroad yard behind the knoll offered a ready escape route for potential assassins whose movements would be obscured not only by the fence (a perfect place to rest a rifle), but also by the shadows of the large, leafy trees that darkened the knoll and contrasted sharply with the bright Texas sunshine that bathed the motorcade.

Regarding the overpass, Agent Lawson later testified to the Warren Commission:

> I recall thinking we were coming to an overpass now, so I glanced up to see if it was clear, the way most of them had been, the way all of them had been until that time on the way downtown, and it was not and I was looking for the officer who should have been there, had been requested to be there, and made a kind of motion through the windshield trying to get his attention to move the

people from over our path the way it should have been. We were just approaching this overpass when I heard a shot.

Along with the failure to secure the overpass and the knoll, agents neglected to check the tall building along the motorcade route either in advance by checking lists of employees against Secret Service files, or at the time of the motorcade, by body searching them before the president passed by. As Secretary of the Treasury Douglas Dillon testified to the Warren Commission in a confidential memorandum:

> Except for inauguration and other parades involving foreign dignitaries accompanied by the president in Washington, it has not been the practice of the Secret Service to make surveys or checks of the building along the route of a presidential motorcade . . . With the numbers of men available to the Secret Service and with the time available, surveys of hundreds of building and thousands of windows are not practical. . . . Nor is it practical to prevent people from entering such buildings or to limit access in every building to those employed or having business there. Even if it were possible with a vastly larger force of security officers to do so, many observers have felt that such a procedure would not be consistent with the nature and purpose of the motorcade to let the people see their President and welcome him to their city.

The number of personnel who performed tasks directly or indirectly relating to presidential protection for the political swing through Dallas was not atypically large, but was impressive nonetheless. There were 445 police and public-safety personnel on duty.

As for Secret Service agents, the combined total from the White House protective detail, vice presidential detail (Vice President Johnson) had come with the president, and the Dallas field office was twenty-eight agents. Even so, Agent Lawson says that the key to improved protection since Dallas is more agents (implicitly, not better agents): "More people [agents] doing advance details. More people per shift . . . a lot more people at a particular event."

Even though the advance security preparations for the Texas trip were adequate according to Secret Service standards and procedures, the performance of some Secret Service agents proved inadequate by any standards. Washington columnist Drew Pearson discovered that at least nine Secret Service agents stayed out late drinking the night of November 21–22, 1963. The first unofficial response from the Service was that the establishment patronized by agents was only a coffeehouse and served no liquor at all, an intriguing assertion because at many clubs and restaurants in the Dallas-Fort Worth area, it was customary, given local liquor laws, for patrons to bring their own liquor, with the management providing setups. The fact that the establishment in question held no license to serve liquor did not assure that none was consumed.

Pearson's allegation gained additional credence when Warren Commission investigators found that a "breach of discipline" involving nine Secret Service agents had occurred. After President and Mrs. Kennedy had retired for the night in their Fort Worth hotel, nine of the twenty-eight agents went to the Fort Worth Press Club for beer and mixed drinks. Agents stayed there for times varying from a half hour to two hours, with two agents heading back to the hotel but a group of seven others gathering at The Cellar, a coffeehouse, until between 1:30 A.M. and 3:00 A.M. One stayed until 5:00 A.M.

Even if the Warren Commission investigation is correct in its conclusions that the agents drank moderately at the Press Club and consumed no alcohol at The Cellar, every one of the agents involved had been assigned protective duties that began no later then 8:00 A.M. on November 22, 1963. The president was scheduled to deliver a breakfast speech in Fort Worth at 8:30 A.M. and then make the very short flight to Dallas.

In Dallas, the nine agents who, at the least, had spent a late night, were handed a range of assignments: one provided security at Love Field, four were assigned to the Trade Mart, and four were in the follow-up car behind the presidential limousine in the motorcade.

Even if the agents had quaffed only a few beers at the Press Club, Secret Service regulations strictly forbade the consumption of alcohol *at any time* during travel that involved protective assignments. Agents accompanying the president were considered to be "on call" at all times during a trip, even if they were off their eight-hour protective shift as were the agents who went out the night of November 21–22. Additionally, Secret Service regulations stated that "violations or slight disregard" for this rule "will be cause for removal from the Service."

The regulations notwithstanding, Secret Service Chief James Rowley later testified before the Warren Commission that a Secret Service investigation of the breach of regulations had found that the performance of the nine agents involved was in no way impaired. He asserted that each of the nine agents reported for duty on time, was in full possession of all mental and physical abilities, and performed all duties satisfactorily on November 22, 1963. Further, he claimed that the agents' activities the previous night did not in even the slightest manner impede an action that might have saved the president's life.

On April 28, 1964, Agent Emory Roberts wrote, "There was no question in my mind as to [agents] physical and mental capacity to function effectively in their assigned duties [November 22]."

Rowley contended that although under ordinary circumstances, some disciplinary action would have been taken against the offending agents, in this case it was not appropriate because it would be "unfair" to agents and their families: It would create the impression that the breach of conduct contributed to the assassination which, according to Rowley, it did not. For the first time, the Service had lost a president, but Rowley's chief concern was weighted to protecting agents who had flaunted the agency's own professional code of conduct. He was more concerned to whitewash the Dallas debacle with his "edict" that none of the nine agents were in a position to have performed any action that might have saved the president, because none were in the president's car, but only in the follow-up car. From Rowley, the Warren Commission learned that the agents involved were aware of the seriousness of their breach of conduct and "would not do it again." The president had been killed, but Rowley was telling the public and Congress that agents derelict in their duties "would not do it again."

Decades later, Lawson would acknowledge that any other organization might have fired him or at least disciplined him as the only advance agent to lose a president. But this did not happen: he worked Kennedy's funeral. Lawson concludes that he "had done everything he could" to protect the president.

At a minimum, the Service's own regulations mandated banishment of the offending agents from any protective assignments for the remainder of their careers. Despite Chief Rowley's assertion that the agents' conduct the previous night did not in the slightest way prevent them from taking any actions that might have averted the tragedy ignores the fact that, for whatever reasons or contributing factors the actions of four of the agents riding in the follow-up car were less than effective. Though there were eight agents in the follow-up car and four had stayed out late, Rowley's blanket assertion that the late-night activity did not impede performance fails to specifically account for what became inarguably the flawed, tardy reaction by agents in the follow-up car.

As a postassassination Secret Service document describes, all agents in the convertible follow-up car were instructed to "watch their routes for signs of trouble, scanning not only the crowds but the windows and roofs of buildings, overpasses and crossings" from their positions on the running boards and inside the car. Chief Justice Earl Warren sharply questioned Rowley about the fact that agents did not spot a rifle or a sniper before the shooting, especially as one witness claimed to have seen a man with a rifle in the depository window before the shooting. Another witness, press photographer Bob Jackson, spotted a rifle in a depository window moments after the shooting. Warren said:

> Now other people, as they went along there, even some people in the crowds, saw a man with a rifle up in this building from which the president was shot. Now don't you think that if a man went to bed reasonably early, and hadn't been drinking the night before, he would be more alert to see those things as a Secret Service agent, than if they stayed up until three or four or five o'clock in the morning, going to beatnik joints and doing some drinking along the way?

In Dallas, the violent thunderstorms that drenched the city in the early morning hours of November 22, 1963, had given way to a bright, cloudless sky by the time Air Force One landed at Love Field. The bubble top would not be needed to keep the president dry.

The "lead car" in the motorcade, an unmarked police car occupied by police and Secret Service agents, led the presidential limousine, driven by Secret Service agent William Greer, out of Love Field and into the city. Beside Greer was Agent Roy Kellerman and seated behind the two agents were Governor and Mrs. Connally. John F. and Jackie Kennedy were in the third seat. No agents were on the running boards, and in the follow-up car, agents, who normally stayed within five feet of the presidential limousine, except at high speeds, were not in place.

Next in the procession came the presidential follow-up car, carrying eight agents and a cache of shotguns and automatic weapons that were concealed in compartments between the seats. Two agents rode on each running board; four others were inside the open car along with two White House staff members. Vice President Johnson's open limousine was next in the motorcade, trailed by his follow-up car.

Potential problems emerged as the motorcade was formed at Love Field, proceeded through downtown Dallas on Main Street, then turned onto Houston Street and finally onto Elm, where the limos passed the Book Depository. Leading the motorcade were Dallas Police motorcycles followed by the pilot car, a police car that preceded the motorcade by a quarter of a mile and looked for trouble in the form of demonstrators or traffic jams. The U.S. House of Representatives Select Committee on Assassinations criticized the procession's motorcycle protection as out of place and position:

> The Secret Service's alteration of the original Dallas Police Department motorcade deployment plan prevented the use of maximum possible security precautions. Surprisingly, the security measure used in the prior motorcades during the same Texas visit shows that the deployment of motorcycles in Dallas by the Secret Service may have been uniquely insecure.

One of the motorcycle detail, Dallas Police Officer Marion Baker, told the Warren Commission, "My partner and I, we got instructions to ride beside the president's car. . . . When we got to the airport, our sergeant instructed me that there wouldn't be anybody riding beside the president's car."

Instead of encircling the presidential limousine, one motorcycle on each fender in a boxlike formation, the cycles pulled back and away. The Secret Service should have noticed the flawed deployment. The House Assassination Committee said that the outriders were "too far from the presidential limousine to afford Kennedy any protection."

Dallas Police Chief Jesse Curry offered: "In the planning of this motorcade, we had more motorcycles lined up to be with the president's car, but the Secret Service didn't want that many."

At first, the trip through the Dallas suburbs to Main Street went smoothly even as the president ordered the motorcade to stop on two occasions: once so that he could respond to a sign asking him to shake hands, a second time to speak to a nun and a group of small children. Contrary to the rock-throwing crowd that had confronted Adlai Stevenson, the crowds were peaceful. On Main Street a boy ran into the street and chased the presidential limousine, but was steered away by agents.

When the motorcycle escort for the presidential limousine got snarled in traffic and dropped back, an agent from the follow-up car "ran up and got on the rear portion of the presidential automobile to be close to Mrs. Kennedy in the event that someone attempted to grab her from the crowd or throw something in the car."

Of all the locations along the route, the Secret Service should have scouted all the potential sniper spots along Dealy Plaza (Elm Street). Several multistory buildings, including the Book Depository, commanded a view of Elm Street. When the president's car turned left from Houston onto one-way Elm Street, the vehicle slowed down significantly.

The turn was a sharp one, a 120-degree hairpin turn requiring that cars— especially an elongated limousine—reduce speed to navigate right in front of the depository. Nor could the president's car suddenly speed up after making the turn. Elm Street was one way and had three lanes, with no breakdown lanes, fences, or grassy areas between the street and the fairly broad sidewalks. For spectators, it offered a prime spot to see the president close up, but because Elm Street was also relatively short, the president would have slighted the throng if his limo had suddenly sped up after making the turn and whizzed toward the Stemmons Freeway just ahead. Kennedy's car slowed for the turn and headed down Elm at a very slow pace, making it an easier target. Instead of the twenty to thirty miles per hour that the Secret Service liked to maintain, the presidential limousine was now crawling along at a mere 11.2 miles per hour.

Just before the limousine made its turn onto Elm, Mrs. Connally remarked, "Mr. President, you can't say Dallas doesn't love you." Moments later, the seven most traumatic seconds in the history of the U.S. Secret Service began.

Gunfire cracked above the motorcade, and Kennedy clutched his throat with both hands. Agent Kellerman, riding in the front seat next to the driver, claims to have heard the president say, "My God, I'm hit."

At the wheel Agent Greer thought that the sound had come from a motorcycle backfire. He twice looked back toward the president, and took no evasive action.

Greer had had no special training in evasive driving, no specialized driving experience at all. Secret Service procedures in operation at this time did not allow Greer to accelerate or take evasive action on his own initiative: He was supposed to wait for a command from his colleague seated next to him, Agent Kellerman. Neither agent took action of any kind during the six to seven seconds that the limousine lumbered down Elm Street.

As Greer turned and looked back at the president a second time, the last shot smashed into Kennedy's head, thrusting him backward, spraying blood and brain matter throughout the limo and even reaching one of the police motorcycles. Finally, much too late, Kellerman blurted, "Let's get out of here, we're hit!" Greer accelerated. Again, much too late.

The Zapruder film proves just how slowly the limo was moving and how long it took Kellerman and Greer to react. Assassination researcher Vincent Palamara combed the literature, documents, and interviews to find the accounts of fifty-nine witnesses—seven Secret Service agents, ten policemen, thirty-seven bystanders, two presidential aids, a Senator, Governor Connally, and Mrs. Kennedy—who all describe what seems like an extreme deceleration, so extreme that some eyewitnesses thought it was a stop. On December 2, 1963, *Newsweek* reported: "For a chaotic moment, the motorcade ground to an uncertain halt." Witness Clemon Earl Johnson said, "And you could see it stop while they threw Mrs. Kennedy back up in the car."

Associated Press photographer Henry Burroughs, riding in a press car, noted: "We heard the shots and the motorcade stopped." *Houston Chronicle* reporter Bo Byers added that the limo "almost came to a stop, a dead stop." Similarly, Dallas Police Officer D. V. Harkness said, "I heard the first shot and the president's car slow[ed] down to almost a stop." United Press International's *Four Days* asserted: "In the right hand picture [photo taken by a bystander], the driver slams on the breaks and the police escort pulls up."

All the accounts paint a damning indictment of Agent Greer's unaccountably slow driving and inept performance—which possibly cost Kennedy his life, as many medical experts believe he could have survived his neck wound. By decelerating from his already slow 11.2 mph and not reacting to the sound of the first shot, Greer allowed the sniper to have a nearly stationary target. His shotgun rider, Roy Kellerman, told him to move out because they were hit, yet Greer only looked back toward the president. Kellerman later said: "Greer then looked in the back of the car. Maybe he didn't believe me."

The possibility exists that if the limousine had accelerated or taken evasive action during the several seconds between the time the first shot hit the president and the time the last shot struck him, the last shot might have missed Kennedy's head. As the Zapruder film amplifies, it is likely that Kennedy would have survived the wounds inflicted upon him prior to the head shot. If the president had been pulled down or covered during the interval between the first and last shots, it is possible that he might have survived the attack even though Governor and Mrs. Connally separated Kennedy from the agents in the presidential limousine.

At least one agent in the vice presidential detail reacted quicker and more effectively than the others. Agent Rufus Youngblood, perched next to the driver of Lyndon Johnson's limousine, recalled:

> As we were beginning to go down this incline [Elm Street sloped downward], all of a sudden there was an explosive noise. I quickly observed unnatural movement of crowds, like ducking or scattering, and quick movements in the presidential follow-up car. So I turned around and hit the vice president on the shoulder and hollered, get down, and then looked around again and saw more of this movement, and so I proceeded to go to the back seat and get on top of him.

The vice presidential car had only two seats, not three, so that Agent Youngblood could get to Johnson without climbing over an intervening seat as Kennedy's agents would have had to do in order to get to the president. Still, Youngblood's quick reaction starkly contrasts with those of the agents in the presidential limousine. According to both Lyndon Johnson and Agent Clifton C. Carter, who observed Youngblood's actions from the vice presidential follow-up car, Youngblood had scrambled into the rear seat before the second shot was fired.

The fact that the president and the vice president were both in slow-moving limos—one behind the other—constituted another security error by the Secret Service. In the immediate aftermath of September 11, 2001, Vice President Cheney was whisked away from his office and hidden at a secure location: he was *never* in the same place as President George W. Bush to deprive terrorists of a dual target that would shove the nation farther down the chain of presidential succession. Yet, in Dallas, the president and vice president rode in slow-moving *open* vehicles on the same route. No bullet-proof safeguards protected either limo, and both men could have been shot at once.

As can be seen from frame 238 of the Zapruder film, the follow-up car closely tailed the presidential limo as the first shot rang out. The second car rolled as close as two to three feet behind, though the distance appears to have increased as the shooting unfolded. At least one agent in the follow-up car heard what he thought was the crack of rifle fire; another asserted that he was close enough to see a bullet hit the president's back. The president clearly reacted to the first shot, clutching his throat with both hands and jerking forward before slumping to his left. White House staff member Dave Powers, the president's longtime friend from Boston and resident funny man, who always had a quip or story to unwind Kennedy, was riding behind the president in the motorcade and recalled:

> After the first shot, I noticed then that the president moved quite far to his left after the shot from the extreme right hand side where he had been sitting. There was a second shot and Governor Connally disappeared from sight and there was a third shot which took off the top of the President's head and had the sickening sound of a grapefruit splattering against the side of a wall.

Agent Clint Hill, in his November 30, 1963, Secret Service report, corroborated the sickening scene:

> As I lay on top of the back seat I noticed a portion of the president's head on the right rear side was missing, and he was bleeding profusely. Part of his brain was gone. I saw part of his skull with hair on it lying on the seat. . . . There was blood and bits of brain all over the entire rear portion of the car.

Author Vincent Palamara described the shooting sequence based upon his own interviews and the Warren Commission documents:

> The first shot, or shots, ring out and the car slows (with brake lights on). Driver William Greer turns around to see JFK [which he denied ever doing]. Roy H. Kellerman, riding shotgun beside Greer, orders Greer to "get out of line; we've been hit." Greer does not. Instead, he turns around a second time and then the fatal shot explodes the president's head.

During the approximately six to seven seconds of gunfire, the agents in the follow-up car froze to varying degrees. At least two agents drew guns while the shooting was in progress, but none reached the presidential limousine until Agent Clint Hill clambered aboard and pushed Mrs. Kennedy back into the car—after the final shot had struck the president in the head.

There is no way to know whether any agent could possibly have reached the president in the few seconds available in time to cover him or to somehow screen him from the final, fatal bullet that slammed into his head. For one thing, the presidential limousine was moving at 11.2 mph., slow for a vehicle but still fast enough that someone trying to catch up with it must sprint to get there. Compounding the difficulty for any agent who might have tried to act heroically, the presidential limousine appeared to drift farther ahead of the follow-up car during the shooting.

At the time of the first shot, the follow-up car was clearly two to three feet behind; at the last shot, before the presidential limousine accelerated, the distance between it and the follow-up car had extended to fifteen to twenty feet. That fact reveals agents' failure to follow procedure because the follow-up car was supposed to stay about five feet from the presidential limousine, except at high speeds when it would be virtually impossible to do so.

As the shots pealed above Dealy Plaza, the mistakes of commission and omission by agents accelerated at an even more rapid clip. Though it is difficult to determine why several agents froze or reacted too late, several clear-cut problems emerge: inadequate training (at least two agents in the follow-up car thought that they were hearing firecrackers instead of gunfire), failure to perceive precipitating clues, fatigue, and a failure to check out potential sniper perches such as the Texas School Book Depository and the grassy knoll. The hard truth is that the reaction time of several agents protecting the president was woeful.

As Assistant Special Agent in Charge and Greer's superior, Kellerman's words to "get out" have been construed by several analysts as an order that Greer failed to follow. William Manchester, who interviewed Greer, says that Greer told Mrs. Kennedy:

> Oh, Mrs. Kennedy, oh my God, oh my God. I didn't mean to do it. I didn't hear [the shots or agent Kellerman's order?]. I should have swerved the car [or at least not let it come to a near dead stop], I couldn't help it. . . . Oh, Mrs. Kennedy, if only I'd seen it in time.

According to the FBI on the night of the assassination, "Greer stated that they have always been instructed to keep the motorcade moving at a considerable speed inasmuch as a moving car offers a much more difficult target than a vehicle travelling at a very slow speed."

One can only wonder why Greer made an exception on the very day he was behind the wheel when bullets were fired at the president.

The Warren Commission Report states:

> The driver, Special Agent William Greer, has testified that he accelerated the limousine after what was probably the second shot. . . . The president's car did not stop or almost come to a complete halt after the firing of the first shot or any other shots.

Greer's statements rank every bit as fictional as the Commission's assertion that Jack Ruby had no ties to organized crime.

To Warren Commission counsel Arlen Specter, the future U.S. senator from Pennsylvania, Greer offered similar "testimony":

> SPECTOR: Did you step on the accelerator before, simultaneously, or after Mr. Kellerman instructed you to accelerate?
>
> GREER: It was about simultaneously.
>
> SPECTER: So that it was your reaction to accelerate prior to the time . . .

GREER: Yes sir.

SPECTER: You had gotten the instruction?

GREER: Yes sir. It was my reaction that caused me to accelerate.

Jacqueline Kennedy evinced little beside fury toward Agent Greer. According to Mary Gallagher, author of *My Life With Jacqueline Kennedy,* Mrs. Kennedy "mentioned one Secret Service man who had not acted during the crucial moment and said bitterly to me: 'He might just as well have been Miss Shaw [the nanny of John and Caroline].' " Mrs. Kennedy added, "You should get yourself a good driver so that nothing happens to you."

Again, making matters worse, the route the motorcade took played right into the hands of any gunman, crouched and waiting inside the Book Depository or on the grassy knoll. The advance man for the Texas trip—Agent Lawson—and Dallas field-office Agent Forrest Sorrels were largely and perhaps wholly responsible for the motorcade route; they mapped out a dreadful course, if only because the dogleg turn of the long limo from Houston onto Elm would slow the motorcade down in the midst of tall buildings, the overpass, and the grassy knoll.

Lawson rode in the lead car in the motorcade and later told the Warren Commission, "I think it [his vehicle] was a little further ahead [of the presidential limo] than it had been in the motorcade [through Dallas], because when I looked back, we were further away." Again, not a good position. President Kennedy was a proverbial sitting duck.

Peter Dale Scott, in his book *Deep Politics and the Death of JFK,* scrutinized the testimony of Agent Lawson's role in placing the motorcycle detail:

> Lawson's first three reports of what happened on or before November 22 raise considerable questions about his performance. For example, he reported that motorcycles were used "on the right and left flanks of the president's car," although photographs show that they accompanied at the rear. Numerous later reports from Dallas police agreed that at Lawson's own instructions the proposed side escorts were deployed to the rear of the car. This change, ostensibly for the sake of security, would appear to leave the President more open to a possible crossfire.

On the night of November 22–23, 1963, the death car was flown back to

Washington; it was full of the grisly evidence of the protective detail's mistakes before and during the assassination. Agents inspected the limo in the White House garage before the FBI showed up: it was the Bureau's task to investigate the President's murder. Skull fragments and bullet fragments were retrieved, and vehicle damage was "noted."

As Palamara writes in *The Third Alternative,* "The Secret Service in Their Own Words," Agent Floyd Boring, who was one of the limo's inspectors, told the Assassinations Record Review Board in 1996 that he found a one- to two-inch piece of skull with brain matter attached in the backseat. Though he did not touch it, he did report it to Paul Paterni, the deputy chief of the Secret Service. Boring did not write a report on this and didn't know if Paterni did. Similarly, Agent Sam Kinney found a piece of skull on the rear seat while the limo was still being flown back to D.C.

The agent's later comments and the various inspections of the limo have spurred controversy, with analysts of the assassination challenging the Secret Service and FBI's accounting of skull fragments and bullet fragments. Even more controversial perhaps, the limo was washed of blood before any detailed forensic exam was conducted. The car also reportedly had a hole in the windshield, but was sent quickly to the repair shop.

Controversy similarly surrounded the Secret Service's handling of President Kennedy's body in the hours after his assassination. In 1963 the murder of a president was not a federal crime, which meant that legally and technically, Kennedy's corpse was under the jurisdiction of Dallas authorities. The agency did fight for his corpse, and won. An hour and a half after the shooting, agents prepared to take the body back to Washington, D.C., but at Parkland Hospital, Dallas County Medical Examiner Dr. Earl Rose, backed by a justice of the peace, blocked their way. Under Texas law, the body of a murder victim could not be removed until an autopsy had been performed. Rose so informed the Service, and J. P. Ward opined: "It's just another homicide as far as I'm concerned."

That proved the wrong thing to say to the men who had just lost the president. "Go screw yourself!" shouted Kennedy's special assistant, Kenny O'Donnell. Agents pressed the doctor and the justice of the peace up against the wall, guns drawn, and whisked the dead president back to Air Force One.

Controversy over the autopsy performed at Bethesda Naval Hospital has long fueled controversy by numerous writers' charges that a cover-up had occurred. One long-running theory postulates that the autopsy actually proved that the fatal headshot came from in front of Kennedy, not from behind (the Texas Book Depository). Today, the lone gunman theory is still questioned by the vast majority of Americans.

The two critical questions hurled by the press and public alike at the Service in the immediate aftermath of the assassination and beyond was, How had the agents failed in Dallas? And how had the Service missed Oswald? Within days the Service was harangued because Oswald was not in its files, either on its list of four hundred dangerous persons or in its general files on more than forty thousand U.S. citizens. The Secret Service had combed through its protective research files and found no dangerous persons in the Dallas area, though there were two in Houston. Unfortunately, the Warren Report revealed just how limited were the resources of the protective research section, "a very small group of twelve specialists and three clerks."

In the weeks before Kennedy arrived in Dallas, the Service did make a special effort to identify the individuals who had fomented a near-riot by throwing rocks during the Adlai Stevenson incident. Agents worked with the Dallas police, who found an informant willing to identify the ring-leaders of the demonstration by viewing a television film of the incident; then the Secret Service made still pictures of these ringleaders and distributed the images to agents and police who would be stationed at Love Field and at the Trade Mart. None of the potential troublemakers was ever spotted before or during the Kennedy visit.

Additionally, the Stevenson episode prompted the Service to pay "special attention to extremist groups known to be active in the Dallas area." Still, in Oswald's case, nothing that would have caused the Secret Service to enter him into their files or onto the "watch list" materialized. He had not threatened the president, had never been convicted of a violent crime, or joined a group who "believes in assassination as a political weapon."

The real question was why Oswald was not brought to the attention of the Secret Service by the FBI, who did have a file on him and knew that he was in Dallas. Oswald had defected to the Soviet Union in 1959 and stayed more than two years before returning to the United States, where he became affiliated with several political groups, including the pro-Castro Fair Play for Cuba Committee (FPCC), the Socialist Workers Party, and the American Civil Liberties Union. None of the groups Oswald seemingly joined was considered violent nor did any of them advocate assassination as a political weapon. The FBI's interest in Oswald was as a potential subversive, a security risk, not as a violence-prone potential assassin. However, the Bureau did interview Oswald on several occasions after his return from the Soviet Union and was monitoring him to see if he joined the Communist Party, which would have made him particularly subversive in the eyes of the Bureau. However, Oswald did not join the Communist Party.

Dallas FBI Agent James Hosty had interviewed both Oswald and his wife, Marina. Oswald resented these interviews and had allegedly written a note to Hosty—the contents of which are not known for certain—warning him not to annoy Marina. The note was destroyed by Agent Hosty shortly after the assassination. A number of Kennedy assassination theorists suspect that the note was threatening and that Hosty should have handed it to his superiors. They imply that he got rid of it to cover himself for having missed Oswald as some sort of potential threat.

If the Bureau made a practice of reporting suspected subversives to the Secret Service, the latter's files would be overwhelmed. The Secret Service told the Warren Commission that federal agencies were supposed to report "all information that they come in contact with that would indicate danger to the president." But the handbook given in 1963 to FBI agents required only the reporting of specific reports of a "threat" against the president, his family, the vice president, or the president-elect and vice president-elect. It cannot be stated, except with the benefit of hindsight, that the Bureau erred in not reporting Oswald to the Secret Service.

Dallas police documents sitting in Warren Commission files show that despite the public attention focused on the Secret Service and the FBI's failure to identify Oswald as a potentially dangerous person, the real failure to discover both Oswald and an extremist group in Dallas lay with the local police. Even though the Service's protective research section had files on more than forty thousand persons, the agency depended in large part on local police for "identifying" and "neutralizing" potentially dangerous persons in the area to be visited by the president. Documents reveal that operational responsibility for identifying and investigating indigenous groups and individuals who might constitute a threat or embarrassment to President Kennedy fell to a twenty-man Dallas Police Department unit—the Criminal Intelligence Section, headed by Lt. Jack Revill.

In and around Dallas, the Criminal Intelligence Section investigated fourteen groups, including the Ku Klux Klan, the Black Muslims, and the local Nazi Party. As its name implied, the Criminal Intelligence Section had a clandestine capability. As a police memo describes:

> This Section [Criminal Intelligence] had previously [before beginning to work on protective research for Kennedy's visit] been successful in infiltrating a number of these organizations; therefore, the activities, personalities and future plans of these groups were known.

The Criminal Intelligence Section made two glaring errors in protective intelligence gathering for the president's visit, errors that cannot be laid upon the Secret Service. One was the omission of notice about Oswald. Unlike the FBI, whose written instructions to agents called for reporting persons who made threats against the president, the Criminal Intelligence Section had a broader mission of identifying persons who *might* threaten or embarrass the president. The Dallas detectives compiled a list of four hundred names, but so broadly was the net cast that four dozen persons who belonged to the Young People Socialist League were placed on the list simply because of the left-wing nature of their group. But Oswald, whose defection to the Soviet Union as a self-pronounced Marxist had been covered in the local press, was not included on the list.

The Criminal Intelligence Section evidently missed a specific chance to catch Oswald in its data net: he had joined one of the fourteen groups under surveillance—the American Civil Liberties Union (ACLU), which many law-enforcement officers deemed a communist organization. In the anti-communist, law-and-order spectrum of Dallas politics in 1963, the police targeted them for reasons cited in a police memo: "This organization is known to have defended communist causes in many cases and has also opposed laws which are detrimental to the communist cause."

Meanwhile, Oswald, with his wife and two children, had been staying at the home of Michael and Ruth Paine. Michael Paine was a member of the ACLU and regularly attended its meetings. Oswald attended an October 25, 1963, meeting of the Dallas ACLU with his host. During the meeting, Oswald spoke and, after it broke up, got into a heated argument with a man who defended the free-enterprise system against Oswald's leftist remarks. The ACLU was under surveillance by police on a continuing basis, even before protective-intelligence-gathering for the president's visit had begun, meaning that they either ignored Oswald or missed him entirely.

Within a few days of the ACLU meeting, Oswald formally joined the ACLU and opened up a post office box in Dallas. On the postal form, he authorized the receipt of mail for the ACLU and also for the pro-Castro FPCC, yet another red flag revealing Oswald's seemingly leftist or pro-communist leanings and one missed or ignored by police intelligence.

Besides missing Oswald, the police Criminal Intelligence Section made another glaring error about a group that would have perhaps tipped off the Service to potential trouble in Dallas. The Stevenson incident had of course caught the attention of the Service, which was especially interested in "extremist groups" in the Dallas area and always seeking out intelligence on any cadre that contemplated assassination as a political weapon. Yet the police intelligence unit failed to report such a group to the agency. The group was called Alpha-66.

The Dallas chapter of Alpha-66 was holding meetings in a house on Harlendale Street in Dallas for several weeks prior to the assassination. Perhaps the most militant and violent of all anti-Castro groups, Alpha-66 was composed of Cuban exiles, many of whom had fought in the ill-fated Bay of Pigs Invasion. Alpha-66 was basically a right-wing commando group that launched missions against Castro's Cuba from the U.S. coast—missions involving both sabotage and assassination.

Before the Kennedy assassination, the Treasury Department's Bureau of Alcohol, Tobacco and Firearms (ATF) had been investigating the owner of a Dallas gun shop regarding illegal arms sales, where they discoved that Alpha-66 had attempted to purchase bazookas and machine guns. The group, according to the gun shop owner, had a large cache of arms somewhere in Dallas, but ATF never reported the allegation to the Secret Service.

The agency would have immediately regarded the presence of a group of commandoes enraged at Kennedy as a potential threat. The Cubans of Alpha-66 were angered that Kennedy had refused to provide U.S. air cover for the Bay of Pigs invasion; many exiles held him personally responsible for their disastrous defeat at the hands of Castro's army. Also, Kennedy had banned Cuban exile groups from launching raids against the island from U.S. soil and had publicly criticized Alpha-66 for violating this ban, to which the national head of Alpha-66 replied, "We are going to attack again and again."

When the Dallas band of Alpha-66 did come to the attention of the Secret Service after the assassination, an FBI informant in Dallas reported that the head of the Dallas chapter, Manuel Rodriguez, "was known to be violently anti-President Kennedy." According to another Warren Commission document that was accidently released in 1976 while it was still classified, Rodriguez was "apparently a survivor of the Bay of Pigs episode."

Although the police Criminal Intelligence Section had missed Alpha-66 and its leader, another local law-enforcement unit with less intelligence-gathering capacity, the Dallas County Sheriff's Office, stumbled onto the group. At 8:00 A.M. on the day after the assassination, the Sheriff's Office passed along a "hot tip" to the Secret Service: For about two months prior to the assassination, Oswald had been meeting in a house on Harlendale Street with a group that the Sheriff's Office assumed to be the pro-Castro FPCC. The group reportedly met there for several weeks, up to either a few days before the assassination or the day after. In reality, the group gathering at the house was actually Alpha-66.

The confusion appears to have resulted from the fact that Manuel Rodriguez, the head of the Dallas chapter, bore a resemblance to Lee Harvey Oswald, a fact that was independently confirmed by the FBI. The Bureau checked into a report that Oswald had been in Oklahoma on November 17, 1963, accompanied by several Cubans, and discovered that the Oklahoma witnesses had seen Rodriguez, not Oswald. According to an FBI memorandum signed by J. Edgar Hoover, Rodriguez was five feet nine inches, 145 pounds, with brown hair; Oswald's autopsy report listed him as five feet, nine inches, 150 pounds, with brown hair.

The Dallas Police Criminal Intelligence Section's inability to find or report on Alpha-66 is all the more inexplicable because of a tape recording that surfaced in 1978 during the reinvestigation of the John F. Kennedy case conducted by the House of Representatives Select Committee on Assassinations, 1976 –1978. Secretly recorded at a meeting of the Dallas John Birch Society the month before the assassination, the tape caught an anti-Castro exile and Bay of Pigs survivor—though not a member of Alpha-66—denouncing Kennedy:

> Get him out. Get him out. The quicker, the sooner the better. He's doing all kind of deals. Mr. Kennedy is kissing Mr. Krushchev. I

wouldn't be surprised if he had kissed Castro too. I wouldn't even call him "President" Kennedy. He stinks. We are waiting for Kennedy the twenty-second [November], buddy. We are going to see him one way or the other. We're going to give him the works when he get in Dallas.

As with the ACLU, the John Birch Society was being monitored by the Criminal Intelligence Section, falling into the realm of extremists meriting scrutiny in the wake of the Stevenson episode. The "Birchers" loathed Kennedy because of his alleged softness on communism and his civil rights policies.

The Secret Service would have taken the Birch Society disdain for the president as a development to monitor. At the least, the diatribe should have precipitated increased efforts to discover and monitor any anti-Castro groups in Dallas. Even though police documents indicate that they attended meetings of the target groups, the Criminal Intelligence Section either missed the speech against Kennedy or failed to act on it. In either case, the Secret Service was given no idea of the possible threat.

One police memorandum stated that the Birch Society "is an active extremist group" in Dallas and that an "effort was made to [somehow stage an event] of an embarrassing nature [to the president]. It was determined that no such action was planned."

The Criminal Intelligence Section's failure to discover or report the anti-Castroite's assertion that "we're going to give him the works when he gets in Dallas" or to uncover or report the presence of Alpha-66 and its allegedly "violently anti-Kennedy" leader comprises a gaffe that may well have contributed to lax or flawed protective measures for Kennedy in Dallas. If the Secret Service had received even an inkling that local Cuban exiles were threatening the president in any way, the agency might well have tightened precautions. Not long before the Dallas trip, the Service had received word of a plot to assassinate President Kennedy; allegedly being planned by an unspecified group of Cuban exiles, the scheme was to ram Air Force One in midair with a small plane as the president approached Miami. Kennedy's itinerary was changed and no threat materialized, a reaction by the agency leading to a logical contention that, in Dallas, the Service would have been wary of any Cuban exile group, especially a commando group such as Alpha-66. Had the presence of Alpha-66 been detected and reported, the Secret Service might have been able to convince the president to accept additional protective measures, or agents might have operated with a keener sense of looming danger.

The copious documentary record of the Secret Service's performance during the agency's most tragic episode does reveal that the failure most often attributed to it—the inability to identify Oswald as a potentially dangerous person—was not a Secret Service error at all. But failures in the gathering of protective intelligence did occur. The Criminal Intelligence Section of the Dallas Police Department had the best opportunity and the best reason to discover both Oswald and Alpha-66, but neither was reported to the Service. If Oswald alone had been reported, there probably would have been nothing in his background that would have caused the Service to "red flag" the trip as especially dangerous.

In terms of protective performance during the shooting, though political priorities had predetermined much of the situation—an open car with no agents allowed on the running boards—agents failed to take immediate evasive and protective action that might have saved the president's life. The extensive postassassination criticism and analysis produced improved protective methods and technology.

Despite the Warren Commission's findings and government insistence on the lone-gunman/Oswald conclusion, several of the agents in the presidential detail did not accept the assertions. Later, some of the men expressed their belief that the case was really a conspiracy, as the vast majority of the U.S. public came to believe. Researcher Vincent Palamara interviewed numerous Kennedy agents and cites Agents Sam Kinney, Abraham Bolden, Maurice Martineau, Marty Underwood, and John Norris as those who "believe this [conspiracy] to be the case." In addition, says Palamara, June Kellerman, the widow of agent Roy Kellerman, stated that both Kellerman and fellow agent Bill Greer, who were in the front seat of Kennedy's limo, asserted that there was more to the assassination than the "official" version let on.

The advance agent for Kennedy's trip to Dallas, Agent Winston Lawson, appearing in 1995 in the Discovery Channel documentary "Inside the Secret Service," recalled the aftermath of the assassination and its impact upon his career. Strangely, Lawson offered that fellow agents had come to him after the assassination and said, "If it had to happen, I'm glad it happened to you." The words seem curious, if not cruel.

Lawson said, "They [fellow agents] didn't mean it in a bad way." In his opinion, they meant they knew he did everything he could.

In a recent interview of Lawson, the retired agent was asked, "Given the improvements in technology, procedure and intelligence, do you think the Dallas tragedy would have been prevented with today's improvements, or would it still be a case of politics over effective protection?"

Lawson replied, "That's a hard one to say. There is so much more now. Not just training but more people. . . . [As a] Political Advance Man— are you familiar with that term?—[he] come[s] to the lead Secret Service advance man and says, 'I want the ropes and stanchions brought down; the crowd will be closer.'

"The best bet [for security] are things that are truly spontaneous"—such as when a president makes an out-of-the-blue stop that no one, including a would-be-assassin could have anticipated. Such a stop is easier to handle than a spontaneous stop that a would-be assassin might well predict.

Lawson sketches an example of the riskier scenario. "A Catholic president goes by a Catholic school with all those Catholic schoolchildren, Kennedy did in Cleveland," Lawson said. "You [meaning a potential assassin] can almost guess he's going to stop.

"There's always gonna be a political side versus a Secret Service side. Sometimes you win and sometimes you lose."

Then, Lawson offered a tidbit previously unheard: "Sometimes the political side will blame the Secret Service for not going to a particular place that they didn't want to go to, using the Secret Service as an excuse."

Lawson does not join agents who stated or implied, in Seymour Hersh's *The Dark Side of Camelot*, that Kennedy's recklessness brought on his death.

Despite all the lapses and failures of the Secret Service agents in Dallas, Agent Kellerman told the FBI the night after the assassination: "The precautions employed in Dallas were the most stringent and thorough ever employed . . . for the visit of a president to an American city." The Commission asked that if this were true, what were the *normal* protective procedures.

Kennedy is alleged to have said to San Antonio Congressman Henry Gonzales, the night before the shooting, "The Secret Service told me they had taken care of everything."

As events proved on that shocking November day, the agency had failed to take care of everything. Agent Clint Hill knew that hard truth within seconds of the first shot. Senator Ralph Yarborough, who rode in Vice President Johnson's limo, saw Hill lying across the trunk of the president's limo after the agent pushed Mrs. Kennedy back into it from the trunk, where she had crawled to retrieve a piece of her husband's skull. Hill "beat the back of the car with one fist, his face controlled by grief, anguish and despair."

The scene continues to haunt the Secret Service and shape the ways in which they protect the president. As a team performance, the agents' actions in Dallas were slipshod. Additional agents would not have saved the day had they reacted and operated as did those at the scene.

# CHAPTER 4

# AGENTS IN ACTION

*Every practical precaution and safeguard should be taken to prevent the actual perpetration of an attack, because:*

*(a) There is seldom any assurance that an attack can be suppressed before its objective has been reached, and*

*(b) Even if the president escapes unharmed, the cost in other lives, injuries or property damage is usually very great before the attacker is subdued.*

*—Secret Service Training Manual*

In September 1964, the President's Commission on the Assassination of President Kennedy—The Warren Commission—submitted its report to President Johnson. Established by Johnson on November 29, 1963, the Commission was granted unrestricted investigative powers to evaluate all the evidence and present a complete report of the assassination to the American people. The members of the Commission were a cross-section of prominent public servants and private citizens: Chief Justice Earl Warren; U.S. Senators Richard B. Russell (Democrat from Georgia) and John Sherman Cooper (Republican from Kentucky); U.S. Representatives Hale Boggs (Democrat from Louisiana) and Gerald R. Ford (Republican from Michigan); Allen W. Dulles, former director of the Central Intelligence Agency; and John J. McCloy, former president of the World Bank. The Commission named former U.S. Solicitor General James Lee Rankin as its general counsel and also appointed fourteen assistant counsels, with twelve additional staff members.

On December 3, 1963, the hearings convened, and the final report was delivered to Johnson on September 24, 1964, after having heard testimony from 552 witnesses and considering the reports of ten federal agencies. The Commission asserted that Lee Harvey Oswald had acted alone.

The commission concluded its report by recommending reform in presidential security measures, and it offered specific recommendations for the protection of the president. The Secret Service had to change the way it did business.

The tragedy revealed an acute need for expansion. Based on the recommendations in the extensive report, the Secret Service increased its number of special agents assigned to presidential protection, expanded its special agents' training, further developed the protective intelligence functions, and increased its liaison with law-enforcement and other federal agencies. The latter had proven a disaster in Dallas, where the Service and local police had failed to coordinate protection, possibly lulling the Service into a sense that the president was safer than, in truth, he was.

The Secret Service added new technical security equipment, automatic data processing, and improved communications systems, and even though it was a traumatic time for the agency, it was also a time of much-needed transformation. Some of the most telling changes came in the Service's internal structure with the creation of four assistant director positions to head the offices of Protective Operations, Protective Research, Investigations, and Administrations. In October 1965, the title of chief was changed to director, a more modern title for the head of the Secret Service.

Although the Warren Commission forced changes in the agency, only another tragedy, one that struck the Kennedys less than five years after the Secret Service failed to protect President Kennedy in Dallas, compelled Congress to expand the Service's mission to include presidential candidates. On June 5, 1968, after Senator Robert F. Kennedy had won the democratic presidential primary in California, he was gunned down an assassin's bullets shortly after midnight. Kennedy had just given his victory speech at the Ambassador Hotel in Los Angles, and private security guards were escorting him through the hotel's semidarkened kitchen. Suddenly Sirhan Sirhan materialized in the front of the crowd. Within seconds, Kennedy lay dying on the hotel kitchen floor. Whether Sirhan actually was the assassin still fuels debate.

Following Robert Kennedy's death, the Secret Service was ordered to secure the Kennedy home, too late to do anything more than help with the preparations for the funeral-train procession from New York to Washington, D.C. President Johnson, who had sat in the limo behind John F. Kennedy's in Dallas, quickly ensured that the Congress passed clear-cut legislation (Public Law 90-331) authorizing the Secret Service to protect presidential and vice presidential candidates. Now, in the 1968 election, the agency shouldered responsibility for an additional twelve protectees. The Service immediately detailed agents to each candidate; these agents stood protective duty without days off for the duration of the campaign and logged over 270,000 hours of uncompensated overtime.

The necessity of protecting presidential candidates from would-be assassins became painfully evident in the 1972 presidential race even to those legislators who had balked at the idea of an expanded, more costly mission for the agency. On May 5, 1972, the wounding of Alabama Governor George Wallace proved the only instance to date in which a presidential candidate under Secret Service protection has been the victim of a shooting. Although Wallace escaped with his life, he was out of politics for several years and remained paralyzed.

Wallace was still a key figure in presidential politics in 1972, his importance often glossed over or neglected, possibly because of the strident, racist political view he still embraced. After running unsuccessfully as an independent candidate for president in 1968, Wallace chased the Democratic nomination four years later, challenging Democrats Hubert Humphrey, Edmund Muskie, and George McGovern. Wallace, an able and energetic campaigner who had garnered more popular votes along the primary trail than any of his rivals heading into May, was gathering enough momentum to play at least the role of spoiler for the mainstream Democratic candidates. Though the Alabama politician did not hold a lead in the number of convention delegates won, his states rights, law-and-order themes had struck a responsive chord with enough voters to reap stronger-than-expected support in several primaries and victories in others, not only in the deep South, but also in Florida, Pennsylvania, and Indiana, as well.

If ever a candidate needed protection, George Wallace was the one. His pugnacious style of politics ignited white-hot political passions even in traditional campaign brawls. This had been true of Wallace on the national stage since 1963, when, as governor of Alabama, he stood in a schoolhouse door to bar black students, vowing, "Segregation now, segregation tomorrow, segregation forever." Throughout his 1972 presidential campaign, hecklers dogged his appearances, and hate mail and threats plagued the campaign every day. His Secret Service detail worked under intense pressure with the knowledge that his campaign venom could stir up a potential assassin at any juncture on the trail.

The race among Wallace, Humphrey, and McGovern grew tighter as the trio headed into the key Maryland presidential primary, with the Alabaman's rhetoric, as well as that of his rivals, growing more volatile. While campaigning, Wallace remarked to an associate, "Somebody's going to get killed before the primary is over, and I hope it's not me."

In Hagerstown, Maryland, police had to break up a clash between black and white youths during a Wallace speech. A man hurled a brick against Wallace's chest in Frederick, Maryland, and at the University of Maryland, students pelted him with Popsicles. A few days later, people tossed tomatoes and eggs at him.

The agents protecting Wallace faced mounting pressure because he would not back away from his populist-style campaign in which pressing the flesh was essential. Still, he cooperated with his security team. He was not one of those politicians who disdained protection and resisted it, and, in fact, Wallace was just the opposite. Although he typically waded into crowds in search of votes, he worried about the spectator who might be concealing a gun or a blade. He did not completely trust his "Washington" agents because of his scorn for the federal government that had forced civil rights down the South's collective throat. He actually had two security forces traveling with him on the primary trail. In addition to the local law-enforcement personnel who would be called upon to help in each town or city that he visited, Wallace had both a Secret Service detail and a contingent of plainclothes Alabama state troopers. His operatives lugged his own six-hundred-pound bulletproof podium, draped in red, white, and blue, to every stop on the campaign trail. As a further precaution, he wore a bulletproof vest.

In comparison to 1968, the Secret Service agents guarding Wallace and the other candidates in the 1972 campaign had tightened protective procedures. All passengers on flights taken by a candidate had to go through X-ray checks, and all bags and cases were inspected. Local press were required to have credentials. Despite all of the stricter security procedures and despite his two units (Secret Service agents and Alabama state troopers), his bulletproof podium, and his grasp of just how big a target he was, Wallace and his agents waded into a nightmare on May 5, 1972, at a Laurel, Maryland, shopping center.

Some two thousand people had gathered to hear what promised to be a vintage Wallace stump speech offering fiery bromides to "send a message to Washington" and punctuated by diatribes against the "ultrafalse liberals" and "the pointy-headed intellectuals who can't park their bicycles straight." Because of the oppressive heat and humidity, Wallace chose for once to shed his cumbersome, heavily insulated, bulletproof vest.

Throughout the speech, several hecklers shouted at Wallace, but by the boisterous standards of his campaign stops, the dissenting voices did not especially alarm his Secret Service detail. Wallace, though tired, rendered a fifty-minute speech, perspiration soaking his shirt and brow, and as he wrapped up his oration, thunderous applause erupted. Country singer Billy Grammer and his band plugged their instruments into the amplifiers and began to twang away as the candidate, flanked by his Secret Service agents, descended the stairs from the makeshift stage.

When he reached ground level, the governor picked up his pace with the intention of a quick exit, but shouts of support from the crowd drew him back. "Over here. Over here," shouted several bystanders. One, a blond man named Arthur Bremer, was among them.

Wallace took off his suit jacket, rolled up his sleeves, and strode toward the cheering crowd. As he moved along the rope barrier that separated him from the crowd, he shook scores of proferred hands, including that of Clyde Merryman, an exercise boy at Pimlico Race Track.

"You've got my vote," said Merryman. Wallace started to reply. From the second row of spectators, a blond man plunged forward with a pistol extended. Arthur Bremer fired a .38-caliber bullet into Wallace's midsection from no more than one-and-a-half feet away; bystanders could feel the sharp heat given off by the explosion. As Wallace fell backward, five more shots echoed—with four tearing into him. He was hit in his midsection, shoulder, chest, and right arm. The crowd's screams were deafening.

Even as Bremer was shooting, Secret Service agents and Alabama troopers had jammed his arm downward and pounced on him, but not before the four bullets slammed into Wallace. He lay bleeding on the pavement. Near him three others were crumpled—Alabama trooper E. C. Dothard was shot in the stomach; Secret Service agent Nicholas Zarvos was hit in the throat; and a female Wallace supporter was wounded in the leg. All would survive.

Police and security men jumped on Bremer, as did bystanders who kicked and punched him as he was pushed to the pavement. People in the crowd shouted, "Kill him! Kill him!" It took ten security men to pry Bremer from the clutches of the crowd and to drag him to a cruiser, where was he slammed inside the vehicle, gasping and spitting blood.

Back on the pavement, Wallace still lay bleeding, surrounded by the crowd. His wife Cornelia had been at a restroom in a nearby bank when the shooting occurred but at the sound of the shots had dashed to her prone husband. She dropped to her knees and embraced him, sobbing. Secret Service agents pulled her away, but she broke loose and ran back to her husband. "I was afraid they'd shoot him again in the head," she said later.

Actually, Mrs. Wallace had a point. As the governor lay sprawled on the pavement, his Secret Service agents and the others left him completely exposed for several seconds after the shooting while security personnel struggled to subdue Bremer. Had there been another assailant intent on finishing Wallace off, there was no Secret Service agent or Alabama trooper covering the governor's body with his own body immediately after the shooting.

Two doctors in the crowd came forward to attend to Wallace. "I feel I can't breathe," the governor whispered. One doctor felt for a pulse but could not find one. Time was running out. First the police and then the Secret Service radioed for an ambulance, and fortunately for the agents, the Laurel rescue squad, an award-winning volunteer ambulance unit, was only four blocks away and raced up within three minutes. Meanwhile, the doctors huddled around Wallace knew he would die unless rushed to an emergency room within minutes. Secret Service agents gingerly picked Wallace up and eased him into to the back of a campaign station wagon for transportation to the hospital, but just as they were ready to move out, the ambulance arrived, and the wounded candidate was loaded into it and whisked away to a hospital where emergency-room physicians saved his life after he nearly died several times on the operating table.

The press and even Secret Service officials viewed the catastrophe as proof that no one could count on stopping a determined assassin willing to take any risk in order to shoot a political leader. As Assistant Secretary of the Treasury Eugene T. Rossides put it, having more agents around Wallace would have "made absolutely no difference." Rossides was bluntly conceding that if a determined gunman gets close enough to take a shot, he will likely get it off no matter how many agents are around. The gunman has to be headed off before he can get close.

Though the statement testifies to the difficulties of thwarting an attack once it starts or attempting to head off the worst by swarming around the protectee, those two last-second tactics comprise but a part of the protective mission. Prevention, the steps taken to protect someone *before* an attack is perpetrated, can be the fine line between life and death for an assassin's target. Identification and neutralization of potential assailants through computer records, local police files, and other information-gathering techniques are and must be the "preventive medicine" against an assailant; though it may be true that additional agents could not have prevented Bremer from thrusting his arm forward and shooting the governor, it is at least possible that the presence of additional personnel might have increased the chances of spotting Bremer as a potential danger *before* the attack materialized. The hard truth for the Secret Service in the Wallace shooting was that even though Arthur Bremer may not have been in the agency's files or on its watch list, he was not simply another face in the crowd, but a face that had appeared with frequency before May 5, 1972: Bremer had been stalking candidates for some time and was conspicuous in his actions.

By most accounts, Bremer originally intended to assassinate President Richard Nixon and only zeroed in on Wallace—reluctantly—when unable to get at the president. Nixon was in Ottawa, Canada, on April 13 and 14, 1972, and after the Wallace shooting, both American and Canadian authorities later identified Bremer as lurking in the crowd outside the Canadian parliament building when Nixon entered to address a joint session. Bremer is clearly visible in news films of the throng.

Bremer's diary indicates that he stalked Nixon in Ottawa, driving around the city from one location to another while shadowing the president, and stayed two nights at a downtown hotel. Having hoped to stay at the same hotel as the press corps so that he could pick up information about Nixon's movements, Bremer could not book a room there; instead, he drank at the bar of the hotel, where the press were staying, and hung around the press room that had been set up there. On his person or in his car were two pistols and ammunition that he had smuggled across the border into Canada. Unable to get close enough to Nixon to attempt an assassination, Bremer lamented in his diary: "Just another goddamn failure."

After the Wallace shooting, federal authorities sifted through a sudden and tardy flurry of credible reports that testified to Bremer's presence at a variety of political events during 1972. Two of Humphrey's campaign workers spotted Bremer at a Humphrey rally on April 3. Then, on April 7–8, Bremer traveled to New York City and registered at the Waldorf Astoria Hotel, where Humphrey was scheduled to spend the night; because of a last minute change of plans, Humphrey did not go to New York. As far back as the fall of 1971, Bremer was arrested in Milwaukee for carrying a concealed weapon. The charge was later reduced to disorderly conduct, for which he paid a $40 fine.

Someone in Wallace's Secret Service or police detail should have spotted Bremer somewhere along the campaign trail: The man flagrantly stalked the controversial candidate. On May 13, less than two weeks before the shooting, Bremer sat in his car for nearly the entire day outside of an armory in Kalamazoo, Michigan, where Wallace was scheduled to speak. A shopkeeper called the police, and Bremer was picked up as a "suspicious person." He told police that he was waiting for the Wallace speech to start, and, satisfied with his explanation, the police released him without searching him for a weapon.

Earlier on the same day that Wallace was shot at the Laurel shopping center, the candidate gave a speech in Wheaton, Maryland. Fred Farrar, a television producer from a Washington, D.C., station, noticed Bremer. "That smirk of his was almost spine tingling," said Farrar, who filmed Bremer for fifteen seconds or so.

Farrar also noticed that after Wallace spoke, Bremer tugged on a policeman's sleeve and asked: "Could you get George to come down and shake hands with me? I'm a great fan of his." The policeman simply moved away.

Bremer tried the same tactic with a Secret Service agent, with the same result. The agent did not sense what Farrar had felt.

As Bremer continued to grin, wave, and cheer, Wallace never did descend the stage and wade into the crowd, for the hecklers had turned out in force. In the midafternoon of that day, Wallace would move into the crowd to shake hands at Laurel, and Bremer would be waiting.

CBS cameraman Laurens Pierce, like Farrar, sensed something wrong with Bremer before the shooting, something that crowd-scanning agents should well have discerned. Recalling Bremer's conspicuous presence at Wallace's Hagerstown, Maryland, speech, Pierce described Bremer as "applauding longer, louder and more vehemently than anyone else. His zeal could not go unnoticed and my camera recorded it."

Pierce also recalled seeing Bremer at a Wallace rallies in Michigan and at Wheaton, Maryland, the latter on the morning of the shooting. At the Wheaton shopping center, Pierce saw Bremer standing in the front row directly in front of Wallace's bulletproof podium and recognized the blond man as someone with a familiar and unnerving face. Pierce approached Bremer. "I've seen you at other Wallace rallies," Pierce said.

"Not me," replied Bremer. "Not me."

Had Bremer been spotted as a stalker by Secret Service agents or by the Service's Protective Intelligence Section, which analyzes films of crowds, or, in fairness, newsmen had reported Bremer to the Service as a suspicious person, the outcome at Laurel, Maryland, might have been different. Maryland had recently banned handguns without permits and allowed police to frisk suspicious persons. Again, with better coordination between police in Michigan and the Service, Bremer, busted for suspicious behavior outside a site where Wallace was supposed to speak, could have ended up in the Secret Service album, pictures of individuals to be watched. No matter what, agents had missed the conspicuous and off-key behavior that had caught the attention of other people. Bremer's trial would reveal that time after time on campaign stops, he showed up with a concealed pistol.

Bremer was apparently immersed in suicidal and homicidal fantasies during the months before the assassination attempt. One evening he placed a noose around his neck and scrawled "KILLER" across his forehead with a felt marker pen. At his trial, the jury rejected the defense's psychiatric testimony and found him guilty; Bremer was sentenced to sixty-three years in prison for his attack on Wallace, and he remains in jail today.

After Wallace was wounded, he still won the Michigan primary with 51 percent of the vote, compared with 27 percent for McGovern and 16 percent for Humphrey. Wallace proved a formidable contender—a cause for alarm, if not outright panic, within the Democratic Party's liberal establishment. If Bremer had not pierced the protection of Wallace's Secret Service detail, the segregationist would have gone to the 1972 Democratic convention with a large block of delegates with which to bargain for policy concessions or future appointments. Bremer's bullets, however, knocked Wallace out of the race. McGovern attained the nomination and was defeated in a Nixon landslide.

As far as motive, Bremer was a cauldron of bizarre emotions. In *American Assassins,* James W. Clarke writes that Bremer had "distorted emotions," even disconnected, but his ability to perceive and reason "remained virtually unimpaired."

The best speculation is perhaps that Bremer wanted to show his contempt for American society by killing its leader, Nixon. Unable to get at

Nixon, Bremer settled for Wallace. Clarke contends, "He [Bremer] needed an audience for his perversity, and someone like the president would ensure that."

For the Secret Service, the ultimate nightmare—a potentially lethal face in the crowd—had emerged on May 5, 1972. It would happen again.

The next attempted assassination of a Secret Service protectee came on September 5, 1975. President Gerald Ford, having just finished breakfast at the Senator Hotel in Sacramento, California, and planning to head to the State Capitol to meet California Governor Jerry Brown, was escorted outside the hotel by his Secret Service agents. Ford stopped to shake hands with and chat a little with the smiling, waving crowd. As he waved, he noticed a small woman standing no more than two feet to his left and wearing a red cape and a turban. Lynette "Squeaky" Fromme looked waiflike, utterly harmless.

Fromme suddenly reached under her cape and drew a .45 caliber automatic pistol. Said Ford, "I saw a hand coming up behind several others in the front row, and obviously there was a pistol in that hand."

At the president's right shoulder, Secret Service Agent Larry Buendorf spotted the weapon and jumped in front of the president to screen him. Then the agent grabbed the weapon and muscled the would-be assassin to the ground.

According to Buendorf, just as he seized her arm Fromme was attempting to pull back the hammer to put a round into the chamber. Fromme blurted, "Oh, shit, it didn't go off; it didn't go off. Don't be so rough." Buendorf wrestled the gun from her hand as other agents surrounded the president and whisked him away.

Agents found four cartridges in the weapon's clip. The only injury from the incident was a cut on Buendorf's hand, the gash likely caused by the pistol's hammer. Grim-faced and shaken, Ford nonetheless went on to meet Governor Brown and to deliver a speech on law and order to the California legislature.

Ford's would-be killer, Lynette Alice "Squeaky" Fromme, was twenty-six years old and had a bizarre history even before the attempted assassination. She was one of the most zealous followers of Charles M. Manson, a blindly loyal member of the "Manson family." In 1971, Manson was convicted of the ritualistic murders of Sharon Tate and six other persons and was sentenced to life in prison, but Fromme was not charged in the murders. She was one of Manson's most vociferous and visible defenders during his seven-month trial.

Two months prior to the attempted assassination, Fromme had sought media attention by issuing a statement claiming that she had received letters from Manson blaming Richard Nixon for his imprisonment. Nixon had remarked to reporters during the spectacular trial that Manson was guilty. Fromme also asserted that Manson blamed President Ford for continuing Nixon's policies.

Fromme, along with another Manson family member, Sandra Good, sought to publicize Manson's letters and his comments on Nixon and Ford as a way of focusing attention on Manson's plight, which they believed to be unjust. Making little headway, both women found another way to dramatize Manson's case: they donned red capes for the cameras and the print media.

In analyzing Fromme, political scientist James W. Clarke concludes, "It is questionable whether Fromme intended to kill the president. Her frustration had never been directed specifically at Ford except to acknowledge that he was simply another willing 'instrument of the ruling corporate elite.' "

Clarke believes that Fromme was in no way motivated by ideology and was attempting to threaten the president with a weapon in order to gain publicity for Manson's cause. Even though the Manson family had a personal hatred of Nixon, there was no such feeling for Ford.

Fromme attempted to turn her trial into a political statement and show-trial much like that of the Chicago Seven; however, her efforts were frustrated by U.S. District Court Judge Thomas J. McBride, who removed her from the courtroom after her disruptive outbursts and had her communicate via closed-circuit television. Her defense was based upon the contention that she did not intend to assassinate the president, but only to receive publicity for Manson. The jury rejected this claim and gave her a life sentence.

In addition to Fromme's notoriety as a Manson follower, she had been arrested more than a dozen times on charges ranging from drug possession, to petty theft, to robbery, to murder (not the Sharon Tate case), but she had been convicted of only minor offenses and had spent only a few months in jail. The murder charge was filed in Stockton, California, in 1972, in the death of a nineteen-year-old woman whose body was found buried under a house in which Fromme had been living. The charge was subsequently dismissed for lack of evidence.

Had the Secret Service "missed" Fromme in a similar way as they had failed to spot Bremer? Should she have merited a place in the agency's files before she pulled a gun on President Ford? The answer is probably not. There is no evidence that Fromme had stalked Ford or any other political leader as Arthur Bremer had done. She was not on the Secret Service watch list of four hundred dangerous persons nor was her name among the forty-seven thousand names in Secret Service files. She had made no threats against any protectees, not even veiled ones.

Not so easily answered as those two questions concerning her absence from Secret Service files is how Fromme managed to get within two to three feet of President Ford while carrying a loaded weapon. Then-Secret Service Director of Public Affairs John W. Warner Jr. refused comment on this matter when asked by the press. No simple answer emerged, but the problem would recur in 1981, when John W. Hinckley slipped within fifteen feet of President Ronald Reagan.

Only two-and-a-half weeks after the Fromme incident, the nightmare scenario erupted for the Secret Service and the country again. President Ford was exiting the St. Francis Hotel in San Francisco, where a crowd of three thousand had gathered to see him. The throng lined the sidewalks for two to three blocks outside the hotel, and was two to three persons deep behind rope barriers. When Ford emerged from the hotel, the crowd cheered, with spectators jostling each other for a glimpse of the president.

Ford, smiling and waving, flanked by agents, walked toward his waiting limousine. As he started to reach out to shake a few hands, a single shot exploded from across the street approximately forty feet away. A .38-caliber exploding bullet screeched past the president, ricocheted off a concrete wall, and struck a taxi driver whose wound fortunately proved minor.

At the report of the shot Ford appeared stunned. As color drained from his face, he doubled over, and his knees appeared to buckle, which caused numerous bystanders to fear that he had been shot. Secret Service Agents Ron Pontious and Jack Merchant quickly pushed Ford down toward the sidewalk to reduce his exposure to any more shots, and amid screams erupting from the crowd, agents pushed the president into the limousine and onto the floor, covering his body with theirs. The limousine quickly sped away. Ford good-naturedly said to the agents covering him, "Hey, will you guys get off me? You're going to smother me."

The president's assailant this time was Sara Jane Moore, who had waited for Ford for more than three hours outside the hotel. A nondescript forty-five-year-old woman, she wore baggy tan pants and a neatly pressed blue raincoat and stood with her hands in her pockets the entire time, except when she fired her .38 caliber revolver at the moment of the shooting.

Secret Service agents are usually on the lookout for persons standing with their hands thrust into coat pockets, because agents know that such persons might have a weapon concealed and could draw it more quickly. If onlookers' hands are inside their pockets, agents will sometimes request that people remove their hands and show them for precisely this reason. In the dense crowd waiting for Ford, no one saw the woman with her hands in her pockets.

Moore drew her revolver and aimed at Ford from the second row of spectators. Thirty-two-year-old bystander Oliver Sepple, a disabled Vietnam veteran, is generally credited with having deflected the gun as it was fired, and causing the shot to miss the president. Still, one policeman at the scene believed that Moore had gotten off her shot in an unobstructed fashion before Sepple could deflect the weapon.

Police pounced on Moore, knocked her to the ground, and tore the gun from her hand. Then they picked her up and carried her into the hotel.

Who was Sara Jane Moore and what were her motives? Among other things, she was a political activist and an FBI informant. When Patricia Hearst was kidnapped by the Symbionese Liberation Army, part of the ransom demand was that Hearst's father, publishing scion William Randolph Hearst, distribute $2 million worth of free food to the poor. Moore volunteered her skills as an accountant to help administer the food distribution and came to the attention of Hearst because of her hard work and efficiency. Soon she took on the role of liaison between Hearst and the political groups distributing the food. Moore appeared to thrive on the importance and excitement provided by her new role and immersed herself in the culture and activities of the radical politics of San Francisco.

By April 1974, Moore was known to the FBI. Her involvements with local radicals were so extensive that the FBI recruited her to work for them as an informant; describing the role as "just like a very bad movie script," she was asked to make contact with radical leaders and funnel information on them to the Bureau.

As with every other assailant who has assassinated or attempted to assassinate a Secret Service protectee since the inception of the protective mission, Moore was not on the Service's watch list or in its files. Nevertheless, she was a very visible figure and was known to both San Francisco police and local Secret Service agents.

On September 20, 1975, two days before Moore attempted to shoot President Ford, a litany of her actions that should have sent up red flags for the police and the Secret Service unfolded. She called the San Francisco Police, identified herself, and told them that she was considering a "test" of the presidential security system and that she had a gun. The next morning, the day before Ford's arrival, San Francisco police officers interviewed her and confiscated her gun, a .44-caliber pistol, along with thirteen bullets found in her purse and one hundred more found in her car.

San Francisco Police Inspector Jack O'Shea would state that Moore, in her call to the police, had said, "I'm going to ask you something that will make you recoil in horror: Can you have me arrested?"

According to O'Shea, he warned her that she could be arrested if she were actually walking around with a concealed weapon. When police went to her home and found her gun unloaded, they decided that, under California law, all they could do was issue a misdemeanor citation and con-fiscate the weapon.

The police did report Moore to the Secret Service, and agents inter-viewed her the night before the president's arrival. By the end of their ses-sion with her, the investigating agents determined that Moore was "not of sufficient protective importance to warrant surveillance during the presi-dent's visit"—a conclusion that not only could have cost Ford his life, but also proved the necessity of training agents more effectively in the psy-chology of interviewing so that they could render more effective judgments about the mental state of potential suspects.

On the morning after the agents dismissed Moore as a threat, she went out and, incredibly, purchased another weapon, a .38-caliber revolver. Evidently remembering what police had told her about the conditions under which she could be arrested, and seemingly still ambivalent about whether to go through with an assassination attempt or just a "test," she sped erratically through San Francisco with her loaded pistol, possibly hoping that she would be stopped and arrested. She was not.

Moore drove downtown and parked. She headed to the St. Francis Hotel and encountered San Francisco *Examiner* reporter Carol Pogash, whom Moore had met when she worked for William Hearst. According to Pogash,

Moore blurted out, "You know the Secret Service visited my house yesterday. They kept me for an hour and questioned me. They could have kept me for seventy-two hours if they wanted to."

Pogash, not taking Moore seriously and not wanting to encourage her to chatter on as she was prone to do, eased away from her.

After San Francisco police claimed that they had fulfilled their responsibilities by reporting Moore to the Secret Service, the agency would not comment to the press about the obvious lapse in protective-intelligence work relating to this case. Said one policeman, "Someone [at Secret Service] apparently made a mistake in judgment."

The Secret Service in the 1970s, as evidenced by the Moore case, looked far more rigorously at direct and specific threats and, to varying degrees, sloughed off vaguer potential threats such as Moore's intimation in the days before Ford's San Francisco visit. Just five hours before Moore's assassination attempt, Secret Service agents arrested a twenty-four-year-old man at a hotel only two blocks from the St. Francis and charged him with threatening the president. The man had allegedly handed a St. Francis employee a note containing a threat against President Ford.

Moore pleaded guilty to the attempted assassination of President Ford. Like Fromme, she received a life sentence. For years, her .38 caliber revolver has been displayed in a glass case in Secret Service headquarters in Washington, D.C.

In an unknown number of instances, the Secret Service takes action—sometimes involving force—in order to prevent an assault on the president; however, because the Service acknowledges thwarted assassination plots, foiled conspiracies, and suspects arrested, no one outside the agency knows the real figures, though there is speculation that they may be a hundred or more.

One strange and complex incident of this type has come to light, involving an alleged plot to assassinate President Nixon. Nixon was scheduled to visit New Orleans in late August 1973, where he was planning to ride in an open car motorcade through the city's French Quarter. The Service uncovered a purported assassination plot and asked Nixon to cancel the motorcade; reluctantly, Nixon did so, issuing the order personally. But in San Clemente, California, where Nixon flew after the cancellation, reporters overheard him say to Rosemary Woods, his secretary, "They called me last night. They canceled. They'll never cancel another time."

He was apparently saying that he, not the Service, would decide whether to back out of an event.

Though a White House spokesman later said that Nixon was not referring to the motorcade, tensions between the White House staff and the Service's White House detail ran high that year, culminating in the removal of Agent Robert S. Taylor as head of the detail. Taylor's departure was sparked by a rift between his detail and the Nixon staff about political priorities versus protective priorities.

Whatever the political machinations between the White House and the protective detail, the Service took the highly unusual step of announcing that it had uncovered a possible plot to assassinate Nixon in New Orleans. Moreover, the announcement came *while* efforts to uncover the plot were still ongoing. The agency was possibly going public to insulate itself against Nixon and his staff's ire at the cancellation of the motorcade.

Suspicion by authorities that an assassination plot might be developing began in early August, with Nixon's visit scheduled for August 20, 1973. New Orleans police initially received a tip, which originated in the predominantly black central city area, warning that trouble awaited Nixon if he visited. Then, three weeks before the visit, a paid informant told police that there had been a meeting of six Black Panthers, who had hatched an assassination plot. A high-powered rifle had "changed hands," warned the informer, who had not attended the alleged meeting but had heard about it. Police alerted both the FBI and Secret Service.

Immediately the Service requested that the six Panthers be detained until the president's visit was over, but the New Orleans police refused because the evidence was only uncorroborated hearsay, not solid enough to act on. Police Superintendent Clarence Giarrusso claimed to have told the Service, "If you want them arrested then you arrest them. We have no grounds." Still, local police did agree to place all six men under surveillance and were granted federal authority to arrest any of the six suspects at the first sign of trouble.

Trouble emerged just five days before Nixon's planned arrival. A female informant told police that she had overheard a black man comment, "Somebody ought to kill President Nixon. If no one has the guts, I'll do it."

When she identified the man as Edwin Gaudet, a former New Orleans policeman whose background was seamy, the Secret Service was alarmed by his possible links to the alleged Black Panther plot against Nixon.

Gaudet had quit the police force in 1966 following an off-duty barroom brawl and had been arrested in 1970 for burning an American flag on the steps of city hall. Far more ominous to the Secret Service was another of Gaudet's episodes in 1970: He had been arrested hurling a burning American flag across the hood of Nixon's limousine during a presidential stop in New Orleans. The incident landed Gaudet in the psychiatric ward of Louisiana State Hospital, but he was later released as an outpatient.

The informant's report about Gaudet and the uncorroborated report of a Black Panther assassination plot took an even more sinister turn for the Service on the day before Nixon's arrival in New Orleans. A police uniform and badge were stolen, which raised the danger that an assassin had gotten his hands on them and could easily walk right up to the president by impersonating a police officer. Although police would later discover that the theft was unrelated to any assassination plot, Gaudet's status as a black ex-policeman and the allegation of a Black Panther plot led the Service to conclude that an orchestrated assassination conspiracy was unfolding. To the president's fury, the Secret Service swayed him to cancel the trip.

On the day after Nixon's visit was scrubbed, the Service told the press that there existed a "very serious, very large" conspiracy by "nonmentals," the term that the agency used and, most likely, coined to distinguish this plot from the more common variety of threats posed by deranged individuals.

The Service launched a nationwide search for Gaudet, who was charged with threatening Nixon's life. Acting on information from Gaudet's father, agents located the suspect at an abandoned commune in the mountains of New Mexico, and local police moved in to arrest him. But when they attempted to serve him with an arrest warrant, Gaudet fired two shots and fled into the peaks carrying a supply of food.

When the police tracked Gaudet to his mountain hiding-place, Secret Service Agent Paul Jones produced Gaudet's wife and cousin, who combined to talk the fugitive into giving himself up. He was arrested twenty hours after his escape.

Two days after Gaudet's surrender, the woman informant who had identified him as the man threatening to kill President Nixon recanted. She claimed that she could not identify Gaudet while she was under oath; the alleged Black Panther plot, reported by another informant, was never corroborated by a second source or by any additional data.

The Secret Service described the threat to Nixon as broad and intense and insisted that the case had not been blown out of proportion. Still, the flimsy intelligence data concerning a plot turned out to be utterly wrong. Though it is certainly prudent for the Secret Service to err on the side of caution in such instances, the question remains as to why the Service publicly announced that it had discovered a plot before it had fully investigated the matter or rounded up the alleged plotters, who might escape and hatch a new conspiracy. Notwithstanding that President Nixon was receiving threats against his life at the rate of about three hundred per year—nearly one per day—the Service reacted to the New Orleans case as especially credible because of Gaudet's past belligerence toward Nixon. Given the volume of threat cases against virtually any president, determining which one demands extensive attention was—and remains—a crucial judgment call for the Service. Its resources are limited; it cannot launch a new, major investigation every day. Because all threats cannot be pursued with equal resources, the agency must be able to determine accurately which protective-intelligence data are worthy of extensive investigation and which are not.

In the case of another would-be assassin of Nixon, the Service did not make the proper call. Samuel Byck had caught the attention of the agency, but deflected his interviewers' scrutiny. The results were tragic and could have been even worse.

Shortly after September 11, 2001, Secretary of Defense Donald Rumsfeld announced at a press conference that until that fateful day, no one had ever imagined an airplane being flown into the White House. Rumsfeld, who was serving as Ambassador to NATO in February 1974, must have forgotten about Byck.

Near 7:00 A.M. on February 22, 1974, a burly, middle-age man ambled up to the front of the line at Gate C at Baltimore-Washington International Airport. A security guard stood with his back to the line.

The heavyset passenger paused behind the guard, pulled a .22 caliber pistol from his dark raincoat, and pumped two shots into the guard's back. The man crumpled—dead before he hit the floor.

As passengers screamed and scattered in all directions, the killer hurdled the security chain, raced down the boarding ramp, and burst into the jet's cockpit. Leveling the .22 at the pilot and copilot, the gunman fired a shot inside the cabin. He shouted, "Fly this plane out of here!"

Forty-four-year-old Samuel Byck planned to crash Delta Flight 523 into the White House to kill President Richard Nixon. He had dubbed his one-man plot "Pandora's Box."

On October 16, 1972, Secret Service investigators had questioned Byck after a tip that he had contended, "Someone ought to kill President Nixon." Byck, described by the agents as "quite intelligent and well-read," struck them as an innocuous type. When Byck's psychiatrist assured the agency that the man was "a big talker who makes verbal threats and never acts on them," he was written off as a harmless crank.

Now, some sixteen months later, Byck turned to Delta 523's pilot and copilot and commanded, "Take off!"

The pilot replied that until the wheel blocks were removed by a ground crew, the plane could not move. In response, Byck shot the copilot in the stomach. Then the gunman yelled, "The next one will be in the head!"

Byck grabbed a female passenger and pushed her toward the control panel. He shouted at her: "Help this man fly this plane!"

Suddenly a pair of shots pealed outside the plane. Byck shoved the woman out of the cockpit, spun around, and fired twice. One bullet hit the wounded copilot above the left eye; the other tore into the pilot's shoulder. The pilot grabbed his cockpit radio and called Ground Control:

> PILOT: Ah, ground control, this is . . . ah . . . Delta at the ramp
> C 8 . . . do you read?
> GROUND CONTROL: Delta C, go ahead.
> PILOT: Do you read?
> GROUND CONTROL: I cut Delta out. Go ahead, Delta.
> PILOT: Emergency, emergency, we're all shot . . . ah . . . can you
> get another pilot here to the airplane . . . ah . . . this fel-
> low he shot us both. Ground . . . I need ground . . . ah .
> . . this is a state of emergency. Get a hold of our ramp and
> ask the people to unhook the tug [the blocks].

An instant later the pilot passed out as Byck reloaded.

The gunman grabbed another woman passenger by the hair, yanked her into the cockpit, and pumped another shot into each of the pilots, who were slumped at the controls. The copilot was already dead. Bullets from police snipers shattered the cockpit windows while the woman screamed for Byck to let her go. He shoved her back toward the cabin.

Two shots cracked from the tarmac and ripped into Byck's stomach and chest. He toppled to the floor, reached for his pistol, and pressed the barrel against his right temple. Then he squeezed the trigger—the weapon's report ending his life.

Who was Samuel Byck, and how had the Secret Service so misjudged his intent to assassinate Nixon? In a series of ranting letters to Jack Anderson, Jonas Salk, Leonard Bernstein, and Senator Abraham Ribicoff and rambling tape recordings made in the hours before the tragedy, Byck left a record of a deeply disturbed man, having mailed rambling letters and tape recordings to various public figures such as Senator Jacob Javits just hours before the hijack attempt.

Byck was a loner about to erupt, one who should not have been regarded so dismissively as just "a big talker" by the agents who had interviewed him. In hindsight, various writers and psychologists have described him as a neurotic personality who, after a lifetime of failure and rejection, lashed out at a public figure as a way to garner recognition. He felt betrayed by his wife, who had divorced him and taken his children, and by his mother, who left the house where she was living with him, and moved to Florida. On February 20, just two days before Byck exploded, he wrote a will in which he wrote: "I will each of my children . . . the sum of one dollar each. They have each other and they deserve each other." His tapes revealed that he held the government's "corruption" and "oppression" as a prime cause of his personal woes.

In the wake of Byck's bloody act, the Service placed increased classroom emphasis on showing agents how to better identify suspects whose mental state forecast genuine danger for the president.

The Secret Service has long repelled threats against protectees other than the president. In 1979, while Senator Edward Kennedy was a presidential candidate, a knife-wielding woman entered the reception room outside his Senate office in Washington, D.C. She was subdued by agents before she got close to the senator, who was working in his inner office. One agent received a minor cut during the scuffle.

Because agents must shield protectees from any kind of harm—not simply an assassination attempt—they have to take action in a wide range of unique situations and settings. President Carter's daughter Amy once attended a pet show hosted by Mrs. Ethel Kennedy at her Hickory Hill, Virginia, estate, where one of the performers was Suzy, a six-thousand-pound elephant who suddenly charged toward Amy Carter. As the crowd scattered in panic, Suzy thundered within thirty-five feet of the president's daughter and was closing rapidly. An agent scooped Amy up and over the top of a split-rail fence as the elephant splintered the fence and continued to charge despite efforts by other agents to distract her. Agents scrambled just ahead of the raging pachyderm to carry Amy safely inside the Kennedy house. The elephant's trainers got the animal under control once Amy was out of sight.

In 1980, two Secret Service agents were killed in separate incidents that did not involve guarding a protectee and that occurred in cities other than Washington, D.C. With a concealed gun, a man named Hugh Ryan walked into the Service's Denver field office on January 15, 1980. Ryan had been committed to a mental hospital the previous year as a result of his attempt to break into the White House grounds, and had later been questioned by the Service for his alleged threat against the president. Now, as Ryan complained to Denver agents that he was being harassed by the Secret Service, a pair of agents, recognizing the man's apparent instability, edged closer to him. Ryan whipped out his .45-caliber pistol and shot agent Stewart Wilkins in the stomach and chest. The second Agent shot and killed Ryan, but too late for Agent Wilkins, who died shortly afterward during surgery.

The Service lost another agent six months later. Special Agents Julie Cross and her partner, Lloyd Bulman, had been assigned to watch a site near Los Angeles International Airport for a gang of counterfeiters. Around 9:00 P.M. on June 4, 1980, two men suddenly appeared behind the car in which the agents were sitting, and opened fire with shotguns. Cross was killed, the first female agent to die in the line of duty. Bulman survived.

According to the Secret Service, the two agents were the victims of a random crime:

> All evidence suggested that the crime was an attempted robbery and not connected to the counterfeit investigation in any way. The suspects took Agent Cross' handgun and a Secret Service folding stock Remington 870 shotgun. For 9 years the suspects remained unknown, despite an enormous effort by a task force of Secret Service agents and members of the Los Angeles Police Department.

For nine years, the Secret Service refused to give up its pursuit of the two nameless gunmen who had killed Agent Cross, employing the television show *Unsolved Mysteries* to run a segment on the Cross case. Eventually, a Los Angeles Police homicide detective arrested a man named Andre Alexander for a 1978 triple murder, and an investigation led to evidence establishing Alexander as the prime suspect in the Cross murder. In 1990, a jury convicted Alexander of three counts of first-degree murder, leading to a sentence of life in prison without possibility of parole.

Alexander was formally charged with Cross's murder in 1992 and stood trial in 1995. When prosecutors convinced the jury that Alexander had murdered the Secret Service agent, the judge handed down the death sentence.

From 1966 to 1972, during the Vietnam War, Secret Service agents accompanied Presidents Johnson and Nixon, Vice Presidents Humphrey and Spiro Agnew, and presidential candidate Curtis LeMay to the ravaged Asian nation. As with Eisenhower's trip to Korea, the hazards facing the Secret Service proved a minute-by-minute challenge, with the politicians' stops and scheduled events revealed at the last possible moment for fear of leaks by South Vietnamese turncoats to the Viet Cong and North Vietnamese Army. With the close cooperation of the American military, agents swept planned stops and monitored them for suspicious activity. "Dummy" motorcades and helicopters were employed. Still, in several instances Secret Service advance agents came under heavy enemy fire from small arms, rifles, machine guns, and recoil-less rockets.

One of the hottest moments for the Secret Service in Vietnam erupted on October 31, 1967. In Saigon, Vice President Humphrey had attended inauguration ceremonies for South Vietnamese President Thieu of South Vietnam; later that evening, Humphrey arrived for a reception at the Independence Palace grounds.

Within a minute of his entry into the Palace, four mortar rounds exploded in the rear of the grounds, wounding two people and demolishing two vehicles. Agents quickly surrounded the vice president.

The Viet Cong had fired the rounds through an opening in the roof of a small hut located six blocks from the Palace, first killing an elderly civilian in an adjacent hut when he went to investigate what they were doing. The agency suspected that Vice President Humphrey was their target.

Back at home, the reality that threats could arise anytime and anywhere for the Service was pointed out yet again in a seemingly innocuous setting.

Presidential candidate George McGovern escaped serious injury when an intoxicated motorist lost control of his automobile while driving on the freeway and his car swerved into the Secret Service follow-up car before crashing into an embankment. The incident killed the drunken driver and injured two agents.

Even though agents fully understood that trouble could erupt at anytime and anywhere, the American public watched in horror as the most dramatic assassination attempt against a president since November 22, 1963, unfolded in split seconds. On March 30, 1981, the television cameras were running when the agency's nightmare of the would-be assassin in the crowd happened again.

## CHAPTER 5

# "GO TO GEORGE WASHINGTON HOSPITAL—FAST!"

*We didn't have that opportunity that day [that the president was wounded] but it is one human being looking into the eyes of another that is the best detector.*
*— Secret Service Agent Jerry Parr, Head of President Ronald Reagan's Protective Detail*

March 30, 1981, when John W. Hinckley opened fire on President Ronald Reagan, proved one of the tensest days and most controversial days in the annals of the Secret Service. Speaking about the attempted assassination of Reagan, Special Agent Jerry Parr relates: "I have a feeling—I've always felt this, and it's what agents know—that the eyes are windows to the soul. If you look at the agents working around the president . . . they'll be looking at [crowds'] faces, eyes, hands . . .

None of the Secret Service detail outside the Washington Hilton Hotel on March 30, 1981, spotted the fidgety Hinckley among the press corps. But from the instant that Agent Tim McCarthy hurled himself in front of Reagan and took a Devastator bullet in the chest, and Agents Parr and Shaddick pushed the president into the limousine, the press and the public alike marveled at the instinctive reactions of the president's protective detail. From the first cracks of Hinckley's handgun to the scant seconds later when agents jumped and disarmed him, they performed with near-textbook efficiency. The detail's heroics in those frenetic seconds, however, cloaked errors that nearly cost Reagan his life. The mistakes left McCarthy, Officer Delahanty, and Press Secretary Jim Brady sprawled and bleeding on the sidewalk outside the hotel.

Behind closed doors at the agency's Washington Field Office, Secret Service headquarters, and the Treasury Department, the internal investigations into what had gone wrong began. How had agents allowed an armed intruder to penetrate the official press "rope line," squeeze within twenty feet of the president, and snap off six shots? Why hadn't the Secret Service secured George Washington Hospital, where Reagan was taken, while agents furnished extra protection for Hinckley in jail? Those questions were just the start. Because the valor of McCarthy would remain fixed in the public's collective eye, the answers were hushed up for a long time.

On March 30, 1981, President Ronald Reagan was scheduled to give a speech at the Washington Hilton Hotel to four thousand members of the Building and Construction Trade Union. The itinerary called for a motorcade from the White House to the Hilton, arriving at 1:50 P.M.; the president would then enter the hotel, deliver a brief speech, exit the hotel into a waiting limousine, and arrive back at the White House by 2:30 P.M.

Such trips to the Hilton to give short speeches to various groups were "standard" events—"home-field advantage"—for the Secret Service and the White House staff. The president had made these appearances every other week for the past several months. The Service's advance preparation work included meetings with hotel and union officials to work out security procedures. Additionally, Agent Mary Ann Gordon drove along the motorcade route to and from the Hilton, accompanied by a representative of the Washington, D.C., Police Department. Gordon, the first woman ever assigned to a presidential protective detail, coordinated Reagan's motorcade routes not only with the local police, but also with the U.S Park Police, who would secure the motorcade route and see to traffic control.

As always, special communications frequencies to be used by police and Secret Service were agreed upon. At a Secret Service briefing of participating police, a system for issuing and checking IDs and color-coded pins was set up. Agent Gordon called the Washington, D.C., Highway and Traffic Department to make sure that there would be no construction along the motorcade route, and then distributed a memo describing the motorcade route to all security personnel.

The Service conducted an advance check of the Hilton Hotel, scrutinizing it for security problems, with agents assigned to guard key areas such as hallways and doorways while the president was inside. Inside the hotel, other agents conducted a walk through of the president's planned routes. The names of union officials who would greet the president and of hotel employees were obtained and checked against the Service's dangerous person files.

Just before the president's arrival, a countersniper team was positioned at an undisclosed location outside the hotel. Technicians from the Service's Technical Security division ran "sweeps" of the ballroom where the speech was to be given, and combed the arrival site outside, searching with a canine team for explosive devices or anything else that could harm the president.

Reagan was to enter and exit the hotel through the VIP entrance facing onto T Street, and from an overall security perspective, this seemed like a secure location. The distance from the hotel door to the street, where the limousine would be parked, was twenty-five to thirty feet, relatively short by hotel standards, reducing the time of the president's exposure to potential assassins. The roof and windows of the Hilton were blocked from a view of the doorway by a high, clifflike, concrete wall that shielded the doorway from the main hotel. Across the street stood an eight-story building with closed windows; its roof was covered by the countersniper team. From a security standpoint, closed windows are considered a good sign, as a sniper is unlikely to place a gun barrel against glass. For a big-city location, the Hilton VIP entrance appeared safe enough from sniper fire, and the street and sidewalk area outside the doorway were quite small so that there was no room for a large crowd to gather.

The crowd who would hear Reagan's speech inside the Hilton was subjected to very strict security, from badge and ID checks to searches. But security outside proved an entirely different matter, one that nearly proved fatal for Reagan. In the precautions taken for the event, the Secret Service scrutinized the crowd inside far more assiduously than the people outside the hotel. Agents had sealed and were guarding the entrances to the ballroom, and spectators were only allowed to enter through two checkpoints. "Explosive ordnance disposal personnel" stood at each checkpoint to inspect handbags and briefcases. At a separate entrance and checkpoint set up for the press, agents inspected cameras and tape recorders for explosives.

Agents and police had set up a rope line outside the Hilton to keep the crowds from getting too close to the president and from blocking the entrance, but the protective detail and police did not search the crowd itself for bombs or guns, nor did agents screen anyone's credentials outside the hotel. According to the Treasury Department's report on the attempted assassination, the total lack of crowd scrutiny in front of the Hilton stemmed from the fact that "the area had not been designated a 'press area,' " implying that the press would have been screened more carefully than the general public. The agency never explained why the press would have constituted more of a threat to Reagan than someone in the crowd.

Inside the hotel, agents noticed that members of the press corps were "straying outside of the designated press area," and quickly escorted reporters back to their preassigned area. However, standing behind the rope barrier was a young man named John W. Hinckley, who soon stole into the ranks of the press corps to within twenty feet of where the president would walk. No agent or police officer stopped him. Because of the tight security inside the hotel, no one there had the opportunity to get so close to the president, but outside was another matter.

If the Secret Service had designated a press area outside the hotel, agents and White House personnel would have controlled access to the area by screening credentials; however, agents felt that setting up an advance press area would have been "impractical" because it could have slowed access to the hotel for the president.

To the Secret Service's way of thinking, stated in a Treasury Department report on the episode, the Hilton trip was uncomplicated from a security standpoint because the visit was to begin and end in the most secure of all locations—the White House. The Hilton was also a site that the president and other protectees visited frequently. The report concluded:

> While the agents conducting the advance for the President's March 30 visit to the Hilton handled their responsibilities capably, their preparation did not address certain details which were included in the standard procedure for an advance. This may be understandable, since the procedures were developed for environments outside of Washington, D.C. and do not take account of the fact that trips in the Capitol have become routine.

Though it is true that the Service tends to regard trips within Washington, D.C., as safer and more routine than in outside locations and that agents seemingly have a more relaxed attitude in the capital toward security, that mind-set definitely eroded effective security for President Reagan. Such complacency could carry to presidential trips to areas that also seem safer, areas such as George W. Bush's remote ranch, in Crawford, Texas. In Reagan's fateful visit to the Hilton, where agents employed a double standard regarding security inside the hotel versus security outside, the Service erred—in large part because visits to the hotel had come to be viewed as "routine."

Then and now, the Service's Washington, D.C., field office handles protective intelligence-gathering for trips within the nation's capital. Before Reagan's visit to the Hilton, field office agents checked with the protective research section at Secret Service headquarters in order to identify dangerous persons who might be in the area and to examine lists of hotel guests and employees against Secret Service files. Agent Timothy McCarthy of the field office checked with headquarters and discovered no problems.

Hinckley was not in Secret Service files. He had been arrested at the Nashville, Tennessee, airport on October 9, 1980, as he attempted to board a plane while carrying three pistols. Then-candidate Ronald Reagan had just canceled a planned trip to Nashville, and President Carter was in Nashville at the time of Hinckley's arrest.

Though many critics have argued that Nashville police or the FBI should have reported Hinckley to the Secret Service, there was no direct threat to either Carter or Reagan involved, and if the Secret Service had to catalog everyone arrested for a firearms violation in any city where a president or candidate was visiting at the time, the list would overwhelm the agency's files. The Service could not possibly interview or monitor all such persons. In fairness to the agency, there was probably no way in which operatives would have been looking for Hinckley on March 30, 1981, even if the Nashville arrest had been reported to the Service. Some have also suggested that the Nashville incident should have caused Hinckley to be spotted as a threat, but one arrest in proximity to a president does not prove that someone is a stalker.

While Hinckley waited outside the Hilton on the raw, blustery March day, President Reagan's motorcade to the hotel and his arrival went smoothly. Reagan strode into a "holding room" where photographers took pictures of him with assembled union leaders. Then he went to the ballroom to deliver a twenty-minute speech as agents scanned the audience of four thousand looking for potential problems. They spotted none.

Outside the hotel, where the press had massed between the parked presidential limousine and the follow-up car, an agent ordered the reporters out of the area so that the vehicles could get into position for the return trip. The agents standing around the limousine scanned the crowd across T Street and on the hotel side of the street as well, looking for signs of trouble.

As the president exited the hotel through the same VIP door used for his entrance, agents took up positions around the waiting limousine. Agents Parr and Shaddick walked just behind Reagan; in front of him walked White House Press Secretary James Brady, Deputy Chief of Staff Michael Deaver, a military aide, and more agents.

While President Reagan strolled directly toward the limousine, Agent Shaddick had to step around a White House staff member in order to maintain his position to the right rear of the president and in close proximity to him. He quickly regained his proper position.

Stationed at the limousine, Agent Timothy McCarthy opened the rear passenger-side door for the president. Shouts of "Mr. President" rang from the crowd. Reagan waved in response as he bent to enter the limousine. Shots suddenly erupted from behind the rope barrier—six of them fired only fifteen to twenty feet from the president in a mere two seconds.

Though the shots sounded like firecrackers to some bystanders, Secret Service agents reacted instantly in clear contrast to the Kennedy assassination, when some agents in Dallas thought that the shots were firecrackers and looked around without taking action. A shot ricocheted off the side of the limousine, passed through the space between the open door and the car's body, and ripped into a spot just under President Reagan's left arm.

At the first sound of the shots near the rope barrier, Agent Jerry Parr shoved Reagan into the backseat of the limousine and began to cover him. Agent Shaddick thrust Parr and the grimacing president into the limousine as McCarthy wheeled around toward the sound of the gunfire and spread his arms and legs to shield the president. A bullet smashed into McCarthy's chest and flung him to the sidewalk. Nearby, Press Secretary Brady, sprawled on the sidewalk, was bleeding profusely from a head wound; D.C. policeman Thomas Delahanty was also crumpled on the concrete, his neck pierced by a bullet.

Carolyn Parr, wife of Jerry, had been working in an office building across from the Hilton. Excited at the prospect of seeing her husband at work protecting the president, she had missed seeing them enter, and so watched to see them exit. As the bodies fell, she could not tell who was who, and she ran out and across the street, trying to break through the law-enforcement net to see if Jerry was all right. She desperately asked one of the agents, "Where *is* he [Parr]?"

"In the car with the man," came the reply. She felt better—but only for a moment. She saw Brady lying on the sidewalk, blood and gray matter oozing from his head. He was "fully alert," she recalls with surprise.

Shaddick slammed shut the door to the limousine and bellowed at the driver to leave the scene. The limousine driver dodged a parked police car and roared away within ten seconds of the first shot.

Bystander Alfred Antenucci jumped Hinckley from behind as he squeezed off the sixth and last shot, and Agent Dennis McCarthy (no relation to Tim McCarthy) dove on the shooter an instant later—as Hinckley continued to pull the trigger of the empty gun. Two D.C. policemen quickly wrestled the pistol away from Hinckley.

Of the six bullets fired from the gun, one had hit Brady; one, Delahanty; the third, a building across the street; the fourth, McCarthy; the fifth, the limo door; and the sixth had ricocheted off the car and into Reagan. Press Secretary Brady had not been scheduled to be at the Hilton, but at the last minute said he would do the chore, and sent Deputy Larry Speakes back to the White House. Because Officer Delahanty's partner was ill, he went to the Hilton, where Hinckley lurked. Agent McCarthy had not been scheduled for this assignment, either, but lost a coin toss with a fellow agent. President Reagan was the only shooting victim who had been scheduled to be at this ill-fated event.

No Secret Service agent had seen the assailant draw his weapon. Once the shooting began, several agents pulled out their pistols and automatic weapons and scanned the crowd for more assailants while other agents covered the limousine's escape with their Uzi machine guns drawn. Neither agents nor police fired a shot.

Agents remaining at the scene radioed that there had been an attack on the president. They held the crowd back from the wounded and tried to preserve the evidence. One agent took Hinckley's weapon, another handcuffed him. Meanwhile, in the presidential limousine, Agent Parr got off of President Reagan and helped him to a sitting position. Parr asked the president if he was all right, and Reagan responded, "Yes."

Despite Reagan's assurances, Parr checked the back of Mr. Reagan's coat for wounds and ran his hands inside the coat. Parr found nothing and ordered the driver to proceed to the White House.

Thirty seconds later, the president complained that he was having trouble breathing and felt a sharp pain in his chest. "I think I cut my mouth," he told Parr. Reagan started blotting his lips with a Hilton napkin.

Parr noticed the foamy blood in the president's mouth and ordered the driver, "Go to George Washington Hospital—fast!"

Agent Mary Ann Gordon, riding in the follow-up car, tried to radio the D.C. police to clear a route to the hospital, but could not get through on her two-way radio. With police frequencies jammed by heavy and chaotic radio traffic ignited by the shooting, Gordon ordered her car's driver to pass the presidential limousine and run interference through traffic. When the president's car suddenly changed direction and turned onto Pennsylvania Avenue to get to the hospital, the lead car in the motorcade and four escorting motorcycles failed to make the turn and were separated from the limousine. The president would have been vulnerable to a second assault if the unfolding drama had been a conspiracy. Also, because the president was in a limo, not an ambulance, the vehicle had to deal with any driver who might have thought that the limo had no right to pass him or her, as well as other potential traffic problems.

Agents who had heard Parr's radio transmission about getting to the hospital fast radioed the hospital that the motorcade would arrive there and that there were injuries. Hospital personnel were not told that the president had been wounded. Agent Parr feared that everyone monitoring his frequency would then know that the president had been hurt—a potential breach of communications security. As the limo raced to the hospital, emergency-room personnel gathered to treat the unspecified "injured."

One Secret Service transmission to the hospital was made, but no one requested that a stretcher be waiting to carry "the injured" inside. Although a later transmission did request a stretcher, none awaited the wounded president when the limo arrived only three minutes after the shooting, and President Reagan actually had to walk from the car to the hospital entrance. Fortunately, the trauma room team was ready.

Agents Parr and Shaddick guided Reagan as he wobbled into the hospital. His knees began to buckle, and the agents and two paramedics carried the president to the emergency room, where he was placed on a cart and whisked to the trauma center. Only upon removing Reagan's clothes did the medical personnel realize how grievously he was wounded. The surgeons' race to save Ronald Reagan's life began.

After touch-and-go surgery in which doctors dealt with the president's collapsed lung and several moments during which his blood pressure plummeted, Reagan made a dramatic recovery. For weeks, however, doctors had to make sure that blood did not begin to pool in his lung again. D.C. Police Officer Delahanty and Agent McCarthy recovered fully from their wounds, but Press Secretary Brady suffered extensive brain damage. The rapidity with which the shots were fired (six in two seconds) made it difficult for the FBI to determine the exact sequence of the wounds. The Bureau concluded that Reagan was hit after he had been doubled over by Agent Parr, who was pushing him into the limousine.

The bullets Hinckley had sprayed outside the Hilton were "Devastators," which contained an aluminum cap that, when detonated, would explode and cause the bullet to fragment and tear through the victim much like shrapnel. Although the round that struck James Brady in the head apparently exploded, the one that hit the president did not, probably because it ricocheted off of the limousine before hitting Reagan, expending its explosive charge. In that regard the president was lucky: if the bullet, lodged close to Reagan's heart, had exploded, he would probably have died. Police officers later found an empty box of Devastators in Hinckley's Washington, D.C., hotel room.

FBI Agent Robert Young described, "These bullets could explode at any time. Anything can make them go off, like heat or pressure or impact." When the doctors removed the bullet from the president's lung, they did not know that they were dealing with a bullet that could have exploded at any moment if its charge were intact. It seems that neither the D.C. police nor the FBI nor the Secret Service communicated the ballistic threat to the president's doctors; however, it remains unclear who knew about the Devastator. The agents who had helped Reagan into the trauma center had no way to know that Hinckley's rounds were Devastators.

Though none of the Secret Service agents or police noticed Hinckley before he opened fire on the president, two military aides who had driven cars in the presidential motorcade and were waiting for the president to exit the Hilton spotted strange behavior by a man in the crowd. The person who displayed "erratic behavior" was not Hinckley, but a man whom agents recognized immediately because they had interviewed him on several previous occasions and had determined that he posed no danger to the president.

Hinckley, the man in the crowd who *was* a danger to the president, was noticed by John M. Dodson, a Pinkerton Detective Agency employee watching the crowd from a seventh-floor window across the street from the Hilton. According to Dodson, Hinckley was conspicuous because he kept turning his body from side to side. Dobson stated, "The best description was fidgety."

Walter C. Rogers, an Associated Press reporter, had also noticed Hinckley before the shooting and claimed that Hinckley was hostile to the group of reporters whose un-credentialed ranks he had joined. ABC television cameraman Henry M. Brown asserted that he had complained directly to a Secret Service agent about people "penetrating" the police line (the rope barrier) and creating crowded conditions that hampered the reporters who were covering the event. Despite Brown's complaint, agents took no action, probably because the area was not defined by the Secret Service as a press area that was off-limits to the public.

Ironworker Samuel Lafta, another bystander outside the Hilton, claimed that one police officer stared at Hinckley several times before the shooting but did not approach him.

Immediately after the assassination attempt, a major flaw in Secret Service protection emerged: Not one Secret Service agent or Uniformed Division officer was posted at George Washington Hospital when the president was brought there. Some additional agents were dispatched to the hospital from the Washington field office, but this was approximately a half hour after the wounded president had been carried to the trauma room. Not only were the reinforcements insufficient to secure the hospital effectively, but there was also no advance detail to secure the entrance to the hospital, the halls, or the emergency room. The agents arriving with the president escorted him inside and then had to set up makeshift security at the hospital.

Though Technical Security Division personnel arrived at the hospital in time to run security checks of the operating room, the recovery room, and the intensive care area, they did not reach the scene in time to check the emergency room where the president was carried upon arrival. Canine teams to sniff out explosives and countersniper teams did not arrive until later that evening. Even if the dogs had been brought earlier, it is doubtful that their handlers would have had time to check the hospital's operating room—saving the president's life would have taken precedence.

The lack of security at the hospital fortunately had no negative consequences for the president's safety—in this particular case. But, under different circumstances, it could have been disastrous, even fatal. At the time that the president was rushed to the hospital minutes after the shooting, no one knew the extent and nature of the attack. There could have been a hit squad following the presidential motorcade to the hospital or other assailants waiting for him there, and they could have finished the job.

According to the Service's protective dictates, all agents should give first priority to the safety of the president. This takes precedence over helping wounded bystanders, capturing assailants, or preserving evidence. When the limousine carrying President Reagan raced up to the hospital, not only was there no advance protection, but also he was being protected by only a portion of his original protective detail. Several agents had remained behind at the scene of the shooting; one, McCarthy, was fighting for his own life. The president's protection was spread perilously thin.

Secret Service Agent Gerald Bechtle, who was acting as assistant director of Protective Operations, sent the agents at the Hilton instructions: members of the president's original security detail should remain at the crime scene in order to implement what Bechtle understood to be an "interim federal presence" (as described in the Service's 1979 memorandum of understanding with the FBI). Yet the Secret Service's first priority has always been the safety of the president. The 1979 agreement with the FBI was more concerned with delegating full investigative responsibility for assassination and attempted-assassination cases to the Bureau rather than the Service, and required that any evidence gathered by the Service should be immediately turned over to the FBI. Because the agreement was never meant to intrude upon the Service's directive to protect the president first, last, and always, Bechtle's order was puzzling. The Service's mission dictated that *all* of the president's security mission should have escorted him to the hospital to guard against any follow-up attack along the way or at the hospital. For the agency, "interim federal presence" did not mean that Reagan's protectors should remain at the crime scene to protect evidence and to help the FBI conduct its investigation.

Some agents seemed to interpret the 1979 agreement as requiring the

Service to stay at the crime scene even after the FBI had arrived, with Secret Service men staying on-site at the Hilton to give interviews to FBI agents. Again, the Service made a mistake: the failure of Secret Service headquarters to properly balance "interim federal presence" against the protective mission could have had serious consequences if Hinckley had proven part of a plot rather than a lone gunman.

Other errors abounded. Neither Secret Service headquarters nor the Washington field office thought to assess the level of security at the hospital and to dispatch the additional agents needed to provide effective protection. With the Washington field office assigned chief responsibility for presidential trips within the Washington, D.C., area, the office naturally handled advance preparations and intelligence gathering for the Hilton visit. Though Secret Service headquarters was brought into the crisis immediately after the shooting, the Washington field office continued to play a major role.

In the aftermath of the shooting, the Washington field office became heavily involved in investigative and law-enforcement activities, even though protection at the hospital did not reach an adequate level until at least three to four hours after the president's arrival. One request for reinforcements made by agents at the hospital to the Washington field office could not get through, apparently as field office's circuits were swamped with calls and transmissions; the field office did not get in touch with the hospital to find out if enough agents were on hand or if more were needed.

The Treasury Department report of the shooting reports that, "Most of the attention of supervisory Washington field office personnel was directed to the arrangements concerning the custody of Hinckley; the transmittal of information derived from Hinckley's personal effects."

The field office responded to a request from Agent Ramsey, who was at the Hilton. His request was likely based on orders he had received from Secret Service headquarters to establish an "interim federal presence." In response to his call, the Washington field office dispatched two additional agents to the Hilton to help the FBI with its investigation. They arrived at the crime scene a little after 2:30 P.M.—about the same time that President Reagan arrived at the hospital with no advance protection and with a diminished protective detail accompanying him.

Shortly after the president had been sped to the hospital, two of the agents in his protective detail escorted Hinckley to police headquarters, where one agent "covered" Hinckley as he was hauled from the car to a cell. The pair of operatives then searched the suspect for weapons and read him his rights.

While one agent stood guard outside Hinckley's cell, the second phoned the Washington field office. Unlike the agent who had called the field office from George Washington Hospital, the agent at the police station did get through, asking that additional agents be sent to the station. The Washington field office quickly sent three more agents to Hinckley's cell block, where they remained while the suspect was interrogated by the police. Then, they loaded him into a Secret Service armored car, took him to an FBI office, and listened to a second interrogation of the disheveled gunman. The agents later reported the gist of the FBI interrogation to the Service's Washington field office. In cases such as Hinckley's, it is the FBI and the police who have jurisdiction once the attempted assassination takes place.

Deep into the evening, the field office probed Hinckley's preattack movements, and Agent Carlton Spriggs determined from Hinckley's personal effects that he had registered at the Park Central Hotel. Two field office agents, along with FBI men, searched the hotel room at 5:45 P.M.

Secret Service headquarters, throughout the first hour of the crisis, assumed that if additional agents were needed at the hospital, someone in Reagan's original protective detail would call for them. Even though a small number of additional agents arrived at the hospital during the afternoon, the crisis managers at Secret Service headquarters had no idea about the level of protection at the hospital, nor did they make any systematic attempt to learn the details. As the Treasury report describes:

> In effect, the headquarters crisis managers followed the implications of existing procedures and assumed that presidential detail personnel on site, and the Washington field office personnel sent there shortly afterward, would request whatever assistance was necessary. The requests they received from the hospital site were few and took some period of time to fulfill; as a consequence, the number of Service personnel at the hospital did not reach a level substantially greater than the security that had been established at the Hilton prior to the shooting until late in the afternoon of March 30.

Inadequate communications facilities at the hospital may have hampered the Service's coordination between headquarters and the protective-detail agents. The Service considered George Washington Hospital to be the primary emergency hospital for trips in the downtown area; however, the White House Communications Agency did not consider it the primary hospital for medical treatment of the president. A military hospital never mentioned in the assassination report had been selected for that role. Because of this, specialized communications at George Washington were limited until agents brought in additional equipment.

At the Treasury Department, as well as the hospital, communications woes plagued the Service. The Treasury's Telecommunications Center first learned of the shooting when one of the operators heard about it from a friend. On her own initiative, the operator immediately began to notify the officials on the Treasury's emergency notification list.

The officer on duty at the Treasury Department Watch Office first heard of the attempted assassination when the news appeared on the press wire. To say the least, it would have been preferable for Treasury's emergency communications system to obtain immediate details from a source within the Secret Service or the Treasury Department.

For Reagan, another problem that could have proven critical was that his medical records were not on file at the hospital nor were they carried along in his limousine. Although the agency had conducted a security survey of George Washington Hospital in July 1980, the report's findings were unclear.

The Service's report on George Washington Hospital contained a security checklist but did not contain a security plan for the placement of guards or the establishment of a "command post." Though the information in the report would have been helpful in planning security, it did not constitute a security plan. The hospital had its own "hospital disaster plan," which was activated by the hospital administrator and called for limiting access to the hospital. The plan proved helpful to the Service, but hardly an effective "game plan" for presidential protection.

The agents who arrived at the hospital with President Reagan, with no advance detail to help them and with their numbers diminished by posting agents at the crime scene, faced the simultaneous tasks of protecting the president and designing security. This made the need for instant reinforcements all the more acute.

In another procedural lapse, the agency had no plan in place for the protection of Vice President George H. W. Bush, who was flying back to Washington, D.C., after attending several Republican events on the West Coast. The Service had no written procedure or policy to automatically increase the protection of the vice president in the event of an attack on the president. Because any attack on the president might be part of a broader attempt to assassinate several top officials, as was the case in the Lincoln assassination, the error was glaring.

Agents in the vice presidential detail did take the initiative in coming up with "quick-fix" special precautions for Bush. When his plane settled onto the tarmac in Austin, Texas, to refuel, the vice president stayed aboard, and agents sealed off all entrances and drew their automatic weapons. Still, as the Treasury Department report on the assassination attempt against Reagan observes, "It is unclear whether the Service made a special check to determine whether trouble might be anticipated at this stop."

Clearly, the Service should always assume the worst—a coordinated attack on the president and vice president might be unfolding. The appropriate response to such an assumption would have been a thorough check of the Austin airport and enhanced security before the plane landed. Because the Austin stop was scheduled in advance and might have therefore been the site of a planned attack, a Secret Service plan to divert the flight if necessary should have been ready.

John W. Hinckley, the man who had nearly killed the president and whose actions had set off a firestorm of questions about the Service's protective performance, turned out to be a deeply disturbed young man with fantasies of a love affair with actress Jodie Foster. A jury found him not guilty by reason of insanity.

The third unsuccessful presidential assassination attempt in six years, Hinckley's attempt compelled the Secret Service to examine every aspect of its March 30, 1981, performance. The agency had constantly implored the genial Reagan not to pause and chat with the press during his exits. "Wave and move, Mr. President," agents had urged.

How did Hinckley get so close? For effective security, agents should never have allowed close-up and unrestricted access to anyone in the area outside the Hilton; Hinckley had worked his way among reporters to a mere fifteen to twenty feet from the president. Either the area should have been designated a press area and credentials should have been checked or an unrestricted area should have been set up at greater distance from the president.

In the aftermath of the shooting, agents tightened security. The president exited events through parking garages instead of out on the street, and the press was kept at much greater distance, which meant fewer opportunities to ask questions of him. Decoy limousines were used on subsequent trips to the Hilton to confuse bystanders as to where the president would exit. Because of the map and newspapers found among Hinckley's possessions, the Service realized that advance publicity about the president's agenda had aided the assailant. The White House halted any release of Reagan's daily itinerary.

The reflexive and heroic actions of the agents flanking Reagan on March 30, 1981, so gripped the public that many of the mistakes escaped close public scrutiny. The image of Agent Tim McCarthy "taking a bullet for the president" was—and remains—unforgettable, and deservedly so.

Recently, McCarthy recalled:

> I scanned the crowd. Hinckley was two or three rows back, pushing forward. He fired. I knew there were shots coming from that location—the noise. I actually never saw Hinckley. It was a reaction to the sound.
>
> Personally, I was pleased to do what I'm trained to do. Whether it's a police officer making an arrest or a Secret Service agent, you never know if you will do what you were trained to. I don't know if I can do it again [a slight chuckle]. But I'm glad I was able to.
>
> The rule is, if the attacker is in arms reach, you go to the attacker. If not, cover and evacuate [the protectee]. You can't leave the president and go to the attacker; you cover and evacuate.

Another agent described both the mind-set and the training that McCarthy displayed in taking a bullet for Ronald Reagan:

> If there's a shot fired, the natural reaction for anyone in law enforcement is to take cover yourself, assess the situation; respond to the situation. The natural reaction for us, if we're

working close to the protectee, is to cover the protectee and to evacuate him or her to the limousine or to an area that we know is going to be safe. So you have to practice a certain amount to be able to instinctively perform that, as opposed to the natural human instinctive performance of trying to save your own skin.

That's [flinging oneself in the line of fire] what everybody says, but that is the essence of the job when you are on protection. We prefer to think that the advance work is done so well that there will not be an incident, but of course there could be an incident anyway and if that does happen, you perform as you have been trained and people do get hurt. You know the famous film with President Reagan where Agent McCarthy turns, and you can tell that he is purposely turning his body the broad way, as opposed to the narrow way, in between the President and the assailant and takes a shot right in the stomach in doing so. That's an instinctive reaction due to his training. It is not the normal reaction that the normal person is going to have. It is something a little unusual, but that's part of the job description.

Despite McCarthy's valor, the assassination attempt outside the Hilton proved that much more than the Secret Service's "exit-security" procedures needed repair. The agents guarding the president performed flawlessly in evacuating him within ten seconds of the shooting, but from then on, the crisis exposed one flawed procedure after another—the flaws had not proven fatal only because the case involved a single attack by a lone shooter rather than multiple attacks in a coordinated plot. Inadequate communications, failure to have a hospital security plan and the president's medical records at the ready, a lapse by several agents who stayed at the crime scene instead of accompanying the president away from the site— these numbered only a few of the mistakes that the Secret Service had made on March 30, 1981. The agency had almost lost a president for the second time.

## CHAPTER 6

# FORTRESS WHITE HOUSE?

*". . . fraught with conflict and symbolism"*

*—Rand Report, Spring 1995*

Security starts at home for the president, but protecting the nation's chief executive where he and his family literally live has not always proven a top priority. Not until William McKinley took office near the turn of the century did the notion begin to take hold. Previously, presidents were often wide open to potential assassins, and trouble sometimes showed up right on the doorstep of the executive mansion.

For much of the White House's nearly two centuries of existence, Thomas Jefferson's adage that the mansion was "the People's House" was taken at face value. The White House was kept as open and accessible to the public as possible. When President George Washington and Secretary of State Thomas Jefferson, both Virginians, were allowed by the Residence Act of 1790 to choose a national capital, they selected a ten-square-mile site perched above the Potomac River. However, the two Virginians wrangled over the most fitting style of a new residence for the president, with Washington, a Federalist, enamored of the plans drawn up by Pierre L'Enfant for a "presidential palace" five times the size of the eventual building. Touted as suitable for "ages to come," L'Enfant's design mirrored the Federalist Party's borderline monarchical belief that Americans wanted a leader a little "above" them. Several Federalists argued that the nation needed the equivalent of an "elected king" and a suitable "palace" for him. Washington asserted that it was his responsibility "to conform to the public desire and expectation with respect to the style proper for the Chief Magistrate to live in." In short, he held that the "Chief Magistrate" should live in a palace.

Jefferson and his fellow Republicans saw things otherwise, loathing the royalist trappings that L'Enfant's plans for a "presidential palace" would feature. Fearing that a "palace" might lend itself to an imperial presidency, Jefferson and company criticized L'Enfant's plan as offensive in a democracy; Jefferson futilely argued that the "President's house" should be constructed of modest brick rather than then granite and marble, contending that the nation's new capital be devoid of any aristocratic structures such as those in Europe. With both sides unable to agree, Washington and Jefferson compromised by opening up the design of the president's house to a national competition. Eventually, Washington acceded to a design by Irishman James Hoban, who dubbed the blueprints the "Executive Mansion or the White House"; both terms were destined to outlive the architect.

The rasps of workmen's saws and peals of hammers and chisels above the Potomac signaled the start of the White House in 1792. Eight years later, in 1800, America's second president, John Adams, and his wife, Abigail, walked into the mansion as its first occupants.

The First Couple soon learned exactly how literal the term "the People's House" was. Throughout the construction of the first White House, citizens would walk on and off the site as they pleased, which forced the marshal of Washington to police the grounds. Eventually, he ordered it closed to anyone who did not possess a written pass.

Presidents have wrestled with the ideas of public access to the White House versus presidential privacy since the Adamses walked through the door of the mansion. Early in Adams's administration, the reality that anyone could enter the house and possibly do anything to the president or his family materialized in the form of a deranged man who visited the White House and threatened to kill President John Adams. Adams, never yelling for help or reaching for a weapon, invited the stranger into the presidential office, sat down with him, and pacified the man. The president made only a brief reference to the incident and noted that the potential assassin never returned.

Adams gave little thought to the matter of security, and even if he had, he would have run into opposition from the Jeffersonian Republicans, who not only preached the gospel of the "People's House" but also embraced free public access to the White House grounds. Throughout much of America's history, the public was granted even more access to the grounds than to the White House proper, and for the first part of the nineteenth century, presidents could look out the windows to see the grounds teeming with people, carts, and stands, as the acreage was used for a public market. The grounds also served a one of the area's chief tourist sites, a spot that offered a panoramic view of the Potomac. The manicured grounds were also a favorite place for visitors to stroll.

President Jefferson threw open the White House doors each day to allow access to the State Rooms for visitors, except early in the morning and during his absences from the mansion. Several times, he turned the White House into an exhibition hall for the public, such as when he displayed plants, animals, and other specimens brought back by Lewis and Clark from their expedition through the Louisiana Purchase territory. Jefferson, practicing what he preached in terms of a more egalitarian nation, hoped that public access to the mansion would strip away any pretention that the president was above the rest of the populace. Famed novelist James Fenimore Cooper noted:

> I have known a cartman to leave his horse in the street and go to a reception room to shake hands with the President. He offended the good taste of all present, because it was not thought decent that a laborer should come in dirty dress on such an occasion; but while he made a trifling mistake in this particular he proved how well he understood the difference between government and society. He knew that a levee was a sort of homage paid to political equality in the first magistrate, but he would not have presumed to enter the house of the same person as a private individual without being invited.

Through the first quarter of the nineteenth century, Jefferson's successors and their wives would greet visitors to the East Room each day at lunchtime, and the presidential inaugurals of Andrew Jackson in 1828 and William Henry Harrison, in 1840, featured raucous, drunken crowds streaming in and out of the White House. Allowing such unfettered access would change drastically, yet the original State Rooms of the mansion have remained open to public view since Jefferson's time, except during the Spanish American War, the two World Wars, and now the post-September

11 era. Until President George W. Bush limited access, more than 1.5 million visitors toured the White House each year.

The protection of the president and the First Family did not much concern Congress or the public until nearly 1900. Still, even Jefferson would look out the windows and give at least passing thought to security from the citizens milling about the grounds, liable to walk through the door at any juncture. He personally drew up plans in 1803 or 1804 to emplace a fence with gates or sentry boxes, for guards, but no one knows if they were ever built. On Jefferson's order, a high stone wall was built to replace the rail-fence that had surrounded the White House grounds, and a series of other walls and iron fences were constructed along and around the White House grounds to force visitors to use adjoining streets when walking the entire length of the grounds. Only with the onset of World War II would public access to the White House grounds during the day be finally halted.

In 1818–1819, President James Monroe, displeased that part of the stone wall blocked his view to the north, ordered that a curving iron fence replace the wall, and workmen erected another iron fence along the east and west boundaries of the White House grounds. Monroe also instructed workers to set up a series of heavily locked gates. The iron fence remained the White House's only public barrier until January 1835, when Richard Lawrence took two shots at President Andrew Jackson, both of his pistols misfiring. Because of the close call, a "watch box" was installed at the gate to the presidential garden, on the south side of the White House, and manned by sentries—the first unofficial presidential security detail.

Even that one sentry box heralded a slow shift in the country's notion of presidential protection. Despite the armed guard, many nineteenth-century Americans and much of Congress recoiled at the idea of staffing the White House grounds with presidential bodyguards; critics called the idea "imperial" and unworthy of a democracy. A popular children's primer of the first half of the century delineated why presidents, unlike kings, should need no protection:

> *How are emperors and kings protected?*
> By great troops of guards; so that it is difficult to approach them.
> *How is the president guarded?*
> He needs no guards at all; he may be visited by any person like a private citizen.

Eventually, guards were retained (later replaced by the Uniformed Division of the Secret Service and its forerunners) to regulate the flow of visitors to the grounds. The sentries opened the iron gates of the grounds at 8:00 A.M. and shut them at sunset. People were allowed to stroll along the paths and gardens. Only the east garden, virtually surrounded by trees and featuring a sentry box, offered a modicum of privacy if a president wanted to step outside during the day without worrying about visitors gawking at him. Visitors were banned from the east garden, though they would stare up at the second-floor windows of the White House for a glimpse of the president or his family, but no one ever did more than look.

The War of 1812 compelled President James Madison to attempt to defend the White House under extenuating—wartime—circumstances that few Americans questioned. With some four thousand British regulars storming toward Washington in August 1814, Madison ordered troops deployed along the White House grounds. A company of one hundred volunteer soldiers bivouacked on the North Lawn and emplaced a cannon at the North Gate. The soldiers, however, as well as the president, fled the grounds as the rampaging British regiments approached Washington. Shortly afterward, red-coated troops set the mansion ablaze, and James Hoban's creation was soon a charred ruin.

The second Executive Mansion, which President Monroe threw open in a public reception on January 1, 1818, sported a facade painted such a brilliant white that the name "White House" took permanent hold. Monroe continued the practice of lunchtime meetings with citizens at the mansion, but was not as comfortable with the notion of the "People's House" as had been his fellow Virginian Jefferson. From the start of his tenure, Monroe, worried that a stranger might stroll unannounced into the White House and assassinate him, employed guards dressed in civilian clothes; the detail was recruited for Monroe by the marshal of the District of Columbia. Whenever the Monroes held a public event inside the mansion, the number of guards was increased, and a doorkeeper—with pistols close at hand—was stationed round the clock in the main entry hall of the White House and granted the authority to admit or refuse entry to virtually anyone who appeared at the door. As further proof of Monroe's concerns for his security, he ordered that an iron fence enclose the White House and that sharpshooters man perches in the trees near the mansion.

The doorkeeper was to remain permanent, but Monroe's guards did not endure. Following Madison into the White House, John Quincy Adams refused to hire guards, as would the next president, Andrew Jackson—even after he repulsed would-be assassin Richard Lawrence in 1835. During Martin Van Buren's administration, however, Congress agreed to dole out the salaries of both a day guard, who often occupied the watch box, and a night sentry. At public receptions at the White house, the blueblood Van Buren hired policemen to guard all the gates and steer away anyone looking like they hailed from the lower classes.

In the early 1840s, John Tyler's turbulent presidency pushed further debate on the issue of presidential protection. When President William Henry Harrison died shortly after taking office in 1841 and Vice President Tyler assumed the office, many Americans did not accept the congressional resolution naming him as the successor. In 1842, an enraged and intoxicated Whig mob, protesting President Tyler's veto of a bill to create the Second Bank of the United States, massed outside the White House's locked gates, throwing stones at the mansion, firing guns in the air, and burning Tyler in effigy; fortunately, the crowd did not storm the mansion. Only one sentry and the doorkeeper would have stood in the throng's way. Not long afterward, as Tyler strolled along the south grounds, a drunken house painter tossed rocks at him.

Fearing for his safety, Tyler acted to establish a permanent company of guards for the Executive Mansion. In 1842, he set Congress a bill requesting the establishment of a "police force for the protection of public and private property in the city of Washington"—namely, the White House and grounds. Kentucky Senator John Crittenden spoke against the proposed measure because it would give the president the power to appoint these officers. During the heated Senate debate over the issue, the official legislative record notes:

> . . . it seemed to [Crittenden] that, by subjecting this matter to the control of the President of the United States, it might be metamorphosed into a political guard for the Executive. . . . [Crittenden] thought that it would not be entirely safe to organize such a corps. It was a little sort of standing guard, which might eventually become a formidable army.

The seeds sown by this bill would soon germinate, and their full development might overshadow the liberties of the people (Congressional Globe, 27th Cong., 2nd sess., 854, 1842).

This fear that a presidential "Praetorian Guard" might allow a strong-willed president to impose his will in an imperial way was and would remain a constant concern among lawmakers and could explain the tight-fisted way in which Congress has so often approached presidential protection as a potential path to unbalanced executive power. As a result, the Senate compromised in 1842 by passing Tyler's security bill but handing the power to choose officers to the mayor of Washington instead of the president. Tyler signed it the amended measure, which created the "auxiliary guard."

Comprised of a captain and fifteen men, the band's official duty was "the protection of public and private property against incendiaries, and . . . the enforcement of the police regulations of the city of Washington." Rules and regulations drawn up by the mayor of Washington, D.C., the corporation counsel of Washington, D.C., and the U.S. attorney for the District of Columbia—"with the approbation of the President of the United States"—governed the officers' tasks. The captain and three guards were assigned to Tyler's White House.

The official presidential detail were called "Doormen" rather than "guards" or "sentries" out of congressional concern that citizens might view them as a "royal bodyguard." Soon the Doormen took on a range of duties that included delivering confidential messages from the president's desk, meeting officials and guests at the stage depot or train station, scrutinizing all callers in the entrance hall, and often escorting them to the president or the first lady. From time to time, the doormen would also escort potential troublemakers out the door—and do it roughly. Despite complaints from some unwelcome guests who found themselves heaved onto the walk or into rosebushes outside the White House, neither Congress not a president criticized the Doormen.

From 1853 to 1857, President Franklin Pierce became the first chief executive to hire a full-time bodyguard, a man who accompanied Pierce wherever he went. Because the doorkeeper and the auxiliaries stood duty only in the White House and on the grounds, Pierce's well-armed bodyguard was at the president's side whenever Pierce set foot outside the mansion. Inside, the guard always stood or sat within easy calling distance of the president. Pierce's measure created the two-tier protective system that remains a Secret Service staple today: guards stationed at the outer perimeters of the White house and grounds and a bodyguard(s) manning the inner perimeter, within the walls of the mansion itself.

Defending the White House took on a new urgency by 1860, as the North and South lurched ever closer to the Civil War. From the moment that the Republican Party nominated Abraham Lincoln as its candidate in the 1860 election, death threats poured in on him. A ring of private bodyguards flanked him throughout the campaign, one of them the renowned detective Alan Pinkerton. After Lincoln gained the presidency, his party increased his security detail.

In a precursor of relations to come between various presidents and their future Secret Service teams, Lincoln loathed being surrounded by guards and worried that their presence made him look unmanly. Still, he understood their role.

Dozens of Washington police officers were posted to the White House soon after Lincoln took office, and because the president did not want the mansion to look like an armed camp, he ordered that all his protectors wear civilian garb and conceal their revolvers. Outside the White House, however, the guards wore their uniforms and carried rifles and carbines in plain view.

Shortly after Confederate batteries opened up on Fort Sumter, South Carolina, in April 1861, the White House was turned into a military position despite Lincoln's disapproval. Union troops actually camped inside the mansion itself until the city's defenses had been buttressed. Soldiers would patrol and guard the house and grounds throughout the Civil War.

Troops guarded Lincoln on his travels, whether to the front or around the capital, and neither Mary Lincoln nor the presidential couple's sons were allowed to leave the White House without a military escort. The Lincolns became the first presidential family to receive such personal protection by the government. No matter where the president went, an armed Metropolitan policeman in plainclothes acted as a bodyguard. On April 14, 1865, as John Wilkes Booth sneaked into Ford's Theatre and put a bullet in the back of the president's head, the bodyguard was tossing down a drink at a nearby saloon.

Lincoln's assassination notwithstanding, Congress decided that with the war over, presidential security could be cut. Lawmakers whittled the White House protective detail to three men who only stood duty inside the mansion, had received bare-bones training, and were derisively labeled "doormen." Once again, presidents leaving the White House risked face-to-face encounters with madmen, disgruntled voters, and potential assassins. After Charles Guiteau shot President Garfield inside the Baltimore and Potomac Railway Station in Washington in 1881, Congress refused to part with the funds for enhanced presidential protection. The old concerns about imperial presidents were still simmering. Garfield's immediate successors would set out from the White House with virtually no protection whatsoever. Even if presidents wanted to hire private detectives as bodyguards, Congress drafted legislation banning any such appropriations.

Not until the rising number of threats directed at President Grover Cleveland in the mid-1890s did the Secret Service begin to provide unofficial presidential protection and did Congress begin to see the need—a limited need in the legislators' view.

In 1902, the West Wing expansion of the White House meant that the early Secret Service protective details had more space to cover. Theodore Roosevelt had moved into the mansion with the largest First Family—five children—to date and was dismayed to find the living quarters too cramped for his brood. To create more space, architects converted the West Wing, then known as the Temporary Executive Office, into the Executive Office of the president; the builders did not intend the structure to become permanent, planning to use it chiefly for the president's personal staff. In 1909, however, the West Wing became the official presidential office.

The East Wing is the most recently built administrative structure within the White House Complex, the addition built as part of the World War II mobilization effort, when President Franklin Roosevelt knew that his staff would swell in wartime. After consulting with architects and the War Department, Roosevelt ordered that an East Wing be added to the White House. Personnel began moving in by 1942, but the attachment was not finished until 1945; Roosevelt and his military staff ran their war operations center in the new wing. After the war, builders fashioned an East Wing reception area, which would be the jump-off point for public tours of the White House and for social events.

At the insistence of the Secret Service, free public access to the White House grounds during daylight hours was ended during World War II—permanently. White House security's fairly relaxed mission was changing for good; from 1942 to the present-day, visitors must report to gates around the perimeter of the White House Complex and are not allowed to stroll up to the front door of the mansion without supervision. No one without an official appointment is allowed onto the grounds until he or she passes Secret Service inspection. One of Roosevelt's staff summed up the lasting security changes ushered in by the war: "No more Congressional constituents, no more government clerks hurrying through the grounds . . . no more Sunday tourists feeding the squirrels, taking snapshots and hanging around the portico hoping someone interesting would come out."

In December 1941, a Secret Service memo recommended that precautions be undertaken "to insure a maximum of safety to the occupants of the White House":

- All skylights covered with a six-inch slab of concrete
- Bulletproof glass
- Antiaircraft crews on the roof
- Dark paint on the roof

The agency issued the dire warning that a direct hit by a Japanese kamikaze "would cause the White House to collapse" and urged that a state-of-the-art bomb shelter be built for Roosevelt. The "FDR bomb shelter" was described in a White House report as the "world's most secure shelter," better than Hitler's bunker (though it is not clear how they knew this). Located beneath the East Wing and boasting a four-foot concrete shell that was reinforced by steel, the bunker was one hundred by fifty feet and contained food, water, and communications equipment, as well as heat and power sources. Oddly, Franklin Roosevelt did not tell Vice President Truman about its existence; Truman found out only when he ascended to the presidency after Roosevelt's death in 1945.

When the White House was almost completely rebuilt during Truman's presidency, with Truman living at Blair House, the Executive Mansion's deepest basement was converted in 1951 into a new bomb shelter for the

"Atomic Age." Truman biographer David McCullough describes the new bunker:

> The entrance, at the end of a subterranean passage at the north-east end of the house, was a four-inch steel door with a narrow window at eye level. . . .
>
> Beyond was a large room with some seventy army cots neatly stacked against one wall, gas masks, chemical toilets, and acetylene torches (in case the occupants had to cut their way out of the steel door). In adjacent rooms were an emergency generator, a larder of Army rations, and a communications center. . . . Accommodations for the President and his family consisted of an 8-by- 10-foot room, four bunk beds, a toilet, and a supply of books.

The Secret Service knew that Truman had determined to stay at the White House if atomic war broke out, citing "morale reasons." Punctuating that resolve, Truman, over his agents' advice, once refused to head to the bunker, even though his staff did, when a radar operator mistakenly reported the sudden presence of twenty-five unidentified aircraft. The planes turned out to be one lone aircraft, off-course.

September 11, 2001, was to drastically change the Secret Service's approach to White House protection, but violent events and threats of violence have fueled a steady upgrade at 1600 Pennsylvania Avenue from the days of Truman to the inauguration of George W. Bush. Even before September 11, visitors to the White House Complex encountered several unmistakable emblems of beefed-up security over the years. In the 1980s, following the terrorist assaults on the Marine barracks and the American Embassy in Beirut, Lebanon, concrete Jersey barriers were installed at the complex's perimeter and have since been replaced by reinforced bollards. The mansion's perimeter fences and gates have been reinforced, with many more guardhouses built at various points on the grounds; both East and West Executive Avenues have been closed to vehicular and, at times, pedestrian traffic. Always, Secret Service Uniformed Division officers are evident, as are park officers and other security personnel. With the ever-increasing dangers of the modern world, the Secret Service's mission to provide the president and his family with the highest level of protection that is consistent with democratic principles grows harder.

After World War II, the agency's chief concern at the White House was to stop random individuals and would-be assassins from getting on the grounds or in the mansion. The attempt by Puerto Rican nationalists to assassinate Truman at

Blair House in 1950 did not bring immediate changes to White House security. The agency reasoned that the problem had been Blair House, not the Executive Mansion. An agency report in the aftermath of the assassination attempt asserted:

> It was reasoned that having President Truman reside in the Blair House while renovations were being completed at the White House had in fact actually amplified the security risk to the President. The Blair House offered, by its architectural design and placement, a limited-security environment. It was separated from the sidewalk by five feet of front lawn, a shoulder-high wrought-iron fence, and numerous sentry posts. The actual physical threat posed to the president, accordingly was deemed to have receded when he and his family moved back in to the comparatively more secure White House.

The "more secure White House" has been the target of more and more would-be assassins and disturbed men and women over the last three decades. Intruders have tried to strike at the mansion, prompting the Secret Service to institute new precautions after each incident.

In February 1974, Private Robert Preston, a U.S. Army helicopter mechanic, sneaked into a military helicopter at Fort Meade, Maryland, switched on the props, and took off toward Washington, D.C., as soldiers on the ground gaped and warnings began to crackle over the airwaves. Preston headed straight for the airspace around 1600 Pennsylvania Avenue.

As he reached the White House and hovered above the mansion, fighter jets zeroed in with missiles at the ready. Preston drifted above the South Lawn. Suddenly he nudged the chopper and touched down about 150 feet from the West Wing; just as suddenly he yanked back the throttle, and the helicopter climbed. The Nixons had never been in danger, as they were not home.

Preston drifted from White House airspace for several minutes before he flew back above the mansion and veered low above the grounds. On the ground Secret Service agents opened up with submachine guns and shot-guns and forced the soldier to land. He was quickly taken into custody.

On Christmas Day of 1974, Marshall Fields, a man dressed in a tur-ban and robes and shouting that he was the Messiah, roared up in his car to the Northwest Gate of the White House complex. He crashed through the gate as Uniformed Agents scrambled out of the way. Fields lurched toward the door of the North Portico and yelled that he had strapped explosives to himself; agents could see that he did have what looked like a bomb taped to his midsection.

Agents backed away, surrounding the car, and a tense, four-hour negoti-ation with Fields began. Finally, he surrendered, with agents discovering that his "bomb" was made of standard flares. Again, none of the Nixons had been home.

Though Secret Service spokesman George Cosper told the press that the security measures for the White House and grounds were adequate, the agency launched a behind-the-scenes security review in the wake of the two incursions, and in 1976 tore down the White House's nineteenth-century wrought-iron gates and replaced them with reinforced steel.

The pay-off from the new gates came quickly. Shortly after they were installed, a man named Stephen B. Williams aimed his pickup truck at the new Northwest Gate and plowed into it. This time, the gate held, and agents swarmed and arrested him.

Because the Service judged that the three incidents were the work of the "cranks," the need of hunkering down the White House from future assaults was not pressing. Terrorism was not considered a real possibility in the 1970s, so any suggestions that sealing off Pennsylvania Avenue would have been dismissed as needless; only once had the agency considered the idea, during the Kennedy administration, and not out of security concerns. In the early 1960s, architects working on a project to preserve nearby Lafayette Square suggested that the street in front of the White House be converted into a pedestrian plaza, with fountains and flower beds. The idea was shelved after the assassination of President Kennedy.

In the early 1980s, during the Reagan administration, presidential secu-rity took on a whole new dimension with a rash of Islamic suicide car and truck bombings in the Middle East. When a small bomb went off outside the U.S. Senate in 1983 and the CIA received reports that pro-Iranian ter-rorists planned to hit major U.S. landmarks and legislative buildings, the

Secret Service went to work on an antiterrorism plan featuring permanent changes to the White House grounds. The agency, reacting to a threat that pro-Iranian Shiite Muslims were possibly planning an attack on the White House on Thanksgiving Day, 1983, parked sand-filled trucks in front of the mansion's gates, as well as those of the State Department. Along the White House's southwest gate, three trucks were deployed, another just inside the northwest gate, and a pair just inside the gates off of 17th Street, which led to the Old Executive Building. A seventh truck was parked on the east side of the building next to the Treasury.

The Secret Service replaced the sand-laden trucks at the White House entrances two weeks later with Jersey Barriers, and also set up the barriers at the intersection of State Place and West Executive Avenue, an entrance for foreign visitors, guests, and other dignitaries. Just across the street in a small park facing the south side of the building, agents emplaced yet another set of barriers.

To further guard against car or truck bombs, the agency installed massive iron bars timed to rise out of the ground when the White House gates were shut. The Secret Service emplaced sturdy masonry slabs in 1984 along the curb on the section of Pennsylvania Avenue fronting the mansion.

It was the grisly truck bombings of the U.S. Marine barracks in Beirut in 1983 that compelled the Secret Service to ponder closing down all of Pennsylvania Avenue, and the Reagan administration asked famed architect Carl Warnecke to draw up plans for a securer Pennsylvania Avenue. Warnecke, who, in less troubled times had earlier proposed the pedestrian plaza near the White House, pitched the idea of controlling traffic through a tunnel that could be built under Pennsylvania Avenue. But the notion foundered.

The agency has tightened security as the threats of both international and domestic terrorism have swelled. From 1984 on, bomb-sniffing dogs checked each car entering the White House Complex for explosives, and media and visitor access to the complex have been restricted to two gates, where uniformed officers check with magnetometers for concealed weapons. Prior to 1984, people entering the White House had only to show official credentials or visitors' permits. Now, state-of-the-art electronic sensors and rooftop surveillance at the White House are constantly updated.

Even before the Oklahoma City bombing in April 1995, the Secret Service had begun instituting, in the early 1990s, the most significant security changes in the annals of the White House. A series of incidents in the fall and winter of 1994 sparked the agency's increased determination to tighten protection along and above Pennsylvania Avenue.

On September 12, 1994, near 2:00 A.M., the drone of a Cessna 150L echoed low above the White House. Thirty-eight-year-old Frank Eugene Corder, a man plagued by alcohol and drug abuse, was at the controls. He had breached air space security above the mansion.

The aircraft drifted for a few moments and then plunged at the White House. Seconds later the Cessna crunched into the South Lawn just short of the mansion's wall and came to rest against the house itself, killing Corder, but harming no one else. The Clintons were not at the mansion.

Corder, who had stolen the small plane from a Maryland airport, was judged to have been suicidal, but no one would ever know if he had taken off with the intent of killing President Clinton.

Just a month later, on October 29, 1994, Francisco Martin Duran, twenty-six years old, positioned himself on a warm October afternoon in front of the White House grounds, pulled a Chinese-made semiautomatic SKS assault rifle concealed beneath his trench coat, slid the barrel between the bars of the fence, and opened fire at the mansion's northern façade. As tourists fled in all directions or hit the ground and Secret Service Uniformed Division officers took cover with weapons drawn, the gunman raced along the fence and kept firing at the White House, peppering it with twenty-nine rounds. He paused to reload, and just as uniformed officers trained their weapons on him, three civilians jumped Duran, slammed him to the ground, and wrestled away his weapon. Three officers rushed up and handcuffed him. Miraculously, none of Duran's shots had struck anyone.

President Clinton had been watching television in a room on the south side of the White House when the shots erupted, and was never in any danger while eleven bullets—including one that pierced a window in the West Wing's press briefing-room—hit the northern face. At trial, Duran pleaded insanity, but was found guilty and sentenced to forty years in prison.

In December 1994, four attacks against the White House fueled a review of all Secret Service protective measures for the complex. The first of these incidents occurred on December 21, 1994, when Secret Service Uniformed Division officers opened the southwest gate for an authorized vehicle to pass, but, as the gate swung open, a man burst past the officers and dashed up West Executive Avenue toward the mansion. The officers quickly caught up with him and soon identified him as a disturbed individual with an obsession about the White House itself, not the president.

The second incident happened later that same day, when twenty-six-year-old Joseph Maggio, of Maryland, parked his car on E Street between the South Lawn of the White House grounds and the Ellipse and climbed out of the vehicle, leaving the motor running. The man raced across the Ellipse toward the Washington Monument and was stopped by Uniformed Division and Park Police officers who told him that he could not leave his car parked there. Then, the man replied that his car was wired with a bomb. The officers instantaneously called for an Explosive Ordnance Disposal (EOD) technician to examine the vehicle. The car proved clean.

Early on the morning of December 23, a staccato burst of gunfire rang out from the southern flank of the White House grounds. Four shots from a 9-mm pistol were fired at the mansion; two shots fell short of the house, but one landed on the State Floor balcony and the fourth penetrated a window of the State Floor Dining Room. As uniformed officers and agents fanned out to search for the gunman, a member of the Secret Service Uniformed Division scanning the South Executive Avenue sidewalk just south of the White House spied a fidgety man. A Park Police officer alerted by the Secret Service rushed up to the man, conducted a "protective search," and seized the 9-mm handgun.

Although the media reported the episodes as "raising further questions about White House Security," the Secret Service did not view them as having been a serious threat to President Clinton and as incidents that never did "pose a serious threat to the security of the President and [were] in fact . . . representative of events commonly faced by the Secret Service and the United States Park Police (Park Police)." Still, a full congressional review of protective procedures and measures was already in progress.

A fourth incident garnered nationwide coverage because it ended with a man shot dead in front of the White House on December 20, 1994. Marcelino Corniel approached a Park Police officer on the north side of Pennsylvania Avenue just across from the Executive Mansion and brandished a knife at him. Then Corniel dashed across the street to the sidewalk in front of the White House and was confronted by Secret Service Uniformed Division officers and additional Park Police who ordered him to drop the knife.

When Marcelino refused and reportedly lunged at the officers, a Park policeman shot and killed him. The incident demonstrated, however, the possible problems inherent in having multiple law enforcement agencies share jurisdiction over the streets and park contiguous to the White House.

All these incidents and the attempt to crash a plane into the White House led Secretary of the Treasury Lloyd Bentsen to begin a "thorough and comprehensive" review of all Secret Service measures for the president, the First Family, and the White House Complex. When the agency complained that immediately after Corder's "suicide crash" on the South Lawn, the media had announced that Clinton was at Blair House, the Secret Service pointed the finger at Clinton's staff. The agency contended that the incident had not been fully investigated, and if it had been a multifaceted terrorist plot, the president's whereabouts and schedule should never have been provided to the media. The White House up to that point had stopped issuing detailed daily schedules after Hinckley shot Reagan, and it was revealed that a copy of the *Washington Post* with Reagan's schedule that day was found in Hinckley's hotel room.

In May 1995, Leland Willima Modjeski scaled the White House fence with an unloaded gun. He was wounded and captured by uniformed officers. But it was another development that same month that led to the most momentous changes for the Secret Service.

The massive truck bomb that shattered the Alfred P. Murragh Federal Office Building, in Oklahoma City, in April 1995, killed 168 people and injured hundreds; among the dead were six Secret Service agents from the field office at the skyscraper. The blast also forced the agency to argue for a controversial counterterrorism measure. Stunned by the loss of the agents and by the ease with which bomber Timothy McVeigh had unleashed the largest domestic-terrorism attack in American history, the Secret Service urged President Clinton to order that part of Pennsylvania Avenue be closed. Unless he agreed, the agency asserted, no one could safeguard the White House from a similar strike. The Age of Terrorism had arrived at the doorstep of the agency and the "People's House."

The need to curtail or even cut off public access and create a "fortress White House" was debated by Congress, the president, and the Service; President Clinton, at the urging of the Secret Service, ordered that Pennsylvania Avenue between 15th and 17th Streets (immediately in front of the White House) be closed to vehicular traffic. In a report by the Rand Corporation, the jarring need for a "closed" White House in a democracy emerged: "Unlike the many subtle or even invisible security enhancements, this measure was fraught with conflict and symbolism."

The conflict and symbolism would swell to unprecedented levels on September 11, 2001.

PART TWO

# ON THE JOB

## CHAPTER 7

# A FEW GOOD MEN AND A VERY
# FEW GOOD WOMEN

*"Worthy of Trust and Confidence"*

—*Secret Service motto*

Bly the standards of the leviathan federal bureaucracy, the U.S. Secret Service is a very small organization: 5,000 field operatives, including 1,200 officers in the Uniformed Division, and approximately 2,700 special agents. The Pentagon has as many public relations officers as the Secret Service has special agents; the Interior Department has twice as many employees as the Secret Service.

Budget-wise, the Secret Service receives a relatively small chunk of the Treasury Department budget. The amount was $857 million in 2002, but the figure will rise sharply as a result of September 11, 2001. Some subdivisions of the Departments of Energy and Agriculture and of the Environmental Protection Agency have budgets that measure in the billions of dollars, in stark contrast to the Secret Service.

Are the agency's resources adequate for effective protection? Like the old Peace Corps recruitment advertisement, the answer depends on whether the viewer thinks the glass is half full or half empty. The Service thinks it is half empty.

The bad news for the Service is that its protective mission has expanded very rapidly and with even greater acceleration in the wake of September 11; in the Service's view, the increased scope of its duties has outstripped the growth of its resources, reflected in the fact that during the Kennedy administration, the agency protected only the president and his immediate family, the vice president, and former presidents. Since then, with its

151

mission broadened to include foreign diplomats stationed in embassies in the United States, presidential and vice presidential candidates, spouses and children of former presidents, and visiting foreign dignitaries, resources have become strained. In the wake of September 11, 2001, the list ballooned to include the Secretary of State, National Security Advisor, and others (the exact list is classified).

Adding to the problem, much of this increased workload is unpredictable, and targeted budgeting becomes difficult, if not impossible. The cost of protecting the president and family can be estimated with ballpark accuracy, but there is no way that the Service can predict how many presidential candidates will crop up in an election year. Protecting a single candidate can easily cost over $500,000 a month, requiring thirty or more agents. This is only the tip of the budgetary iceberg: protective research and field office work also increase with each additional protectee, as the number of incidents, cases, or threats confronting agents has to be investigated.

A former Secret Service public affairs director, Robert Snow, has said, "It's easier to manage criminals than protectees"—meaning that the Service can predict its money and personnel needs for dealing with forgers and counterfeiters more easily than it can for its protective mission. Snow said that the Service is in constant contact with the staffs of ex-presidents who inform the agency about travel plans. The problem, according to Snow, is that ex-presidents do not always plan their agendas very far ahead of time. Nor can the Service predict the cost of protecting visiting foreign dignitaries. For many years the number of dignitaries was fairly stable at eighty to ninety per year. Recently the tally has equaled two hundred or more, further straining Service resources.

To meet these unpredictable demands, the Service is forced to live hand-to-mouth, constantly asking the Congress for supplemental funds and frequently borrowing personnel from other Treasury Department agencies (Custom Bureau, Internal Revenue Service, and the Bureau of Alcohol, Tobacco and Firearms). The Service also borrows personnel from the National Parks Service and the Department of the Interior to help with work in Washington, D.C., especially with controlling the White House tour line, which was shut down in response to the terrorist attacks of September 11 but may reopen in the future and become a significant drain on agency personnel. Sometimes, during a presidential campaign year, there are more non–Secret Service Treasury Department personnel doing protective work than there are Secret Service agents.

The Secret Service's budget is reviewed by the Treasury Department and by the Office of Management and Budget (OMB) before it goes to Congress. Usually, the Treasury review results in a cutting of the Service's requests, and the agency is hamstrung by a time-honored Treasury gag rule (typical of many federal agencies) that prevents the Secret Service from appealing directly to Congress for a larger budget.

The need to borrow personnel from other Treasury agencies has disturbing results for the quality of protection, for as professional and diligent as these "second stringers" may be, the fact remains that they are not Secret Service agents. The borrowed agents' training and work experience are not the same; their protective assignments are given sporadically. Though these Other Treasury Personnel (OTP) are "retained" for protective work or are given refresher courses and though many OTPs may have worked with Secret Service agents many times in the past, they are still not full-time security personnel. Yet, these are the people helping the Secret Service to protect presidential candidates in frenetic political campaigning.

Despite the stress that congressional underfunding and the dual mission piles upon the Service, agents embrace both their protection and anticounterfeiting duties. Former Agent Timothy J. McCarthy, the man who took a Hinckley bullet meant for President Reagan, said, "The theory of the Secret Service is that a good criminal investigator who has good sense [and] judgment will carry over to the protective mission: arrests, stressful situations, effective reactions. If they excel in that, they will excel in the protective mission as well."

Ex-Agent Bill Carter also endorsed the dual mission: "I liked the divided responsibility. . . . There was more of a mental challenge in following the trail of counterfeiters. I enjoyed it more than presidential protection."

As with personnel, the Service often borrows from, or is trained, by other agencies when specific types of technical expertise are required. Traditionally—though secretively—the Service has received training and equipment from the CIA. In 1976, a House Intelligence Committee hearing revealed that the CIA had manufactured the color-coded lapel pins worn by agents as an unobtrusive identity badge. The Service has also requested such things as "technical countermeasures equipment" (antibugging devices) and has received "briefing/training" of a classified nature from the CIA.

One of the few declassified CIA documents dealing with aid to the Service indicates that in 1973 alone, the Service was provided with such equipment as "6 portable X-ray units; 1 frequency counter; Nohawk printer; motor drive; receiver; transmitter; 1 [item deleted]."

The CIA's vast expertise in sophisticated technologies of surveillance, countersurveillance, bomb detection, and espionage remains a crucial resource that the Service cannot generate on its own. Still, the Secret Service holds the responsibility for making sure that every room entered by the president is free of eavesdropping devices and explosives. Although the precise nature and extent of Secret Service dependence on the CIA remains top secret, the relationship covertly stands as a critical one, given the Service's limitations of personnel and resources.

That the Secret Service can use all the free technical assistance it can get became embarrassingly clear in 1978, when Congress provided a special appropriation of $4 million for the purpose of developing "audio counter-measure equipment." In the absence of such equipment, at the time the average ham radio operator could easily monitor the often top-secret trans-missions of the U.S. premier protective organization.

Today, the U.S Secret Service is an organization that Lafayette Baker and William P. Wood could never have imagined. About the only aspects they would have recognized are that the agency is still under the aegis of the Treasury Department and still chasing counterfeiters. The Treasury Department also houses the Internal Revenue Service (IRS), Customs, and the Bureau of Alcohol, Tobacco and Firearms.

The secretary of the treasury oversees the Secret Service and its sister agencies, but the current director of the Secret Service, Brian L. Stafford, has extensive autonomy and actually runs the organization. Though an assistant secretary of the treasury is assigned administrative oversight of Secret Service, this position is more a liaison from the Cabinet Department to Director Stafford. The man who serves in the titular footsteps of William P. Wood, Stafford is the twentieth director of the agency, appointed to the post on March 4, 1999. Previously, he served as the Service's assistant director of the Office of Protective Operations and as the special agent in charge of the Presidential Protective Division. In the U.S. Army, he served from 1969 to 1971, completing a tour of duty in Vietnam.

Stafford's career with the Secret Service began in 1971, when he was a special agent assigned to the Cleveland Field Office. Rising through the field and managerial ranks, he has served in the West Palm Beach Resident Office and the Presidential Protective Division and has held key positions in the Special Investigations and Security Division, the Technical Security Division, the Miami Field Office, and the Office of Protective Service. In the course of his career, Director Stafford has earned an array of achievement and performance awards.

Stafford oversees an organization that, in the 1870s, once had barely twenty agents and now numbers some 5,000 operatives. Approximately 2,700 special agents are rotated throughout their careers in the organization's dual missions of protection of leaders and money-related investigations. The remaining employees beyond the special agents and officers are technical, professional, and administrative support personnel.

Stafford, as with all modern directors of the Secret Service, is not a political appointee from outside the organization, nor is he selected from the larger Treasury Department. Instead, the director is chosen by the secretary of the treasury from the ranks of career agents subject to the approval of the Civil Service Commission. Under the director are five assistant directors, each handling a distinct functional area and running a separate office: investigation, protective operations, inspection, administration, and protective research. The modern Secret Service has a complex internal structure for such a relatively small federal agency, primarily a result of the score and diversity of its duties.

Today's Secret Service has 121 field offices, 115 in the United States and the other six in Puerto Rico, Canada (2), Paris, Nicosia, and Rome. The most populous states have several offices: nine in California and eight each in New York and Texas. These offices perform the bulk of their duties in counterfeiting and forgery cases and on protective missions when the need arises. The Washington, D.C., field office, by virtue of its location at the center of political power and leadership, handles more protective work than any other office. More typical of big-city field offices is Boston, where as many as forty to sixty agents may be assigned at any juncture; they usually pursue more than five thousand forgery and counterfeiting cases a year, an activity that consumes most of their time. Forgery and fraud investigations and arrests are more frequent than those involving actual counterfeiting. Though many people figure that the Service's list of "Most Wanted Fugitives" would likely be dominated by the mug shots of people who pose a threat to the president, the reality is that the list is heavy with alleged fraud perpetrators, whether involving credit cards, "access device fraud," or banks. The Service considers any attempt to tamper with the nation's money—whether someone mints or prints phony money, treasury bills, ATM cards, or any other such scheme—as falling within the purview of the agency's anticounterfeiting duties.

In every presidential administration, some of the agency's field offices besides Washington, D.C., will become heavily involved in prot1ective work because of their location. The Texas field offices play an important role today as President George W. Bush travels back and forth between Washington, D.C., and his ranch in Crawford, Texas.

At the Secret Service's Washington headquarters, the Office of Investigation's forgery division reviews cases—of treasury checks, government bonds, and food stamps—and assigns them to field offices for investigation.* The Washington office also performs handwriting analysis and helps the field office to present evidence in the courtroom.

Working as a subdivision of the Office of Investigation is the Special Investigation and Security Division, whose experts pore over questionable documents to determine if they are forgeries. They also analyze fingerprints, and conduct forensic analyses relating to presidential protection, as opposed to anticounterfeiting.

The agency's arm whose mission is crime-related research and analysis is the Office of Protective Research's Forensic Service Divisions, which is staffed with clerks, laboratory personnel, and polygraph experts who administer and interpret lie detector tests.

Another task performed by the Office of Investigations is to conduct background checks on government employees. Perhaps surprisingly, this office does not investigate assassination attempts or successful assassinations of political leaders or assaults on political leaders. The Secret Service investigates threats, but it is the FBI that has investigative responsibility

---

* Melanson's repeated attempts to obtain accurate information regarding the internal setup of the secret Service's bureaucracy were given only selective responses by the Service's Office of Public Affairs. The portrait provided here comes from interviews, media descriptions, and government documents and reports. Therefore, it may contain some outdated information, especially in the wake of government-wide and agency reorganizations in the aftermath of September 11. It should be noted that the agency would not fully respond to the authors' fact-checking queries.

*after* the incident has occurred. The FBI also determines whether an assassination incident was a conspiracy or an assailant acting alone.

By means of a "delineation agreement," a common practice among federal agencies, the Secret Service and the FBI have arranged that the Service shoulders responsibility over the scene of an assassination or assault only until a "logical and coordinated transition of control of the investigation can be delegated to the FBI." In essence, the Service is supposed to hold suspects at the scene and preserve evidence until the Bureau can take over. The agreement further specifies that the Service must give the Bureau immediate access to all evidence and investigative materials; however, all the activities covered by the agreement are secondary for the Secret Service's primary responsibility, which has priority over the pursuit of suspects or the preservation of evidence, that is, the safety of the president or other people under Service protection.

The Office of Investigations also contained the Treasury Security Force, a small unit of more than one hundred officers. This unit, which became part of the Service's Uniformed Division, provides twenty-four-hour protection for the main Treasury Building and the Treasury Annex, both located near the White House, and for the grounds surrounding these mammoth stone buildings.

In connection with crimes or violations of law occurring within these buildings or on their grounds, officers of the Treasury Security Force possess special powers of arrest. The officers' primary task is to control access to the buildings, and except for the public tour of the exhibit hall located in the basement of the Treasury Building, access is limited to employees or persons with valid visitor's badges. At the doors to the buildings and at small guard shacks near the gates that guard the vehicular entrances, Security Force guards are on duty. They also patrol the roof of the Treasury Building, which overlooks the White House, and have the authority to search the belongings of persons entering the buildings.

In addition to the main building and the annex, the Treasury Department occupies other buildings in Washington, for example, Secret Service headquarters. These other locations are not protected by the Treasury Security Force, but by the landlords or the occupants.

The Service's Office of Protective Operations contains the Uniformed Division, a unit of twelve hundred officers who guard the White House and foreign missions within the Washington area. Along with its White House and diplomatic protective mission, the Uniformed Division has provided security for Middle Eastern missions to the United Nations because of increased threats of terrorism, especially after September 11, 2001.

The Office of Protective Operations also contains the security details for current and former presidents and spouses. The Fords, the Carters, the Reagans, the Clintons, and both George Bushes and their wives—all have Secret Service details. The number of such divisions depends on the number of protectees—former presidents, widowed first ladies, and so forth.

Over the past few decades, the Secret Service has evolved into an intricate organization—too intricate, critics have charged—in which the Presidential Protective Division alone features three distinct units: Support and Logistics, Operations, and Training and Special Programs. The operational subunit is broken down even further into three separate entities— one for presidential protection, one for presidential families, and one for transportation.

The Candidate/Nominee Protective Division, a more recent creation, was formed because the Service was faced by the ever-increasing length and complexity of the presidential nominating process which demanded months of full-time attention. Though this division has only a handful of agents and a small administrative staff, it performs the key role of coordinating protection for presidential candidates. As the need arises during an election year, agents are borrowed from field offices to form protective details. Before the creation of this skeletal division, the candidate-protection mission had no permanent staff and was entirely ad hoc.

To protect visiting foreign dignitaries, the Secret Service deploys the Dignitary Protective Division, and despite its impressive title, the unit is a skeleton operation, with its only permanent personnel a detail leader and assistant leader. Unlike other protective details, except the Candidate/Nominee Division, the agents who staff the dignitary division are field office personnel who are assigned on a temporary basis, as dignitaries visit the country and depart.

The Office of Protective Research, which works very closely with the Office of Protective Operations, constitutes the nerve center of the agency's protective mission. It is responsible for collecting, analyzing, storing, and disseminating vital data gathered by the Service itself or provided to it by other local, state, and federal agencies. There are files on over forty thousand U.S. citizens who, for one reason or another, have come to the Service's attention. The office also compiles data on threats against political leaders and on the names and faces, as well as their methods and means. This role has taken on dramatic new resonance since the tragedy of September 11. On the Service's "Watch List" are four hundred persons considered dangerous to protectees, a process augmented by an in-house team of research psychologists that works on the identification of dangerous persons.

To ensure the president's safety at home or on the road, the Office of Protective Research's Technical Security Division conducts manual and electronic surveys, "sweeping" the Oval Office, hotel rooms, and other sites for surveillance devices; testing food for poison; and measuring air quality to check for deadly bacteria. The office's highly trained researchers and engineers furnish technical support and expertise for the sweeps, and in another critical role, the Technical Security Division manufactures and issues the passes and credentials that afford access to the White House and the Executive Office Building.

The Technical Development and Planning Division of the Office of Protective Research conducts long-range analyses in various areas of Secret Service endeavor, functioning as something of an in-house think tank and maintaining extensive contact with private industry to keep abreast of the latest technological developments in interpersonal warfare and security. This division installed the original Capitol Building's security system—a system that has several hundred surveillance cameras, numerous X-ray scanners, and sensors that are distributed throughout the building and grounds, including a new state-of-the-art system of heat and water pipes that runs under the Capitol grounds. Keyed in to a control center within the Capitol, the division's Capitol security system serves today as the prototype for that of the White House. Recently, the system was redesigned by outside experts working with the Service and the Capitol Police.

The Office of Protective Research's Communications Division installs and maintains all the various radio, telephone, and cryptographic equipment used by the Service. With its own communications personnel, the agency is always in direct contact with Washington, D.C., police and with the National Crime Reporting Center.

Because of a recommendation of the Warren Commission, which, in the wake of the John F. Kennedy assassination, contended that the Secret

Service of 1963 did not maintain sufficient contact with state, local, and federal agencies and was therefore not receiving enough of the kind of data it needed to perform its protective mission effectively, the agency created the Office of Protective Research's Liaison Division. For the next eighteen years, the division made surface changes; however, cooperation between the Service and local law-enforcement bodies remained ragged. Subsequently, the liaison function was fused with public affairs, creating the Office of Public Affairs and Government Liaison.

Although the primary purpose of the Liaison Division was to increase the Service's ability to gather intelligence, the Treasury Department's report on the attempted assassination of President Reagan in 1981 criticized the division's alleged passivity:

> Insofar as the Liaison Division is involved in intelligence support, the process is largely ad hoc. Liaison agents operated in an informal manner and, by and large, take their inte ligence support roles to be passive ones, responding to Intelligence Division requests rather than generating more and better intelligence and sources.

For the day-to-day operations that enable the protective and investigative arms of the Secret Service to do their jobs, the agency's Office of Administration has four divisions that perform management-analysis and administrative-housekeeping functions in such areas as personnel, budgeting, and purchasing. A fifth office, the Office of Inspection, conducts internal audits. This unit is similar to that of the internal affairs office of a major police department and conducts investigations of employees when conditions warrant.

In addition to the five major offices that are under the director of the Secret Service, Director Stafford has units that work very closely with his office: public affairs, training, and legal counsel. Public affairs deals with the press, Congress, and the public, disseminating issues-brochures, talking with reporters and researchers, and maintaining a clipping file of articles about the Secret Service appearing in newspapers throughout the country.

The director's training office gives Secret Service agents specialized courses in protective and investigative work. It also instructs the Uniformed Division (and former Treasury Security Forces) in the latest profiling techniques and maintains an in-house reference library where personnel can read the latest reports and studies on protective duties and anticounterfeiting.

The legal counsel provides advice to the director and works for the Secret Service, but reports directly to the Treasury Department's general counsel. The legal counsel's role is to inform the agency about changes in the law and about Supreme Court rulings that relate to the detention and arrest of suspects and the rights of the accused. Secret Service agents make as many as several thousand arrests each year, and the bulk still involve forgery. Over the years, the Service can boast of a trial conviction-rate of 98.8 percent, a lofty statistic aided by agents' familiarity with required constitutional procedures. The legal counsel, in addition to helping with cases headed to court, works with the director in drafting new legislation and amendments to existing laws and submitting the proposed changes to Congress.

In 1982, the protective mission of the Secret Service expanded once again. Congress passed a law making it a crime to threaten candidates or officials, a change from previous laws making it illegal to threaten presidents, presidents-elect, vice presidents, and vice presidents–elect, punishable by a $1,000 fine, up to five years in jail, or both. Before the 1982 law, there were only vague, indirect statutes relating to threats against presidential candidates or other officials. With this 1982 law, the Service could and would prosecute a threat against a candidate or congressman with the same legal tools used for presidential threats. The protective mission now had a more solid legal foundation.

One proposed reorganization within the Treasury Department that would have had a profound impact on the Secret Service was the 1982 legislation that would have abolished the Service's sister agency, the Bureau of Alcohol, Tobacco and Firearms (ATF). ATF's main function is to enforce laws regarding firearms, explosives, liquor, and tobacco, but it was the enforcement of firearms laws that earned the Bureau the enmity of the very powerful National Rifle Association (NRA). Pushed by the NRA, the Reagan administration introduced a bill to eliminate ATF. Despite a personal plea to congressmen by White House advisor Edwin Meese and despite hard work by Reagan's close friend Senator Paul Laxalt (Republican, Nevada), the bill died in committee in the Senate.

Had ATF met its demise, most of its agents would have been transferred to the Secret Service. The NRA, which originally backed the idea, reversed its position on abolishing ATF when it began to fear that the Secret Service would inherit ATF functions and would use its superior intelligence-gathering system and renowned investigative talents to enforce the gun laws more strictly than ATF ever could. Senator John Dingell (Democrat, Michigan) had another concern: he feared that the large infusion of ATF agents would dilute the quality of the Service, which he regarded as the superior organization of the two. Other senators worried that if the Secret Service took over ATF functions, it would become politicized and have to battle the NRA over gun control to the detriment of the protective mission. Fortunately for the Service and for its protective mission, the measure failed. But after September 11, 2001, the most drastic reorganization of all was proposed by the Bush Administration: moving the Service from the Treasury Department to the newly proposed Department of Homeland Security.

Though counterfeiting and forgery have comprised the Secret Service's mission from the very start, the agency's later mission stands as its "trademark" to Americans. This is the Secret Service's most publicized, best-known activity. From the protective mission's formal inception in 1906, to the thirty-six presidential protection bills presented to Congress in the wake of President Kennedy's assassination, in 1963, to the 1982 legislation providing protection to presidential candidates and other public officials, and beyond, the Secret Service's "public face" has been the collective faces of the men and, later, the women, who must stand ready to take a bullet for the president.

In 1963, in direct response to the national shock and tragedy of President Kennedy's assassination, Congress authorized the Secret Service to protect Jacqueline Kennedy and her two children for a makeshift period of two years. In 1965 this was extended to all wives and children of former presidents.

Congress, in that same year, finally made it a federal crime to assassinate, assault, or kidnap the president, vice president, president–elect, vice president–elect, or the next in line for succession to the presidency. Additional legislation was passed that same year to extend protection to former presidents and their wives, and to widows of former presidents until their remarriage or death. This bill also provides protection for children of former presidents until they reach the age of sixteen.

In addition to protecting the president, vice president, and other officials who enter the line of succession to the presidency (Speaker of the House and president pro tem of the Senate), the immediate families of these individuals are also protected. The children of former presidents are protected for ten years or until they reach age sixteen. Former president's spouses can continue to receive protection except when they remarry (an interesting cultural side effect of the idea of having a man around to "protect" you) or when they divorce the former president or the ex-president dies. If a president dies in office, the wife receives protection for one year from the date of death.

In 1997, Congress put a ceiling on the protection of "formers": a period of ten years after they leave office (for presidents who leave after 1997). For presidents who departed before 1997, protection is theirs for life or until they refuse it. This makes Bill Clinton the first president to be restricted to a decade. The first George Bush is the last to have open-ended protection for life.

Richard Nixon refused protection in 1985. In the year before Nixon gave up this perk, the government spent $12.6 million to protect ex-presidents Nixon, Ford, Carter, and their spouses. Columnists Jack W. Germand and Jules Witcover observed:

> Nixon did something right. His decision to give up costly Secret Service protection is a welcome surprise. That Nixon now has plenty of money to provide his own security does not take away from the gesture. Gerald R. Ford is in a financial position to do the same and all he's saying is that he'll consider emulating Nixon. The reply suggests Ford would have preferred that Nixon keep his mouth shut.

As of 2002, the Secret Service protects five former presidents and their spouses: the Fords, the Carters, the Reagans, George and Barbara Bush, and the Clintons. Any of the persons defined by law as eligible to receive protection may decline it, as Nixon did. If presidential candidates wish to refuse protection, the Secret Service asks them to sign an official waiver of protection. Normally, the total number of protectees at a given time is about thirty, but this number increases greatly during a presidential election year.

The agency's protective mission can also be increased at any juncture because Congress added a catchall phrase to the 1971 legislation with a statute allowing Secret Service protection to be granted "at the direction of the president." This has resulted in a mixed bag of assignments over the years: protection of foreign missions to the United States located outside of Washington, D.C.; President Carter ordering protection for Ted Kennedy before he became a legally qualified presidential candidate; and President Reagan providing protection to his three top White House aides—James Baker, Edwin Meese, and Michael Deaver. As previously stated, the list has swelled since September 11, 2001.

Responding to the assassination of presidential candidate Robert F. Kennedy, allegedly gunned down by Sirhan Sirhan in June 1968, Congress granted Secret Service protection to major presidential and vice presidential candidates. Ten received protection in 1968; thirteen in 1972. This was one of the broadest extensions of the protective mission because of the greatly increased number of protectees and the frenzied scheduling of presidential campaigns. In 1976, Congress extended protection to include the wives of presidential and vice presidential nominees during the election cycle.

In terms of numbers of agents needed and protective research to be done, it is much more demanding for the Service to protect candidates who were seeking enthusiastic crowds of potential voters than it is for ex-presidents or Ike's widow, Mamie Eisenhower, who almost never left her farm.

Although the Secret Service's Candidate Nominee Operations Section is responsible for planning and coordinating protection for presidential candidates, the agency itself has no role in determining who is eligible for campaign protection. A candidate cannot simply "declare" that he or she is running for office and expect a unit of elite agents to show up at campaign headquarters. An exception was Rev. Jesse Jackson in 1983. As soon as he announced his candidacy, he asked for Secret Service protection and was granted it even before the first primary in New Hampshire.

When is a presidential candidate credible or serious enough to deserve personal protection at taxpayers' expense? According to law, the secretary of the treasury determines which candidates qualify, but does so only after consultation with an advisory committee composed of the Speaker of the House of Representatives, the Senate majority and minority leaders, the House minority whip, and one additional member selected by the other members.

They can consider the level of support a candidate has drawn, the amount of money raised, the votes won in early primaries, and other political factors. Of course, there is one possible exception to this process: a sitting president can simply assign protection to any candidate he or she sees fit.

The major candidates who make the cut are provided protection, and even though they can decline, fewer than a dozen have done so (Carter thought of declining in 1976, then thought better of it). Protection is given to presidential and vice presidential candidates for the 120 days before Election Day.

The duties and decorum of agents covering candidates is spelled out in organizational procedure. The protection is twenty-four hours a day, seven days a week. As federal employees, agents are forbidden by law from engaging in partisan political activities of any kind. On the campaign trail, agents duties are tense and far-ranging:

- Coordinating all security matters, including coordination with other law enforcement agencies
- Providing security for the candidate's residence, mail, luggage, and transportation
- Facilitating appropriate access by the traveling and local press
- Providing a system of identification, permanent and temporary, to facilitate movement of necessary personnel within secure areas

The Service's "don't" list forbids agents from providing any personal services unrelated to security or providing any protective or personal services to the campaign staff. As is the case with the sitting president, each candidate is assigned a protective detail of agents. The key difference is that, in what the Service describes as "some cases," the detail will be rounded out with agents borrowed from other federal agencies: the Bureau of Alcohol, Tobacco and Firearms; Internal Revenue Service; the Treasury, the Inspector General's Office for Tax Administration; and the U.S. Customs Service. As a result, some of the protectors we see flanking a candidate are actually agents who are more accustomed to tracking tax cheats or illegal immigrants than to protecting political leaders.

One of the flaws covered-up—then and now—in a system trying to protect a large field of presidential candidates is that manpower can be dangerously overextended, forcing the Secret Service to draw from other agencies such as ATF to augment campaign security details. These substitutes hardly receive the protective training required of Secret Service agents. In an interview with Thomas O'Reilly, a retired ATF agent, the potential problems of the arrangement materialize. An ATF agent for thirty years, he was "loaned" to the Secret Service a number of times in the late 1960s and 1970s to cover presidential candidates when the field had swelled. He covered Jesse Jackson.

Almost every ATF agent gets loaned sometime during his career, but as O'Reilly notes, the Secret Service did have a preference for "younger guys." Though the agency would prefer not to borrow personnel for the presidential primaries, they have no choice. "They borrow from Customs, ATF, IRS—any Treasury agency," said O'Reilly.

He never saw any conflicts between politics and protection because, he asserts, that was handled by the Secret Service. He did know, however, that "some candidates wanted it [protection], some didn't." He added, "Some guys [candidates] were hard to get along with, some weren't."

His duties consisted of scanning crowds, standing guard on rooftops, and riding in motorcades. The borrowing was geographic. O'Reilly mainly worked New England details, which usually lasted days or weeks. When candidates became frontrunners or the field narrowed, the protectee was given real Secret Service agents. O'Reilly did some advance work, for example, checking a place before the protectee got there. Sometimes a candidate would be in ten different places in one day. O'Reilly would stay in New Hampshire for weeks at a time, not even commuting back to his home in Boston. "These New Hampshire roads in winter," he lamented.

ATF agents guarded John F. Kennedy's Hyannis house when he wasn't there. When Kennedy would arrive, his Secret Service presidential detail would take over (protection).

O'Reilly found the work "boring."

"A lot of standing around waiting," he reflected. "Especially in motels. You'd sit in a motel room, waiting, and then they [the Secret Service] would tell you, 'OK, we're going,' so we would line up in the procession [cars]."

The ATF loaners never knew in advance what their duties would be. They were always handed spontaneous assignments. That's how he did "a little bit of everything."

He admitted, almost apologetically, "They [ATF agents] get a little training." Still, even though there were "protective classes" given at ATF by Secret Service agents, "they [the classes] were not very extensive."

The leader of the protective detail and assistant leader are responsible for liaison and coordination with the candidate and his or her senior staff. For each candidate, the Service will set up an "Operations Office" located usually in the candidate's city of residence; coordination between the Service and the campaign is crucial to safety, given all the stops, changes of plans and schedules, and, always, the potential threats hidden in crowds.

The dramatic expansion of the Secret Service's protective mission in the modern era is a result not only of the increased number of legally mandated protectees, but also of the pace of modern politics as presidents and candidates travel much more now than in past decades. At the turn of the twentieth century, Theodore Roosevelt became the first U.S. president to travel outside the country while in office. Now, a century later, both the presidential office and the modern presidential campaign demand extensive travel which greatly increases the scope of agents' work. As late as World War II, the White House detail consisted of only sixteen agents; in 2002, the exact number is classified, according to a member of George W. Bush's detail, but the best estimate places the number as over one hundred.

Although it is a relatively small federal agency, the modern Secret Service has a very complex organizational structure in terms of the number and diversity of its divisions and subdivisions. It is true that modern bureaucracies appear to have an innate tendency toward proliferation and compartmentalization, but the Secret Service's intricate structure accurately reflects the complexity and diversity of its responsibilities although some streamlining would appear to be helpful. The agency is a dual-mission organization—protection and investigation of counterfeiting and forgery—with overlapping yet distinct activities for each basic mission and with increasingly varied and numerous responsibilities that have grown out of these two basic missions. Today, the organization that once consisted of a dozen plainclothes operatives and a director now includes handwriting experts, intelligence analysts, psychologists, uniformed officers, and canine teams.

Since September 11, 2001, conflicting messages about the number of Secret Service personnel have emerged publicly. Many agents and uniformed officers are citing burnout and reportedly seeking transfer to other divisions or retirement; at the same time, though no hard numbers are available, many men and women are still seeking to join the agency. Despite the stress and problems of resources, Secret Service employment remains perceived as good work, if you can get it. The Service claims that applications have remained high and turnover low, especially for the job of agent, so that the agency can afford to pick only the qualified applicants.

Applicants for Secret Service positions within the Uniformed Division must be U.S. citizens who have a high school diploma or equivalent and a valid driver's license. Though the requirements are not as stringent as those for special agents, a rigorous federal background check takes place before a uniformed officer candidate can obtain a "top secret" clearance. They must also be over twenty-one and under thirty-seven years of age. Candidates take a written exam, and those who pass are given a series of personal interviews. If they get through these, they must pass a polygraph test before being selected. Given the controversies and vagaries of the "lie detector," this is no small hurdle, even for the most upstanding candidates. Drug screening is also done.

Candidates for the Uniformed Service must also meet the physical requirements: passing a medical exam and an eye exam certifying 20/40 vision in each eye, "correctable to 20/20." Weight must be proportionate to height. As the Service's brochure warns, "Selected applicants should be prepared to wait an extended period of time while a thorough background investigation is conducted."

Uniformed personnel have no investigative duties concerning protection or financial and communications crimes as do special agents for the Service.

With a legacy whose origins stretch back to the 1860s, one of the hallmark branches of the Secret Service is its Uniformed Division. The first formal attempt to provide security at the White House and its grounds came during the Civil War, when the "Bucktail Brigade"—soldiers from the 150th Pennsylvania Volunteer Regiment—and four Washington, D.C., police officers were assigned to protect the mansion. The White House military aide oversaw the unit. In 1922, President Warren G. Harding created his own self-serving "White House Police Force," and the true precursor of the Secret Service Uniformed Division began in 1930, with President Herbert Hoover's proposal to merge the White House Police and the Secret Service, who would supervise the police detail.

Today, even though the Uniformed Division is a subdivision of the Service's Office of Protective Operations, it is practically a separate organization within an organization. In 1970, the unit, known as the White House Police Force, was revamped as the Executive Protection Service, with increased personnel and expanded duties which included responsibility for protecting foreign diplomatic missions in the D.C. area. In 1977, the unit again received a new name, this time changed to the U.S. Secret Service Uniformed Division—its present title. In the division's protective role, it buttresses the regular Service through a series of special support units: Counter-Sniper, Canine Explosive Detection Team, Emergency Response Team, Crime Scene Search Technicians, Special Operations Section, and Magnetometers. The division also provides a support infrastructure of fixed security posts and foot, bicycle, vehicular, and motorcycle patrols.

What was formerly the Treasury Security Force, a uniformed-officer corps within the Treasury Department, was merged into the Uniformed Division in 1986. This relatively small unit of several hundred men and women had responsibility for protecting Treasury Department buildings and facilities, duties that are now officially handled by officers/agents of the combined Uniformed Division.

In its protective duties, the Uniformed Division overlaps with those of the protective details staffed by regular Secret Service agents. The Division protects the president and immediate family, primarily at the White House, the vice president and immediate family, the White House grounds, foreign missions, buildings in which presidential offices are located (such as the Old Executive Office Building and the official Washington residence of the vice president).

The Division's protective responsibilities extend around the clock. Even when foreign ambassadors are traveling away from their Washington, D.C., embassies, the buildings are protected twenty-four hours a day. As is the case with regular Secret Service agents, presidents can assign the Uniformed Division personnel to protect any foreign diplomatic mission whenever they perceive it to be necessary, whether it be a Japanese mission in San Francisco or a Saudi Arabian mission in New York. Since 1973, the Division has, at presidential request, protected several United Nations missions in New York belonging to Middle Eastern countries, on a more or less permanent basis. In 1975, President Ford vetoed a bill passed by Congress that would have placed the burden for such protection on the local government of the cities outside of Washington in which such missions were located.

When tourists visit the White House, they see firsthand one of the Uniformed Division's key roles: to police the tours to the White House tours. Over two million visitors come each year, and they queue up in lines that extend halfway around the mansion. Keeping the lines orderly and directing traffic around the White House while guarding the mansion's extensive grounds and its numerous gates and guardhouses requires a large contingent of uniformed officers. The tours were canceled for months after September 11, 2001, and have been restored only on a limited and selective basis.

The Uniformed Division executes its protective duties through a network of foot and vehicular patrols. Lightweight motorcycles are used to patrol the streets around the White House, where canine teams are in place. A subdivision of the Uniformed Division, the canine unit consists of a dozen teams of extensively trained officers and dogs. Although the dogs undergo training in attack and in scouting, techniques similar to those used with police dogs, the Secret Service dogs' primary use is in explosive detection.

It takes thirteen weeks to train a team of dogs and handlers. First comes a four-week session at Lackland Air Force Base, in Texas, where dogs and handlers are monitored for compatibility so that they can ultimately perform as a well-integrated team. The second phase of the training is a nine-week session at Andrews Air Force Base, in Maryland, and it is here that explosive detection is emphasized. The dogs are taught to sniff out all kinds of explosive substances, snarl at them, and sit in front of them. Canine teams are given frequent refresher courses after basic training.

For the Uniformed Division, fixed guard-duty can be both boring and hazardous. An eight-hour stint standing near the gate of a foreign embassy can be tedious and uncomfortable during Washington's sultry summer heat. Yet officers must remain alert because burglaries and bombings do occur. In 1980, the Yugoslavian Embassy was bombed by a Croatian independence group.

The responsibility for guarding foreign missions was given to the Uniformed Division in 1971, when it was called the Executive Protection Service, because of a rising concern among foreign diplomats about possible terror attacks. In the late 1960s and early 1970s, Washington, D.C., police were inundated with requests from foreign ambassadors who wanted increased protection because of what State Department Security Officer William P. De Coury called an "upsurge of terrorism around the world." Several incidents of more run-of-the-mill crime on Embassy Row—an embassy was robbed and an ambassador mugged—led to beefed-up uniformed officer details for diplomats in 1970–1971.

Because the Washington police did not have the personnel to respond to the demands for increased protection for foreign dignitaries, Congress turned the safety of diplomats and their families and staffs into a federal responsibility. The Uniformed Division was officially charged with the task of protecting the approximately twenty-five hundred foreign diplomats living and working in the D.C. area in numerous residences and office buildings.

The Uniformed Officers have a narrowly defined law-enforcement role when protecting foreign missions. If officers see a burglary taking place a block away from their post, they must remain where they are and radio to the D.C. police or to a Uniformed Division patrol car, which will then proceed to the scene of the crime. Even if such help is too far away to stop the robbery, the Uniformed Division officer must not stray from his or her post. If there is a political demonstration at an embassy, it is the D.C. police and U.S. Park Police who arrest unruly demonstrators in the streets. The Uniformed Officers' main task is to protect the embassy, and they can make an arrest only once a demonstrator tries to enter the building.

The law giving the Service a permanent protective mission for visiting representatives of foreign governments and for official U.S. representatives on foreign visits covers some one hundred to one hundred and fifty foreign representatives who visit the United States each year, staying for periods of a few days to several weeks; some of them travel extensively within the United States during their stay. Depending upon the number of visiting dignitaries and their itineraries, this responsibility often puts a genuine strain on the Service's uniformed and regular personnel, stretching the agency far too thin.

In sharp contrast to the tailored business suits worn by regular Secret Service agents, the Uniformed Division wear uniforms that are a cross between police and military dress: distinctive black pants with bright gold striping, white shirts with gold trim, gold and blue badges, name tags that include the officer's home state, highly polished black shoes, police-style caps, and shoulder chevrons indicating rank. Though regular agents' revolvers are carefully concealed under their specially tailored suits, uniformed officers wear theirs in hip holsters. Uniformed personnel also carry radios and nightsticks.

It was the Uniformed Division, still called the Executive Protection Service in the early 1970s, that was the focus of President Nixon's attempt to add imperial luster to his presidency by dictating that his uniformed guards don lavish costumes. To the Uniformed Division's embarrassment, the Nixon White House outfitted the officers in chocolate-brown costumes with white tunics draped with gold braid, topped with sharply sloping hats. The new outfits looked like they might have been borrowed from the Vatican or from a sixteenth-century French palace. Criticism from the media and the public was universal: People felt that the new uniforms made the officers look imperial at best, foolish at worst. As soon as Nixon left office, the uniforms were quickly packed away.

Even with less ostentatious uniforms, the Uniformed Division has come in for its share of criticism. Many congressional budget-cutters have moaned that the Division's protection of foreign missions is really an expensive subsidy to foreign governments. Critics point out that uniformed personnel provide "more" than protection: they also handle such chores such as unsnarling traffic jams after big parties at the embassies—with American taxpayers footing the bill.

Since 1978, when Washington columnist and television commentator Howard Kurtz, in his early career as an investigator for columnist Jack Anderson, derided even the protective duties performed by the Uniformed Division as a misappropriation of scarce resources, the debate over the need for the division has swung back and forth:

> The inescapable irony is that the nation's taxpayers, many of
> whom live in high-crime areas without adequate police protec-
> tion, are paying over $17 million a year to support a special
> police force in the one area of the of the nation's capital that
> needs it the least.

Nonetheless, the Uniformed Division points with pride to the relative absence of crime on Embassy Row as evidence of its effectiveness. Congress continues to view the Uniformed Division's domestic protection of other nations' diplomats and heads of state as an agency duty that helps maintain better international relations.

For special agents, the age requirements for entry, as with the Uni–formed Division, are that they be at least twenty-one and no more than thirty-seven years old when first appointed; the age range reflects a general barometer of one's peak physical years. The average age of the approximately twenty-seven hundred Special Agents is around thirty-five. They must be in excellent physical condition, and are required to pass a comprehensive medical exam provided by the Service with frequent reexaminations.

The physical stipulations, mirroring those of the Uniformed division, demand that "weight must be in proportionate to height" and vision at least 20/40 in each eye, uncorrected; near vision must be at least 20/40 corrected. To the Service's carefully cultivated public image, proportionate weight to height—fit, trim agents—is essential.

The importance of good eyesight to an agent cannot be overstated. There are few occupations where vision is so crucial to the prevention of violence or in life-and-death situations.

For prospective special agents, a bachelor's degree from any accredited college is required, and any major will do. Decades ago, many agents were former lawyers or teachers. Now it is more diverse. Former Agent Timothy J. McCarthy has said, "Because of the increased white-collar crime, they [the agency] were seeking people with a business background. But even a physical education major fits in somewhere. You want people with diverse backgrounds, not all accountants."

A current member of President George W. Bush's protective detail relates that years ago, military and law-enforcement backgrounds were predominant, but that has all changed: "Ours is a people job, and those with 'people skills' will get the nod in recruitment. Although in the 1990s, with the Service policing computer fraud, there were some recruits who worked for IBM. Scientific and computer skills are in demand right now in [2002]."

In lieu of a degree, the Service makes exceptions "in some cases" for candidates with a minimum of three-years' experience in law enforcement, two of which are in criminal investigation, or with "a comparable combination of experience and education."

For men and women aspiring to make the cut as Special Agents, the application materials are extensive and somewhat intimidating: fifteen pages of forms, waivers, and an exceedingly detailed questionnaire. Applicants are warned that any omissions or inaccuracies will delay their application; any "misrepresentations" will end it. On the forms, the applicants must fully reveal family and employment history and all tax-return filings with the Internal Revenue Service.

*"Did you ever use illegal drugs?"* The query leaps out at all candidates, and the questionnaire is especially concerned with marijuana: Ever use it? How many times? When was the last time?

A question asks open-endedly: "Are there any incidents in your own background, or that of the members of your family, which might compromise your performance as a Secret Service employee?" This intimidating question not only takes considerable thought to answer accurately, but also requires the applicant to imagine the "compromising" impact of virtually every negative incident or condition in the person's life.

Applicants must write a series of eight miniessays about their experiences and abilities, dealing with everything from working with people to using firearms to accepting responsibility. The candidates sign waivers that their tax records and consumer-credit files can be accessed by the Service, and agree to take a polygraph.

Finally, the three-page cover letter from the Special Agent in charge of the field office to the prospective applicant states ominously the pressures and demands of the job regarding risk, stamina, and personal life, which should be "prudently discussed with your family and significant others." The fainthearted need not apply.

Would-be Special Agents must pass the Treasury Enforcement Agent Exam, which is not specific to the Secret Service, as it is given to all applicants for Customs, IRS, and Alcohol, Tobacco and Firearms. Those Secret Service candidates who pass are waiting listed by the agency, and those with the highest scores are eventually invited to a series of in-depth interviews in which they are judged by their "personal appearance, bearing and manner; ability to speak logically and effectively, ability to adapt easily to a variety of situations."

For the applicants, the tests do not end with acceptance: agents are required to undergo semiannual physical fitness tests administered by the Service, checking "cardiovascular fitness, upper body strength, and flexibility."

If prospective agents pass the vigorous background checks on their character, honesty, and "loyalty to the United States," the new recruits receive a top secret clearance. The recruits' next step is a Special Agent training course at the Federal Law Enforcement Facility in Brunswick, Georgia, the prelude to more specialized training at the Secret Service's facility in Maryland.

The Service continues to be concerned at all times about the appearance and demeanor of potential agents, for someday they might serve on the White House detail, which often operates under the media spotlight. Though they will remain anonymous, agents will be seen by millions of Americans. Neither the Service nor the president wants any odd-looking, mean-looking, or scruffy types spoiling the president's image or that of the agency.

Agents have a clean-cut appearance and dress conservatively; their suits are specially tailored to conceal their pistols and automatic weapons. Except for the radio transmitters in their ears, they look like business executives.

It is indicative of the kind of young men that the Service prefers to recruit that one agency outreach program, designed in part to aid recruitment, involved the Eagle Scouts. What better source of clean-cut, loyal young men, the Service reasoned. Though the Service has more paper-qualified applicants than it needs and though it is notoriously reclusive and publicity shy, it created the Law Enforcement Assistance Award in 1972, given annually to an Explorer Scout who has helped some law-enforcement agency by preventing a crime or helping to catch a suspect. Each spring the Service used to host a one-day seminar for the presidents of Explorer posts around the country, complete with a tour of the agency's highly secretive Maryland facilities. There, scouts could watch agents being trained.

Starting salaries for Secret Service agents are not high by federal standards. Agents are usually hired at the GS-5, GS-7, or GS-9 level, "depending upon qualifications and/or education": GS-5, $22,737; GS-7, $28,164; GS-9, $34,451. Pay scales are "adjusted geographically" in response to cost of living, and most jobs pay a higher salary than the stated figures (local U.S. payments can increase from 8 percent to 19.4 percent depending on the area; outside the continental United States, it is 10 percent to 25 percent). In addition, Special Agents also receive "Law Enforcement Availability Pay (LEAP)," which gives them a 25 percent boost over their base pay. Typically, agents will attain GS-12 to GS-13 fairly rapidly, with a base pay of $49,000 to $59,000. GS-15, $82,580, is usually attained later. Agents are civil service employees and are eligible for retirement at age fifty, with twenty years of service. In protective work, the average age of agents tends to be younger than that of supervisory personnel, with an average retirement age of fifty-five for the organization as a whole and a turnover rate of only 3.8 percent annually.

Any of the Service's twenty-seven hundred special agents can aspire to one day be the director of the organization, for unlike many federal agencies, the director is not an outside political appointee but is chosen from within the organization by the secretary of the treasury. Most directors have served "on-the-line"—performing difficult protective assignments. Typical of this are agents such as former Director H. Stuart Knight (1973–1981) who served in the vice presidential protective detail in Caracas in 1958 and was outside Nixon's limousine repelling assaults by angry demonstrators, and current Director Stafford, who headed the Presidential Protective Division.

In a recent interview, Boston field office Agent Mark Carleton discussed career paths, as well as training and recruitment, in today's Secret Service. According to Carleton, agents typically spend four to six ("ideally" six) years in a field office on their first assignment learning various facets of the job, which includes protective as well as investigative duties. But now, since September 11, agents are being "launched," or sent to protective duties or details beyond the field office, in a much shorter time of two to three years. In "Track I," says Carleton, new agents start in field offices and go to protective duty. On this track "the agency owns you." The agents have little or no say in where they are sent or what they do. Later, in "Track II," a permanent protective assignment or support assignment for the protective function, agents have more say and more control over their lives.

Carleton relates that a major, if not *the,* major key to success is "following the rules." Agents who can't or won't adhere to that code end up as permanent "journeymen." Generally, the Secret Service now takes 60 percent to 70 percent of its recruits from people with law-enforcement or military backgrounds—around twenty-seven-years old, old enough "to have lived," young enough to be trained. The typical pattern is field office to protection and back to a field office.

Carleton says that one of the in-house truths is "you *will* travel and *will* relocate." But the most important adage remains: "Follow the rules and succeed."

Special Agents In Charge (SAIC) of field offices do not work their way up through the ranks in one office. They hop around getting promotions, going "up the ladder" until they are a SAIC ("Sack"). There are management slots, "senior management," then SAIC, with agents sometimes having worked in ATF or IRS before beginning their Secret Service careers. SAIC's rule is "You talk to the Sack before you talk to God.

Carleton's Sack went from the Chicago field office to a protective detail and then to Miami and Houston, moving up the ladder until he made SAIC in Boston about four years ago.

Carleton expresses pride at the levels in post-Service positions that agents have attained: security heads for Fortune 500 companies and high-level jobs in other law-enforcement agencies. Still, he insists that most agents retire out of the Secret Service and *then* go on. "The attrition rate [agent dropout] is low," he maintains.

One the most prestigious duties agents can draw is assignment to the select group of more than one hundred men and, to a far lesser degree, women comprising the White House detail, the all-star team of protective duty. Even though an agent's original posting to presidential protection may be strictly according to merit and experience, as the Service claims, the effectiveness and tenure of an agent on the presidential security team depends on a variety of factors, not the least of which is how his or her personality and operating style mesh with those of the president and the White House staff.

Today, women can serve as special agents, and the Uniformed Division has long had women officers. Anyone taking the White House tour will find that one-third to one-half of the uniformed guards stationed at the White House gates, around the grounds, and inside the mansion are women. Not surprisingly, women have long filled many clerical jobs in the Service. However, not until 1971 were the first four female special agents appointed. Since then, there have not been any glaring episodes of institutional prejudice against female agents.

The biggest breakthrough for women in the Service did not come until 1978, during the Carter administration. Special Agent Mary Ann Gordon was assigned to the White House detail on a permanent basis, where, previously, women had been given only temporary assignments. That same year, one woman agent was assigned to Vice President Mondale's detail.

In an interview with the author, Gordon, who went on to work at the Service's Division of Public Affairs in Washington, described her landmark appointment as "a matter of timing." Part of the "timing" involved the

Carter administration's emphasis on affirmative action. Still, despite Gordon's milestone, her appointment to the presidential detail did not fuel an influx of women into the ranks of special agents, and the number of women overall remains conspicuously small in comparison to the proportion of women involved in other kinds of Secret Service work such as the protective duties performed by the Uniformed Division.

The Service's organizational treatment of African Americans has been a subject of considerable contention. In February 2000, a group of black agents filed a class action suit against the agency and charged that they were passed over for promotion because of racial discrimination.

One of the plaintiffs is Agent Reginald Moore. This sixteen-year veteran had risen through the ranks to the highly prestigious position of lead agent in the presidential detail (protecting Bill Clinton). Moore alleges that he was on track for a higher management position but was passed over for a white agent whom he had trained. A frustrated Moore contended that after following all the rules and defined career steps for years—"doing things the way they should be done," as he put it—he was blocked from the step upward to the administrative elite.

Jay Branegan, *Time* magazine's Washington correspondent, observed: "This story is rife with ironies. In the last couple of years, there have been quite a few women and minorities in the presidential detail—an incredibly elite and dangerous position. They are willing to take a bullet for the president [but encounter resistance when seeking managerial positions]."

According to the agency's most recent figures, African Americans make up approximately 10 percent of the special agent corps but less than 5 percent of management. Secret Service spokespersons retort that there are a number of women and blacks in the higher administrative echelons: of seven assistant directors in 2000, there were two blacks and one woman.

In several ways, the lawsuit by its own agents poses a public relations dilemma for the Service. The action is bad press for such a well-respected agency, subjecting the secretive agency to legal probe and public scrutiny, and possibly eroding morale and the internal cooperation that is essential for any organization to function at peak effectiveness.

In contrast to the furor, or perhaps because of it, the Service promoted African American Agent Larry Cockell to the position of assistant director of training just a month before the lawsuit was formally announced. Cockell is one of the most photographed agents in the history of the organization; he became familiar to the nation by holding Clinton's belt or hips as the president worked rope lines. Cockell was one of the agents forced by Ken Starr to testify before the grand jury in the Monica Lewinsky case. In June 2001, the trim, handsome fifty year old rose to an even higher rank: deputy director of the agency. This makes him the first African American with a potential career path to the pinnacle—director of the U.S. Secret Service.

Whether Service candidates are African American, white, Hispanic, male, or female, their training does not vary in their first year, their probationary year. The preparation is intense. They receive both formal instruction and on-the-job training, and the degree to which the first-year job experience involves protective work or investigative work (counterfeit and forgery cases and protection-related cases) depends on the Service's personnel needs at the time.

All agents take sixteen weeks of formal instruction: eight weeks at the Treasury Department's Federal Law Enforcement Training Center in Georgia and another eight weeks at the Secret Service's Maryland training facility. The quality of training has improved markedly in the past decades and is now much more extensive and sophisticated than it once was, a reflection of how the trauma of the Kennedy assassination changed so many aspects of Secret Service training. It is not forgotten that several of the agents who guarded President Kennedy could not even recognize the sound of gunfire in Dealy Plaza, Dallas and that agents in Kennedy's motorcade mistook the rifle fire for a motorcycle backfire, firecrackers, or the blowout of a tire. Texas politicians with hunting experience (Governor John Connolly, Senator Ralph Yarborough) immediately recognized the sound as gunfire, but the agents had practiced with firearms only on a firing range while wearing earmuffs and had not been trained to recognize the sound of gunfire under natural conditions.

Apart from the improved quality of training today, two other key factors influence the substance and effectiveness of Secret Service training. The first part of the process seeks to develop combat-ready skills and instant reflexes for use in real life-and-death situations such as an assassination attempt. Although these worst-case scenarios might occur only once every few years or once in a decade, agents must be trained to react within a split second even for situations that, fortunately, occur too infrequently to provide much actual experience. Hence, the necessity of stepped-up training.

The second key component of Secret Service training is "dual purpose," referring to the Service's dual missions. Former Secret Service Director Eljay Bowron III (1993–1997) commented, "In fact, we find that they [the dual missions] complement one another." He alleged that the counterfeiting investigative training inculcates "powers of observation and the ability to read people. . . . Investigative assignments are invaluable in protection-learning variety and flexibility." In truth, Bowron's assertion is a wide stretch. An agent's ability to observe a phony $20 bill has no applicability to protection. Counterfeiters are confronted and arrested by agents who very often raid their dens, basements, and warehouses. This is a world apart from the skills needed on the rope line: counterfeiters do not show up in or outside Secret Service field offices waiting to draw a gun and assassinate agents while giving up their own lives in the process. In seeking out coun-terfeiters, agents do not scan crowds looking for the guy with the ink on his fingers or a wallet stuffed with phony bills.

For agents who make it through their probationary year, those who rise to the rarified post of presidential detail generally have to pay their dues with nine to ten years in the field. Today's agents are not only far better trained than their predecessors, but also come from a wider range of back-grounds. In years past, the Secret Service did not have to actively recruit very much, but now they seek candidates with some measure of technical expertise and computer skills—such candidates do not always come to the agency in the supply needed.

All agents do both investigative (counterfeit and forgery cases) and protective work and are trained for both. For many agents, a typical career pattern would be to spend the first three to four years after the pro-bationary period in one or more of the Service's field offices. Then, if the organizational needs and an agent's skills permit, he or she may enter full-time protective work. Tours of duty in protective work are from a minimum of three years to as many as five or six years; afterward, an agent is trans-ferred back to a field office. Unlike the first field office assignment, the agent has some choice of location and is allowed to "bid" (apply for) for an administrative post.

The career of Agent Tim McCarthy is fairly typical in the Service. He entered the Secret Service after graduating from the University of Illinois with a B.S. in finance and a minor in accounting. "Because of the increase in white-collar crime, at that time they were seeking people with a business background," he recalls. "But even a physical education major fits in somewhere. You [Secret Service] want a diversity of backgrounds, not all accountants."

McCarthy participated in protection of every president from Nixon to Clinton through protective work in the field office, when a president would travel to his area, and nine years of permanent assignment to the presidential detail: Carter, Reagan, and George H. W. Every agent usually ends up with a protective-detail assignment, but McCarthy was atypical in doing two stints. In a recent interview, McCarthy notes that the usual stint was four to five years and that his lasted "too long."

After he was shot protecting Reagan, McCarthy was assigned to the "counterfeit squad" in the Chicago office, then back to Reagan's presidential detail. He says, "It's an eight-hour shift at the White House. But otherwise, the sky's the limit."

McCarthy relates that at the White House, there are a number of fixed security posts that must be manned by the presidential detail, and they can program in breaks and meals. But on the road there are much more prolonged, open-ended assignments.

From 1989–1993 McCarthy was in charge of the Chicago office, overseeing approximately 100 agents in his main office, 10 more in a Milwaukee substation, 10 in Springfield, Illinois, and 3 in Madison, Wisconsin. McCarthy's job was, in major part, "coordination": coordinating both the investigative and protective missions. In protection, he would liaison with the protective detail of the protectee coming to Chicago and work everything out: routes, events, and so forth. Sometimes, a neighboring field office (Detroit) would borrow thirty agents when a protectee was coming to their turf.

Limiting protective duty to a three-to-five-year span helps reduce stress and prevent agent burnout. Onetime Secret Service Public Affairs Director Robert Snow told the author that the dual-mission career pattern has benefited the Service. He related, "We find that it works well. Protective agents are better, sharper because of their investigative training."

Agent Timothy McCarthy told Melanson: "The theory of the Secret Service is that a good criminal investigator who has good sense, [and] good judgment will carry over to the protective mission: arrests, stressful situations, effective reactions. If they excel at that, they will need excel in the protective mission as well." Another former agent told Melanson: "I liked the divided responsibility because it was mentally challenging . . . There was more of a mental challenge in following the trail of counterfeiters. I enjoyed it more than presidential protection."

Snow also claimed that even when working a field office, half of the agent's time is spent in "protective work." Though this may be literally true, "protective work" in the field offices primarily involves protective intelligence gathering and case work—checking out threats or monitoring dangerous persons—rather than guarding a protectee (providing direct on-the-line protection).

Even though both are law-enforcement functions, as the Service is fond of pointing out, the actual relationship of the two kinds of work is such that it would be equally accurate for a young man who worked in both stage lighting and choreography to point out that both are related to the theater.

Because the training of agents is relatively short and intense, it does not maximize the effectiveness of the protective mission when much of the training received is not directly related to the mission. The Secret Service counters that protective training is continuous and prefers that each agent gain experience at two successive field offices, one large and one small, but costs and logistics do not always make the measure possible.

Agents involved in protective work must take refresher courses periodically and learn about relevant changes in the law and about new protective techniques. This, however, does not deflect the agency's commitment to the dual nature of the basic, most important training received by agents. The Service claims that "it is impractical to have agents specialize in only one area," in large part because of the Service's dual mission, but a separation of the two could heighten the effectiveness of protection.

In preparing candidates for their twofold duties, the Service boasts that its agents receive "the finest law-enforcement training in the world." Rookie agents are first sent to the Federal Law Enforcement Training Center, in Glynco, Georgia, where they enroll in the Criminal Investigation Training Program for nine weeks. This is a general course for all federal investigators and covers such areas as criminal law and investigative techniques, providing prospective agents a general foundation for specific Secret Service courses to come later. The curriculum covers a wide range of subjects:

Ethics and Conduct for Investigators
Organized Crime
Orientation of Federal Law-Enforcement Agencies
Orientation on Contraband Narcotics
Civil Rights
Conduct and Testifying in Court
Conspiracy
Constitutional Law and Rules of Evidence
Federal Court Procedure
Preparation for Trials
Searches and Seizures
Arrest Techniques
Bombs and Explosives
Surveillance Techniques (including the use of electronic devices)
Undercover Operations
Firearms Training (including night shooting)

As the relevance of most of these to the protective mission is limited, the rookie agents' real training lies ahead.

After graduation from Glynco, agents go to the Secret Service Training Academy in Beltsville, Maryland, for their specialized schooling. They take an eleven-week course that covers both investigation of counterfeiting and protection techniques. Beltsville, a sprawling facility that encompasses 420 acres, boasts administrative offices, a cafeteria, student lounges, ammunition and firearms storage rooms, a canine training area (where dogs learn to sniff out bombs), an armorer's workshop, locker rooms, classrooms, and firing ranges. At the facility, the rookies study the history of the organization, preparation of reports, and anticounterfeiting techniques that include finding fingerprints on government checks and bonds, learning about the paper and metal used to make currency, and training in "access device fraud"—how criminals gain access to ATMs and other electronic transfers of money.

Throughout the grueling eleven weeks at Beltsville, the agents also study measures against financial crimes, protective intelligence, physical protection techniques, and emergency medicine. The training also encompasses firearms, crowd-control tactics, water-survival skills, physical fitness, and defensive driving techniques. Class field trips are not to museums but to mills that produce currency paper and to the Bureau of Printing and Engraving, in Washington, D.C.

Some of the most important moments of the training are practical exercises and stimulations such as questioning a suspect (played by an instructor) and conducting handwriting and typewriting analyses to catch forgers. Then there is a simulated raid on a counterfeiting operation and an exercise featuring how to take photographs that will be useful in court if an arrest can be made. Arrest techniques range from subduing to handcuffing. The Service will not reveal how much of the eleven weeks of training is consumed by investigative training and how much is left for protective training. But it is clear from the depth and scope of investigative training received that it claims a major chunk of the available time.

Some of the training received in Maryland is relevant to both protective and investigative work—care and use of firearms, karate, wrestling, and boxing. A "ten-minute medicine" course teaches agents how to keep a heart-attack victim or an injured or wounded person alive for the ten critical minutes until professional help arrives. Cardiopulmonary resuscitation (CPR) is taught for a full day, as are techniques for controlling bleeding and for treating shock and bullet wounds. Agents even receive a basic knowledge of firefighting.

All of this is, of course, potentially useful to protectees. Since 1973, agents have saved over a hundred lives through CPR and other lifesaving techniques. When the president and his family are at a secluded retreat, an agent's life-saving skills could be crucial in case of emergency.

Last, but not least, agents receive their detailed training in protective methods and procedures, conducted in the classroom and via practical exercises. Topics covered include protective research (intelligence gathering), bomb detection and disposal, and methods and techniques of counterterrorism. In a minicourse given by psychiatrists on the distinctions between normal and abnormal behavior, agents are taught to detect potential assassins. In a more physical lesson, agents are taught how to fall from a moving limousine without getting hurt.

Firearms training is extensive and, unlike the previous training at the Treasury's Georgia facility, focuses specifically on the special problems of protective work. Trainees learn how to shoot in the dark and how to shoot from inside a limousine at both moving and stationary targets. In the "running man" simulation course, trainees shoot at a target as it runs through a

RIGHT: Pete McCartney, the counterfeiter who fooled America with his well-crafted bogus greenbacks from the 1850s to the 1880s. The Secret Service finally put him out of business in the 1880s. Source: Library of Congress

BELOW: Four early and unidentified Secret Service men (c. 1866). Source: *Harper's Weekly*, Library of Congress.

*Some of the first Secret Service operatives.*

ABOVE: Three Secret Service operatives guarding President Teddy Roosevelt (in carriage, left), circa 1903. Source: Library of Congress.
BELOW: German spy Dr. Heinrich Albert, whose capture by the Secret Service in 1917 shattered a German spy ring in the U.S. Source: Library of Congress.

How the Secret Service Solved
**THE MYSTERY OF THE LITTLE BLACK BAG**
BY EDMOND VAN TYNE

LOST—On Saturday, on 3:30 Harlem elevated train, at 50th St. station, brown leather bag containing documents. Deliver to G. H. Hoffman, 5 East 47th St., against $20 reward.

*Albert's reward advertisement, which appeared in the Lost and Found section of the New York*

ABOVE: Retiring Secret Service Agent Frank Burke (left), the man who seized Dr. Albert's briefcase, which contained plans for a German invasion of the U. S. in 1917-18. Source: Library of Congress
BELOW: Mrs. Edith Wilson, the First Lady, guarded by Secret Service operative Myles McCahill (in straw hat) on Memorial Day 1919 near Paris. Source: Library of Congress

Agents John Marshall (left) and Jim Beary (right), who helped protect FDR on his over-seas trips during World War II.  Source: Library of Congress

# COUNTERFEIT RING BELIEVED SMASHED BY SECRET AGENTS

## 'Count' Victor Lustig Associate of Al Capone, 'Legs' Diamond Always Worked Fake Money Games

**By BARTON BLACK**
*Times Staff Correspondent*

NEW YORK, June 1.—Federal agents today were preparing what they termed an "acquittal-proof case" against Victor Lustig, whom they described as one of the most versatile criminals of the age—a sort of Public Swindler No. 1.

Often has Lustig let it out that he is the scapegrace son of a Prussian nobleman and that, except for machinations in

ABOVE: Count Lustig, a world-renowned counterfeiter, captured in 1935 by the Secret Service. Source: Library of Congress

BELOW: Agents (L to R) Deckard and Rowley (future Director of the Secret Service) shield FDR (center) at Casablanca in 1943. Source: Library of Congress

ABOVE: President Harry Truman signs bill outlining the Secret Service's protective duties on July 16, 1951. Source: Library of Congress
BELOW: A presidential motorcade forming in front of the White House during the Eisenhower administration, Secret Service agents positioned around the president's limo. Source: National Archives

ABOVE: Agents on the firing range in the late 1950s. Source: National Archives

BELOW: A World War II-era Secret Service "bomb carrier." Source: Library of Congress

WILLIAM P. WOOD
1865–1869

HERMAN C. WHITLEY
1869–1874

ELMER WASHBURN
1874–1876

JAMES J. BROOKS
1876–1888

JOHN S. BELL
1888–1890

A. L. DRUMMOND
1891–1894

CHIEF
U. E. BAUGHMAN

WILLIAM P. HAZEN
1894–1898

JOHN E. WILKIE
1898–1911

WILLIAM J. FLYNN
1912–1917

WILLIAM H. MORAN
1917–1936

FRANK J. WILSON
1937–1946

JAMES J. MALONEY
1947–1948

A gallery of Secret Service directors from the end of the Civil War through the beginning of the Cold War; in 2002 the director is Brian Stafford, who has worked on presidential security details from Nixon to Clinton.  Source: National Archives crowd of innocent bystanders. Agents learn to handle submachine guns and shotguns. All this, even though agents rarely use their weapons and are taught that their first priority is to cover the protectee rather than return fire.

As the site of the weapons training, the Beltsville facility is one of the most sophisticated firearms training centers in the country, used by all federal law enforcement agencies except the FBI, which has its own modern practice range in the J. Edgar Hoover building, and housing the Secret Service's arsenal of weapons and ammo. Beltsville has several firing ranges; the indoor ranges are able to host twenty-four shooters at one time, and each range is equipped with a control booth that can simulate daytime or nighttime conditions. Agents are also taken to a pair of outdoor ranges, one for rifles, another for pistols.

In firearms training, agents "must be aggressive." They learn to fire "two rounds in 4 seconds" and draw and holster their weapons with reflexive smoothness. From the control booth at the state-of-the-art firing range, trainees get their instructions on loading and firing. On-floor instructors provide individualized help. Each trainee must fire one thousand rounds each before they go out to the simulations, which involve both cutouts and live action.

Issued a 9-mm Sig Sauer semiautomatic pistol, the standard Secret Service weapon, each trainee is responsible for the cleaning, maintenance, and action readiness of his or her weapon. At the end of the eleven-week course, agents possess the weapon full-time—it becomes theirs and not just for use in training exercises. Agents are also trained in the use of the Service's other weapons of choice: the M 16, the Uzi, and the Agent K-MPS.

Indoors at Beltsville, agents pore over movies of assassinations and attempted assassination. The screen is filled with the Zapruder film of President Kennedy's assassination, tapes of the two attempts on President Ford, and the assault that nearly killed President Reagan. Numerous other assassinations and attempted assassinations flicker on the screen; agents at Beltsville analyze both domestic and foreign incidents—Robert F. Kennedy, President Park of South Korea, George Wallace, Martin Luther King Jr., Malcolm X, Jack Ruby's murder of Oswald, and Mrs. Ferdinand Marcos.

Called the "James Rowley Training Center" after former Director James Rowley (1961–1973), the facility's very name testifies to the Secret

Service's so-called "troubled years," the era when Rowley's agency became the first to lose a president (Kennedy) and faced political sabotage of the Service by the political cutthroats in the Nixon White House. Hiring additional agents and instituting both changes recommended by the Warren Commission and by his own staff, Rowley is credited with strengthening the Service after the tragedy in Dallas.

The "teachers" at the Rowley Training Center are agents with special expertise in a given area or outside experts (especially in counterfeiting courses). The faculty tutors agents in "unarmed combat skills" and put them through rigorous weight training for bulk and stamina.

At Beltsville, the constant screech of tires and grinding of gears prove how seriously the Service takes driver training. All agents take a course in evasive driving, learning behind the wheel of high-speed "performance" vehicles, such as the Chevy Camaro, how to maintain "correct lines" in guiding the vehicle through "difficult corners" and to operate at high speed. The centerpiece of evasive action is the "J-Turn," in which the vehicle executes a screeching pivot to turn on a dime and blast off in the opposite direction. At Beltsville, agents come way from the track with the ability to perform J-turns without losing much momentum and are able to totally shake a threat or tailing car.

Though the Service's usual follow-up car behind the presidential limo is a Chevy Suburban, the Beltsville philosophy is that if agents can learn to drive fast and safely in a fast car, their skills in the driver's seat will carry over to less-responsive vehicles such as the bulky Suburban. Perhaps most important, an agent at the wheel of the presidential limo—difficult to drive fast because they are so heavy—can even J-turn them, which is an impressive piece of driving: the vehicle executes a screeching pivot, turning on a dime and blasting off in the opposite direction without losing much momentum.

In the driver-training courses, agents not only learn how to drive an armored limousine and a follow-up car and to use evasive steering, but also how to handle blowouts from bullets and to control braking. Once the techniques are learned on a track at Beltsville, agents wheel out into the nearby cities and suburbs of Maryland for practice under real traffic conditions. Though trainees are carefully supervised by instructors, no sign atop the limousine announces "student driver."

Simulation and instant reply are also primary training methods. Agents practice escorting a make-believe president through crowds and in and out of vehicles in exercises during which spontaneous simulated attacks or medical emergency procedures are videotaped. Later, they are played back and discussed by Beltsville's students and instructors.

The centerpieces of Beltsville are its two massive mock-ups—"Hogan's Alley" and the "White House." Hogan's Alley looks much like a Hollywood back lot, containing a street and a façade of several buildings approximately one city block in length. On foot and in passing "motorcades," agents sharpen their protective skills at the "Alley," where a computer-controlled program sends cutout figures popping up without warning in windows and doorways and along the street. The figures are movable and bullet sensitive, that is, a handful of "assassins" having an audio "shooting" capacity, and appear for different lengths of time, carrying a variety of objects from briefcases and umbrellas to guns. The agent's task is to quickly determine which figures are assassins and which are innocent civilians and to react without gunning down an ordinary citizen whom the wily computer has programmed to appear suddenly in a second-story window holding what looks like a gun but is only an umbrella. The simulations are complex and demanding: a cutout of a woman pushing a baby carriage may move in front of a figure who begins "firing" at the presidential limousine.

The scene of these tests and exercises, the "tactical village," is an eerie, Disneyesque mock-up of "Main Street USA," not just a façade but three dimensional. With laser pistols aimed and fired by trainees at the cutout targets that pop up in various structures and places, agents are scored on hitting correct targets and lose points for hitting "friendly" targets. Sometimes the targets are live and not cutouts: "Much active Secret Service training is designed to make the student fail. The theory is, you learn by your mistakes."

In April 1982, the Service announced its plans to build the ultimate mock-up—the White House and vicinity. The $1.6 million project was part of an expansion program that extended Beltsville's mock-ups to include an entire minicity complete with shopping mall and numerous streets. Agent James Boyle said "Most of our agents work there [in and around the White House] at one time or another on temporary or permanent assignment. Each of those environments have their idiosyncracies, and that's what we want our people to be familiar with."

Secret Service agents used to be taken to the actual area for training—to the White House and to Lafayette Park. "It's not feasible to run them through there," said one Secret Service instructor.

The mock White House lacks realism in some respects. There is no Oval Office for agents to train in. On the other hand, at the Beltsville White House, trainees can conduct exercises that would be impractical in the real setting, such as engaging in a simulated firefight with terrorists on the "south lawn" and chasing them along Pennsylvania Avenue.

At Beltsville, agents learn how to handle potential attacks on a presidential helicopter. Choppers are used frequently for the president and other protectees, especially on jaunts from the White House to one of Washington's airports or vice versa. Agents are strapped during "Helicopter Evacuation Training" into the "dunker," an open metal structure containing a helicopter seat. Suddenly the dunker plunges underwater and often goes in upside down. Disoriented from crashing into the water, agents must escape the dunker while putting on a portable breathing device called a "canister." When one device runs out, antipanic training requires the trainee to switch to a new device without running out of air; eventually, the student activates a floatation device that propels him to the surface. Presumably, in the "real thing," agents would calmly put their canisters on and help the president or other dignitaries escape a chopper in water and guide them to the surface.

Beltsville also produces another type of Secret Service graduate—of the four-legged variety. At the facility's Canine Training center, the Service trains Belgian Malinois, a specialized breed the size of a German Shepherd, to detect bombs and explosives by smell. The highly intelligent dogs are also trained to attack "if necessary."

As the Beltsville complex proves, Secret Service training is highly sophisticated in its technology and techniques and ambitious in its scope. Still, eleven weeks is not a long time to turn rookies into professional agents, considering the dual-purpose nature of the training—investigative and protective. Some protective skills, such as falling off a moving limousine without getting hurt, can be mastered in a short time; others, such as scanning a crowd to watch for quick and threatening movements, cannot be learned simply "in the classroom." Looking for the faces of dangerous individuals and simultaneously holding a specified proximity to the protectee are skills that need time, practice, and, most of all, field experience. Complicating the already daunting task of protecting a president and other dignitaries, the range and "delivery means" of potential threats faced by agents has changed in recent years as international terrorism soars. The dangers of real-world protection means that there is even more ground to cover during the portion of the eleven weeks the Secret Service devotes to protective training.

The Service's training does not and cannot end with a Beltsville diploma. Agents receive continuous advanced training during their entire careers in areas from firearms requalifications to emergency-medical refresher courses. In "simulated crisis training scenarios," agents assigned to protective details are required to participate in exercises termed "Attack on Principal" (AOP) and simulating real-world situations of attack, crowd control, and other spontaneous incidents. Agents get immediate feedback on the effectiveness and correctness of their responses.

Agents assigned to investigative duties in field offices have a different kind of postgraduate training. In such "continuing education" Secret Service courses as Fundamentals of Banking, Advanced Access Device Fraud, Questioned Documents, Undercover Operations, Telecommunications Fraud and Financial Institutions Fraud, agents refine the skills learned at Beltsville. Agents are also "encouraged" to attend training sessions offered by other law-enforcement agencies.

A cultural sign of the times emerges in what the Servicel labels "management and individual development" courses of the kind that many private and public-sector organizations suggest or require for their employee. Ethics, Diversity, Interpersonal Awareness, Practical Leadership, and Introduction to Supervision are all topics that are part of an agent's education today.

Though nearly all professions benefit from periodic reeducation, the Service is one of those organizations for whom it is an absolute necessity rather than a professional-development luxury or self-improvement tangent. Like CPAs or tax lawyers who could cost their clients millions or place them under the penalties of the IRS by providing outmoded advice, the Service's dual missions demand new techniques to keep up with the times. Faced with people committing credit-card fraud or producing phony Treasury bonds, an ever-expanding arsenal of new weapons for assassination, and new delivery systems for such potential threats as germ or chemical warfare, the Service must constantly teach even its most veteran agents state-of-the-art methods to fight counterfeiters, assassins, and terrorists.

# THE SECRET SERVICE

Despite all the protective duties, the bulk of the agency's investigations focus upon counterfeiting and forgery. These activities generate a combined total of several hundred thousand cases a year. Counterfeiting remains a daunting problem even if not as severe as during Civil War, when nearly one-third of all money in circulation was phony.

Today's counterfeiters use a wide range of sophisticated techniques and technology. Scanners, photocopiers, plates for printing bills made by etching with acid rather than engraving by hand—these and many other tools can churn out a flood of bogus bills. The more that technology advances, the greater grows the pressure on the Secret Service to put counterfeiters out of business before huge amounts of phony bills get into circulation.

Of all the agency's duties, catching counterfeiters is the one that depends most upon public cooperation, and the Service actively cultivates public support for this mission. Quick recognition of phony money and prompt reporting by citizens enables the Service to zero in on the counterfeiters more rapidly.

The Service's public relations efforts, meager as they are in comparison with some federal agencies, emphasize public education and participation in stopping counterfeiters. Its glossy brochure "Know Your Money," the descendant of the successful anticounterfeiting campaign of World War II, is the largest, most ambitious one the Service publishes. The brochure features blowups of bills with instructions on how to detect counterfeit money by scrutinizing the presidential portrait, the serial number, and the paper. The usually publicity-shy Service even awards U.S. Savings Bonds to citizens whose alert reporting helps nab counterfeiters, and it presents these awards with as much press coverage as possible.

According to the Service, the modern counterfeiter is usually someone with expertise in photography and/or printing. Phony bills are usually wholesaled to some group or criminal organization that will attempt to pass them, with the counterfeiter typically netting 10 to 50 percent of the face value.

Secret Service laboratories analyze phony bills for fingerprints and also trace the materials used in making them. Using special chemicals that react to traces of human perspiration, the Service can detect latent prints on bills, bonds, and checks. Each year, agents seize massive stashes of counterfeit bills before they hit the nation's businesses and banks.

Agents frequently work undercover to infiltrate counterfeiting operations, sometimes posing as underworld buyers who are looking to purchase large blocks of counterfeit money, stock certificates, or bonds. Such purchases usually involve large amounts of cash. In one case, a counterfeiter offered an undercover agent $5 million in phony Treasury notes for the price of $450,000. The Service will also set up pseudo "fencing" operations so that they can make contact with a number of counterfeit rings.

In 2002, forgery is the second major area of the Secret Service's money mission. Each year staggering sums of money are lost nationwide because of forged bonds and checks. Blank checks or bonds stolen from mail boxes or banks are cashed with forged signatures, and, in a single year, the Secret Service will investigate well over 100,000 cases involving (forged) government checks. In one case, a postal clerk swiped 600 blank government checks and sold them before the Service caught him.

As with counterfeiting, the Service believes that public alertness is the key to prevention of check forgery and fraud. The agency publishes a pamphlet entitled "Know Your Endorser," which encourages people to check carefully the endorser's identification and to watch for obvious clues, such as a woman in her twenties cashing a Social Security check.

The Service's Office of Investigations has "questioned-document examiners," experts who determine whether signatures on bonds, checks, and letters are real, as well as whether the document is otherwise counterfeit. These analysts are annually called upon to work with nearly 100,000 questionable documents relating to thousands of the agency's cases.

Over the past four decades, the agency's array of anticounterfeiting cases reveals how hard it is to keep pace with, let alone stay ahead of, innovative countefeiters. In 1961, a group of seasoned criminals set up a counterfeiting operation that churned out $250,000 worth of topnotch bogus $20 federal reserve notes by January 1962. Cunningly, the counterfeiters destroyed their "factory" and tossed the debris into a river to cover their trail before passing any of the notes. Next, the ringleaders deployed "shovers" to circulate the bills in a range of cities such as Philadelphia, Detroit, New York, and Washington, D.C.; the phony notes soon turned up in over thirty states. Acting on a tip, the Service's Special Detail, veteran investigative agents hailing from field offices across the nation, were assigned to the Cleveland office where they launched a skillful undercover operation to "rope"— infiltrate—the murky world of local counterfeiters. Several agents traced the defunct counterfeiting plant to the basement of a home leased by several people in a Cleveland suburb. Within three months, the Special Detail not only rounded up thirty-five suspects, but also found the broken equipment and plates on the rive bottom. The ring's architects were convicted, with only some $74,000 of the $250,000 in bogus bills making it into circulation.

A decade later, in 1973, Secret Service agents reaped the agency's largest haul (to that date) of counterfeit bills. Seven counterfeiters had established several "supply (distribution) houses" in Florida and set up their equipment at the home of one of the plotters in North Carolina. When the Secret Service discovered that a suspected counterfeiter had ordered high-grade paper from a paper supply company, agents launched an investigation. The man was the partner of the North Carolina counterfeiter.

The Secret Service arrested the man who had ordered the paper, but he would not give up his partner. Then, the Nashville field office learned of a similar order of high-quality paper. According to the Secret Service's account of the case, the Nashville clue led straight to the counterfeiters:

> The license plate on the car used was registered to the same individual making the North Carolina purchase. Efforts to locate the man were intensified. Several days later, agents in Cincinnati received information indicating that the fugitive and another man had been questioned by local police and released following the passing of a single counterfeit note. Ten days later, one of the principals was apprehended in Minnesota. Agents found a telephone number in his possession and traced it to a residence near Chattanooga, Tennessee, where they observed the vehicle used in the North Carolina supply house purchase.

They obtained search and arrest warrants and raided the premises on January 4, 1973. Five suspects were arrested at the plant site, and a sixth was arrested in Florida. It took agents three days to sort and count the bogus notes. Of the $6.2 million in counterfeit bills produced by the group, later investigations revealed only $160 had been passed on to the public.

In a far more exotic locale, the Secret Service broke up a counterfeiting ring in 1985 in what became known as the "King Kong Case." The story began in Hong Kong in 1972 with the arrest of a skilled counterfeiter named Tin Cheung Wong. Released from prison in 1974, he moved to

Bangkok in 1975 and created another counterfeiting operation, training graphic artist Ah Sin Lee, nicknamed "King Kong, " in the counterfeiter's craft. With Tin Cheung Wong's death, in 1979, King Kong and Wong's chief distributor, travel agent Ming Cheung Wong (not related), took over the operation.

Lee traveled to Malaysia, where he spent a year or so crafting near-flawless $100 counterfeit bills. As the Secret Service notes, "The excellent quality of the notes assured their acceptance all over the world. Because of the counterfeit's very deceptive nature, even the banks were unable to detect them."

As the Secret Service became increasingly aware of the notes passing from the Far East into American banks, the agency's Forensic Services Division pored over the paper used in the counterfeit notes and tried to unravel the techniques the unknown artist or artists were using. The agency discovered that the bills were circulating in as many as ten different makes of paper.

Meticulously tracking the bills' circulation routes to a Hong Kong Chinese crime syndicate, the Secret Service and Hong Kong police fingered Ming Cheung Wong as the man supplying the notes to the gangsters. They arrested him and three accomplices in May 1984, but the search went on for the man who was actually creating the notes.

The eighteen-monthlong pursuit of the counterfeiter led to Bangkok on June 13. Special Agents—along with U.S. Embassy personnel in Bangkok, U.S. Drug Enforcement Administration investigators assigned to the Bangkok Embassy, and the Bangkok Metropolitan Narcotics Unit—busted King Kong, who was caught red-handed as he was working on a new $50 bill. Agents not only seized him, but also his press and tools, ending the run of a counterfeiter who had printed and circulated nearly $4 million in counterfeit $100 bills and $1 million in counterfeit travelers' checks.

As counterfeiters and forgers turn to ever-changing technology to improve their bogus bills and launch new methods of financial fraud, the Secret Service works hard to keep pace. In May 1993, an agency investigation uncovered a scheme that could have brought millions of illicit dollars to three suspects. Their "tool" was an Automated Teller Machine (ATM).

The trio, presenting themselves as representatives of a financial services company, installed a portable ATM in a mall in Manchester, Connecticut. Over the next two weeks, this ATM seemingly functioned as any other such machine did, handling transactions at the mall while logging account information and the Personal Identification Numbers (PINs) of customers. But there was one transaction the machine did not handle: it had been programmed to inform customers that it was "out of cash" whenever someone tried to make a withdrawal. Unwitting customers walked away thinking that they had been "inconvenienced, not defrauded." The three men had clandestinely shut down the mall's ATMs, forcing people to use the fraudulent machine.

After two weeks, the men hauled away the ATM—with its account and PIN numbers. The con men encoded the information onto blank white plastic cards, and, using the PIN and account numbers on the new "bank cards," traveled to ATMs along the East Coast, emptying people's accounts.

As the scam surfaced, Secret Service agents sprang into action. With the investigation underway, agents obtained search warrants that resulted in the seizure of six additional ATMs, computer equipment, and other paraphernalia used in the manufacture of the counterfeit credit cards. Agents learned that two of the suspects had been involved in financial crimes for over ten years and that they had bankrolled this ATM operation, utilizing "kiting" schemes with fraudulent credit cards and loan applications. In addition, they produced counterfeit cashier's checks, which were used for defrauding two auction houses of more than $300,000 and $400,000, respectively, in fraud against a major credit card company. One of the suspects was also involved in illegal arms sales to drug cartel members and Mexican nationals through his gun shop. More than three hundred weapons were sold, many of which had been converted to fully automatic machine guns equipped with silencers. The suspects were arrested, found guilty, and sentenced to prison terms.

The Service's running battle against innovative counterfeiting, forgery, and other financial fraud notwithstanding, the agency's protective mission remains its "trademark" in the public's view. In post–September 11 America, terrorism has begun to reshape the Secret Service. More changes will come as they did in the traumatic days following the assassination of President John F. Kennedy on November 22, 1963.

# CHAPTER 8
# THE POLITICS OF PROTECTION

*"A Living Nightmare in a Democracy"*
—*Secret Service Director H. Stuart Knight, 1971–1983*

T here is no Democratic or Republican way to pave a street."
So goes the hoary political bromide. Ideally, there should
also be no partisan or political dimension to presidential protection. It is the image that the Secret Service cultivates for the public,
and who would argue that protecting the lives of political leaders is a
governmental function that *should* be divorced from politics? The truth
is somewhat different.

To much of the public, the Secret Service does appear to have an apolitical image akin to that of the British civil service, which prides itself on
serving Conservative or Labor governments with equal effectiveness.
People genuinely believe that the agency will protect any occupant of the
White House and take a bullet for him or her without question, let alone
question of ideology, whether Democrat or Republican. Further fostering
the image, the agency has a merit system complete with entrance exams and
civil service job protections, which are designed to insulate the organization
from patronage politics.

Traditionally, the director of the Secret Service is a career agent who has
come up through the ranks. Although the director serves at the pleasure of
the secretary of the treasury, a presidential political appointee, there is no
tradition of sacking the old Secret Service head when a new president takes
office. Even the agents who head up the White House protective detail
sometimes continue in their post after a change of presidents—testimony to

the neutral, nonpolitical nature in some aspects of the job. Agent Jerry Parr headed the White House detail under Carter and continued for the first year of the Reagan presidency, even though the somber Carter and the charismatic Reagan possessed personalities as different as the men's party labels.

This kind of stability suggests that the Service's protective mission keeps the agency steady amid the strong currents of politics that roil the American presidency. After all, the protective mission is a consensual one: neither the Congress, nor the press, nor political interest groups will argue against trying to keep presidents alive or against the necessity for a protective organization. Other bureaucracies such as the Department of Education have their very existence questioned by warring legislators, and organizations such as the Environmental Protection Agency must constantly try to carry out a mission redefined by the push and pull of presidents and Congress alike. Americans, however, see the Secret Service differently; they view it as somehow above the political fray. And yet the day-to-day operation of the Secret Service is highly political. Though Robert F. Kennedy once asserted, "Politics and protection don't mix," they actually do mix in every area of the Service's protective mission.

Political considerations, dynamics, and realities do—and always have—shape the style and effectiveness of protection. The Service's operations and duties are in many ways dominated not by merit and consensus, but by the vagaries of politics. As with every other government body, the agency encounters *politics* in the best sense—the presidency as the highest political office in the land, an elective office beholden to the governed for its powers—and *politics* in the worse sense—patronage, corruption of the agency's mission, and partisan subversion of protective methods and procedures.

The Secret Service's most vital mission is to protect the president, the nation's single most vaunted *political* office, but because there are no laws or accepted rules governing the interaction of agents and the president, the Service has no set guidelines to buffer its men and women from the overwhelming sense of politics that dominates the presidency. And the manner in which each president conducts his own brand of politics can make him the bane or the buddy—sometimes both—of the agents sworn to protect him.

The Treasury Department report on the attempted assassination of President Reagan concluded, "The means exist to fully protect the president; unfortunately, he must decide whether in availing himself of these means he will reduce his ability to lead and his effectiveness in office."

The report does not seek to blame presidents for any protective problems; it simply points out that only a presidential "recluse" can count on foolproof security. By nature and training, presidents are politicians, highly successful ones. They do not reach the White House by isolating themselves but by wading into and winning over a majority of voters. Once a man sits in the Oval Office, he cannot effectively exercise the presidential power by being a recluse, and Americans expect that politicians will get out and campaign to be president and to remain president. As George McGovern's former campaign manager Frank Mankiewicz put it: "There's no way you can run for President on TV or riding around in a bubble-top limousine."

The life of Secret Service agents would be far easier if a president could campaign that way, but the public will have none of it. When voters turn out to greet or take the measure of a presidential candidate and are thwarted by Secret Service protection, they don't like it one bit. One reporter describes an incident in the 1980 presidential campaign, a scene that recurs frequently on the primary trail and in the general election:

> In Iowa, George Tans, a *New York Times* photographer, said that many of those who went to see Governor Reagan told him the protection "was overdone and they resented it." Said one disaffected Republican, "I shook George Bush's hand; when Reagan was here I couldn't get near him."

As the Secret Service understands but will never embrace, politics is a marketplace seething with potential threats at any instant and in any location. The agency knows that if one candidate appears too distant or reclusive, one or more of his challengers will—by virtue of his personality or of advice from his campaign managers—go out of his way to appear accessible and gregarious, a strategy that worked beautifully for Reagan and Clinton. Both men understood that "pressing the flesh" works; for their protective details, the two presidents' love of working a crowd made every trip outside the White House a challenge for agents scanning the throngs for that one flash of menace. In many ways, a candidate or a president's personal style of politics dictates the type of protection his agents must use.

# THE SECRET SERVICE

The reality for the Secret Service is that the political, as well as the protective, timbre of the job never stops, not even once a president is elected. Agents realize that if their protectee tries to hole up in the Rose Garden, his opponents and the press will criticize his unwillingness to "stay in touch with the people" and his "increasing isolation." Even if the public accepts presidential isolation because of some protracted crisis—such as President George W. Bush has faced since September 11, 2001—or because the president has an immense reserve of popularity, the political marketplace will eventually allow a presidential challenger or successor to lambaste a "reclusive" president as out of touch. And the political reality for the agency is that it will have to protect the president or candidate who is wading into crowds and always into potential harm's way.

Agents have witnessed several modern presidents who became increasingly reclusive with their power already in decline or with lame-duck status, such as Richard Nixon and Lyndon B. Johnson. When Jimmy Carter's detail was guarding him during the Iranian hostage crisis of 1980, they saw a man with a valid excuse for not getting out much on the campaign trail, but a president who suffered the costs of that isolation at the ballot box. Daily, the agents protecting challenger Reagan and President Carter experienced the political climate of a hard-charging campaign for one and a crisis preventing the other from hitting the political stump often enough.

For Secret Service agents of any era, the job would be easier if Americans really behaved according to a Gallup poll that shows that as much as 45 percent of the public agrees that the "old-style" politics— shaking hands, kissing babies—is just too risky for our leaders. Agents know that presidents, candidates, and the public only buy that idea in the abstract; once presidential primary and caucus time rolls around, the public wants to see their candidates up close and resent it if the Secret Service details keep citizens from getting that handshake, a few words, or a wink from the candidate.

The politics of protection take a different tack in the wake of an assassination attempt. Everyone talks differently. "This macho stuff has to stop," snapped a Ford aide, referring to direct public contact in the aftermath of Ford's second brush with a would-be assassin. Former Senate Majority Leader Mike Mansfield concurred, "I do not think a president has a right to place his life in danger. It is not the man concerned, it is the office, in effect, which is of paramount importance."

# THE POLITICS OF PROTECTION

The agency has learned that such public sentiments for a president's or candidate's safety soon ebb and that politics as usual regains its hold; officeholders are even more afraid to be labeled a "wimp" than to face a potential assassin. In the view of presidents, Gerald Ford's words ring true, "The American people ought to have an opportunity to see firsthand or to listen more directly with their president."

For agents assigned to protect a president or presidential candidate, the "face in the crowd" along the campaign trail is not the only nightmare. Incessant political fund-raisers of all sizes and varieties from high rollers' party dinners to giant venues could always be the one where an assassin is lurking. Whether as candidate or president, such fund-raising requires dinners, cocktail parties, handshakes, and contact with thousands of people who are courted primarily for their dollars instead of their votes. Agents can never assume that everyone in the room is "okay."

Because most presidents and candidates are politicians at their very core, they often relish contact with the public, thriving on the attention and even adulation. With Lyndon Johnson, agents discovered that his "pressing the flesh" bordered on an obsession. As Hubert Humphrey explained, there are two reasons that politicians do it, "First, it is good politics; second, and most important, it makes you feel good. It makes you feel very good."

It always makes the Secret Service wary.

The shifting political tides of the past three decades have drastically changed the "campaign hours" that agents put in long before the general election. It was once possible to become the party nominee by meeting with only a few dozen people, the political bosses who tightly controlled large blocks of convention delegates via their state or city political machines. As late as 1968, when Humphrey and Nixon were nominated, there were only seventeen primaries, and the vast majority of convention delegates were selected without the direct input of the voters. Now, in state after state, the voters are given a chance to express their preference for a nominee, to have *their* chance to see the candidates, which means that agents are on duty round-the-clock at stops all over the nation.

A one-day nationwide primary would make the Service's protective mission infinitely easier, but politics dictate otherwise. In every presidential election cycle, agents must do advance and protective work on a seemingly endless trail of primaries, with candidates stumping all over the map, as agents fight exhaustion and the omnipresent fear that the wrong face in the crowd is out there. From truck stops to big cities, the public and the possible danger await.

Throughout a campaign, politics and protection constantly clash. Politics often win out—over the Secret Service's objections. With personal contact so crucial to getting elected, politicians frequently buck their protective agents in favor of pressing the flesh. The 1980 presidential campaign featured seven candidates who qualified for Secret Service protection but refused it at various points along the election trail. John Connally—no stranger to political violence, having been wounded in the assassination of President Kennedy—was one who refused. George H. W. Bush turned down protection in Iowa, preferring not "to look like a big shot" and wanting to "roll up his sleeves and talk with people."

Five Republican candidates refused protection at one time or another in 1980, as did independent candidate John Anderson and Democratic candidate Jerry Brown, who said, "Agents get between me and the people."

A Brown aide added, "In Iowa we saw Senator Kennedy's protection blocking highways, getting in the way the kind of one-to-one contact we prefer—we don't need that."

In the 1990s, Bill Clinton drove his agents crazy with his frequent unscheduled forays into crowds. The sight of Agent Larry Cockell clutching him by the belt, the arm, or his coattails became a familiar one.

The agency's perennial battle of protection versus politics extends far beyond the campaign and fund-raising trail. Any president's foreign-policy role takes on political shapes that often play havoc with protection. President Johnson's 1964 trip to Mexico offers a classic example. Because Mexican politics feature an even more pronounced variety of public contact and political symbolism than in America, it was an unwritten law in Mexican politics that presidents can never appear in public with any barrier between themselves and their people—no bulletproof shields, no bubble-top cars, nothing. The same was expected of visiting leaders of foreign nations.

In the furor after President Kennedy's assassination, many in the Secret Service assumed and hoped that his successors would never again ride in an open car. However, Johnson had two choices regarding his motorcade into Mexico City: he could ride in an open car with the president of Mexico, or he could ride in a closed car without his host. It was *not* an agonizing decision for the garrulous Johnson, who approached life fearlessly. The choice created anxiety among his staff and near-apoplexy for the White House protective detail. In the interests of diplomatic harmony and political courtesy, Johnson opted to ride in an open car alongside the Mexican president. Forced to accede to political considerations, agents did grueling advance work in Mexico City; the Service's security checks of potential sniper sites and roadways were far more intensive than had been the case in Dallas in 1963.

One Secret Service director, H. Stuart Knight (1973–1981), described presidential protection as "a living nightmare in a democracy." Because the Service operates in a democracy, agents cannot employ tactics or measures that strike the public and Congress as redolent of a police state. If agents are perceived as bullies or show even a glimmer of insensitivity to constitutional rights, they become an instant political liability to the president. The mere appearance of toughness or a chip-on-the-shoulder attitude by Secret Service agents can unleash political flak aimed at the White House, as well as the Service.

When the Service overreacts or appears overzealous in handling a crowd or screening a press corps, agents are excoriated by the public and the press—sometimes by the White House itself. The Service is aware of its place in a democratic system, and John Warner, a former public affairs director for the agency, describes the problem of establishing protective barriers in America, "We would like to move people back farther, but those we protect and the media would not allow it and it's not realistic in a democracy."

After an assassination attempt, the press and the politicians usually beat the drums for tighter security, for tougher controls. However, if the Service implements stricter security when there has been no recent assassination attempt or when the trauma of the attempt has passed, the media, politicians, and the public decry such "undemocratic" procedures, and political pressure engulfs the Service until agents accede to politics and ease up once again.

Melody Miller, an assistant press officer for Senator Edward M. Kennedy and a veteran of his 1980 presidential run, describes the intersection of politics and protection: "I was very good at being diplomatic: No you cannot do that; this you can do [Miller to the Secret Service]. The head of the detail [Agent Tom Quinn] was extraordinarily competent and professional, and gained the utmost respect [from the Kennedy staff]."

Also addressing politics versus protection, Eileen Parise, who has worked as an advance person in several administrations and is currently working in public relations for President George W. Bush, says: "Our job is to convey politics and message for that week [of a public event]. . . . It's our job to get the President seen and heard in near-perfect political settings; it's their [the Secret Service's] job to protect him as completely as possible. They want 99% level of confidence for the protectee."

In her experience, she finds her dealings with the agency a "wonderful relationship." Though acknowledging that disagreements between the Service and political staffers are "fairly common but not extreme," she adds, "We solve it on the ground, so that nothing goes back to the White House [in a disagreement between advance staff and the Secret Service, the dispute is taken to the president or White House chief of staff, a mode of resolution that neither the staff nor the Secret Service wants]. They [the Secret Service] never say 'No.' It is a negotiative process. Agents are colleagues, comrades. We consult them on what is and isn't going to fly. We agree to disagree."

Parise sees agents not as protective robots or security-wonk zealots, but as politically sensitive. She marvels at their ability to "persuade" other law-enforcement bodies and agencies to cooperate on the state, local, and foreign levels. "They *are* politics," she says of their political skills. "But when they overcompensate [for security] we draw the line."

In part, Parise says, the cooperative relationship comes from the staffers learning what the concerns and needs of the Secret Service are, and when they can be addressed, they are. "They teach us," she says. "They're very good at teaching us. . . .We really respect them, and, God knows, we don't want the president hurt. . . .They like stairs instead of elevators. They like to avoid glass. We think, in advance, how to help them."

One of the reasons Parise and her political advance colleagues listen to the Service is that they know that the agency is privy to intelligence reports about potential threats—reports that the staffers do not get, even though Parise has a top secret clearance. "They are better informed [than political staffs]," she observes.

Advance work for presidential trips and local events point out the constant tug between politics and protection. Four to five advance teams do work for the president, the vice president, and their wives. Always, the Secret Service wants a week or more to check out and plan any trip or event, but White House staffs are on a different time line: they try to plan five to seven days in advance, but cannot always do this because politics are often too spontaneous. It is particularly difficult during campaigns when there are several cities visited during a week. Both the White House staffers and the Secret Servce must coordinate with their local counterparts, trying to build trust in a frenzied period that is often days rather than weeks. Though a longer lead time for presidential trips is often possible—sometimes ten to fourteen days—other situations demand that protectees barnstorm somewhere in two days.

Three people head the coordination of events on the road: the lead White House staff person, the lead Secret Service agent, and the lead person from the White House Communications Office. Additionally, a "site person" usually coordinates events from fund-raisers to rallies; motorcades usually have a White House "motorcade staff person" who is assigned to work with the Secret Service.

According to Parise, Secret Service agents handle their assignments in a more stable and professional manner than political staffers. Staffers, she notes, are in and out of the administration, as they take on other assignments. Since September 11, 2001, the assignments of the Secret Service have been more of a "fire drill," the list of protectees expanded to include Bush's National Security Advisor, Condoleezza Rice, Senate Majority Leader Tom Daschle, and other congressional leaders. In her political dealing with the Service, Parise evinces her "utmost respect" for the agency as a "very elite group of people, well read, articulate, having political sense—all smart."

Not every political staffer seconds Parise's views. A highly placed staffer who worked for Democratic presidential candidates in the 1980s offers, "There is conflict every day between staff and Secret Service. They [agents] want to limit exposure and access. There is a lot of tension between the two. . . . Every day was back and forth. . . . As individuals [agents] you can get along, but as an institution, they are just not sensitive to the tension."

He says that the agents on the permanent detail, who you would ride the plane with, were "okay." But the "local agents" went "way out of the way" to hinder politics. "This agent was being a jerk. Got tough on student radios being on. It was a never-ending hassle. The guys in the pool [permanent protective detail] were okay. They get to know you. But the local agents try to ride the advance people. Local agents were overbearing jerks."

Another Democratic staffer supports Parise's assertions, "These guys [the Secret Service] were very professional. There was a tremendous imbalance. I was in my early 20s and given all this great authority, to set the vice presidential calendar, to call and say, 'I'm calling from the White House.' But in the field, you had an organization that is more professional than the political side. It always amazed me how young the [political] advance people were. We used to laugh as we boarded a plane at some airport to set up a vice presidential trip, 'If they only knew who we really were.' . . . The Secret Service was a real job. We [political staffers] were stringers, consultants with no training or routine. We had to integrate with the Secret Service."

He saw his relationship with the Secret Service as a "fairly reasonable" thing to work out when it came to the conflicts between politics and protection. "Others saw it as a relationship full of conflict," he says, "but there seemed to be a way of working things out.

"Guys in the lead-agent position were okay. There was no instance where they pulled us away [from the rope line or a stop]. . . . Rural Iowa was more casual for them. Urban settings were more intense. But there was a way of working it out."

Despite the politico's youth and stringer status, he did not feel condescended to or rebuffed by most of the agents he dealt with. Still, he did notice some "attitude" on the part of a handful: "More police-like, militaristic types, real cut-and-dried, never saw their eyes behind the sunglasses."

Conversely, he also points a finger at the political advance teams and staffers: "A lot of people who did advance work were hotshots. Always feeling that they must get results [even if it meant] abusing and offending people."

As the ex-political staffer says, it is not always White House Chief of Staff Andy Card dealing with the head of the White House Secret Service detail. In other venues, Secret Service agents who are not on the presidential protection "all-star team" deal with kid politicos who often have more political authority than political experience.

The former political aide states, "As a general rule, most of the agents I worked with were pretty real guys. I was surprised. They really believe in what they're doing . . . fully prepared to take the hit a [bullet for a protectee]. Political people don't treat the Secret Service particularly well. But they [the Secret Service] get great respect from their law-enforcement peers."

# THE POLITICS OF PROTECTION

Providing a Secret Service view of politics versus protection, a retired agent contends:

> It's difficult to find a medium. The Secret Service *can* overrule a president, but you'd better be on solid ground when you do it. Agents must be political themselves, show good political judgment: "Mr. President, I don't think we should do this. I'm not going to approve this stop [on the campaign trail]." Agents need to be sure of themselves and not just challenge the president unprepared. You need the support of the presidential staff. This is "politics." You must rally staff support and have good reasoning, then the president will agree. Internal politics and how it works is the key. . . . A Secret Service agent is a security person, an investigator, and a politician. And you better cover all bases to be effective.

Another retired agent, Chris Von Holt, discusses the effort to get both politicians and agents to work together as best they can:

> About a week or so ahead of time the advance team would come in from the President's full-time detail in Washington, D.C., and they would interact with our office . . . set up the advance of where he is going to be and what he is going to do, in conjunction with the political staff that would also come from out of town. There are a lot of entities that are involved in anything the President does: there's us, the political staff, military components. . . . If he's going to go to a hotel you have the hotel staff and people in various functions there. . . . If he's going to go to a speech site you've got the host committee at the speech. . . . So there are a lot of entities that all have to act together.

Today, the enhanced security since September 11, 2001, has compelled political staffers and agents to work more closely with each other but has created tremendous friction between the Secret Service and the Washington press corps, with agents unrelenting in instituting heightened procedures for checking credentials and screening the White House press pool. If reporters feel abused by agents and uniformed officers, the president and his staff notice. As former Nixon aide John Erlichman once described it, the proper "care and feeding" of the White House press corps is a key element in the success of any administration, and the president cannot risk having a press constantly at odds with his protective detail. Both the press and the agency know that the chief executive has the political wherewithal to pressure the Service into loosening up on faces they know and see every day, faces that pose no threat whatsoever to the president's safety.

Part of the ongoing uneasiness between the press and the agency is a Secret Service belief that a would-be assassin can infiltrate the press corps. In 1981, John Hinckley sneaked in among the reporters outside the Washington Hilton to open up on President Reagan. In 1972, the Service tried to strengthen security for the president and for presidential candidates by implementing tighter security checks on the press, precisely to prevent a would-be assassin from hiding among the press corps and gaining close access to the candidate. The Service informed all reporters who wished to cover the 1972 Democratic national convention in Miami that they had to submit their names and considerable personal data to the Service for a security check. Tougher procedures for the White House Press Corps were also instituted. Of course, many in the press retorted that the Service had failed to adequately scan the *crowd*—not the press corps—outside the Hilton.

Reaction from the media and the public was swift and intense, with a committee of reporters accusing the Secret Service of usurping the press-accreditation process for the Democratic Convention. When several well-known reporters were denied convention press passes on security grounds, they took the Service to court. One news organization branded the stricter procedures "an unprecedented veto over who might cover the convention," and a "threat" to freedom of the press.

Although the *New York Times* and the *Washington Post* were singled out by the Service and the FBI, the Secret Service responded that it had no interest in any reporter's ideology or associations. It simply wanted to make sure that no individual who had previously made threats against any protectee would gain special access provided by a press pass. As the constitutional issues involved in conflicts between freedom of the press and effective security were hotly debated, public pressure mounted against the agency. In the end, the reporters generated enough political pressure to force the Service to back down and abandon its stricter standards. But the conflicts between freedom and protection remained unresolved. Today, as the war against terrorism unfolds, the conflicts are flaring again.

As Director Stafford and his predecessors have all learned, the Secret Service's balancing act of providing tight protection without trampling on constitutional rights is a tough proposition and one exacerbated in moments of national crisis. The Service pays a heavy political and sometimes legal price when it strays too far in its pursuit of protection. After the back-to-back assassination attempts on President Ford, agents were especially keyed up when dealing with crowds. In Skokie, Illinois, a young man, his hands thrust deep into his pockets, stood in a crowd of spectators as President Ford approached. An alert Secret Service agent ordered the young bystander to take his hands out of his pockets as a security precaution. The man refused. The agent and several policemen jumped him and hauled him away; afterward, it was determined that the man had presented no threat to the president. A number of reporters criticized the agency, but most of the public did not view the incident as troubling.

Still, other such incidents do not end so painlessly for the Service. In 1980, the organization made a public apology to Jane Margolis, a militant San Francisco union leader, and gave her $3,500 as an out-of-court settlement for her lawsuit for false arrest against the Service. In 1979, Margolis had shown up at a Detroit union convention intending to berate President Carter for his alleged "antilabor practices" when he arrived to address the gathering. Agents spotted her and decided she posed trouble. They dragged her in handcuffs from the hall and held her for forty minutes before releasing her.

When reporters pressed the Service about the case, the agency's rejoinder was that it was all a misunderstanding. The agent involved was merely assisting a Detroit police officer who "believed that the arrest was being made for violation of federal law." Margolis, however, sued the agrency for false arrest, winning not only the settlement but also a formal public apology from the agency.

When agents become fatigued or unusually tense, they have sometimes proven heavy-handed in protecting a president or candidate, and the political fallout can be intense, depending upon the status of persons who are the targets of alleged overzealousness by agents. Immediately after Arthur Bremer shot George Wallace, *New York Times* reporter Nan Robertson ran into a problem at the hospital where the grievously wounded Alabama governor had been taken. Robertson, using a telephone in the hospital's out-patient clinic to phone in her story, was ordered by a Secret Service agent to leave, but she ignored him and continued to dictate her story. According to the *Times,* Special Agent Joseph Herman then picked Robertson up, put an armlock on her, and threw her out into the hall. The diminutive reporter was alleged to have "crashed on the floor and skidded down the corridor head first into the opposite wall."

Media and public outrage exploded around the agency. The Washington Press Club filed a formal protest with the Service, as did the Reporters' Committee For a Free Press and the *New York Times.* To Secret Service Director James Rowley, Max Frankel, the *Times*'s Washington bureau chief, snapped off a letter calling the incident "an unprovoked and malicious assault." The Service was compelled to offer a public apology to Robertson.

With both constitutional and political factors constantly colliding with security, the Service has long griped that they cannot always conduct intel-ligence gathering or set up protective measures without complaints from the president, the public, and the press. Some agents complain that they are afraid to place suspects under surveillance for fear of being sued or being accused of using "Gestapo tactics." Despite such fears, the Service must—and usually does—operate within the boundaries of an assumption of innocence until proven guilty and of citizens' rights to privacy.

According to Professor Charles R. Halpern, director of the Institute for Public Representation at Georgetown University Law Center, being identi-fied by the Secret Service as a "threat" to the president can have "devastat-ing effects on the life of the person" so identified. Halpern asserts that the Service can legally intervene to incarcerate a person identified as a poten-tial threat only if the person is "arguably mental ill." But the problem for the agency is that many individuals whom the Service perceives as a threat do not fall into this category.

The politics surrounding such explosive social issues as mental illness also encroach upon the protective mission of the Secret Service. The hard evidence that a person who is a potential threat might be mentally ill can be difficult to come by, even if the Service regards the person as unstable; under existing privacy laws, the Service cannot talk to the psychiatrist of any suspect, no matter how "dangerous" the person appears to be, without the person's permission. Without psychiatric data in many cases, the agency is hard-pressed to demonstrate mental illness and stands wide open to lawsuits for false arrest if it takes action against an individual without sufficient proof of mental problems.

Privacy rights also prevent the Service from employing its own psychiatrists to analyze agency files of potentially dangerous persons in order to discern patterns or develop clues that a citizen might be planning to kill a president. Without such guideposts, the Service is not only hampered in using its own data files, but is also legally forbidden from opening its files of at least forty thousand names to consultants without the permission of the subjects.

Even though the mental health and psychiatric professions cooperate extensively with the Service in its efforts to identify dangerous persons and to predict violent behavior, the cooperation is informal. These professions seem committed to keeping a safe distance between themselves and the Service from fears that they might be somehow "taken over" by government interests that are not always in the best interests of a patient. Some psychiatrists fear that extensive linkage with the government might create the appearance of an alarming trend in which definitions of "insanity" become political.

Part of the Service's problem is that the boundaries of constitutional rights are far from clear-cut. Also, the agency is always caught up in conflicting and shifting political views from the press and the public, who will both demand tougher protective measures in the wake of an event such as Hinckley's attempt on Reagan's life but will then turn on the Service and charge it with running amok. One Secret Service agent observed bitterly, "The congressmen who are howling now [for tougher security] are the first to complain when one of their constituent's rights have been violated."

Even the Service's arsenal of protective devices is as much a product of American political culture as American technology. The National Commission on the Causes and Prevention of Violence concluded that an impressive array of awesome, James Bond–style protective devices such as poison pellets and darts were available to the agency, but that "they could not be utilized when the dangers inherent in them or the impression they would make upon onlookers were considered."

Like all public agencies, the Secret Service also has its share of internal politics. Its relationships with Congress, with the Treasury Department, and with federal and local agencies create a rich, often troubling political tableau. Sometimes, informal treaties between agencies produce cooperation; other times, bureaucratic guerrilla warfare erupts—as is presently the case between the FBI and the CIA.

Today, reflecting how agency relationships can change over time, the FBI and the Secret Service, once at odds in the J. Edgar Hoover days, have a better rapport sparked in large part by joint political interest in pressuring Congress for changes in Freedom of Information and privacy laws. Gone are the years of the 1930s, when the FBI was the Service's fiercest bureaucratic enemy and Hoover's G-men actually muscled onto the Service's turf, performing duties of presidential protection for President Franklin D. Roosevelt.

Local and regional politics plague the Secret Service every time that a president leaves Washington, D.C., for the agency is hugely dependent on local police for data concerning potential threats and for help in setting up security. Yet there are no laws or even accepted rules governing the Service's relationship to the police departments with whom it must work intimately in order to protect presidents, candidates, and visiting dignitaries. The agency's relationships to various police departments range from cordial to hostile.

Throughout the decades, the tension between the Service and the New York City Police Department has proven deeply rooted. One twenty-year veteran of the NYPD chided the Service for "treating local police as if they were Keystone Cops"—a complaint that many other police forces have leveled in private against the agency. When President Carter visited New York City in 1976, coordination of protective efforts between police and Secret Service was fractious as a result of the agency's stance that agents armed with rifles be positioned on selected rooftops. Police Commissioner Michael Codd had an icy response: "If anybody does that he'll be arrested. That's basically a job for us."

The Service deferred to New York's men in blue. In many other cities, local police would have deferred to the agency and allowed them to deploy its countersniper teams.

Similarly politics swirl around the agency's efforts to gather intelligence, as does the efforts of every government agency with an intelligence-or data-gathering mission (FBI, CIA, military intelligences, National Security Agency, etc.). The organizations all fight each other for federal dollars, seeking to expand their own data nets while trading information with friendly agencies: Since September 11, 2001, the war on terrorism has brought controversial intelligence-gathering moves by the Justice Department, affording the Secret Service greater latitude in monitoring persons and groups that might pose a security threat.

In the late 1970s, the Service joined with the CIA and FBI in lobbying for congressional relief from the Freedom of Information and privacy laws of the mid-1970s, and in 2002, the campaign for further relief from those laws continues, especially with fears that terrorist cells, which may pose a grave and continuing threat to the president, are operating in the United States. Director Knight, a tough, square-jawed ex-police officer who had joined the Secret Service in 1950 and climbed through the ranks, told Congress that in 1976 alone, there had been a 50 percent decrease in the quantity of information that the Service received from local police and federal agencies and that the quality of data had declined an estimated 20 to 25 percent. Even with the full development of the computer age in the 1990s, the Service feels it does not receive enough data from other departments and local police forces, fueling the "Washington-versus-everywhere-else-in-the-nation" mentality.

The Service, like other data-gathering agencies, continually argues that the Freedom of Information Act (FOIA), which provides public access to government documents under certain specified conditions, has destroyed the confidence of informants about their anonymity and has made the agency timid about using data about individuals, for fear of being sued. But neither the Secret Service nor any other federal agency has been able to offer direct evidence of this alleged cause-and-effect. In the wake of September 11, however, Attorney General John Ashcroft instructed agencies to refuse FOIA requests if they could legally do so, as a tightening of information systems against terrorism.

One of the problems noted by both the Warren Commission in 1964 and the Treasury Department report on the attempted assassination of President Reagan in 1981 is that there are no set policies governing what information other agencies should provide to the Secret Service. Again, the political climate—whether civil libertarians or conservatives have the upper hand—effects how much information about potential threats the Secret Service can gather and exchange with other agencies.

In the turbulent political climate of the 1960s, the Secret Service and the FBI swapped information that was less about presidential security than about the FBI's surveillance campaign against antiwar groups. Some of the exchanges, of the type later outlawed by the Privacy Act of 1974, were controversial. The FBI provided the Service with data form its COIN-TELPRO project, a massive surveillance of hundreds of dissident groups and thousands of persons; in return, the Service gave the Bureau data on potentially threatening persons. In truth, the FBI data contained very little protective intelligence; the vast majority of groups and persons targeted in COINTELPRO posed no threat of violence. Most persons in the Secret Service files were not violent either, and critics charged that the exchange fed each organization's lust for data more than it aided the performance of their missions.

In the early 1960s, the political muscle of the Johnson administration altered the Secret Service's mission in a way that made the FBI data more useful. The Johnson White House pressured the Service into protecting the president from "embarrassment" as well as from harm, and the agency began to use the FBI data to focus on political dissidents in advance work for presidential travel and appearances. As the Service tried to avoid stops where Johnson might have to encounter peaceful demonstrations and suffer "embarrassment," the highly political mission proved a dubious departure from the real purpose of presidential protection. There is no evidence that Johnson and his staff did so out of any residual fears from November 22, 1963, to justify the measure.

Straying even farther from its protective mission, the Service became one of the users of the National Security Agency's project MINARET, which was created to intercept and open the mail of thousands of American citizens and hundreds of organizations—in clear violation of federal statutes for the mail. Although the FBI and CIA were the main abusers, the Service got in on the act, by requesting the National Security Agency (NSA) to intercept the mail of groups and individuals who were on the Service's Watch List. Utterly illegal, the practice at least related to the Secret Service's protective mission. The same, however, cannot be said about the agency's other use of MINARET, to protect presidents not from threats, but from public embarrassments. Frank Donner, in *The Age of Surveillance,* his detailed chronicle of domestic spying, notes:

> The functional responsibilities of the requestors [for MINARET data] were largely ignored, notably in the case of the Secret Service, which submitted the names of individuals

and organizations active in anti-war and civil rights movements not considered a direct threat to protectees [,] on the theory that they might participate in demonstrations against U.S. policy that would endanger the physical well-being of government officials.

In exchange for the illegally opened mail, the Secret Service traded its Watch List, providing the NSA with all of its data on groups and persons potentially threatening to protectees. The fact that the NSA had no protective mission was ignored by the Service; the fact that the Service had no legitimate political-surveillance mission was ignored by NSA.

Under pressure from the Johnson and Nixon administrations and under the watch of Directors Rowley and Knight, the Service had shifted its mission beyond protection. Its forays into gathering data on political dissidents, running political interference for beleaguered presidents by "protecting" against peaceful demonstrators as well as physical threats, and trading its threat files to any agency that had something to give in return were clearly beyond the Service's legitimate protective mission. And the agency could not simply cite White House pressures: the lure of trading data with the illustrious agencies of the American intelligence community— CIA, FBI, NSA—proved irresistible for an organization that had always aspired to be a full-fledged intelligence agency but had not succeeded since World War I.

The extensive use of the Service in the Johnson and Nixon years to serve as an advance political detail as well as a protective detail was and remains part of a larger problem: the way in which modern presidents and their staffs politicize and shade the Service's mission. Secrecy is a mixed blessing for the protective mission. On the one hand, it provides a certain advantage in dealing with congressional oversight committees, with the public, and with the press: "The Secret Service cannot discuss its protective methods and procedures." This helps shield the agency from some criticism and second-guessing. Still, because of the need for secrecy in protecting a president, the Secret Service cannot or will not blow the whistle when presidents misuse it for political or personal purposes. Not until Ken Starr subpoenaed several members of Bill Clinton's Secret Service team was the code of silence pierced for a sitting president.

If a president misuses the National Park Service, a ranger or Park Service administrator can leak to the *Washington Post* or complain to a congressional Committee, with only the usual career risks of whistle-blowing to worry about. But the Secret Service, much like the CIA, lives by a code of secrecy dictating that any disclosure of who does what, when, and how can place a president in mortal danger. Even when presidents misuse the Service for political or personal reasons, the cloak of secrecy has prevailed, at least until the Starr investigation of the Whitewater and Monica Lewinsky scandals. The Secret Service believes that it cannot tell what is wrong without disclosing what is right—how it protects a president.

The Service cannot work with a president in a give-and-take situation with no formal rules if it becomes his critic or if he views it as a political enemy. A president could retaliate by freezing the Service out, by not cooperating, or by using other federal employees to provide protection, as Franklin D. Roosevelt did with the FBI. If an individual agent refuses to do a president's bidding or criticizes orders, he or she might be yanked from the White House protective detail even if the agent is right and the president or his staff are technically wrong. With the Service so steeped in secrecy and so accessible for a president, the temptation for the White House to misuse agents for personal and political gain is pronounced.

Over the decades, one misuse loathed by agents have been administrations that pressure the Secret Service to perform political chores unrelated to its protective mission. President Nixon asked the Service to tap his brother Donald's phone. They did, even though Donald Nixon was no threat to the president in the protective sense, only in the political sphere.

Lyndon B. Johnson's aforementioned desire to avoid public embarrassment as he escalated the Vietnam War in the mid-1960s pressed the Secret Service into increasing political tasks. Prior to a Johnson speech at the University of Rhode Island, Secret Service intelligence learned that a professor planned to walk off of the platform in the middle of the speech in protest against the war. The Service was ready for the professor. As he started to stride from the stage, two uniformed nurses placed by the agency rushed up and escorted him to create the impression that it was illness rather than political opposition that caused the sudden departure.

Richard Nixon often used agents to help him stage political dramas. During the 1970 congressional elections when he was stumping for candidates who backed his Vietnam policy, he instructed the Service to allow a few hecklers to remain in the crowd to provide a foil for his speeches. Besides suspending judgment about whether the hecklers presented a threat to the president and should have been removed, the Service had the delicate and distracting political chore of ensuring that there was just enough heckling to provide drama, but not enough to disrupt the speech.

On other occasions, Nixon used the Service to prevent protest. He ordered agents to disperse protesters or remove them at his public appearances regardless of whether they posed any possible threat to the president. The tactic resulted in an injunction issued by Federal District Court Judge James B. McMillan against Secret Service agents, preventing them from depriving protesters of their political rights. The injunction required that a threat to the president's personal safety be identified before demonstrations could be disbanded.

The press complains that presidents avoiding questions use agents to keep reporters at a distance. During the Nixon years, the Washington press corps alleged that sometimes agents would physically intervene to squelch a reporter's question during Nixon's press encounters. Sometimes the Service is tougher with the press than with the general public, fueling press suspicions that the Service is running political interference for the president. The charge has begun to surface again in the tightened security surrounding President George W. Bush since September 11, 2001.

The problem arises with candidates, too. In New Hampshire in 1980, one reporter was turned away by an agent guarding Ronald Reagan. Though the reporter had no fewer than six security badges, one required badge was missing; the reporter simply stashed all of his badges and walked into the event unchallenged as an ordinary citizen.

In addition to politicizing the Secret Service in ways that hinder its protective mission, the president and his family tend to personalize the Service—again, to require agents to run personal errands and do chores unrelated to security. This may seem like a minor corruption of the Service's mission compared with using it to perform political chores, some of which are of dubious legality. But the erosion upon maximum protection can prove equally serious, perhaps more so. No agent can adequately guard the First Lady when his arms are full of shopping bags; no agent can guard the president while toting a beer cooler.

Still, the agents are always there, standing around. The temptation for presidents and their families to use them as errand boys is usually irresistible, with agents not in a position to complain. As one agent put it, "You do what the man wants."

Some presidents want more than others. As Governor of Georgia, Jimmy Carter had been accustomed to being surrounded by a phalanx of state troopers whom he used to run menial errands. At first, he viewed the Service in much the same way—as bag carriers. Eventually, he stopped.

The "favors" requested of agents by presidents and first families run the gamut from baby-sitting to carrying packages, to providing a fourth for bridge. All detract from an agent's ability to provide protection.

One of the most personal uses of the Service by presidents and perhaps the most awkward for agents is covering presidential trysts. If a president entertains or visits a female friend, he cannot do so without Secret Service complicity. Not often, anyway. In the alleged liaisons of various presidents from Harding to Kennedy, the Service's stealth and secrecy may well have been necessary for "protection" of a different kind—protection of the president's political career, of his image with friends and family, of the safety and anonymity of his female companions.

Presidential residences present another tempatation, a financial one, for misuse of the Secret Service. The agency has the legal authority to request improvements on a president's private home if the Service believes that such improvements will reduce threats to safety or enhance security. Before 1973, the Service had to request the necessary funds from the General Accounting Office; in 1973, the Service was given its own fund for security improvements, though it still has to answer to congressional oversight committees about how it spends the money.

Congress may be increasingly cost conscious, but presidential-protection expenses are as difficult for it to deal with as those related to national defense, and for similar reasons. Congress wants the best possible protection for presidents, and it usually defers to the Service's expert judgment in such matters about whether a new communications center at Reagan's ranch is an absolute necessity. At the moment, virtually no one would question any Service requests for state-of-the-art security measures at the Bush ranch in Crawford, Texas.

If Congress balks at allocating funds for security at presidential homes, the chief executive could be endangered, a risk that most legislators would rather avoid. So unless the expenditure appears blatantly unrelated to security, Congress usually loosens up the cash, especially if both the Service and the White House agree on what needs to be done. They usually do. As a staff member for the House Appropriations subcommittee that oversees Secret Service expenditures remarked, "We can't afford to have a president killed. My God, the whole country goes into shock."

Despite such fears, legislators have sometimes questioned security improvements on presidential homes. One notable example came during the Nixon administration, which, with Secret Service support, spent roughly $10 million in "security" improvements on three Nixon residences—San Clemente, California; Key Biscayne, Florida; and Grand Cay, the Bahamas, as well as at the home of Nixon's daughter. The range of improvements included communications facilities, guards, offices, Coast Guard patrols, boats, fences, heaters, bulletproof windows, and landscaping. In an article written with James P. Kelly, private security consultant N. C. Livingstone asserted that not only the president was abusing tax dollars, but also that Vice President Spiro Agnew had "disguised hundreds of thousands of dollars in non-security improvements to his home under the cachet of security."

The press and Congress questioned whether Nixon's improvements, particularly the landscaping, were legitimately related to security. When critics alleged that the improvements benefited Nixon friends such as businessman Bebe Rebozo, the White House responded that the Rebozo house in question was rented by Julie Nixon Eisenhower and her husband, David, which justified the expenditure, and that the president's frequent visits to another friend's island home at Grand Cay necessitated improvements there. The White House also pointed out that the Secret Service had ordered all of the work to be done. Though this was technically true, the Service remained closemouthed about whether the requests for the renovations had come from the agency or the White House. Of course, the Service would not publicly criticize the White House.

Public criticism mounted when it was discovered that the Service was paying a California firm $12,000 a year for special care of the grounds on Nixon's San Clemente home in order to "keep the landscape from interfering with security." In all, the government spent $500,000 more on improvements for the San Clemente and Key Biscayne properties than Nixon had originally paid for them, prompting Senator Howard Baker to quip, "Someone might decide to run for president so the Secret Service could make improvements on his home."

The Secret Service's view of the security-improvements fund is that the agency is required by law to immediately correct any situation that threatens presidential security and that there is no choice but to pay for "justifiable security improvements." In truth, the Service believes it has little discretion because of the word "justifiable." When $70,000 was spent for a communications command post at the Ford residence in Alexandria, Virginia, or if George W. Bush's Crawford ranch is similarly equipped, there is no problem. But what happens if, like Nixon, a president decides that less-than-perfect landscaping constitutes a threat to his security? The Service can acquiesce and authorize the expenditure, or it can buck the president and risk a public, and private, feud with the White House. Traditionally, the Service complies with a president's "request."

Since the furor over the Nixon repairs and renovations, the Service has not been called to task by Congress to explain its use of taxpayer money for refurbishing presidential homes. Perhaps succeeding presidents have shied away from the potential political fallout for a chief executive who is discovered to be remodeling his house at the public's expense. Still, the potential for abuse exists as long as the Service is legally compelled to spend money for anything related to security and tends to accede to White House definitions of what is justifiable.

In 1981, President Reagan's Pacific Palisades home was put up for sale at $1.9 million, even though the first family had not been seen there in eight months. Despite this the Secret Service was providing round-the-clock guards for the expensive piece of real estate. Protecting presidential investments by baby-sitting property until it sold is not within the Service's job description, but the agency did not complain—not publicly, anyway.

The dynamics of presidential politics pervade every facet of the Service's existence down to the nuts and bolts of protective methods and procedures. In classically understated "bureaucratese," the 1981 Treasury report on the attempted assassination of President Reagan asserts, "The political mission of the White House staff conflicts at times with the security mission of the Secret Service; security measures taken to protect the presidents are often determined by give-and-take between the two groups."

What the report didn't say is that, typically, the White House staff takes much more than it gives and usually gets its way. Former Agent Charles M. Vance told a Senate committee:

I have personally seen many, many incidents during which the

> Secret Service strongly objected to a movement or situation involving a president or vice president and stated that agents could in no way provide adequate security under the circumstances and yet were overruled . . . by White House staff members who wanted more "press exposure" or "public impact" or "a good camera angle."

Whenever there is a close-up look at the operation of the White House protective detail, the primacy of politics can be seen clearly. In most administrations the tail wags the dog from a security point of view: The White House staff often tells the Secret Service what to do. Sometimes, the conflicts between the political mission of the White House staff and the protective mission of the Secret Service spark intense animosity. One agent assigned to the White House detail confided to an associate his frustration with Nixon's top aides: "You know what we say to each other now, don't you?" asked the agent. "We say that 'come the revolution be sure and save two bullets—one for Haldeman and one for Erlichman.' "

The White House staff's political goals frequently overrule the Secret Service's judgments and trump its procedures. In virtually every administration, the interference of the White House staff and the infighting between staff and agents can erode the Service's morale and hinder the agency's ability to do its full job. Another politically bred danger is that the agents on the White House detail may get so accustomed to White House notions of protection that they lose their edge—their training and professionalism may take a backseat to the administration's ideas. For example, agents are trained to stay in close proximity to the protectee at all times and to do so in tight formation. Nixon White House staffer Bruce Whelihan recalled that in order to give the press a clear view of Nixon interacting with friendly crowds, "I'll sometimes go in with a hook and yank out agents who are too close." It is likely that after a few months of such treatment, agents were distracted from the intense concentration demanded by crowd control, second-guessing themselves about whether they were so close to the president that they would suffer the embarrassment of being hooked.

These problems are compounded by the fact that agents serving on the White House detail are in the same position that House Speaker Sam Rayburn described for junior members of Congress: *they have to go along to get along*. Despite their civil service status and protections, agents on the

White House detail who feud with the White House staff or who displease the president or the First Family will probably find themselves transferred to other duty. Civil service may protect their job with the Secret Service but not their assignment to the presidential detail.

That arrangement reveals a fundamental weakness in the agency's protective system. It is one thing for the protectee to overrule or ignore protective procedures; it is another thing when the protectee has the power to remove agents who displease him. The White House detail is selected on the basis of merit, but while they serve on the White House detail, they serve—at least to some degree—at the pleasure of the president. Much of the time this is not a problem. Agents do the best job they can, and their particular assignments are left to Service brass. Sometimes, however, personal influences upon the agents and the men and women they protect can hamper maximum security.

When a president or a First Lady take a liking to an agent, they sometimes request that the agent go along on this or that trip. Jacqueline Kennedy felt comfortable with Agent Clint Hill; often, presidents discover that certain agents are fun to chat with. Such rapport, as natural as it is, can create problems if it interferes with the normal rotation of assignments and shifts within the seventy-agent White House detail.

What happens if an agent and a protectee develop a friendly relationship? One possible outcome is that the agent may use his "in" to persuade the protectee to accept more security, to follow protective procedures. But the leverage can also work the other way: the rapport makes it more difficult for an agent to avoid running errands or to insist that proper procedures always be followed.

A retired "all-star" agent carefully says that his loyalty to the job and the protective mission was not compromised at a conscious level by the contrast of really liking one president and disrespecting another. What he worried about was the "subconscious" effect this might have on his reactions and reaction time in an instant, life-or-death situation. This is an interesting admission that has never been offered anywhere before. It comes close to acknowledging that, contrary to the Service's code of silence, *who* the protectee is as a person—and perhaps politically—does factor into the human psyche and *could* affect events.

As in all other aspects of life, personalities come into play between agents and those they protect. Stern, humorless agents who unnerve the president by acting like a robot or a jailer will have little influence in persuading the president to do anything he doesn't want to do. As competent and efficient as such an agent might be, he will prove useless if he is always "getting the hook" because the White House media advisor dislikes the agent's somber image, or if the agent becomes such an unsettling presence that he is booted from the White House detail. For agents working with the president, the job is truly a Catch-22.

The degree to which the president, First Family, or White House staff meddles in agent assignments varies with administrations and with the situation. The Service steadfastly denies that the problem exists, claiming that assignments are strictly based on merit, and transfers from the White House detail to other kinds of work are solely by the book of established personnel rotation.

Agents know better. A classic illustration of White House power over the presidential detail occurred in 1973, when the head of Nixon's detail, Robert H. Taylor, and his second-in-command, William L. Duncan, were transferred out of presidential protection after four years of service. Secret Service Director James M. Rowley claimed that the reassignments were in no way political but were simply in keeping with the Service's standard policy for rotating supervisory personnel. The record proves otherwise.

Sources close to both the Service and the White House said that Taylor's departure was triggered by a feud with H. R. Haldeman about protection versus politics. In one incident in Providence, Rhode Island, Haldeman allegedly ordered that a protective barrier be removed so that Nixon could get closer to the crowd. Taylor refused, on security grounds. At the inaugural parade, Nixon's White House staff was irritated because agents trotted alongside the presidential limousine, deploying between Nixon and the crowds that lined Pennsylvania Avenue. After these incidents, Haldeman reportedly demanded that Taylor be transferred out of the presidential detail, and White House sources told the press that Director Rowley had acquiesced.

Such "transfers" certainly have a chilling effect upon the Service. Agents were said to have been deeply demoralized and worried about the sanctions that might ensue from just doing their job.

Because the White House detail is a niche within a highly charged political arena, the job is shaped by personality and patronage. Presidential protection is most effective when it is allowed to function professionally and autonomously, but it functions this way only to the extent that the president and his staff adopt a give-and-take attitude. Typically, political pressures and priorities compel the politicos to intervene into the Secret Service's professional domain—to the detriment of protection. Behind a cloak of secrecy with no rules of the game to help ensure the integrity of its mission, the Service's White House operation succumbs to one of the American presidency's most public and private weapons, politics.

Despite the political realities of the job, past and present agents generally do all they can to convey an apolitical image to the public. Agent Jerry Parr, who pushed Reagan into the limo after the attack by Hinckley, and who was special agent in charge of the White House detail during parts of the Carter and Reagan administrations, says: "Many agents take to the grave what they know."

The Service will "go public"—under certain circumstances—to foster the nonpolitical image, cooperating occasionally with Hollywood. For Clint Eastwood's movie *In the Line of Fire,* retired agent and Head of the Public Affairs Office Robert Snow was a consultant. "We'll provide technical assistance for virtually any project provided it portrays us in a positive light," Carl Meyer, a Secret Service spokesman, said in 1998.

For Eastwood's production, the agency exercised "editorial control," a line-by-line review of the script, and also helped with wardrobes and the filming of motorcades and campaign rallies. Snow, taking a page from the Hoover book—Hoover had nearly complete creative control of the FBI TV series starring Efram Zimbalist Jr.—used Eastwood's movie as a public-relations tool. Meyer approves of Eastwood: "I can't think of many actors who could do a better portrayal [of a Secret Service agent] than Clint Eastwood. It's the whole Clint Eastwood mystique."

Secret Service spokeswoman Gayle Moore justifies the agency's control of its "apolitical," on-screen depiction:

> There aren't any secrets leaked in the movie. The bottom line is the filmmakers came to us and said, "We want this to be authentic; we want it to be accurate." If someone's going to make a movie they're going to make it with or without us, so why not become involved?

The Secret Service is far less forthcoming with authors, including these authors, than Hollywood because the agency does not have line-by-line veto power. Even with that power, not everyone at the agency agrees with the Hollywood treatment. Some worry about the issue of assassinations "copycatted" from films: John Hinckley was inspired in part by the Travis Bickle character in *Taxi Driver*.

The Secret Service also helped with a 1993 TV series that dramatized cases from agency files but was canceled after two episodes. Even though the agency gave advice to the makers of the Kevin Kline film *Dave,* the Service was less than thrilled about the plot line—a presidential imposter subverts the twenty-fifth Amendment, which deals with the constitutional line of succession to the office.

The Service remains highly sensitive about symbols and images. During the Carter administration, several agents printed some T-shirts that featured a presidential seal riddled with bullet holes and bearing the motto, "You Elect Them, We Protect Them." When agents wore them to a Carter softball game, "Carter fumed," according to ex-Agent Marty Venker. Shortly afterward, the Service sent its agents a memo forbidding improper depictions of the presidential seal.

In 1995 came the Service's most extensive media and public-relations outreach. The Discovery Channel produced a ninety-minute documentary entitled "Inside the Secret Service." A flattering puff piece, it portrayed the Agency as patriotic, competent, apolitical, and dedicated, while glossing over the Service's many problems and failures.

The program, said the announcer, had the "full cooperation" of the Service, the "first time" this had happened. After a glowing introduction by none other than President Reagan, who intoned that if it were not for the Secret Service he "might not be here," the cameras filmed Secret Service facilities and former agents and directors. The training facility at Beltsville, Maryland, was extensively photographed for the first time, as were anticounterfeiting labs and techniques. Former agents Clint Hill and Jerry Parr and former director Robert Simpson and then-Director Eljay Bowron III did most of the glowing, cheerleading voiceovers when the announcer fell quiet. There were no critics or detached analysts.

Notwithstanding the laudatory documentary, it is only in an ideal world that "politics and protection don't mix." In our present system of presidential protection, politics mixes with virtually *every* aspect of protection.

## CHAPTER 9
# "THE SIXTH SENSE"

*A reporter asked Secret Service Director of Public Affairs John Warner whether agents were trained to use their bodies as shields in the event of an attack on the president. A pained expression crossed Warner's face. He waved his hand, thereby dismissing the question.*
— Robert Blain Kaiser, "Presidential Candidates Disagree on
*Value of Secret Service Watch,"* The New York Times, *February 10, 1980*

The Service does not like to discuss its protection methods. But in the aftermath of the assassination of President Kennedy, the agency launched the most complete overhaul of its protective methods in the history of organization, seeking the help of outside experts who authored detailed reports for the Service's review. Traumatized by "losing Lancer," the Secret Service turned for aid to the Department of Defense, which opened its vast research and development resources available to the Service to find ways of reducing the vulnerability of political leaders to assassination. The agency also received help from the Office of Science and Technology, the Office of the Director of Defense Research and Engineering, the Advance Research Projects Agency, and a range of think tanks: the Rand Corporation, the Research Analysis Corporation, and the Institute for Defense Analysis. With the vast expertise of the defense establishment, the Secret Service had one goal in mind: to never lose another president to an assassin.

Attempting to cover all the possible methods an assassin might use, the agency studied how it could improve coordination among agents, the White House, federal agencies, and local police. Because of Dallas, where the advance team truly dropped the ball, the agency pored over ways to tighten advance planning and control publicity for a president's forays outside the White House. The Service, with a rash of reports from defense and outside sources, pored over the use of body armor, attacks on the protectee from the air, tighter methods of screening crowds and press credentials, the use of shields, evasive action, surveillance techniques, and the collection and processing of data about potential threats. In many ways, the Secret Service grasped that it must move into the modern age, that the outdated protective methods may well have cost John F. Kennedy his life and the entire nation its president.

The Research Analysis Corporation, studying ways to better protect a president during travel and public appearances, proposed that the Secret Service turn to the most sophisticated weaponry, such as "cold liquid" weapons and "liquid stream projectors." For months, the agency's brass pondered data on how attackers might penetrate protective barriers and confuse or distract Secret Service agents. It examined the possible use of non-lethal protective weapons such as "gas-propelled impact projectiles." Embarrassed by the accounts of agents who had failed to recognize the sound of gunshots in Dallas or had mistake them for motorcycle back-fires, the Service explored the use of acoustical early warning devices that instantly identified small-arms fire. A rush to armor everything gripped the agency—cars, chairs, helicopters—anything in which a president might appear.

At the same time, in the months following the John F. Kennedy assassi-nation, the Institute for Defense Analysis studied threats for the Secret Service: What motivates assassins? What methods and weapons are they likely to use? Computerized simulations and war-game techniques tested the effectiveness of various protective methods, and the reaction times of agents—so slow and ineffective on November 22, 1963—were measured. Even the use of body doubles and false identities by assassins were studied. To repel threats, the Institute proposed some highly futuristic devices such as special lighting systems that would blind an attacker and an energy field that would deflect ballistic projectiles away from the protectee.

The results of these studies were presented to the Service in the STAR reports between 1963 and 1966, but the revolutionary improvements in pro-tective methods that the think tanks and defense strategists envisioned never came about. The Secret Service was not transformed into something like a corps of Jedi warriors wielding light sabers and other fantastic devices.

In truth, it was not that the Secret Service rejected out of hand the experts who dreamed up the avant-garde techniques. The agency was constrained by the political nature of its mission: The experts did not have to worry about a White House staff or anti-democratic images or media reaction. To the ivory tower consultants, it was perfectly logical to protect the president by any means possible, allowing the think tanks to propose such things as a huge truck-mounted optical scanner that would roll along in motorcades and provide complete electronic surveillance of crowds and buildings and a smoke screen device on the president's limousine designed to go off when anything went wrong. The outside experts could suggest a complete suit of body armor for the president, a device that created high-pitched noises that would disorient attackers, and a protective shield that would automatically pop up and surround the president whenever there was a threatening noise. The Service knew what the White House would think of such measures: "no way."

The Service turned to none of this hardware, not anything even approximating it. It was not for lack of money or technology: It was because the Service knew full well that no president could accept the political image created by the presence of smoke screens, pop-up shields, leviathan monitoring devices, and weird noises. Even the far less obtrusive, standard methods adopted by the Service are applied only when the president and the White House staff will permit it.

Since the outside reports following the John F. Kennedy assassination, the Service has continued to draw upon outside experts from both public and private organizations in order to modernize protective methods. Still, this ongoing solicitation of expert advice remains tied to the political realities the Service encounters every day in each administration. One measure that presidents and other politicians have not resisted is bulletproofing of everything from podiums to windows and limousines.

There has been tremendous improvement in the armor and maneuverability of limousines, with no sacrifice of style or comfort, since the days of the Kennedy "death car." When the growth of the automobile sounded the end of the presidential horse and carriage in the early 1900s, the Secret Service purchased a 1907 H. White Steamer that became the first motor vehicle used at the White House; but President Theodore Roosevelt did not climb into the vehicle—the Secret Service drove it behind his horse-drawn carriage, marking the agency's first "follow-up vehicle."

Not until December 1941, in the wake of Pearl Harbor, did the Service employ its first partially armored presidential car. The limo had once belonged to Capone and had been seized by the government because of the mobster's failure to pay income tax. The "armor," however, was merely bulletproof glass. In 1942, the agency bought fully armored limousines and also, for the first time, used agents as drivers for the president.

At first, Secret Service advance details would drive the president's limousine and Service follow-up vehicles across the country for use upon the president's arrival, but wear and tear on the vehicles, travel distances, and driver fatigue led the agency to convert a railroad car into a platform for four vehicles. The railway car was fitted with portable ramps so that the limos could be loaded on and off quickly. The railway car was also equipped with water tanks to wash the cars and had racks for extra tires and accessories for emergency use. For destinations overseas, the limos were loaded aboard a ship, and since the 1950s, have been driven inside huge military cargo planes and flown to sites across the globe.

The Secret Service continues to be responsible for the procuring, driving, maintaining, and securing of the vehicles, each designed and equipped with state-of-the-art technology and armor.

Whenever a president is "on the road," whether by limo, helicopter, or Air Force One, the challenges for his Secret Service detail are immense. A sizable chunk of the Service's training manual is devoted to protecting a president when he travels, full of such rules as the following:

> Roll back and examine all rugs insofar as practical. Then go over the entire surface of rugs. Pressing down firmly with fingertips to locate any small objects that might be concealed therein. . . . Carefully examine all pictures—tap for hollow frames. . . . All lights in the area should be monitored with a photo cell to detect the presence of sound modulated light waves.

Presidential travel presents more of a challenge to the Service than providing protection at the White House. Any stop on a presidential trip poses the chance of changing from friendly or at least familiar to hostile in a blink. As a result, advance scouting is crucial to protection. But the amount and quality of advance security preparations are not consistent, varying with the number of agents available for a particular advance mission and with the amount of cooperation and information provided by the White House staff. Although agents always follow certain procedures when the president (or any other protectee) travels, no predesigned protective packages for advance work have been set in motion. The Treasury Department admits the flaw:

> Thus, the [advanced] procedures do not include such matters as how far from the president crowds should be kept, under what circumstances doors should or should not be locked or guarded, or even how many Special Agents should be assigned to a particular visit. The standards which Special Agents apply as individual cases seem to be the product of their experience in similar circumstances, modified by two other factors: the level of manpower available to the Service; and the needs to reach a practical accommodation—there being no written agreements—with the occasionally conflicting demands of the White House advance staff for greater exposure of the presidents.

Good advance work requires consistent coordination among the White House staff, Service field offices, the White House detail, and local police, and if any of this breaks down, lapses in protection can arise and possibly prove fatal. For a presidential trip, one or more agents are assigned to do the advance work, depending, in part, on the scope of the itinerary. Usually, at least one agent from the White House detail will meet with the agent in charge of the field office closest to the destination, and they will work with local police.

Depending on the president's travel agenda and the amount of preparation that is possible for the Service, agents set up a secure area on tarmacs for Air Force One, closing off entry routes for possible assassins. The agency uses military airfields whenever possible: traffic is always restricted at them, and a ready supply of trained military security is always available.

Motorcade routes remain a constant concern because of the specter of the Kennedy assassination, and during the advance work, agents pore over not only the main route, but also alternate routes selected in case of a blockage or emergency. Emergency sites—hospitals to which the president can be taken if he has a medical problem or injury—are selected, and routes to them are planned. Agents survey buildings, subways, and streets all along the route to search for potential sniper perches and deploy countersniper teams carrying binoculars and high-powered rifles. Rooftops are the preferred sites.

Since Hinckley's attempt against Reagan, agents pay special attention to the placement of rope barriers. Still, the Secret Service cannot protect the president away from the White House without the aid of local police—without them, the job simply could not be done, as the agency does not have anything approaching the personnel needed to perform all of these tasks.

One of the Service's tasks on the road is to set up credentialing procedures to make sure that only bona fide reporters can get near the president the image of Hinckley having wormed his way among the press is still a potent one. In times of strict security, such as the days following President Reagan's near-assassination, agents may even search reporters after checking their IDs.

The White House staff and the president's media advisor play a crucial role in advance work involving the press, for they know reporters much better than the Service does. One of the major problems in checking credentials on the road is that there are local reporters in addition to the national press. If the president goes to Rapid City, South Dakota, to dedicate a dam, the familiar faces from the Washington press corps might tag along, but for the agency, there will also be local press who must be screened. The Service may know the *New York Times* reporter by sight, but must check whether a *Rapid City Bugle* exists and whether a Joe Woodstein is really a *Bugle* reporter. That is the task of the closest Secret Service field office working with White House media people.

Even thousands-of-dollars-a-plate dinners attended by a political party's high rollers come under strict agency scrutiny. After September 11, agents subject the elite to metal detectors as they file in for a black-tie dinner with the president, and, to the fury of some bigwigs, pat them down from time to time.

On the road, every room the president will enter is scoured by agents for electronic surveillance devices, bombs, toxins, and fire hazards; in Washington, D.C., the Service has its own bomb carrier in which it can transport any bombs it discovers, drive them to secure areas, and examine and detonate them. The bomb carrier looks like a cement mixer on a trailer and is pulled by a small van. Outside the Washington area, the Service must rely on local police bomb-disposal vehicles.

Agents map out a secure presidential escape route for every room, garage, and corridor that the president will enter. They inspect hotel elevator cables and plot exit routes in the case of a stalled elevator, and at every location where the president will sleep, eat, or visit, study lists of employees from hotels, catering services, and airports, cross-checked against the names in the Secret Service files to identify dangerous persons.

In recent years, the agency has convinced presidents to don—at least occasionally—bulletproof vests, such as when President George W. Bush threw out the ceremonial first pitch in New York at the 2001 World Series. The practice has become more common since the attempt against Reagan, who would wear a bulletproof vest at most public appearances after he was nearly killed and at all events where the Service had any hint of danger. On his European diplomatic tour of June 1982, he wore it constantly.

Despite the agency's urgings that presidents wear vests, some chief executives resist the suggestion. The Service wanted Gerald Ford to put one on in public after the two attempts on his life, but he did so for only one day after the second attempt on his life. The president told his security detail that he found the vest too bulky and uncomfortable.

Reagan's consistent use of the vest, in contrast to Ford, may not be due entirely to the fact that Reagan was seriously wounded and Ford was fortunate enough to escape unharmed. The advent of lighter, less bulky bulletproofing probably made Reagan's model considerably more comfortable than the one Ford rejected seven years earlier. Today even lighter models are the norm.

At presidential speeches, national political conventions, and dinners, bulletproof podium shields are now universal—the glass reviewing stands for inaugurations are now entirely bulletproof. As far back as the Knoxville World's Fair, in May 1982, Reagan addressed the crowd from behind a glass shield that protected him from head to toe.

At every moment in the president's itinerary, whether he is in a banquet room, exiting an airplane, or riding in a motorcade, the agency's primary protective goal is to maintain a *safe zone*. Also called "the outer perimeter," a "zone of security," or the "sanitized zone," the safe zone is the actual area surrounding the protectee, the zone's size and shape varying with such factors as the number of agents on duty, the situation, and what the protectee will allow. Ideally, from the Service's viewpoint, the zone ought to be the size of a football field; in reality, it is usually measured in feet rather than dozens of yards. It is supposed to surround the protectee completely (360 degrees), whether the protectee is stationary or moving. Whatever threats arise, the zone will give agents a better chance to prevent an attack or, failing that, to blunt an attack, or, as a Secret Service manual describes it, "to absorb the shock to such an extent that the results will not be tragic."

Unfortunately for the Service, the zone is often more imaginary than real. Presidents will frequently sprint out of it in order to reach outstretched hands, but enlarging the zone so that the protectee has more leeway is usually prohibited by lack of personnel and by the fact that it is not politically smart to clear out several city blocks just because a president is about to enter a hotel. Though a zone may be small and fairly fragile, it is better than no zone at all.

As with protective procedures, the ultimate effectiveness of the zone is dependent upon the eyes, ears, and reflexes of agents. No matter how big or small the zone is, it is up to agents to detect and stop threats—the zone only buys them more time. Agents attempt to divide the 360-degree perimeter into visual surveillance zones, so that every inch of the zone's imaginary boundary is being watched. But, these zones may have holes. Lapses can occur when the Secret Service's protectee is moving rapidly or, worse, erratically.

If the worst should happen and an assassin breaches the zone, other advance work comes into play, details that, if neglected, could prove fatal to a president. For example, emergency blood of the correct type is stocked for the president at the designated emergency hospitals wherever he travels.

Advance work also means homework for agents—a great deal of it. Lists of key telephone numbers must be committed to memory (police, hospitals). Photos and dossiers of dangerous persons known to be in the area being visited are studied carefully.

In recent years, as foreign terrorists have slipped in and out of the United States seemingly at will, the agency has tried to institute greater secrecy about presidential travel, fearing that easily affordable weapons such as shoulder-held missiles might be used against the chief executive. The Service has always wanted the White House to keep travel plans secret, and now, more and more, the Service is getting the secrecy it wants. Details of an itinerary are no longer announced in advance, to the extent that it is politically feasible to avoid doing so. Precise arrival and departure times, travel routes to and from hotels and airports, and even the location of certain appearances are often hushed up so that would-be assassins cannot stalk the president. For the first time in the history of the modern presidency, the

Reagan administration quit publishing the daily presidential schedule with geographic details, cities, hotels, and times of arrival and departure.

When Reagan decided to visit a black family in Maryland who had been subjected to a cross burning, the Service instructed the family not to tell anyone about their upcoming meeting with the president, ordering them to invent other excuses for absences from school and work. So secretive was the visit that the family actually thought they were going to the White House; instead, without advance warning, the president showed up at their house.

Sometimes the element of surprise works against protection rather than for it. When a president, or any protectee, suddenly has a whim to do this or that, with little or no advance warning to the Service, problems flare. In 2001, President Bush's daughter "lost" her security detail when she slipped off to a concert at Madison Square Garden. Frantic Secret Service agents searched all over the arena for her. In such instances, the kind of careful advance work required for effective security is impossible. A Service training manual politely refers to these events as "off-the-record trips." In agent jargon they are called "pop-ups," such as when a president spontaneously decides that he must visit the home of a friend or confidant within the hour or decides that he has to play golf—in fifteen minutes. In the latter case, there is nothing agents can do but sprint for their golf bags, stuff a high-powered rifle in with their clubs, and rush to tee off either with the president or right behind him. For the Service, pop-ups reduce protective methods to catch-as-catch-can.

Still, agents must go where the protectee goes. Skiing with Ford or horseback riding with Reagan was not considered difficult duty, but, sometimes, the protectee's idea of a fun trip creates logistical and lifestyle nightmares for agents. On Vice President Walter Mondale's vacation to Lakes Elsie, Manitou, and Brennan, in the Canadian Rockies, the wilderness trek proved a culture shock for the Washington-based protective detail, whose main exposure to nature consisted of walking across perfectly manicured lawns under the stately shade trees that dot the nation's capital.

For ten days at Lake Brennan, a small tent city was erected, with supplies and equipment ferried by helicopter; agents had to unload fourteen hundred pounds of food, electric generators, and seven motorboats. The Service took on so many duties in their combined role of Boy Scout–Indian guide that it was a wonder they had any energy left to devote to preserving the safety zone. Pitching tents, toting and assembling communications gear, policing the site for trash and garbage so as not to offend their Canadian hosts, and paddling Mondale on his long fishing expeditions, agents were truly out of their elements—especially as they came under ceaseless attack from swarms of "no-see-um" flies whose bites swelled and itched. Because the Canadians would not allow helicopters to disturb the most pristine areas of their wilderness, the agents were forced to trudge and paddle on long portages to satisfy the vice president's passion for trout. In one instance, agents lugged boats and equipment for six miles between lakes. At least Mondale brought his own cook, so agents were spared that duty.

Surprisingly, foreign travel is not always more difficult for the Service than domestic travel. It depends on how cooperative the foreign hosts are, what the political climate is, and the purpose of the protectee's mission. Overseas, the Service gets plenty of help from American military personnel and from the security forces of the host country. Yet a visit to a country in which domestic unrest or international terrorist attacks are commonplace presents obvious dangers to a president. In 1982, President Reagan visited West Germany and Italy at a time when both countries were having problem with assaults on political leaders by hard core terrorists such as the Red Brigade and the Baader-Meinhof Gang. With the Secret Service working with the West German and Italian police and armies to cordon off motorcade routes and buildings where the president visited, the terrorists never got close to him. Similarly, one of the toughest overseas visits for the Service was the advance work when former Presidents Nixon, Ford, and Carter all flew to Cairo for the funeral of assassinated President Anwar Sadat.

Most of the agents who accompanied President Nixon on his 1972 trip to China fondly remember the sojourn as a logistical dream, superior in coordination and cooperation to most domestic trips. The Chinese regime, firmly in control of its country, provided an army of unobtrusive security men and plenty of English-speaking liaison personnel to see that everything ran smoothly. To the delight of the Service, the hosts made sure that every Chinese citizen who came in contact with the American visitors—waiters, chauffeurs, guards—could speak fluent English: this was critical to security, affording agents the ability to exercise more control over people and settings with no language barrier to confuse things.

Chinese planning for the trip was described by one observer as "absolutely meticulous in every respect." The Chinese politely looked the other way at Secret Service agents carrying weapons even though long-standing tradition forbids anyone from carrying weapons in China. Even though the hosts provided an enormous security force of both plainclothes agents and militiary personnel, the government allowed the Service such latitude in implementing its own security that American agents, not Chinese, were allowed to check credentials and screen guests at the doors of the Great Hall of the People, where Nixon and Mao were to watch a ballet. The Chinese even allowed the Black Box—the locked briefcase carried by a military officer, holding the codes to activate America's nuclear arsenal—to be brought into the Great Hall.

Whether a president, a candidate, or another protectee, foreign stops with totalitarian regimes do tend to make the job of the Secret Service easier. An agent on Jesse Jackson's 1988 trip to Cuba recalls:

> I got involved in this aspect of the Jackson campaign since, as the Secret Service liaison officer with the State Department at that time, I was supposed to secure visas for the agents who would accompany the candidate on the trip. The countries on Jackson's itinerary changed daily, and sometimes hourly. I would be on my way to an embassy to get visas, only to receive a call saying that Jackson wasn't going to that nation anymore.
>
> One of the countries finally decided on was Cuba. At first the official I dealt with at the Cuban Interest Section in Washington was very suspicious of my application for visas. I went out of my way to convince him that our only interest was in having agents with Jackson and that the Secret Service wasn't trying to pull any tricks to get agents into Cuba. After a couple of days, the official became very cordial and cooperative, and the agents who went on the trip said the Cuban security officials were very cooperative while they were there.

In April 1999, retired Agent Chris Von Holt discussed "on-the-road" details. Recalling how he helped protect Tipper Gore as she attended a Grateful Dead concert, he relates: "It was interesting, entertaining. She's a music fan and we went with her to various concerts. Just another one of those interesting days on the job."

Chris Von Holt elaborated in an interview with radio host Mark Harlan:

> HARLAN: Why don't you talk a little bit about the setup for pro-
> tection. Let's say the president is going to come into town.
> What do you do?
>
> CHRIS VON HOLT: About a week or so ahead of time the Advance
> Team would come in from the president's full-time detail
> in Washington DC, and they would interact with our office
> ... set up the advance of where he is going to be and what
> he is going to do, in conjunction with the political staff that
> would also come from out of town. There are a lot of enti-
> ties that are involved in anything the president does:
> there's us, the political staff, military components. . . . If
> he's going to go to a hotel you have the hotel staff and
> people in various functions there. . . . If he's going to go to
> a speech site you've got the host committee at the
> speech. . . . So there are a lot of entities that all have to act
> together.
>
> HARLAN: Now I assume that one of the things they teach you
> when you're becoming a protection person is to look for
> things out of the ordinary, look for the anomaly. Situations
> like: everyone's cheering and clapping and one guy isn't, or
> everyone's walking to the left and some guy's moving to
> the right. It seems like, if you're in that type of situation
> where someone else has protection on them, that the other
> protection people are more likely to be more anomalous—
> it's more likely for them to stand out of the crowd. What
> I'm thinking here, is there any chance for something to go
> horribly wrong and two agents end up just going at each
> other? Or do they give you some sort of special instruction
> on how that might work?
>
> VON HOLT: Well that's all worked out by the advance detail.
> Especially with the president, everything is choreo-
> graphed, literally down to the minute, so we know exactly
> where he's going to be, exactly where Mr. Yeltsin will be
> and exactly where all of his protective detail will be.
> There's also usually either a pin system worked out for

recognition between us and them or, on big events, a pass system with your face on the front it, along with a color/letter coding system. That way we know that that pass is foreign security and this pass is our security and the staff will have one, the press will too.

HARLAN: So what do you do? How do you compensate, or compromise, these two sets of guards when you know that the Russian standing right over there is packing heat in the same room as the president?

VON HOLT: Well, the advance team would go to Russia a week, maybe 10 days, ahead of time and iron all of that out . . . who is going to be where, who is going to assume what responsibilities. We would work the protective formation around the president, even if he's with Mr. Yeltsin. Sometimes that is going to coincide with the Russian security detail around Mr. Yeltsin. So it's almost, again, something along the lines of a football play, where you know where your people are and hopefully you know where their people are.

There may be some tension between the two groups, but not a lot. Generally speaking we get along pretty well with the other protective services. We're over in so many countries now that they know what we do, and we know what they do, so generally speaking it's all worked out pretty smoothly ahead of time.

We, of course, rely very heavily on the local police departments . . . we rely on their intelligence section and their uniformed officers very heavily.

It's all put together in that week, basically with a bunch of meetings and walk-throughs. We go over inch-by-inch where he's going to be and what he's going to do, and assign responsibilities to everyone. So by the time he gets here it's all mapped out, literally minute-by-minute, and when he steps off the plane, it's almost like a football play in motion where everyone has responsibilities and he's really the only one that can do whatever he wants. Everyone else has things very well set that they need to cover.

Retired agent Dennis V. N. McCarthy, in *Protecting the President: The Inside Story of a Secret Service Agent,* remembers:

> When members of the First Family move around the country they don't usually generate as much advance publicity or public interest as the president does when he takes a trip. While protecting family members, the Secret Service is more concerned about the possibility of a kidnapping than an assassination.

At home and abroad, the possibility that an attack on the president or a protectee can come anywhere and anytime fuels every tactic and detail of the agency's days and nights. The Service's manual emphasizes that agents should shoot only in worst-case scenarios: "Usually weapons should not be used to subdue an attacker if any other defense will effectively suppress a threat." As every agent is taught, the Service's role is "reactive": protection depends on instant and appropriative reaction to an assault. The hard truth, one agent puts it, is that "we have to give away the first shot."

Even then, the agent's first priority is *defense.* "Our job," said former Secret Service Public Affairs Director Jack Warner, "is to protect the person from being hit by an object any way we can."

Agents closest to the president do not really need guns for their first response to a crisis, for their job is to immediately surround the president, shield him, move with him to a safe place, and once there, cover him with their bodies as agents did to Vice President Johnson when shots were fired in Dallas, and with Ford after he was pushed into his limousine following a shot that narrowly missed him. This is defensive protection, not offensive. After the president is shielded from the immediate threat, his agents' mission is to rush him to a safer spot as quickly as possible, preferably to a safe home base (the White House) or to a hospital if he has been injured.

Early in 1976, candidate Ronald Reagan watched agents taking target practice. As a former cowboy actor, Reagan noticed that the agents fired from a standing position instead of a crouch. "Doesn't that make you too big a target?" Reagan inquired.

"That's just the point," an agent answered. "The reason we shoot standing is to better protect your body with ours."

Agents are trained to remain upright at all times and to make themselves as large a target as possible, while interposing themselves between the president and the attacker. Agent Timothy McCarthy performed the technique to the letter during the attempted assassination of President Reagan, walking directly toward Hinckley as Hinckley fired at the president. McCarthy neither crouched nor dodged but created as big a screen as possible and was hit by a bullet meant for Reagan.

If an assault explodes around the president, the agents' duty is to protect him above anything else—even if it means ignoring the attacker or not helping those injured in the attack. Despite their training in lifesaving and first aid, agents cannot assist others until the president has been safely evacuated. However, agents not directly involved in getting the president away from harm are allowed to tend to the wounded or subdue, capture, or even shoot an assailant, as well as seal off the scene of the attack to preserve evidence.

Protecting a captured attacker from furious bystanders or from trigger-happy local police is a critical duty for agents. Only a full investigation and interrogation of a suspect can unravel the nature, scope, and origin of an assassination attempt and answer key questions. Was it a lone assassin, a domestic conspiracy, a foreign terrorist plot, an isolated incident, or a coordinated attack on all political leaders? Dead suspects cannot be interrogated.

In April 1979, the Service developed written procedures for agents with a protectee under attack. But the guidelines are flawed. They make no provision for an automatic reinforcement of presidential protection in case of attack. If the second-in-command of the protective detail, whose decision it is whether reinforcements are needed, is too distracted or too injured to give the order, then reinforcements could be delayed or might not arrive at all. Without quick reinforcements, it is conceivable that the presidential detail could be pinned down by snipers, unable to evacuate the president.

In another blind spot of the guidelines, the agents under fire might not be able to see the full picture. If the second-in-command perceives that there is only one attacker, that the attacker is in custody, and that the president, though wounded, has left for the hospital, there seems to be no need for reinforcements. At the scene, things might appear under control, but this could be illusory. Other attackers may await the president at the hospital or might be positioned to assault his limousine on the way. Lacking reinforcements, the protective detail, diminished by casualties or simply by having left some personnel at the scene, may not be strong enough to repel a second attack. That scenario during the attempt on Reagan would have left the Service powerless to protect him on the way to the hospital or during the first hours there.

The weakness lingers today. The Service fears that a natural influx in presidential protection immediately following an attack such as occurred on September 11 might overcommit personnel, putting too many agents in the wrong place at the wrong time—"overmanning," the Service calls it. If, for example, there were a massive increase in the number of agents assigned to the president but the attack on the president was only one of a series of attacks, on the vice president and several other protectees, the Service would likely be unable to respond effectively to the additional attacks. Some middle ground must be found. Hopefully, it has been.

Pursuing their goal of thwarting an assault before it ignites, Secret Service agents rely on what they call "the sixth sense." It might sound mystical, but what it means is relying upon one's instincts and training. Agents are trained to combine perception and reaction: "Be alert for signs of danger. . . . Look for persons who are acting unnaturally. . . . Look for unnatural appearance of places, objects, and situations."

To agents, the sixth sense means an ability to anticipate danger and to take quick preventive action. Alertness and swift reactions comprise the cornerstones of a good agent—no matter how sound or technically advanced their equipment and protective techniques may be. Safety zones, bulletproof vests, and good intelligence data can help, but it is the reflexes and skills of agents surrounding the protectee that make the biggest difference in the outcome of an attack, spelling the difference between life and death.

Former agent Rufus Youngblood, who dove atop Johnson as the shots rang out above Dallas on November 22, 1963, describes how agents view the sixth sense in a practical manner, "You are constantly on the alert for the individual who somehow does not fit. You scan the crowd, the rooftops, the doorways, the windows, ready to take whatever action necessary."

Each agent watches some portion of the 360-degree safety zone, and if an agent fails to spot a quick or suspicious movement within his zone or if the zone breaks down, they may find themselves screening the president from a hail of bullets instead of clamping down on a menacing person *before* he or she strikes. All it takes is one agent whose perception wanes for an instant.

Hand in hand with the sixth sense, agents must react quickly and instinctively to threats; the slow and questionable actions of Kennedy's detail in Dallas left a blemish that the Secret Service has labored to erase or at least rectify. Good reactions, unlike any Hollywood version of agents "quick on the draw," do not mean that agents immediately open fire on someone taking shots at a president. Agents' first priority is to protect the president, not draw and shoot, which is described in a training manual:

> In some instances the time needed to put weapons into action may be sufficient for the attacker to accomplish his mission. Example: on the average it takes an officer at least 2 1/2 seconds to react, draw, and aim his revolver from a hip holster. During this time the attacker could run 75 feet. If the president is in a car which is moving in a direction generally toward an attacker at 20 miles per hour, [the car] would travel 73 feet in 2 1/2 seconds. Therefore, the attacker and the president could cover a distance separating them at 148 feet (approximately 9 car lengths) while the officer is attempting to draw and fire his gun.

Despite the emphasis placed on lightning-fast reaction to an attack, agents must further rely on their own instincts to immediately let them discern proper versus "over-the-top" responses. Agents, their jobs already tough enough, have to grapple with myriad questions in the heat of an incident. What happens if agents react too quickly and unnecessarily to a strange face, movement, or sound nearby? They could embarrass the president by pushing him to the ground and smothering him with cover before shoving him into a limo. The scenario, all too possible, could ruin an agent's career. And what if bystanders are pushed around or trampled if agents think an assault is erupting? Bad press or even litigation may await.

Although the Secret Service does not have the media and public's luxury of hindsight as to whether a threat exists, agents simply cannot afford to operate like frontier marshals or Latin American security forces that use force first, ask questions later. Agents turn to their instincts, their sixth sense—and hope it does not let them down in a crisis.

The old adage "prevention is the best defense" governs nearly as much of the Service's attention as actual physical protection. In all that the agency does, deterrence and vigilance—protective intelligence—are the watchwords:

> Obtain pertinent protective information—names, photos, descriptive information on known subjects in area to be visited. Determine as to current status of subjects—hospitalized, in custody, at liberty and where.

Unfortunately, manpower and budgetary concerns often intrude on protective intelligence gathering designed to sift through strategic warnings that are gathered from the FBI and other agencies. The information ranges from potential threats and tactical warnings to specific plots in progress. Because the Service's staff and database are limited, the Service must concentrate on known menaces: It does not have the resources or expertise to monitor every conceivable threat to a president or to speculate that a problem *might* develop. The Service's data system is small compared with that of the CIA and the FBI, so Secret Service agents cannot even hope to gather dossiers on every person or group. The agency must too often guess what kinds of individuals and groups present the likeliest danger to protectees.

The Service's Office of Protective Research gets its data from three main sources: the White House, Secret Service field offices, and other federal agencies. From the White House staff come reports on any calls or letters that appear ominous in any degree. Anyone who comes into or near the mansion and acts threateningly or strangely is automatically reported to the Service, which then interviews the person or, in extreme cases, sends them for psychiatric observation. All self-announced oddballs or belligerent and surly types who step into or near the White House end up in the Service's data bank.

In the field, the Service's field offices depend almost entirely upon the help and data of other federal agencies (especially the FBI). State and local agencies also provide information on possible trouble. But the Service claims that in recent decades there has been a drastic decline in the amount of intelligence it receives from these sources, a result of the Privacy Act of 1974, which restricts governmental circulation of information on individuals, and from the Freedom of Information Act. Agents contend that the latter has sliced information provided by the public and by undercover informants because sources fear that no one can protect their anonymity. According to the Service, it has suffered a 40 percent reduction in data, with the biggest dips in the raw data needed to predict threats to the president and others.

In addition to information laws, the Service argues that since 1976, when Attorney General Edward Levi issued restrictive guidelines for the investigation of individuals, agents have been severely hampered in their ability to follow up on information that fingers dangerous people. Making matter worse, according to the agency, the FBI, which remains the Service's major supplier of raw data, has moved away from the general domestic intelligence needed by the Service and toward specialized criminal intelligence demanded by prosecutors. With all of the declines in data cited by the Service, it still obtains nearly ten thousand new pieces of information every month, and the agency's undermanned Office of Protective Research must wade through reams of this material, aware that any note or file might prove that of an evolving assassin or terror plot. With the post–September 11, 2001, edicts for a greater sharing of raw intelligence reports among agencies, the Service could be swamped with data.

Although the Service has "memoranda of understanding" with other federal agencies about the kind of information passed on to the Office of Protective Research, the so-called guidelines are too general, even vague. Out of habit and a lack of resources, no one effectively monitors whether other federal agencies cooperate fully with the Service, a frightening prospect given the lack of communication between the FBI and CIA in the months before September 11, 2001.

In theory, the typical memorandum of understanding specifies seven categories of data that other agencies should provide to the Secret Service:

1. Information concerning attempts, threats, or conspiracies to injure, kill, or kidnap persons protected by the USSS [U.S. Secret Service] or other U.S. or foreign officials in the U.S. or abroad.
2. Information concerning attempts or threats to redress a grievance against any public official by other than legal means, or attempts personally to contact such official for that purpose.

3. Information concerning threatening, irrational, or abusive written oral statements about U.S. Government or foreign officials.
4. Information concerning civil disturbances, anti-U.S. demonstrations or incidents or demonstrations against foreign diplomatic establishments.
5. Information concerning illegal bombings or bomb-making; concealment of caches of firearms, explosives, or other implements of war; or other terrorist activity.
6. Information concerning persons who defect or indicate a desire to defect from the United States and who demonstrate one or more of the following characteristics:
   a. irrational or suicidal behavior or other emotional instability
   b. strong or violent anti-U.S. sentiment
   c. a propensity toward violence.
7. Information concerning persons who may be considered potentially dangerous to individuals protected by the USSS because of their background or activities, including evidence of emotional instability or participation in groups engaging in activities inimical to the United States.

In Washington, D.C., the Secret Service "Watch Office," complete with a switchboard that operates twenty-four hours a day, seven days a week, screens incoming data—State Department cables, intelligence reports from the CIA, FBI, Defense Department, National Security Agency; and countless other private and public sources—alerting Secret Service and Treasury officials via the switchboard when there is an unusual event or emergency.

The on-duty officer at the Watch Office confronts a daunting mission every day, for there are no written guidelines to define an *emergency* or an *unusual event.* Upon the officer falls the decision about what is important enough to warrant an alert. When in doubt, the watch officer can consult with the White House or with intelligence agency personnel, but he or she must make the final judgment about an emergency. Once again, the sixth sense, instinct honed by training, is crucial to agents.

The Service's Protective Research data bank is crammed with files on groups, organizations, people, and past events and incidents, all of them indexed and cross-indexed. What most Americans do not know is that a simple call or e-mail from someone with a personal ax to grind can land virtually anyone on the Watch List. Many thousands of citizens—most of them harmless—are on file as having been checked out for one reason or another as potential threats, and each year the file swells with several thousand new names. Among these, there can be as many as a thousand individuals arrested and several hundred convicted for threats against public officials. Still, a lot of Americans would be stunned to discover that they are on this list.

The system is, as the Service describes it, is "primarily directed toward identifying dangerous individuals." There are over fifty thousand Americans in the Protective Research files, ostensibly because of some actual or potential threat or some problem or characteristic that makes them potentially dangerous. Cross-checked against lists of employees at the hotels and airports where protectees appear, the group is constantly monitored.

When the president is on the road, the file is whittled down to identify dangerous people in the specific areas that he will visit. Dubbed the "Trip File," it may contain as many as one hundred names, and with state and local law-enforcement officers and federal field officers, the Service attempts to check out and account for every person in the trip file. In their advance work, agents try to learn whether these individuals are still in the area; whether they are in jail, hospitalized, or at liberty; and what their current condition is, which usually means seeking to interview them. Sometimes, if a red flag of some sort goes up in the interview, a few people will actually be detained for the duration of the president's visit.

A second and more menacing list of names is prepared for each trip: These are the individuals in the area who are considered to *definitely* be dangerous, as opposed to potentially dangerous, or who remain unaccounted for after the efforts to check out each person in the Trip File. Known as "The Album," the second file includes a photo and profile of each individual and is studied by every agent in the protective detail. Particularly dangerous cases are red flagged with a "look out," as are previously accounted-for individuals in the Trip File who suddenly become unaccounted for because of escape from prison or a mental institution.

To scan crowds for faces from the file or album, agents pose as newsmen or photographers and mingle in crowds both at the White House and on the road, hoping to spot anyone whose picture is in the album—especially a person tagged with a "Look Out." Equally important, the Service's own "faces in the crowd" can pick out men or women who seem to be turning up at several presidential events at the White House and elsewhere, and identify the next would-be Hinckley or Bremer before he can cross from stalker to gunman.

Along with crowd screening for presidential venues, Protective Intelligence maintains a special, smaller Watch List of four hundred or so persons considered particularly volatile, and tracks these people even when no protectee is visiting their area. Field agents run checks on each name every three or four months to update their status, location, and condition; violent persons who are incarcerated are not on the list, but are again added as soon as they are released from mental hospitals or prisons.

The Watch List is far from foolproof no matter how vigilant agents and analysts are. Strict legal limitations hamper the Service's ability to deal with dangerous persons on the Watch List or in the album. By law, agents cannot scoop people up and lock them away on speculation or simply because the president is coming to town. The Service must demonstrate grounds for the arrest of anyone. More often than not, agents have a hard time making a case that a person is dangerous. Problems arise because budgetary restraints and the Service's dependency on other agencies for data do not always allow a clear legal blueprint of a person's menace to a president or other protectee. Compounding the problems, privacy laws ban the Service from presenting data from psychiatrists without the patient's permission. In some cases, however, the family of a person on the Watch List will voluntarily cooperate with the Service and will commit a troubled individual to a hospital for the duration of a presidential visit. Without this kind of family cooperation, agents must have specific, concrete data to confine a person. In many cases, this is legally out of their reach.

During the late 1960s and early 1970s, the Secret Service made its future job more difficult by requesting and receiving the National Security Agency's "watch list" of civil rights and anti–Vietnam War activists. The Secret Service stepped far beyond its protective mission to ferret out persons potentially dangerous to protectees and was reined in by the Privacy Act of 1974, which forbids federal agencies from gathering data on or opening a file on citizens who are simply exercising their constitutional rights of free speech and free assembly—unless they are specifically suspected of criminal or terrorist activity. Protesting a war does not make one a danger to the president, but that did not stop the Secret Service from fishing in dubious political waters. One question never answered is whether the unconstitutional measure was the agency's idea or that of the Nixon White House.

The Justice Department, in an embarrassing moment for the Secret Service, ordered the agency in 1973 to "cease and desist" in its use of NSA data on groups and individuals obtained through wiretaps and other secret electronic surveillance. In a further rebuke of the Service, Attorney General Elliot Richardson ordered that the agency must obtain approval from the Justice Department to make any further requests from other agencies for data.

Adapting to the new rules, the Secret Service's Protective Intelligence Department has continued to turn up constant threats to the president. In one case, a person anointing himself "catman" penned a number of menacing missives to the Reagan White House. In a crowd outside Gracie Mansion, the residence of the mayor of New York City, where Reagan was the guest at an event, Secret Service agents surveying the crowd snapped a photo of a jittery man. When the agency added him to their files and ran a check on him, they found not only that he lived in New York—the postmark on the threatening letters—but the photo also indicated he had moved within a close shot of Reagan, even though screened off by the president's detail. Agents from the New York field office pounced on "catman" in a subway station and arrested him.

Civil libertarians loathe profiling even if it turns up a "catman," but the Secret Service views the technique as invaluable. In 1998, the agency developed a new and improved profile of dangerous persons, but unlike the previous profiles, the new model is based on behavioral traits and actions rather than on socioeconomic or psychological traits. Drawing upon the cooperation of the FBI and the Bureau of Prisons, the Service "conducted an operational study of the thinking and behavior of eighty-three persons known to have attacked or come close to attacking prominent public officials and figures in the United States during the last fifty years."

The Secret Service's analysis of the eighty-three cases took six years to conduct (1992–1997), and its premise is that similarities of "characteristics, thoughts, or behaviors among past assassins could be the key" in finding future ones. Because the subjects had stepped onto the public stage of political violence between 1949 and 1996, the study has a problem: not all of them were still alive. The agency could try to interview Sirhan Sirhan but not Lee Harvey Oswald, presenting a huge discrepancy in the relevance of the data. One key finding was that it is not the "self-announcers," the braggarts who craft threatening letters and menacing phone calls, who present the most danger; less than one-tenth of the eighty-three attackers communicated any threat to the target or to any agency before their attack.

Even though the Secret Service trumpeted the intensive research effort as a powerful protective tool, the new profile is not a significant leap forward. As with previous profiles, vagueness and generality plague any real formula to sort out would-be assassins from troubled persons in the general population, millions of which never hurt anyone, including themselves. The agency's eighty-three case studies cull eight motives for the attacks: notoriety, attention to a personal problem, avenging a wrong, ending personal pain, saving the county or the world, fixating on the target, making money, and effecting political change.

What leads today's agency to open a protective-intelligence case file on an individual? Anyone who exhibits "inappropriate or unusual interest in a protected person or by threatening a protected person" can garner the Service's scrutiny. For agency analysts assessing whether someone constitutes a threat, one criterion is "behaviors of concern":

1. An interest in assassination
2. Ideas and plans about attacking a public official
3. Communicating inappropriate interest in a protectee, especially comments that imply an attack
4. Visiting a site linked to a protectee
5. Approaching a protectee ("traveling to an event site where the public official or figure is scheduled to be")

As the Secret Service develops profiles to identify would-be assassins and combs the known cases for clues of who assassins really are and what motivates them, the answers remain complex and elusive. Webster's Dictionary states that an assassin is "one that murders a politically important person either for hire or from fanatical motive." So it is a term of relative status that includes not only presidential-level leaders, but mayors, John Lennon, and Malcolm X. The assassination of a political leader has a profound political impact no matter the motive or method of the killer or killers. In an instant, the will of the people expressed at the polling places is shattered—bullets for ballots.

Policies change, such as Kennedy's and Johnson's different outlooks on Vietnam. Policy debates and electoral contests are altered, as when presidential candidates George Wallace and Robert Kennedy were gunned down. For decades, the domino effect regarding leaders and policies and historical events can unfold: If John F. Kennedy had won a second term, there would probably not have been a Johnson presidency, particularly as Kennedy was thinking of jettisoning Johnson from the 1964 ticket; had Robert Kennedy survived, been the Democratic nominee, and won the presidency, Nixon might have never been elected—the nation might have been spared Watergate and the prolongation of the Vietnam War.

Certain conspiracies have a more profound impact on a democratic political system than the lone gunman or a few men. Though the impact on policies and the political dominoes of President Kennedy's assassination are the same whether his assassin was a disaffected loner, a team of Mafia hitmen, or a CIA executive action squad, there is a key difference. When powerful organized interests conspire to remove those leaders who threaten them, the very core of democracy is compromised. If it happens frequently, there is no democracy (and no set standard on how often is too often). It is proudly asserted that the United States has never suffered a coup d'état—an overthrow of a duly elected leadership. If, however, John F. Kennedy was killed by organized political interests, then there was one, even if the perpetrators were not the Joint Chiefs of Staff. And the Secret Service knows it.

There are lone nuts, and there are conspiracies. By the legal definition of the knowing participation of more than one person, the assaults against Lincoln, Truman, and Malcolm X were undeniably conspiracies. A conspiracy of lone nuts is not as politically threatening as a conspiracy involving a foreign government, a criminal organization (the Mafia, the Cali drug cartel) or elements of the U.S. intelligence community. In a fictional scenario illustrating a potential conspiracy of lone nuts, John W. Hinckley happens to meet another unstable young man at the hotel bar just before attempting to kill President Reagan. After a couple of beers, Hinckley confides that he is about to kill the president to impress actress Jodi Foster. His muddled soul mate asks if this would work for Raquel Welch as well, since she also had refused to respond to overtures by phone and mail. Hinckley is certain it would work, and they're off together. In contrast, if CIA case officers and anti-Castro Cuban commandos successfully plotted to kill President Kennedy and frame a patsy while they escaped, it is truly a *political* murder instead of a murder that happens to be political in its target and impact. If Hinckley had decided that to really impress Jodi Foster he needed to kill Elton John, the politics would disappear.

So when is the murder of a political leader a *political* assassination? And when is an assassin politically motivated as opposed to being insane? The historical record tells us these are not easy questions. Hinckley was judged insane: If he had announced that he sought to kill Reagan to make Vice President Bush chief executive (Hinckley's parents had supported Bush's campaign for the Republican nomination against Reagan), would that make him an insane *political* assassin?

Arthur Bremer, who gunned down George Wallace, smiled strangely in crowds and allegedly scrawled "killer" on his forehead while putting his neck in a noose a few weeks before he shot Wallace. Bremer was deemed sane. Did the fact that he seemed also to be stalking Carter, Reagan, Humphrey, and Nixon make him politically motivated, or just a political junkie? Booth's killing of Lincoln for the disintegrating Confederacy and Leon Czolgas's killing of President McKinley for the cause of anarchy were clearly political with no issues of diminished mental capacity. Still, Booth was part of an intricate conspiracy, whereas Czolgas acted alone. Sarah Jane Moore, the assailant of President Ford, announced no political motive and had no diminished capacity. However, she seemed intent on bringing herself to the attention of the authorities so that they could prevent her from "testing" the presidential security system. She was somewhat involved in radical politics in San Francisco and had allegedly served as an FBI informant. This is a rich political context, but it was never translated by Moore or her captors into a political motive.

An alleged "political" motive can almost always be found, however weak it may be, even if it is not immediately espoused by the assailant, who may have come from a troubled area of the world, been affiliated with a political organization, or known people who championed a political cause. Yet tens of millions of persons who have some political element in their lives never attempt an assassination. Often, those who do, have major emotional problems unrelated to whatever might pass for their politics. Some, such as Arthur Bremer, do not care who the politician is or what he stands for, so long as he is highly visible or powerful. This maze of psychological and political factors resists simple categorization, and may be glossed over with superficial stereotypes or composites. For the Secret Service, the quest for an assassin's "profile" continues, perhaps never to be fully realized.

Every now and then, profiling is turned on the profilers. On Christmas Day of 2001, roughly ten weeks after September 11, a Secret Service agent trained to spot dangerous persons by using the agency's profiles was singled out by suspicious airlines security. Arab-American Secret Service Agent Walled Shater, a member of President George W. Bush's protective detail and a seven-year veteran of the Service, was flying from Washington to Crawford, Texas, to report for duty at the Bush ranch.

The thirty-three-year-old agent boarded an American Airlines flight and was introduced to the captain to provide the required paperwork for federal agents to carry weapons on planes. However, Shater was asked to leave the aircraft for additional security checks, along with several other passengers. One source said that Shater was allowed to board three times but then was asked to leave.

Two accounts of Shater's problem in boarding the plane have emerged. The pilot filed a complaint with the Secret Service, accusing the agent of unprofessional conduct and claiming that he (the pilot) was concerned that Shater might be misrepresenting himself as a federal agent and that he was "confrontational, hostile, and argumentative." In the complaint, the pilot urged the Service to address Shater's behavior before "he interferes with another commercial airline flight crew in the course of their lawful duties, and compromises the safety and security of the crew and the passengers on board."

The pilot alleged that the incident began when a flight attendant said she and her colleagues were worried by the actions of a passenger who reputedly departed the aircraft while leaving a carry-on bag in his seat and demanding that the flight attendants not leave without him. The pilot wrote that the flight crew "observed books in the individuals [sic] seat which was [sic] written in what she assessed was Arabic-style print."

Additionally, the pilot contended that Shater was asked to leave the plane to fill out new paperwork: "The form was unreadable because it was a carbon copy and there were items missing. I then had the agent come back and recheck his credentials," but the new form was allegedly "filled out improperly." The pilot charged that the agent "came up to me with loud and abusive comments." For an hour and fifteen minutes, the plane was delayed. It finally took off—without Agent Shater. He was temporarily blocked from taking *any* American Airlines flights but was finally flown to Texas the next day, after an airline manager spoke to a Secret Service supervisor.

On January 4, 2002, Shater's attorneys fired back. "Pure and simple," said attorney John Relman, "this is a case of discrimination. This wouldn't have happened if he wasn't of Arab descent."

Another attorney, Christy Lopez, asserted that Shater had shown valid credentials and a badge and that three law-enforcement officials at the airport verified them. His ticket showed that it was government issue. According to the attorneys, the agent had "acted in a cool and professional manner throughout."

Two other passengers told CNN that Shater seemed calm and professional, but they did not see him interact with the pilot. Passenger Mark Puschel, who occupied the seat behind the agent, revealed that a flight attendant twice patted down a jacket that Shater had left on his seat and asked Puschel if he found the agent suspicious. Puschel responded that he did not, and apprised CNN that when the flight attendant examined the book Shater had left, she made a hand gesture "like she was grossed out." Shater's attorneys said that the book was about Middle East history and was in English, and questioned why his belongings were searched.

In response, airline spokesman Todd Burke offered, "This has nothing to do with the ethnicity of the agent." Shater's attorneys said that any money he might receive from the airline by way of a settlement or a ruling against them would be donated to the victims of the September 11 attacks.

As for President Bush, he asserted that, "If he [Shater] was treated that way because of his ethnicity, that will make me madder than heck. . . . I told him how proud I was that he is at my side."

So how effective is the profiling and protective intelligence of the Secret Service in the "big picture" of rooting out and preventing attacks on presidents, candidates, First Families, and other protectees? No one except the agency knows just how many would-be assassins have been foiled and how many potential assassins have been identified, investigated, and incarcerated. There are dozens of arrests each year of "very dangerous" persons, each annual catch containing perhaps two or eight or twenty people who would have shot at the president if they had not been arrested. But it is still a problem of the first magnitude that those who actually show up and shoot at our political leaders are, by definition, unknown to the U.S. Secret Service.

By itself, this indicates that significant deficiencies in the protective intelligence system exist. One involves the system's technical capacity. Though the Service's main complaint is that raw domestic-intelligence data have decreased drastically in recent decades, the agency struggles to process whatever data—police reports, memos from the FBI and CIA, e-mails, phone tips, reports from field offices, and other sources—the Service gets. By the Treasury Department's own admission, the quality of data analysis has suffered because of the Service's inability to develop the statistical tools needed to mine it if collected. Though these capacities were presumably upgraded significantly with the creation of the Service's Threat Assessment Center in 1996, the broadened mission has meant more and different kinds of data to process, as in the recent study profiling violent offenders in America's schools.

The Service takes the position that "more is better"—if it could only obtain sufficient raw data, the agency's intelligence system would better meet the demands of the protective mission. The new policies of agency data sharing after September 11, 2001, will doubtlessly provide more. Still, the system may need considerable upgrading before it can efficiently deal with the data already on hand: increasing reams of data are only useful if the Service knows what to look for and if its data system knows how to find it.

Critics of the Service still point to the data-gathering breakdown regarding John Hinckley after he was arrested at the Nashville Airport on October 9, 1980, as he attempted to board a plane while carrying three pistols. With candidate Reagan having just canceled a Nashville trip and President Carter at the Grand Old Opry, mere proximity should have landed Hinckley on the Service's Watch List. Even today, the fact that this incident did not send up a red flag about Hinckley seems like a classic bureaucratic foul-up to many people: either the Nashville police or the FBI should have reported him, and agents should have been looking for him as they protected President Reagan.

Then and now, the Service looks at things differently. As logical as this criticism seems, a Secret Service agent in charge of a field office said of the Hinckley case:

> Take the same situation of someone in New York City being arrested for carrying a gun before a president is supposed to visit. Is the Secret Service supposed to look into every incident? We'd need ten thousand agents [to check out everyone arrested with a gun in sites a president intends to visit] in New York City.

No one can dispute that the Service has limited personnel, 2,700 agents. It can only interview or check out a tiny sample of its more than 50,000 files, with the real problem how to choose *which* cases should be selected for the Watch List of 400 persons and then given special attention. The problem remains unresolved, and this is the critical weakness of the protective intelligence system. Currently, there are no precise profiles or techniques for picking out the next Bremer or the next Hinckley, a fact even if the Service had 120,000 dossiers.

The Watch List contains three to four hundred persons not because that is the actual number of dangerous people in America but because, in addition to representing the Service's best guess as to who the most dangerous persons are, it represents the number of cases that the agency can handle at one time. Despite the impressive progress in the fields of computer technology and psychiatry, the Service still has few solid clues as to how to look for potential assassins, how to decide between those who are actually dangerous or *potentially* dangerous. Computers, no matter how sophisticated, can only be programmed on what to look for when the Secret Service tries to select one truly dangerous person from a group of one thousand seemingly menacing persons. To date, no such knowledge exists for the Service or any other law-enforcement agency.

In choosing its four hundred entries for the Watch List, the Service does not depend upon hard scientific concepts of psychology and psychiatry; instead, the choices are analysts' own best judgment. The Watch List is the product of educated guesswork, with some individuals dropped from the list because they no longer appear to be acutely dangerous and others added, and is checked for consistency to ensure that it never deteriorates into a hodgepodge of cases. For the Watch List, the human element still trumps computers: agents bring their own judgment, based on experience and insight, to bear. There is nothing automatic or scientific about it.

The human touch can be fraught with mistakes, such as when former Director Robert Simpson (1981–1982), sounding like a pop-psychology simpleton, revealed his and the Service's surprise when a main element in their profile was erased in 1975—gender. All previous assassins had been males until Fromm and Moore showed up. Simpson says that the Service had to "rethink" the profile: "Didn't make any difference, the sex of the individual. Anybody can be an assassin."

An area in which computer science does dominate is in the agency's analysis of threatening letters and fingerprinting. Breaking down the typing and comparing it to previous ominous letters in mere seconds, computers can identify the writer if he or she is on file virtually anywhere. For fingerprints on letters, laser probes can discern prints invisible to the human eye or normal microscopic analysis. Then the agency's computers trace the print through a file shared by many law-enforcement agencies (the AFIS system). The computer unearths the best ten matches.

In the Service's dependence on intelligence organizations for much of its data, the agency can sometimes be at the mercy of specious information. The Service's biggest concern throughout November and December 1981 was protecting against a Libyan hit team allegedly dispatched to the United States by Moammar Kaddafi to assassinate President Reagan. Reagan himself announced that there was "hard evidence" of the plot, which was presumably provided by the CIA. Much of the mainstream news coverage concurred that intelligence about the Libyan plot was detailed and reliable: The hit team was reportedly composed of three Libyans, three Iranians, and an East German. According to "sources," the hit squad had landed in Mexico and entered the United States, and in the newspapers, readers were apprised that one assassin wore cowboy boots and smoked English cigarettes; sketches of the assassins also ran in the press, which cited the chief sources as "security officials" or "Capitol Hill sources." A number of publications simply used the vague phrase "It's been learned."

The "hard intelligence" that put the Secret Service on perpetual alert for two months was less-than-solid to say the least. Though one has to assume that the agency had access to better intelligence than reporters, ABC newsman Sam Donaldson said, "We've never confirmed any hard evidence about a hit team inside the United States." Two members of the Senate Intelligence Committee who were primary media sources for the Libyan story subsequently felt that they were misled—"entrapped" by the CIA briefers who told them about the plot and about the alleged evidence. Was the whole affair the result of faulty intelligence gathering or analysis? Was it all a CIA concoction designed to provide leverage against Kaddafi or to discredit him? Like the rest of America, even the Secret Service may have been unable to learn the truth from closemouthed CIA officials.

The Service has adopted a more hard-nosed, skeptical attitude about the validity of all CIA bombshells, but in the post–September 11 era, they cannot afford to ignore any CIA data on alleged threats against the president and other officials. Even now, the Service has neither the personnel nor the sources to develop its own intelligence networks in a league with the CIA or the FBI or even to verify the work of other agencies. Director Stafford and his agents must take intelligence reports at face value, perhaps with a little discount for past performance. In the final analysis, no matter how weak or dubious the intelligence appears, the Secret Service is in no position to dismiss a report that Al Quaeda or any other group is out to get the president, and must risk the distraction and embarrassment of a wild goose chase rather than the parade of the riderless horse.

PART THREE

THE HUMAN FACTOR

## CHAPTER 10

# BOOZE, BURNOUT, DEMANDS, AND DEPRESSION

*"The Mission Comes First"*

—*A Secret Service Field Agent, March 2002*

Some might think that the men and women of the Secret Service, in their crisp suits and dark sunglasses, operate at peak efficiency every day, the very embodiment of image presented in the documentary "Inside the Secret Service" (1995). But for many agents, the image belies the truth. Fatigue, stress, fear, domestic woes, alcohol and drug abuse, and every frailty of human nature permeate the Secret Service, and though the bulk of the force either rises above or tamps down the pressures, many agents battle a range of demons from the bottle to burnout.

The Secret Service has a team of in-house psychologists who counsel agents about stress and about the problems it can create, such as alcoholism, and as part of an ongoing program of stress evaluation, agents are given physical exams yearly and agility tests every six months. However, like police officers concerned that a visit to a psychiatrist or psychologist can scuttle a career, agents have traditionally wrestled with their problems alone, which, unchecked, can ruin not only an agent's career, but also his or her family life. According to Secret Service spokesmen, self-awareness is the key: Agents are taught to discern warning signs of severe stress manifested by themselves or their colleagues. Still, many of those agents avoid therapy at all costs, and the costs can prove severe.

As far back as 1975, former Agent Clint Hill stated, "A lot of agents are getting tired." He claimed that some were discovered by doctors to show the same type of fatigue experienced by soldiers in combat. Hill retired that same year as head of the White House detail at only age forty-three.

In 1978, the Secret Service commissioned a study of the effects of stress on agents, the first such check that the agency had done on itself in its 114 years. The agency turned to the same renowned psychiatrist, Dr. Frank Ochberg, who had helped profile assassins in the past. Ochberg, from the University of Michigan and an associate director of the National Institute of Mental Health, spent a year interviewing agents around the country. When the study was finished, Secret Service spokesman Robert Snow said that the agency had presented a "pretty general" portion of it before Congress in the course of seeking appropriations and allowed agents themselves to read selected pages of the report so long as they didn't take them out of the office. Ochberg's findings remain as sobering and as unresolved in 2002 as they did in the late 1970s.

Though the findings and data of the psychiatrist and his research team have stayed under Service lock and key, Ochberg and several agents have discussed many aspects of the yearlong study, completed in 1979. Ochberg indicates that the travel routine, grueling hours without relief, and the stress of looking for that lone face in the crowd and realizing that one might have to take a bullet for the president piles exhaustion and fatigue upon agents. Their reflexes and reactions suffer, placing the lives of protectees at risk. The problem has not gone away since 1979; in fact, it has swelled in the months since September 11, 2001.

For the men and women who guard the president, the eight-hour shifts can prove nearly debilitating as they try to maintain a heightened state of alertness every minute they are on the job. Presidents and candidates travel so extensively that jet lag becomes chronic, exacerbated by "shift lag"—the protective detail works in three 8-hour shifts, and agents are rotated among shifts. With shift lag, jet lag, and tension, it is a wonder that agents are not perennially exhausted. The agency grasps that it could instantly reduce stress and fatigue by shorter shifts and more stable assignments, but the measures require drastic increases in Service personnel levels and a conspicuous rise in budget. Neither has been on the horizon, and stress and manpower problems have escalated since September 11, 2001. How the coming reorganization of Homeland Security unfolds could well produce improvements and help for the Secret Service.

For many kinds of the agency's work, an eight-hour shift is appropriate, but, depending on what the president or another protectee is doing, eight hours can prove far too long for agents to maintain the unblinking concentration required for effective protection. There is a great deal of difference between an eight-hour shift when the president is asleep and when he hosts a breakfast for businessmen at the White House, meets with a foreign ambassador, and then goes out to attend a luncheon.

In an interview given shortly after his report to the Secret Service, Ochberg said, "Law enforcement agencies across the country have all recognized that there is a need to understand how officers deal with and tolerate stress. The Federal Government has at last recognized it should be the same. The idea that the Secret Service is supposed to be beyond stress is not true."

Though the threat of being shot haunts agents, Ochberg noted that highly trained agents standing guard in hallways found the sheer boredom versus the need for constant vigilance a major source of stress and tiredness. The boredom factor—incessant stretches where nothing happens, but *could* happen in an instant—especially plagues the Service's thousand or so uniformed officers. They must stand guard for hours at a variety of locations, from the White House gates to the doors of foreign embassies along Embassy Row in Washington. As one uniformed officer describes it, "If you're standing guard on the midnight shift and no one comes by to say hello for hours—well, that can get very boring." Another officer says of fixed-post guard duty, "Sometimes you wish something would happen so you could see some action."

Several years ago, the Uniformed Division tried rotating duty assignments every two hours. Uniformed guards would be on duty for two hours and off for two, but the schedule drew heavy public and congressional criticism for being too "cushy," which fueled a quick return to standard eight-hour shifts. Although guard-post assignments are changed frequently to ease boredom, no matter how novel the surroundings, eight hours of standing and watching can numb one's thoughts and reactions.

Because of September 11, 2001, the already undermanned Secret Service has heaped additional hours and even double shifts upon both plainclothes and uniformed personnel, and more and more agents and officers are "flaking" or burning out. Director Stafford has admitted that the strains are causing havoc for the Service as men and women are resigning for other jobs or performing at substandard levels because of too many hours, too little support, and too much stress. Fighting a "continuous loss of personnel" because of "enormous overtime burdens" at a time when the need for enhanced presidential protection has never been higher, Stafford says, "I'm well aware that the attrition rate of the Uniformed Division is at a critical level."

Of all the personal burdens that dog agents, the impact of their job upon their family life might well be the worst. The men and women of the Secret Service, in many ways, have two families: their wives and children, and the agency. Before anyone is hired by the Secret Service, the agency interviews spouses and family members to determine not only if a recruit is well adjusted, but also to determine whether his/her family can handle the strains to come. The wife of a twenty-nine-year agency veteran says, "There are many, many lonely hours. When his responsibilities of the job increase, so do the tensions at home. You just force yourself to cope with all the problems. But since you don't know any other life, you get used to it."

Despite the stoicism of those words, many agents' families resent that the agency comes first. According to Ochberg, "It gets so that they can never invite people for dinner, because they might have to leave at the last moment." The daughter of one agent told Ochberg sarcastically that she didn't expect her father to be at her wedding.

Another agent's wife, speaking only on condition her name not be mentioned, related, "I have nothing good to say about what it's like being married to a Secret Service agent, so I'd rather not say anything at all."

For agents, a normal social life is virtually out of the question. Still, most agents' spouses apparently come to grips with "sharing" their husbands with his mission, as the divorce rate among agents is no higher than that of the general population.

Another agent acknowledges the overlapping relationships between his "two families." He acknowledged that a career in the Secret Service "is tough on your personal and family life, but it's made up for in a real sense because it *is* your family, or a family."

He says, "There's little room for family: mission comes first." He notes than an agent could be plucked to spend six weeks in Salt Lake for the Olympics at short notice. In contrast, if an agent has a family crisis of injury, the Service will quickly fly him home. Yet he may miss his daughter's birthday party while he is on the road with a protectee. Higher-ups have more control over their lives, but until you're that far up the ladder, there's an agency saying: "If the Secret Service wanted you to have a family they would have issued you one."

In one instance, an agent suffered a "training accident," and it was touch-and-go that he would survive his injuries. The Service brought his parents to the hospital, with an agent to take care of them, and placed another agent outside the hospital-room door. Such attention is part of the Service's code and culture.

One agent's view is that the Service is comprised of "civilian soldiers, a paramilitary organization," and it is key that no matter the pressures, agents must "follow the rules." An agent who doesn't "play by the rules will be a journeyman agent his entire career," he asserts. "We are a very tight family, and mission comes before family." But there is "extraordinary support for personal problems—beyond belief—to help out."

Not everyone can withstand the pressures and the personal problems. Former Agent Marty Venker, who worked ten years of presidential protection for Nixon, Ford, Carter, and a host of foreign dignitaries, burned out on the presidential fast track and had a nervous breakdown. More bluntly than any agent on the record, Venker described his own problems and those of other agents to writer George Rush. No other agent has come close to such public airing of his personal demons and the stress afflicting agents on the "presidential fast track."

"First chance I got," says Marty, "I stopped by W-16 at the White House and took a look. The [Dr. Ochberg] report said that, roughly speaking, in terms of tension faced by an average person, an agent aged two years for every year he guarded the president.

"Maybe it was just as well, then, that I never touched down long enough for any romance to take root," Marty admits. "In those ten years, I could count my relationships on one hand. That's how often I'd meet someone with the will and the means to keep up with me. I met one woman in Paris. I was walking out of the American Embassy toward my car and she saw me. She was standing at the fence, so I walked up to her and we started talking. She came from a real rich family in Chicago. She was gorgeous and great fun and she spoke French better than the French. She'd fly around the world to meet me. That was the only way we could keep it up."

Describing the pressures and fatigue of agents protecting a president on the road, Venker says: "Seven o'clock P.M. You've only got a couple of hours before you're on duty again at midnight. After a while clocks just become decorative objects.

"There were many nights when I used to wake up in some dark hotel room and not know where in the world I was. I'd look at my watch and it'd say seven o'clock. Great. A.M. or P.M.? And by the way, what day is it? I'd get up and search around for a pack of matches: Oh, Geneva, Switzerland. Then clunk, back to bed. Sometimes we'd have to hammer on an agent's door, practically break it down, and the guy still wouldn't get up. On the plane guys who'd never had a nosebleed would suddenly find blood gushing out their noses—from not getting enough rest."

Other agents have concurred with Venker's observations of the strains that presidential travel pours upon agents. Former Agent Chuck Rochner observes, "The burnout factor was a problem for a lot of us. Just when you got some kind of a reprieve in a field office, you found yourself back on a detail."

Chuck Vance, the agent who married Susan Ford, daughter of President Ford, and left the Service soon afterward, after sixteen years, discussed the crushing stress of the job. "Every year," he points out, "[the agents] have a physical examination and monitor their vital signs. Every year, those signs begin to deteriorate: high blood pressure, things like that . . . I [still] find it hard to relax."

Ex-agent Donald Bendickson said that for two decades, he lived "at the whim of somebody else—maybe three years with my family during Christmas. . . . Stress is an individual thing. Some people handle it and some people can't, but it takes its toll . . . inwardly or outwardly."

Nineteen-year agent Jim Kalafatis offers, "We had two agents die within a month, of sudden heart attacks. They were athletic guys, in good shape. The first thing you do is call down to the office and ask, Was there any history of angina? You think, maybe this guy abused himself: drinking, rich food; maybe he didn't listen to his doctor. But when a guy dies suddenly, it kind of scares everybody. You say, 'I'm healthy. I don't have heart problems. I don't think the medical guys know completely what stress does to you. You have other weird things. We've had several guys die of brain tumors. Maybe it was related, maybe not. You don't know."

For Agent Venker, the pressures he felt accumulated until they exploded in an argument with the head of his detail over a relatively innocuous matter—the proper dress for agents guarding Nixon.

Venker tells Rush, "We headed for the airport. Nixon had taken the train to Vienna, where we were supposed to relieve the earlier shift at four P.M. We should've had plenty of time to make it, but we ran into some bad plane connections, so we didn't get to the hotel in Vienna till almost nine. When the shift finally showed up, Mike Endicott [Venker's superior] was mad. My men were still in their casual clothes."

"I took a pretty good piece out of him," Endicott recalls. "We had people who had been on for quite a while. Not that they were complaining. But I was Marty's boss and I told him he had a responsibility to make the relief as expeditiously as possible, and that he didn't have anything to do but travel that day. He didn't care for the criticism. A few words were exchanged."

[Venker] said to him, "What are you flipping out about? It'll take us two minutes to change into our suits.

"My shift changed into their suits, and we walked Nixon to dinner. I took him into this banquet hall that was about seventy feet long. Nixon was eating by himself at a table. I was about thirty feet away sitting in a chair. I'd been hyped up all day. And then suddenly I was alone with *him* again. As he ate, we just kept staring at each other. That's when things started spinning. I could hear Nixon's knife and fork *screeching* against his plate. It got to be deafening. Nixon cutting his meat in this depressing city with its overtones of the centuries—dead kings, ostentatious waste . . .

"I [Venker] suddenly felt that if I didn't get up from that chair, I never would. I heard a referee counting: 'Seven . . . eight . . . nine.' So I got out a piece of paper and I wrote to Mike asking if I could talk with him when the shift was over. I passed it to an agent in the hall. The agent came back and told me that Mike said if I wanted to talk to him, I should talk to him right now. Somebody filled in for me and I went outside in the hall and told Mike, 'I can't stand one more minute of this. I've got to quit. I'll try to finish my shift, but if you can find anybody to fill in for me, it'd be a big help.' He started getting into the argument about the clothes again."

"He was wrong in what he did," says Endicott, "it wasn't me he offended or hurt. He hurt the other guys. . . . That wasn't very considerate."

Venker told Endicott, 'It doesn't have anything to do with the argument we had. I just can't take it anymore.' Mike said that if that's the way I felt, he thought I should leave right away. He started talking again about who was right and wrong about the suits and I said, 'I don't think you understand. As of this moment I don't work for you anymore.' I was trying not to get any more emotional than I already was, but he didn't seem to understand me. So I said something like, 'You can't tell me shit! It's over!' That's when he told me he would contact the U.S. Embassy, that there'd be a ticket waiting for me there."

Endicott remembers, "I suggested that he return to the United States. I was taking him off the trip . . . he said he was going to quit and I said, 'Fine.'"

Typically, many agents contend that it is not the stress that causes problems for some, but that agents who can't take it are somehow not "wired" physically or emotionally for the daily rigors. Jerry Parr, one of the heroic detail whose quick reactions saved President Reagan's life, said of Venker, "Marty was a very sensitive guy. He did his duty, but I think his focus was elsewhere. It was my sense that he really wasn't a law-enforcement type. Some that aren't can keep it up and end up retiring and do quite well. Others don't do as well."

Agent Rochner believes that for many members of the Service's presidential detail, there is a point where it's time to leave: "There are burn-out cases, and they're caused by many different things. You can be on the front line too much. You can take your job seriously, do it day after day, year after year. When I left the White House, the last thing I wanted to do was take a foreign trip. It was really tough on me to take that last foreign trip. It was too much. There is a percentage of us for whom enough is enough."

According to Secret Service data, only about 3 percent of those who become agents leave before retirement, and most of those people drop out within the first year or two. After 20 years, agents can retire if they are 50 or older, with most stepping down at the mandatory retirement age, 55, to receive a full pension. Many critics charge that the Service is "playing" with the real figures about agents leaving before age 55.

Rochner says, "I didn't go out under the best of circumstances. And I've kind of resolved it in my mind. It's a very competitive outfit with a lot of hard-charging guys who . . . really claw to the top."

Those "circumstances" thrust Rochner into a battle for agency control between Director H. Stuart Knight (1973–1981) and Assistant Director Robert Powis, a member of Reagan's detail since the 1976 campaign. In 1980, Knight accused Powis of financial mismanagement, reprimanded him, and tried to demote him; however, Powis, with the support of powerful Reagan confidant Edwin Meese, took the matter to court, cleared his name and reputation, and was promoted to deputy assistant secretary of the treasury. Knight soon resigned as director of the Secret Service and was replaced by John R. Simpson (1981–1992).

Rochner reflects, "There's a lot wrong with the Secret Service. Many who stayed on after Marty [Venker] found out that there was only a certain number of leadership positions and most of the agents were overqualified. Probably the majority of the agents go out bitter in one way or another. It seems as if none of them ever meet their expectations. It's a special group of men, extremely competitive and I'm no exception; I should have been director. Most guys felt that way. They really worked hard for that position. Many retired with disappointment." They still do.

After retirement from the Service, Agent Mike Endicott spoke evasively about one of the whispered fears of the agency—nervous breakdowns: "I'm sure if there were incidents of nervous breakdowns, they certainly wouldn't publicize them to everybody."

Venker addresses the matter head on: "I know others beside the agent who dreamt of the 'faceless assassin.' There was a period when I was in the New York field office when we heard about a couple of agents flipping out. One guy was found stalking through a forest in New Jersey. He had a gun and he was wearing next to nothing but combat boots. The police found him. Another agent got 'lost in the crowd'—that's what it's called. He just wandered away for the detail and kept going 'Gotta take a break.' The plane took off without him. A couple of these breakdowns happened, by coincidence, around the same time. Naturally our reaction was to laugh it off. Somebody came into the field office one day and made some wisecrack about 'What's happening to his place?' A bunch of us pulled out our pistols, held them up to our heads and screamed, 'Aaaaahhh!' "

For many agents then and now, the ideal is Clint Hill, the symbol of Secret Service courage since November 22, 1963, when he raced from the follow-up car to hurl himself across the back of John F. Kennedy's limo and shove Jackie Kennedy down onto the blood-spattered backseat. The thirty-one-year-old Hill placed his jacket over the president's shattered skull. Hill was never the same after those horrible minutes in Dallas, as he told Mike Wallace on *60 Minutes* in 1975. Breaking into tears several times during the interview, the agent expressed guilt for having failed to react faster at the sound of the first shot. Hill told Mike Wallace and the nation that he felt guilty for not reacting faster. He admitted his need for psychiatric help.

Jerry Parr, who went from the hero of Hinckley's attempt on Reagan to a counselor to the terminally ill and the homeless, says, "Clint Hill is probably a person who should have had an opportunity to talk about it more, to ventilate. The organization didn't provide it. I'm not blaming the organization. Sometimes organizations have to grow, like people."

In 1973, Agent Jim Connolly, battling alcohol abuse, killed himself, and Rochner states that another agent took his life "in the late sixties, in Washington, with his own weapon. There were signs he was beginning to buckle."

Jerry Parr reasons, "The Service ought to talk about fear. I gave my people an opportunity to talk about it after the attempt on Reagan. Sure there's fear. But a macho organization doesn't like to put it out it's afraid."

In the years since Ochberg's study, the Service has tried to do a more "mature job of self-scrutiny" about the pressures of the job. Whenever possible, agents no longer have to share hotel rooms, providing welcome solitude for a few hours on the road. It has reduced the number of days agents can spend traveling during campaigns. On the pressure-packed White House detail, most agents are limited now to three to five years of service before reassignment. In theory, the Service will send any agent, as well as anyone in his or her immediate family, to psychotherapists and experts in substance abuse, marital counseling, and personal finance.

Ex-agent Rochner told Rush, "As with many law-enforcement agencies, I think we're just catching up. . . . The last ten years, they got a handle on it, or were moving in the right direction. They were actually looking for people who showed stress."

Venker's comments broke the code of silence about emotional problems among agents, but his peers still view him as more of an aberration, an agent who just couldn't "tough it out." Endicott asserts, "Marty's quitting was a matter of stress, but we weren't conscious of him having a nervous breakdown . . . . Certainly there was nothing abnormal in his behavior that would cause me to call the Director. If Marty had a breakdown, he certainly didn't convey it to me. There was nothing that led me to believe he was anything other than frustrated with the job and with his social life. . . . Many agents like to leave their job at work. But with Marty, it became almost impossible for him to come back to work. It got to the point where he had to decide what he was going to do with the rest of his life . . . Marty was a hell of an agent and one heck of a dedicated employee, but it was probably in his best interests that he left. . . . You could see that he was not necessarily comfortable with his colleagues anymore. . . . It's just like a marriage that goes bad. Sometimes you just grow apart. Nobody's fault. You just change. Marty changed"

In 2002, the Service has family and individual assistance programs implemented in the years after Venker's breakdown, in 1974. But, as many critics point out, the programs are mere institutional "makeup," for most agents still recoil from the thought of counseling, which they believe will end any chance of their climbing to the Service's highest positions.

Words that Venker uttered in 1988 ring true in 2002: "The thought of getting 'counseled' never crossed my mind. I felt so different from the rest of them. I didn't have a wife. I didn't have an alcohol problem. What advice could they give me? I just didn't want to be a Secret Service agent anymore. So . . . I had a nervous breakdown. I was okay for a couple of weeks after Vienna. I partied some. But all of a sudden, after all that running around, it was like I'd smashed into a brick wall. I couldn't get out of bed. After all those days when I didn't need any sleep, now I couldn't stay awake. When I opened my eyes, I'd just stare at the ceiling above my bed. I can't remember what I thought about. . . .

"On one of my first ventures [back] among the living, I visited Dr. [Bertram] Newman. Newman diagnosed me as suffering from something akin to post-traumatic stress disorder."

The "partying" and drinking to which Venker turned to relieve stress continue among some—though certainly not the bulk—of agents today. In February 2002, several of Vice President Dick Cheney's agents wrapped up their shift on his visit to San Diego and decided to toss down a few beers at a local watering hole called the Daley Double. Many drinks later, fists and feet began flying in all directions just outside the bar—the four agents were battling fifteen civilians. In the melee one of the agents clamped his teeth around a man's ear and tore off the tip, which was never found. When police finally broke up the brawl, they were stunned to learn that four of the "miscreants" were Secret Service officers. The agency, sorting out what happened that night, has yet to make a final decision on how the quartet will be disciplined.

Though the majority of agents do not abuse alcohol or drugs, the simple fact that even a handful might is cause for concern, if not outright alarm. An agent under the influence or even nursing a hangover might not spot the face in the crowd, and even if he or she does, might not be able to react quickly enough because of dulled reflexes. A president or a protectee could die if just one member of a protective detail is not 100 percent in command of their faculties. An intoxicated or drugged agent is a menace, pure and simple.

Beyond the immediate jeopardy an impaired agent places fellow agents and protectees in, the fallout of the problem cuts at both the Service's public image and could erode confidence in the agency's ability to protect the president and others. Recent reports of several agents driving drunk—several times to report for duty at the White House—have blemished the Service publicly. Just as disturbing to many in Congress and the White House was the agency's "discipline" against the offenders: One agent received a pass, and the other, who had a prior drunk-driving episode, was yanked from the presidential Protective Detail, but received no other sanction. Despite the drunkenness, the agent had still been promoted to the White House detail.

A twenty-page report released in 2002 by the inspector general of the Treasury Department revealed that the Secret Service glossed over or ignored incidents involving agents, uniformed officers, and alcohol. Typical of the agency's response to the problem was an episode in which an officer suspected of four drunk driving incidents within eight months in 1995 received only a "fitness for duty" medical examination. On one of the four occasions, police had seized the Secret Service man's weapon. Only in early 1999, when a court convicted the officer of driving under the influence, did the agency consider sacking him. To date, his status remains unclear.

In the early morning hours of January 31 and February 1, 2002, some twenty Secret Service agents assigned to the Salt Lake City Winter Olympics were drinking and partying at the Western Inn Motel in Provo, Utah. When the motel manager requested that the revelers tone things down and not smoke, several drunken agents reportedly retorted, "We don't have to do anything we don't want." Soon the party grew louder, and the manager, Casey Clements, returned to the room, where his appearance enraged an agent. Clements told reporters, "That upset him. He pushed me out of the door and said if I did that again, he'd throw me to the ground, put a gun to my head, and I'd be sorry."

Allegations later surfaced that the Secret Service contingent may have been drinking with local teenage girls and that one of the girls might have been sexually assaulted. These reports are being investigated by the Utah County attorney's office with the cooperation of the agency. A spokesman for the Service stated that one of the agents at the party resigned and two others could face charges.

A *U.S. News & World Report* investigation also uncovered other embarrassing flaps involving agents and liquor. In August 1999, at Lulu's Bar—"where every day is Mardi Gras"—in Washington, D.C., police rushed into the men's room to break up a shooting that had injured two men; one of them was an Air Force recruit, the other Secret Service Agent Manuel Puente. Puente, a member of the White house detail, was dismissed from the force for "conduct unbecoming."

In October 1999, small-time thief Kenneth Blake slipped into the Chicago Fairmont Hotel, looking to lift a handbag or two. First Lady Hillary Clinton was staying there, and Secret Service Agent Mary Drury was knocking back a few drinks in the hotel bar with another agent near 11:00 P.M. She was off-duty, but carrying her .357 Sig Sauer service weapon in her pocketbook—in violation of the agency's edict that forbids any agent to drink while carrying a gun.

Blake sidled alongside the agent and took off with her handbag—and weapon. According to reporters, "It was the second time Drury had lost her gun . . . and she had been promoted a grade between the first and second incident. The *U.S. News & World Report* also asserted: "In another incident, in 1993, Drury was driving home from a Chicago bar when she rammed her government car into a Chicago Transit Authority bus so hard that several items flew out of the trunk. Drury has not received any significant sanction from the Secret Service."

With stress and hours mounting since September 11, 2001, many agents and uniformed officer of the Service are, in their own words, "burning out." Days off have become scarce, with manpower to guard the White House, the president, the vice president, their families, and an expanded list of others stretched to the limit. The political campaigns of 2002 and 2004 will surely present even more difficult situations, with many new protectees for the service to cover. A special agent relates that the number of available agents is in great flux, estimating that right now there are some twenty-seven hundred agents and twelve hundred in the uniformed division, but this number changes daily. Clearly, the Secret Service is straining to bulk up as rapidly as possible since September 11, 2001.

The special agent pointed to the Service's current shorthandedness. Within a three-week period they had the Super Bowl, Olympics, and the United Nations to secure. "Luckily, New Orleans agents flew to Salt Lake City to bolster the Olympics [because the Super Bowl was a one-day event]," he says. "'Every agent with a badge and a gun was working." Even the agency's Public Affairs Office was practically emptied to cover the protective workload.

With that ever-escalating workload since September 11, agents' nerves and energy are stretched to the limit, and with the danger of burnout rising, the Secret Service must devise new ways to help their people cope. Otherwise, even the president's protective detail might have one or two agents so stressed, so exhausted that the chief executive or someone else will be vulnerable to attack.

## CHAPTER 11

# FAMILY MATTERS—PROTECTING
# FIRST LADIES AND FIRST KIDS

*Often, however, agents develop genuine and often long-lasting friendships with the people they protect. Still, agents know they must maintain a discrete distance in public from the people they guard, especially if the protectee is a young, attractive woman or the teenage daughter of the president.*

—*Ex-Agent Dennis V. N. McCarthy*

For First Ladies and their children, the initial days in the White House can be exciting. Watched by Secret Service agents with their sunglasses, earpieces, deferential manners, and rugged good looks, presidents' wives and kids feel important—and to the Service, they are. Often, however, the novelty of round-the-clock protection begins to erode, and residents of the White House turn annoyed and rebellious when it comes to their protectors. Agents understand this, but their mission cannot change: they must keep the First Lady and the First Kids in sight and out of harm's way.

In the 1930s and 1940s, Eleanor Roosevelt refused Secret Service protection, believing that their presence made her look more like a queen flanked by an imperial guard than the nation's first truly public First Lady. Agents tailed her surreptitiously; she just refused to acknowledge them.

In contrast to many First Ladies of the modern era, Jackie Kennedy, who traveled widely and often unaccompanied by her husband, had a favorite agent, Clint Hill, and always asked that he be assigned to her detail whenever she was on the road. Hill liked the First Lady, but in 1995 told the makers of "Inside the Secret Service" that there was "a lack of support" [from the Secret Service] on the First Lady detail. Though there was always lots of "help" on a presidential detail, he notes, on a First Lady detail agents [operated] "pretty much on [their] own." Perhaps that is why Hill admits performing duties for Mrs. Kennedy beyond agency guidelines:

"I dealt with the maid and nanny . . . a lot of things she would deal directly with me instead of going through a social secretary."

Pat Nixon viewed the Secret Service as necessary, but tried to set her own conditions for protection. One of her agents recalls, "Mrs. Nixon always wanted as little security as possible around her and more than once complained to the president about the number of agents assigned to her. She was also genuinely concerned about not creating problems for other people when she traveled around Washington or any other city."

She did not buck the Service about an agent driving her to her weekly appointment at the Washington, D.C., Elizabeth Arden beauty parlor, where another agent would sit inside while she had her hair done. But she was angry to learn that whenever she went out for her beautician appointment, several agents in a back-up car trailed her limo at a distance because they feared that if she spotted them, she would complain to the president. She demanded an explanation for the presence of the "trail car," and her driver replied that it was simply a precaution in case her own car broke down.

Although she was not as extreme as Eleanor Roosevelt, who flatly refused protection, Mrs. Nixon often gave the agency fits. She once informed her detail that she would be heading to Los Angeles to visit a friend for a few days—without full Secret Service protection. In no uncertain terms, she told the agency that she wished to be left alone on the trip.

Agent Dennis V. N. McCarthy recalls, "Instead of being driven in a government car with me riding shotgun in the front seat—our usual procedure—she said she was going to ride to Los Angeles with her friend alone."

Mrs. Nixon allowed McCarthy to follow her in another car, but was adamant that agents could not come near her friend's house during the visit. Faced by a First Lady demanding that he abdicate the most basic protective procedures and knowing that she could have him yanked off the prestigious White House detail, he notes, "The 'order' put me in a delicate position."

McCarthy turned to Agent Bill Duncan, the man in charge of the First Family's protection, for help. Duncan called Mrs. Nixon, but could not get her to back down from her vacation demands. When Duncan called McCarthy back, the head of the protective detail said that they would have to do their job by "tricking" the First Lady into thinking she was getting her way. McCarthy says, "It was agreed that I would follow Mrs. Nixon and her friend in a Secret Service car. I was to be the only one she would ever see, but Bill assigned a carload of other agents to follow far enough behind me so that Mrs. Nixon wouldn't know they were there." If there were trouble of any kind, the agents could close on the scene quickly.

The ruse worked, because the press thought that Mrs. Nixon had traveled to the couple's ranch at San Clemente.

No one, friend or foe, would likely dispute that Hillary Clinton is a fiercely independent person who has her own way of doing things. Early in her husband's first term, however, Mrs. Clinton, code-named "Eagle" by the Secret Service, learned the realities of protecting a First Lady in an era growing more and more dangerous. As she attended an event on Georgia Avenue in Washington, shaking hands and chatting with the crowd, Secret Service sharpshooters lined the rooftops, and spectators were herded through metal detectors. Among the crowd mingled plainclothes agents scanning for any hint of danger to the First Lady.

"We try to make our protection the least intrusive as possible and still maintain safety," says Secret Service spokesman William Burch. "But the bubble is created not only by Secret Service but staff and press."

Still, with the gregarious Bill Clinton and Hillary, the Secret Service knew they would be in for a challenging time. "I suspect there will be more 'off the record' movements, more spur-of-the-moment visits," said former Secret Service Agent Richard McCann, who guarded presidents Richard Nixon and Gerald Ford and Vice President George Bush. "Yeah, they're [the Clintons] living in a fish bowl, and it's going to be difficult for them. But you try to work it out."

According to agents, Hillary was easier to guard in public, as she was not prone to the same need for "crowd worship" as her husband. In that regard, Hillary Clinton and Barbara Bush actually shared something in common: on forays outside the White House, both First Ladies tended to meet their public at actual events and did not "work the crowds" much, making life just a little easier for their agents. On the other hand, throughout the Clinton presidency, stories reputedly leaked by unnamed agents alleged that Hillary had no compunction about cursing at anyone—including her detail—and firing objects in their direction on a number of occasions. Those stories of Hillary Clinton's temper, of course, seemed to run again and again on Fox News, Rush Limbaugh, and other decidedly conservative outlets.

In protecting Hillary and Bill Clinton's daughter, Chelsea, and the off-spring of other presidents, the Secret Service has had to guard, baby-sit, run errands, and look the other way at times when their protectees are having fun with their friends. Agents try to let "kids be kids"—within reason.

The need to protect presidential children was first recognized in 1894, when Mrs. Grover Cleveland became alarmed not only about threats to her husband, but also rumors of plots to kidnap the First Couple's children. Informally and unofficially, several Secret Service agents had guarded the Clevelands both at the White House and at their Massachusetts summer home. A decade later, Mrs. Teddy Roosevelt requested and received additional agents to help protect her large family.

From the days of John and Jackie Kennedy to the era of George W. and Laura Bush, only the Reagans and the first President Bush did not require protection for presidential children or teens. And the agents assigned to guard the "First Kids" face some far different challenges than their colleagues on the other protective details. Retired Agent Dennis McCarthy relates, "Often, however, agents develop genuine and often long-lasting friendships with the people they protect. Still, agents know they must maintain a discrete distance in public from the people they guard, especially if the protectee is a young, attractive woman or the teenage daughter of the president.

"The ever-present security [for First Children] makes it very difficult for these young people to go on dates, to go to parties with their friends, to do any of the things that average young people enjoy."

For some presidential kids, it's hard to get past their first look at their new protectors, the quintessential Secret Service "look"—the dark shades, the suits, wires in their ears, microphones concealed in sleeves, and trim to muscular physiques. Still, at some point, a number of presidential kids either rebel against their watchers or make their lives miserable.

High among the "problem kids" for the Secret Service was Tricia Nixon, whom Richard Nixon's confidante John Ehrlichman called a "tough and troubled cookie." Tricia allegedly treated White House aides and agents alike as "the help," once getting an Air Force One steward in hot water for for reportedly staring at her legs. According to author Anthony Summers, Tricia once ordered a White House usher to fetch pillows to the garden for herself and a friend and then demanded that he lift her friend's legs to "create a hassock," as Secret Service agents looked on.

Her agents sarcastically nicknamed her "Tricia Goody Two-Shoes," and when she ordered them to water her plants while she was on a trip, the agents complied—sort of. One of her detail would later claim that they urinated on her flowers and plants.

Another presidential daughter who posed problems for her agents was Luci Johnson, who shared her father's disdain for Secret Service protection and delighted in making their lives miserable. She loved to race to the White House garage, hop into her car, and tear into the streets as her detail scrambled furiously to their vehicles and chased after her. After she had given her agents the slip several times, the head of her detail took away her keys and defied her to complain to her father. She didn't. One of her protectors adds, "After that, she didn't go anywhere without agents."

Luci Johnson found other ways to drive her detail crazy. Shortly before her wedding to Pat Nugent, she and her fiancé went to a private party in a Washington home, with her agents accompanying the couple. The head of the detail agreed to Luci's request that she and Nugent be allowed to go to the party while the agents waited outside, which they often did—and still do—if the party is small and they know the guest list. Luci assured the agents that she would tell them of any change in plans once the couple went inside the house. Outside, the detail took up positions to watch the house.

Not long after Luci and Nugent entered the home, they sneaked out a back entrance for a night on the town without the Secret Service. As the other guests started to leave several hours later without any sign of the couple, agents went inside and asked the hostess where Luci and Nugent were. The hostess replied blithely that they had already left. Frantic agents asked the few remaining guests if anyone knew where the couple had headed. All claimed they had no idea.

The thought of Lyndon Johnson learning that his daughter had given them the slip and was somewhere unprotected in the city could unsettle even the most fearless agent. With no idea of her whereabouts, the detail drove back to the White House, went inside, and waited, seething that they had tried to give the couple some privacy but had still been duped.

When the couple returned unscathed, their laughter almost mocking, Luci's agents said nothing. Nugent escorted her upstairs to the family's quarters, on the second floor; meanwhile, the agents waited for him to come back down the stairs.

At the first sound of Nugent's feet on the steps, the head of Luci's detail moved to the stairwell. He had decided that Nugent and Luci alike needed a dose of reality.

The agent, much smaller than Nugent but a gifted boxer and extremely strong, grabbed the startled fiancé by his coat's lapels, lifted him off the floor, pressed him against a wall, and explained the way that the couple's future dates were going to be. From that moment, Nugent and Luci never again pulled such a caper.

Agent McCarthy remarks, "As far as I know, President Johnson never heard about the incident. If he had, I suspect that one of two things would have happened. Either he would have fired the agent in charge of Luci's detail, or he would have administered one of his Texas tongue-lashings to his daughter and future son-in-law. My guess is that it would have been the latter."

For agents trained to take a bullet for the president, presidential "kiddie patrol" can prove alternately boring and unique. Jimmy and Rosalyn Carter enrolled their daughter Amy in a public elementary school when the former Georgia governor moved into the Oval Office in 1977, and each day, an agent had to go to school—fourth grade—with Amy. Agents had to sit in class all day, go to recess, and "enjoy" all the other the other aspects of a fourth-grader's day, "protecting" Amy from classmates and teachers.

Agent McCarthy notes that sometimes he or other agents had to play something of a parental role for Amy. On a frigid day, he had taken her to school. When her teacher told the children that it was too cold for them to pile outside for recess, ten-year-old Amy argued to McCarthy that she would be warm enough if she went out with her coat on and demanded that he allow her to do so. McCarthy responded, "Amy . . . not all the children in the class have coats as warm as yours and the teachers have to look out for the best interests of all the students."

Though pouting, Amy stayed inside with the other children.

A vice presidential daughter sent the Secret Service springing into action in the late 1970s. In a 1998 interview with *Swing* magazine, Eleanor Mondale, the daughter of Carter's Vice President, Walter Mondale, asserted that she was asleep in Blair House one night and suddenly awoke to find a stranger prowling around her bedroom. "I was so scared I fainted," she claims. "Upon coming to I reached for the phone and picked up the 'hot line' to the Secret Service Command Post. I whispered that there was a man in my room and hung up. Minutes later, two agents burst into the room with guns drawn. When I told them that the man was actually a ghost, they requested that I *never do it again!*"

Eleanor Mondale, like several other presidential and vice presidential kids, went off to college while her father was in office, and the Secret Service discovered that protecting a president or vice president's daughters on campus and off raises a host of problems, dilemmas, and considerations of tact. All around the "political kids," other students hit as many late-night parties as they do books, experiment with alcohol and marijuana, date up a storm, and otherwise act like what they are—kids generally away from their home and parents for the first time, testing their proverbial wings in every way. A bevy of Secret Service agents flanking a girl wherever she goes on campus can cramp any hopes of a normal social life unless agents and protected daughters can work out some tacit agreements. Agent McCarthy says, "Secret Service protection can be an onerous wet blanket to the academic, social, and life style changes and experiments pursued by most college youths, whether in the classroom, the dorm, the sorority, the dance clubs.

What happens if the new look includes spiked, green hair: Does *this* get reported to the White House or is it off limits? How difficult dating must be, especially if it leads to a desire for physical intimacy. Did agents in Chelsea Clinton's biology class have to take notes to blend in? Write gibberish in blue books during final exams? It surely burdens their peers as well as the First Children. Does a young man fear that he will undergo a background check if he dates a First Daughter, and that a high-school marijuana bust will be writ large in his college experience? Do peers really want to toss a few pints down with federal agents watching? Do professors want federal agents undercover in their classrooms during the war on terrorism in which their opinions might seem unpatriotic?

McCarthy experienced all of those factors firsthand during his time on duty in Julie Nixon's dormitory at Smith College, in Northhampton, Massachusetts:

> Those of us on the detail didn't live on campus, but we spent most of our time there.
>
> We maintained a post outside her dorm room throughout the night, and at first our presence was very inhibiting to the other girls on the floor, especially since they shared a communal

bathroom at the end of the hallway. When we first arrived, all the girls would scurry past clutching their robes over their night-clothes trying to maintain their composure. As the weeks passed, however, the girls adjusted to our eternal presence on the floor and began to behave normally around us. Everyone became casual again and propriety was discarded, as were most of the robes.

I began to wonder if the girls even noticed us at all anymore. Early one morning after having been on duty all night, I decided to test just how much we had become fixtures of the floor. I had a newspaper with me, which I folded so a page full of large pic-tures faced out. Then I turned the paper upside down so that any-one who even glanced at it would notice. Pretty soon I heard a door open as one of the young women came out of her room to go to the bath. I didn't even glance up but sat there engrossed in "reading" my newspaper. As the girl walked by, she slowed her pace. I knew she had seen the paper, but I didn't budge and she continued on down the hallway. As she reached the corner, I saw her looking over her shoulder so I raised my head and gave her a big wink. After a second she broke into laughter, relieved, I think, to find out it had been a joke. That was how I found out the girls did notice us as they walked past.

Anytime Julie was going to leave the dorm, we waited for her in the 'dating parlor.' I was sitting there one evening waiting for her when one of the other girls in the dorm came over and struck up a conversation. By this time, all the young women on campus knew us and more or less considered us to be part of their lives. Pretty soon a couple of other girls came over and we began jok-ing and sharing the latest campus gossip. Before long, more and more girls joined the impromptu gathering. By the time Julie arrived, she found me sitting in a big armchair in the corner sur-rounded by a harem of twenty-five or so of her dormmates. Julie seemed surprised, but I just shrugged my shoulders to indi-cate that I had no idea how it had happened. I said good-bye to the girls and made no explanation to Julie.

Since Julie and the other girls on campus were required to eat all their meals in the college dining hall, Julie's agents also ate there most of the time.

During Chelsea Clinton's matriculation at Stanford, her agents allowed her to be a college kid, to go to parties at frats and sororities, to date, and to move about campus with some degree of freedom. Yet the agents were always close at hand, and, yes, the Service scrupulously ran background checks on the boys she dated.

Recently, the college antics of George W. and Laura Bush's twins, Jenna and Barbara, led much of the public to pose a question: Where were the young women's Secret Service agents when the presidential daughters were busted for underage drinking, twice in Jenna's case? Several agents have hinted that the twins' protective details have been told to "let the girls be girls" at college and let the family handle such incidents as "margaritas at Chuy's."

At the Austin, Texas, bar in June 2001, the twins ordered drinks with Jenna's fake ID. Someone recognized the two young women and called the police, and when Officers Clifford Rogers and Clay Crabb arrived at Chuy's and saw the twins, Rogers headed toward Jenna. At the same instant, Crabb told *The Hightower Report* (August 6, 2001), "I was tapped on the shoulder by a subject identifying himself as a member of the Secret Service."

Crabb called Rogers back before he reached Jenna's table, and both officers discussed the situation with the twins' agents, one of the latter calling a superior for instructions. As the conversation went on, a Secret Service agent gathered Jenna and Barbara, escorted them to an SUV in the parking lot, and got them to climb inside the vehicle.

The pair of police officers stood their ground, asserting their jurisdiction and telling the agents that they could not yet take the twins home. Crabb told Jim Hightower, "We told the agents that the girls needed to stay until we talked to our supervisor." He ordered Jenna to hand him her fake ID. She did so, and moments later the Secret Service whisked the twins away.

In the June 11, 2001, issue of *Time,* Josh Tyrangiel, writing about the underage drinking episode and the role of the Bush twins' Secret Service detail, asked, "This is what you call protection?" Tyrangiel writes, "The most beguiling question . . . is . . . why the Secret Service agents . . . didn't do anything to stop her [Jenna].

"'It's not our job to be substitute parents,' the [Secret Service] source says. 'Our function is to keep her [Jenna] safe and secure and get her home every night. . . . If they push us away, we can't do our job.'"

College-age kids remain a balancing act for agents who must weigh how much latitude to give their high-spirited protectees without incurring the wrath of the president or his wife. However, no matter what, the agents' mission is to keep the First Daughters from harm, if not always out of trouble. Agent McCarthy describes the ongoing dilemmas that agents "on campus" face:

> Protecting the older children of a President can be difficult for the agents involved. If, for example, the young person they're protecting goes to a party where marijuana is present, it an uncomfortable situation for the Secret Service detail. Whatever their own personal views about smoking pot, they are, after all, federal law-enforcement officers.

For agents who drew duty watching young presidential kids such as John F. Kennedy Jr., his sister, Caroline, or Amy Carter, far less serious but, for some, "uncomfortable" duties emerge—such as the annual White House Easter Egg Hunt, where a lucky agent gets to put away the sunglasses and suit and don floppy ears and cottontail as the event's star attraction.

## CHAPTER 12

# GETTING TO KNOW YOU— PRESIDENTIAL PSYCHOLOGY

*To understand what actual presidents do and what potential Presidents might do, the first need is to see the man whole—not as some abstract embodiment of civic virtue, some scorecard of issue stands, or some reflection of a faction, but as a human being like the rest of us, a person trying to cope with a difficult environment*

*—James David Barber,* The Presidential Character

Ow does it feel to have a grown man or woman gripping your belt from behind, practically thrusting a hand into your pants as you walk a rope line to greet people? Americans need only recall Agent Larry Cockell grabbing Bill Clinton this way on countless occasions, including one in which a beaming intern named Monica Lewinsky greeted the president from behind the rope line.

Agents working the rope line never know how a George W. Bush, an Eisenhower, or a John F. Kennedy might react when an agent's hand suddenly clutches the president's belt or his hip so that he can be yanked out of harm's way at any instant. Former Secret Service Director John R. Simpson, who retired in 1992, recalls, "I had one individual [protectee] tell me, 'Get your hands off me.' And I told him, 'Well, I guess when somebody shoots at you, you're going to take it.' "

On the campaign trail, agents and candidates take the first measure of each other, of the acceptance or resistance to protection from a potential president. Though the Secret Service develops strict rules concerning what presidents should and should not do, presidents actually make up their own rules as to what advice, restrictions, and security procedures they will follow. There is a law that requires that presidents must be given Secret Service protection; however, there is no law requiring presidents to accept protection or to comply with agents' procedures. Personality—a president's psychology—permeates every aspect of how the Service protects him and how well or poorly protected our commander-in-chief is at any given time. At times, the relationship between a president and his agents is downright adversarial.

Many Americans still view the presidents as somehow larger than life, to the point that they become national symbols rather than flesh-and-blood human beings. The Service knows all too well just how human—with human frailties—a president is. For agents, the everyday stress faced by all presidents effects their relationship with them; even though some chief executives pride themselves on their machoism, they and their agents know that the threat of assassination shadows every moment. A president needs protection, but often recoils from it. Fatalism enters every president's psyche: They, as well as the Service, grasp that if a president obsesses about the risk of death, his performance in the Oval Office will suffer. Most presidents adopt the view that the risks to their person come with the territory—an occupational fact of life.

John F. Kennedy's fatalism is now legend. According to White House advisor Kenneth O'Donnell, Kennedy viewed the risk of assassination as part of the price for an open Democratic process and was not at all perturbed by it; he even asserted that assassination was the Secret Service's worry, not his. Still, this did not banish the problem from Kennedy's mind. The night before his assassination he remarked to O'Donnell, "Last night would have been a hell of a night to assassinate a president. . . . Anyone perched above the crowd with a rifle could do it."

On the morning after his election, Kennedy learned that there was a higher value on his life than he had pondered. He stepped onto the sweeping oceanfront porch of the family's Hyannisport home and saw the yard and the beach beyond swarming with Secret Service agents. He realized that his solitary walks along the Cape Cod shoreline were over.

Kennedy's outgoing personality won over most of his agents, to the possible detriment of effective protection. A former agent who guarded him says, "I loved John Kennedy. Had no respect for LBJ whatsoever. And subconsciously, you don't know how you'll react. I probably would have given my life [for LBJ]. When I left [the presidential detail], I worried about giving my life for someone I'm better than." [He laughs.]

The former agent was careful to distinguish that his loyalty to the job and the protective mission were not compromised at a conscious level by the contrast of really liking one president and disrespecting another. What he worried about was the "subconscious" effect this might have on his reactions and reaction time in an instant, life-or-death situation. No other agent has ever before come close to this admission, which hints that, contrary to the code and the public image of the Secret Service, the protectee's personality—if not his politics—does seep into agents' psyches and could effect events. An ex-agent acknowledges that the prospect is one of the reasons why he got out of protective work—the subconscious factor and the continual second-guessing.

In this agent's time on the job, he and his colleagues came to know a great deal more about a president than do today's agents. The reason was largely logistical: in past decades, there was not as much rotation of agents, and they stayed on protective details "for a long period." He feels that the rotation system in 2002 is a good thing, and says, "Rotating in and out so they don't get too close [with the protectee]. . . . Agents stayed too long and got too familiar [with a president]—too friendly and emotional. It does effect one's judgment."

Discussing Kennedy and his detail, the agent contends: "The Secret Service was too close to him. They liked him too much and they made decisions. . . . He told them to 'stay away' and they did, 'cause they liked him too much."

The former agent referred particularly to Kennedy's order that agents stay off the running boards of his limo, which he still sees as a major factor in Kennedy's death. "If they didn't like him," the former agent says, "they might have pushed the president [into accepting their presence on the running boards].

"The bond is there whether you like it or not: like relatives tied by blood even though you don't like them."

Unlike Agent Clint Hill, this agent was not especially fond of Mrs. Kennedy at first, but he came to admire her over the years: "I wasn't wild about Jacqueline Kennedy. I was a young man from the deep south—cultures away. I didn't quite understand her life style or attitude. But now I realize what a great lady she was."

He felt sorrow at her death even though he hadn't seen her in person for over three decades. In a similar vein, he had one of his old Secret Service colleagues stop by his house after Nixon died. The agent confessed, "I couldn't stand Nixon, but when he died I felt sad." That's the inevitable bonding, the agent says, that evolves between agents and presidents even when they do not like each other.

Reflecting upon the relationship between Kennedy and agents, former Agent Dennis McCarthy remembers:

> The parties Brooks [Agent Brooks Keller] arranged on the press plane and at hotels on presidential trips during the Kennedy administration were so popular that one day President Kennedy asked him to report to Air Force One. When he got the message, Brooks thought he had done something wrong, but Kennedy said he just wanted to meet Brooks and find out how he could get invited to some of those "wild parties" he's been hearing about.

While funny, the incident reflects how a protective line had been crossed. Secret Service agents traveling with the president were considered to be always on duty, even if they were not on their eight-hour shift of protection, and consumption of alcohol while on duty was strictly forbidden.

John F. Kennedy's personal relationship with his agents may not have been the norm among modern presidents, but his fatalism was shared by other men in the Oval Office. As Franklin D. Roosevelt put it, "Since you can't control these things [the threat of assassination], you don't worry about them." President Lyndon B. Johnson opined, "If anyone wants to do it, no amount of protection is enough. All a man needs is a willingness to trade his life for mine."

Dwight D. Eisenhower remarked to his friend and confidante Sherman Adams, "If anybody really wanted to climb up there and shoot me [he pointed to a fire escape outside his Denver hotel room], it would be an easy thing to do. So why worry about it."

Even though presidents must accept the reality that they are vulnerable to someone determined enough to die in an assassination attempt, that reality is yet another worry for the Secret Service: A fatalistic attitude enables a president to go from crowd to crowd, handshake to handshake, without dwelling on the possibility that an outstretched hand may hold a gun. Presidents steel themselves not to flinch, jump, or duck at every loud noise or sudden movement. But the Secret Service agents around the president must react to those same noises, must check everything out; in short, they must worry about everything that the president would like to ignore. The more the president puts the dangers out of his mind, the more that agents must keep them in mind; moreover, the Service's warnings and restrictions pose an intrusive reminder of vulnerability and mortality.

After a threat against President Carter turned out to be a hoax, a Secret Service agent remarked, "They [presidents] never think it can happen to them, and when something like this happens, it reminds them of the hazards."

Still, most presidents seem acutely aware that it *can* happen to them, which is precisely why they tend to be fatalistic. Under normal conditions and on a day-to-day basis, it is Secret Service personnel and procedures that provide the most graphic reminders of "the hazards."

Agents agree that it is the president's personality more than the depth of his fatalism that will determine his willingness to comply with protective requirements. Both Eisenhower and Kennedy—men who had seen combat and death—were very fatalistic about assassination, but Kennedy rebuffed Secret Service advice to a degree that at times appeared to some agents as bordering on a disregard for his personal safety. Although Eisenhower felt that the Service's sometimes intricate protective procedures were largely a waste of time and energy, he complied graciously and cooperatively.

Another built-in tension between protectors and protectee is that most presidents get tired of having their lives managed, while the Secret Service precisely aspires to extensively manage its protectees. Because presidents normally win election after a long, punishing campaign now measured in years rather than months, Elizabeth Drew, who has interviewed many presidential candidates, has concluded that the process is "both strange and brutal" and that "few human being could emerge whole."

Virtually every facet of a candidate's life—from speech, to clothing, to makeup and hairstyle—is managed by professional experts, until the distinction between and public and private life, between the candidate and the campaign, blurs or disappears altogether, as the candidate is programmed for electoral success. According to Drew, it is a truism in presidential politics that "candidates' wives hate schedulers and advance men." And why not? These men and women control a candidate's or a president's life to such a huge degree that it must sometimes feel like a kind of emotional prison. And the Secret Service is part and parcel—the most suffocating symbol, perhaps—of the control that others take over a president's life.

Presidents and their agents have waged a battle between proximity and personal space throughout the twentieth century. Retired agent Edward P. Walsh says, "If you don't have trust and confidence, you don't have proximity. If you don't have proximity, you have an open door. . . . Some bad guy is going to walk through that door."

Presidents, however, rebel in many ways against having an agent always at their side, in front of them, or behind even during moments when all that any human being craves is a little solitude, a little silence. In 1914, shortly before the onset of World War I, President Woodrow Wilson's first wife, Ellen, died. When his daughter arrived at the White House to comfort him, neither she nor his staff nor his agents could find him in a room-to-room search. Finally, she discovered the president sitting alone in a dark corner of the cavernous East Room, but only after she sensed, rather than saw, him in the pitch blackness, with all the lights out and the curtains tightly drawn.

Today, Wilson would never have been allowed to slip away from his agents. His every movement in the White House would be known to someone.

Herbert Hoover used to take morning walks around the White House grounds accompanied by Secret Service agents. Soon, he changed his routine to tossing around a medicine ball with staff or friends because he did not find his agents "lively company." Truman, however, enjoyed strolling and talking with his agents.

When Jimmy Carter took office in January 1977, he decided to set some guidelines regarding agents and his own personal space. He ordered the Secret Service to unlock all the doors that connected three floors of the White House so that the First Family would have more freedom of movement in addition to the elevators. Because Carter viewed the lawns and gardens as part of the family's living space, agents had to constantly patrol the area, as the president was likely to step outside at any moment. He also ordered agents to keep their distance from him in and around the mansion, and he would later laud his agents for the way they usually managed to keep a discreet distance from him at the White House.

In keeping with his common-folk personality, Carter told the Secret Service that he wanted to visit his hometown, Plains, Georgia, three weeks after his inauguration (1977), but wanted to arrive by motorcade instead of a helicopter. The Service, however, explained to him that the amount of money they would have to spend to secure intersections and for crowd control would dwarf the tally for a helicopter trip. Carter later said, "It was obvious that I was not simply one of the people anymore."

Carter's tweaks to the usual protocol between agents and a president did not go down well with his detail, making him one of the more unpopular modern presidents to the Service's way of thinking. A former agent would note the difference between Carter, who could be austere, and his successor, the genial Ronald Reagan. Not long after Reagan's first inauguration, in January 1981, the agent, who had guarded Carter, was escorting Reagan from his White House living quarters to the Oval Office. Reagan started to chat, and it took the agent a few moments to respond. "All of a sudden," the agent recalled, "I realized he [Reagan] was talking to me."

As another agent later grasped, Carter was aloof because he thought his agents disliked him. In turn, his protective detail believed that the president did not like them.

For the Service, Carter's personality stood in stark contrast to that of his predecessor, Gerald Ford, who ranks as one of the most popular presidents in the agency's annals. A "man's man"—a former All-American football player at the University of Michigan—Ford, in the Service's view, was a regular guy who happened to be the president. An agent says, "He [Ford] was friendly and easy to get along with, and agents who were close to him say he was exactly what he appeared to be— a nice guy trying his best to do one of the most difficult jobs in the world."

Agents would never have dreamed of pulling a stunt on Ford such as they once did to Carter. Carter loathed the use of sirens in his motorcades, and after he delivered a speech at the Washington Hilton Hotel and was driven back to the White House, every motorcycle officer in the motorcade turned on their sirens and kept them blaring, with the full complicity of the Secret Service, until his limo reached 1600 Pennsylvania Avenue. According to one of the agents, Carter did not say anything about the incident.

Candidates themselves can become testy or even downright rebellious toward their Secret Service agents. During Ronald Reagan's unsuccessful 1976 campaign for the Republican nomination, he insisted on getting eight hours sleep per night, arguing that he could not function well on less sleep. His inventive managers, frantic to overcome Gerald Ford's slim delegate lead, took to resetting clocks and watches and manipulating time-zone changes, to give the candidate the impression that had he had a full eight hours, while actually working him longer. The Secret Service knew, and when Reagan caught on, he instructed them to make sure that he got his eight hours.

When the candidate wins and enters the White House, the intensity of the control exercised by political managers often subsides in favor of the greater control assumed by the Secret Service, whose necessary intrusions on privacy and mobility on the campaign trail can seem mild compared with the fishbowl in which agents try to protect the president. The successful candidate has now ascended to the most powerful political office in the world, becoming, in Lyndon Johnson's phrase, "the leader of the free world." Yet, according to the Secret Service, the world's most powerful man cannot shake hands with everyone he wants to, must sometimes stay inside when he wants to be outside, and cannot go to his favorite restaurant unless Secret Service agents dine at the next table and unless the kitchen and food are checked, causing long delays.

Of all the century's presidents, Lyndon Johnson probably had the most turbulent personal relationship with his agents. Agent Dennis McCarthy's hard feelings toward Johnson linger, "I believe that because of Johnson's he-man image of himself, he resented having agents around him all the time. He didn't like the idea of needing 'protection' from anyone."

At the White House, Lyndon Johnson would demonstrate his independence from Secret Service agents by walking outside without informing them, jumping into the limousine, and ordering the driver to "just drive," which forced the White House detail to scramble and catch up. But it was on Johnson's home turf, the Texas ranch, where the chase really became frenzied. There, Johnson would drive himself, speeding his big Lincoln over the endless maze of dusty roads that criss-crossed his vast acreage.

The Secret Service pursued in his dusty wake, and the agent usually did catch up. All through the chase, Johnson, whose Lincoln always carried a packed cooler of beer, would cradle a can between his legs and quaff it as he zoomed around the ranch. Eventually, he would need to make increasing pit stops, which gave agents an opportunity to catch him.

At one such stop, the earthy Johnson accomplished literally what many presidents may well have thought about doing figuratively. When he pulled up his Lincoln to the side of the road and got out to relieve himself, agents quickly surrounded him. As a stiff breeze swept across the plains, a surprised agent sputtered, "Sir, you're pissing on my leg." Johnson continued.

"I know," he drawled. "That's my prerogative."

Even when presidents are inclined to use indoor plumbing exclusively, agents are not far away. Aboard Air Force One, when a president or member of the First Family goes to the lavatory, protective procedures call for an agent to stand outside the door. Betty Ford recalled a flight during which there was some unexpected turbulence while she was in the lavatory. The Secret Service agent standing guard outside the door yelled, "Sit down, Mrs. Ford! Please sit down." The First Lady responded, "I *am* sitting down."

Eventually, most presidents come to feel that Service agents intrude upon them much more than they should. When the agency requested additional White House office space during Johnson's term, he replied, "No, hell no. Secret Service would have absolutely no hesitancy in occupying my bedroom!"

Agents who protected Johnson still regard him as one of the toughest presidents the agency ever had to guard. To Johnson, spontaneous contact with the public was as much a compulsion of his personality as a political necessity, as it was with Bill Clinton, and both men liked to do it as often and as extensively as possible. On one occasion when Johnson unexpectedly waded into a crowd to pump hands, kiss women, and pose for the cameras, an agent blurted: "We've got to have some restraints."

Johnson responded, "I've got to press the flesh."

Johnson's chronically cutting demeanor toward agents rankled them. The president treated them more as flunkies and errand boys than as the men entrusted with his life. He delighted in insulting any agent newly assigned to the presidential detail, trying to intimidate him from the first moments on the job; sometimes, Johnson would mimic agents, his bullying patter cowing new agents and grating the veterans.

Johnson's disdain for having agents around compelled his detail to take some unusual steps when he "strayed off the reservation." Not only did agents have to hop into cars to keep him in sight, but also boats. Johnson loved to buzz in his sleek speedboat across a lake at his ranch and forced agents in an accompanying boat to race him. The fact was that the agency's speedboat was always a faster model than the president's, as the Service could never allow a president to surge far away from them. Still, the agents deferred to Johnson's office and his ego. According to one of them, "We were afraid that if we ever beat him in a race, Johnson would take our red boat for his own use. So we always let him win."

To be watched over, escorted, and chauffeured by dozens of deferential, well-dressed agents is a visible reminder of the power and prestige of the presidency. But presidential protection is not a nine-to-five operation conducted only at the president's office or place of work. It is constant and, as far as the Service is concerned, applies to the president's private as well as public life. Because of this, the Secret Service's welcome can quickly wear thin.

When a president wants to shake the burdens of office for a few hours by perhaps visiting a friend, the Secret Service is there to turn the outing into a complex logistical problem that tears away any semblance of leisure or normalcy. John F. Kennedy was rankled to discover that stepping out of the White House to a party in nearby Georgetown for a few hours of fun and relaxation turned into a protective production by his agents.

The Secret Service's policy of inspecting all foodstuffs brought into the White House has been a particular problem for the more epicurean chief executives. Franklin D. Roosevelt's well-known fondness for exotic fish and game resulted in a continuous stream of gifts to the White House kitchen—everything from Peking duck to Maine lobster. When Secret Service agents insisted on sidetracking all of the incoming treats to a laboratory where they could be analyzed, Roosevelt was furious. Even worse for Roosevelt's adventuresome palate, agents took to consuming some of the allegedly more questionable gifts; others they simply tossed into the garbage.

The Service's intrusion into the private lives of presidents and their families, to the extent that they have a private life, has always proven a source of friction. When even a trip to the bathroom brings security precautions, privacy dissipates. Johnson once admonished an agent who was on his first tour of duty at the Texas ranch, "If you hear rustling in the bushes near the old man's bedroom door during the night, don't shoot. It's probably him taking a leak."

Although "Mr. President" can rattle the entire globe with a few words, he discovers that there is one group whose role it is to say "no" to him—no sudden zig-zags on the golf course, no unescorted nature walks on his own ranch, no popping into McDonald's for a burger and fries. Like rebellious children constrained by overbearing parents, all presidents to one degree or another feel like overriding, like saying, "no." The games of hide and seek among agents, presidents, first ladies, and first kids are constant: Bess Truman trying to ditch them, Gerald Ford sneaking to the golf course, John Kennedy slipping off to see a mistress, Bill Clinton strolling from a tee to press the flesh with crowds along a golf course fence.

Many agents understand that any president has a strong urge for "normalcy" in a highly abnormal existence of power, privilege, and danger. Truman's "everyman" makeup urged him to take walks, buy newspapers, walk the dog, and preserve a "normal" family life with the wife and children. It is not normal to have an armed guard silently positioned outside your bedroom while you argue or make love. If you head to the kitchen for a snack, an agent follows you or hands you off to another agent for the short trip. It is not normal for Chelsea Clinton or the Bush twins to be followed on their dates by someone who is not even their father. Understandably, the stress of political life causes First Families to crave some dose of "real life." But the Service is, and must be, always there in one way or another to intrude on the illusion with their requests, rules, and its very presence.

Eventually there often develops a kind of game or contest between presidents and their protectors—one in which both sides attempt to define to their advantage the boundaries of the president's privacy. Sometimes the game is good natured, sometimes not. Harry Truman's desire to stay close to his plain-folks roots caused him to seek out ordinary activities as if he were still a private citizen. For example, he liked to leave Blair House, where he was living while the White House was being refurbished, and walk to the bank a few blocks away. Of course, the problem was that Truman was not an ordinary citizen depositing his paycheck, and the pied-piper effect of the president strolling the busy streets of downtown Washington soon caused vehicular and pedestrian traffic to snarl, creating a potentially dangerous situation for presidential security.

The Service responded imaginatively: It had the traffic lights along the president's walking route fixed in advance so that they would turn red in all directions, stopping all traffic and clearing the way for a swift and safe presidential walk. But Truman soon noticed the strange phenomenon of the four-way red lights and ordered the practice stopped. "I'll wait for the light like any other pedestrian," he huffed.

What Truman had a hard time accepting was the agency's need to guard not just against assassins, but also the chance that a car could careen out of control and mow down the president or that he might try to cross a street against the light. To agents, the words "accidents happen" have always been a part of the protective lexicon.

After the assassination attempt on Truman at Blair House, he did allow the Service to give him more restrictive protection than he would have preferred.

One of the more interesting cat-and-mouse takes between the Service and a First Family involved First Lady Eleanor Roosevelt. Both she and the president loathed the Service's ubiquitous presence and restrictions. In retaliation, the First Lady allegedly made life unpleasant for agents whose unlucky assignment was to hover around her. Finally, the frustrated Secret Service took the unusual step of letting the First Lady protect herself: they issued her a revolver and taught her to use it for self-defense. In exchange for her promise to carry the weapon with her at all times, the Service promised to allow Mrs. Roosevelt to gallivant on her own. As is often the case in a game without enforceable rules, both sides cheated. The First Lady kept the gun in her dresser drawer and never carried it at all; the Service planted undercover agents at all of her public appearances.

In 1981, then Secret Service Director H. Stuart Knight described the ego-induced dimension of the conflicts between presidents and the Service: "To tell a president he can't do something because he might get hurt assaults his ego. He has to feel like a man, not a puppet, and you've got to figure out a way he can save face."

The problem is that there is not always—or even usually—a way for the Service to protect in a face-saving manner without assaulting the president's ego, or privacy, or even his psychological defense mechanisms for coping with the threat of assassination. One result is that most presidents eventually rebel against their protectors, the degree and kinds of rebellion hinging upon the presidential personality. Sometimes the "uprisings" are good-natured, other times vindictive. The common denominator is that the president finds a way to assert himself against those who intrude upon his style, his privacy, or his psyche by lashing out at them, besting them, or perhaps humiliating them.

Although John F. Kennedy was liked by many of his agents, he would sometimes snarl at agents who cramped his political style—mingling with crowds, shaking hands, driving his agents crazy with his lack of concern for his safety. "Get those Ivy League types off my back!" he ordered the head of the White House detail. The two agents who were riding on the back bumper of the President's limousine were promptly withdrawn. Of course, President Kennedy himself was a bona fide Ivy Leaguer, Harvard.

President Franklin D. Roosevelt delighted in unleashing inventive pranks on his protectors. Roosevelt, who liked to relax in the White House swimming pool, which was actually several pools connected by underwater passageways, would splash about until the agents guarding him would look in another direction, then dive deep underwater, and swim through a passageway to surface in another pool out of the agents' view. Acutely aware that Roosevelt was partially paralyzed from polio and assuming that he was still underwater, the agents would plunge in—suits and ties and all—as Roosevelt chuckled in the other pool.

Another of Roosevelt's pranks was to persuade an agent to fetch a ladder and climb onto the roof of the president's home in Hyde Park, New York, under the pretext of having the agent retrieve something or check something. Then, the president would order a handyman to remove the ladder, leaving the agent stranded and temporarily out of Roosevelt's way for a while, or at least until another agent found a ladder.

Always keeping agents on their toes, Roosevelt pioneered the stunt that Lyndon Johnson would later elevate to an art form—vehicular hide-and-seek with his detail. While driving near his rural Hyde Park home, Roosevelt once made a quick U-turn on a narrow country lane. The maneuver posed no problem for his small and sleek roadster, but the more cumbersome Secret Service vehicles following slipped all over the "road," allowing Roosevelt to speed away and escape surveillance for a short time.

From the day that a Roosevelt or any president first steps into the White House, the questions regarding presidential personality surface for agents. How much will a president resent protective intrusions upon what remains of his private life? To what degree will he rebel against them? How fatalistic will he be concerning danger? Will his attitude toward the Service be one of cooperation, indifference, or stubborn resistance? The adage "only time will tell" holds true, and sometimes it does not take long for agents to realize just how many or few difficulties a chief executive will present.

Political scientist Dwight L. Tays has offered a means to classify presidents according to the way in which they react to security precautions. He asserts that presidents fall into three basic types for the Service. In the "less-restrictive" category are presidents who largely discount the need for protective procedures and attempt to conduct their activities with "as little regard for security as possible"; the Johnsons, Kennedys, Clintons, and Trumans are examples. The second type, the "passive-cooperative" president, does not see the need for protective measures but goes along with them anyway, usually trying to make things less difficult for the Service; Ronald Reagan is an example.

Falling into the third division is the "supportive-preference" president, a George H. W. Bush or George W. Bush type who is generally receptive to protective procedures and tends to enjoy the isolation from the public that such procedures provide. At the least, Tays's analysis highlights the significant differences in presidential personality.

According to Tays, John F. Kennedy was the prime example of a less-restrictive president, proving to be one of the most difficult and recalcitrant of modern presidents as far as Secret Service protection was concerned. A strong-willed man who was accustomed to doing what he wanted to do, Kennedy complained to friends shortly after taking office that he felt like a virtual prisoner in the White House because of protective restrictions imposed upon him.

Though Kennedy could charm his agents, his relations with them were sometimes tense and even abrasive. He groused about procedures, snapped at agents, and constantly ordered them not to do what they perceived as essential for his protection. To the chagrin of agents, he would spontaneously command his limousine driver to stop. Then he would climb from the car and plunge into a crowd to shake hands with no thought of his own safety.

Much like Kennedy, Franklin D. Roosevelt despised protective measures and not only challenged his agents with pranks, but also with active resistance. Colonel Edmund Starling of the Secret Service described Roosevelt as "utterly fearless, contemptuous of danger, and full of desire to go places and do things, preferably unorthodox places and unorthodox things—for a president." Over a half-century later, agents would mutter similar sentiments about Bill Clinton.

At the opposite end of the personality spectrum are several presidents who were very cooperative with the Service and much easier to protect, the ones whom Tays would label the supportive-preference type—Eisenhower, Nixon, Reagan, and both Bushes. Eisenhower did not believe that security was necessary, but like a good soldier he acceded to his agents' requests. Ike was in many ways a dream protectee for the Service, a man who felt no compulsive need for public contact or independence from his agents and described the Service as "one of the finest, most efficient organizations of men I ever known." As a military man, he liked the little things about the Service that reminded him of the Army, and, ever the commander concerned for his men, made sure to personally thank his agents who had to stand duty at Christmas away from their families. Of course, in contrast to Ike, Kennedy and Roosevelt would have probably have been pleased if all of the agents had just gone home for the holidays and stayed there until the next Christmas.

When the Secret Service suggested that Eisenhower should not sit out on the White House lawn to do his oil painting, one of his favorite pastimes, because he presented too good a target, he moved his easel indoors with no rancor toward his agents. Ike once reflected ruefully that he "apparently worried these protectors by my unthinking disregard for their advice." In fact, he did understand their worry that his personal fearlessness or fatalism might cause him to be easy prey for a determined assassin. Still, he was the Secret Service dream come true—a president who felt guilty about not following procedures.

It might surprise many people that the Secret Service found Nixon one of the easiest of all presidents to protect. "Protecting Richard Nixon," says one veteran agent, "was like protecting a robot."

Nixon, hating contact with the public and especially spontaneous outings, preferred to retreat to the confines of the White House or his San Clemente, California, home. He was generally cooperative with the Secret Service, but the same could not be said of his political aides. At times, he would even request additional protection—a request that the Service is not used to receiving.

Still, even a cooperative president like Nixon can present problems for the Service by rebelling against procedure. During the 1973 inaugural parade, the Service requested that Nixon keep the windows of his limousine closed because agents expected trouble from demonstrators. The request infuriated Nixon. He opened his windows as protestors opened up with a barrage of eggs and rotten fruit. Though the "missiles" turned out to be harmless, neither Nixon nor the agents knew this would be the case.

Ronald Reagan also cooperated with his agents even before John

Hinckley tried to kill him. Then-Secret Service Director H. Stuart Knight told the press that Reagan "will wear protective attire anytime we ask him to," which has not been true of most presidents.

After the assassination attempt in March 1981, the Service escalated security for Reagan, cutting further into his privacy, but he never complained much. Understandably, he proved even more cooperative with the Service after the attempt. He always was impressed with and grateful to his agents, especially Timothy J. McCarthy, who took a bullet for him, and after the shooting, Reagan evinced a kind of combat-born camaraderie with agents.

One might think that Reagan's attitude was predictable, that a president would gladly accept increased security without complaint since he had nearly lost his life. But two assassination attempts on President Ford seemed to have the opposite result: he became almost more resistant to precautions in his attempt to prove that he would not be intimidated by the threat of assassination.

Between the two extremes are Tays's passive-cooperative presidents— the middle-range group that does not regard protection as all that necessary but, for the most part, go along with it anyway. Truman; Ford, except for his aversion to bulletproof vests; and Carter fall into this category. Yet Carter pulled one of the most sudden and nerve-wracking stunts in recent memory for the Service: At his inaugural parade, in January 1977, he decided—without warning to his agents—to walk the length of Pennsylvania Avenue, from the Capitol to the White House, instantly creating a logistical and security nightmare for the unprepared Secret Service. They scrambled to cover him from all angles as he strolled to 1600 Pennsylvania to the applause of throngs in which the dangerous face in the crowd could have been lurking.

For the most part, Carter did not buck the men and the woman, Mary Ann Gordon, who protected him, but his aloofness galled his agents. He never developed the friendly relationship with agents that Ford and Reagan had and was regarded as a "cold fish."

A man who was decidedly not a cold fish, "Give 'Em Hell" Harry Truman had come to terms with the Secret Service presence while he was vice president. Although he did not deem protection as necessary and it inhibited his desire to do things in an ordinary manner, he generally accepted it.

Shortly after becoming vice president, Truman spotted a man hanging around outside his Senate office. When the president asked an aide who the man was and what he wanted, the staffer responded that the man was a Secret Service agent.

"Well, what the hell is this? When did this happen?" Truman asked. He approached the agent and shook his hand. "I don't see much sense in this," he said, "but if you fellows are detailed to do it I'll give you the all the cooperation I can."

With Lyndon Johnson, such a loose cannon for the Service in the first years of his presidency, larger events made protection of him easier for agents. Johnson, so cantankerous and capricious a protectee for most of his tenure, changed during his last two years in office. As opposition to his conduct of the Vietnam War soared, he became a political recluse. The man who once thrived on "pressing the flesh" now holed up in the White House or visited only those few places—mostly military bases—where he might find a friendly audience. With his loss of enthusiasm for public contact, he became a much more docile protectee.

As Johnson's sense of isolation waxed, he seemed to worry more about the possibility of assassination, especially after the assassinations of Robert F. Kennedy and Martin Luther King Jr., both in 1968. After King's murder, Johnson was scheduled to attend a memorial service, and the president telephoned agent Clint Hill, head of the White House detail, three times the night before the event, once at 4:00 A.M. According to Hill, Johnson "had a premonition that something was going to happen to him." The president requested that Hill stay as close to him as possible.

Gerald Ford perceived assassination attempts as a direct challenge to America's democratic system. The day after the second attempt on his life, he asserted, "The American people are a good people and under no circumstances will I—and I hope no others—capitulate to those who want to undercut what's good for America."

Ford declared that if a president could not walk among the people "something has gone wrong in our society," and vowed to continue personal contact with the public. Ford kept his promise but, in the process, became a less cautious, almost Kennedy-style, protectee. In his effort to prove that American democracy would not be paralyzed by the fear of assassination, he campaigned for a second term from open limousines and stepped into crowd after crowd. In Dallas, he rode in an open limousine along a preannounced parade route, constantly waving at the crowds that lined the streets, refusing to wear a bulletproof vest. Having beaten back a bruising primaries challenge from Ronald Reagan and suffered media condemnation for pardoning Nixon, Ford faced a dogged and swelling challenge from Democrat Jimmy Carter and perhaps grasped that the last thing he could afford to do was to eschew public appearances.

The relationship between a president and his agents is comparable to that of a doctor and a patient. The agent is akin to the doctor: He or she can't force a patient to stop smoking or lose weight but has a superior knowledge of the specific risks and dangers. The patient—or president—can ignore the agent, but at the president's peril. Inevitably, personalities determine the dynamics among agents, presidents, and First Families. If agents are unfriendly, unsmiling, stern or just plain unnerving for any reason, the president and family find tolerating the intrusions more difficult. Transfers of agents have occurred because of this. But even if the protectees chat with agents and develop an easy rapport that makes the time pass more easily and the conflicts more bearably, the agents will continue to do their job—make unpleasant requests or enforce constricting "rules" as much as possible.

The Service's most recent presidential protectees, George W. Bush and Bill Clinton, have been a contrast in styles. As Bush's term evolves, both his own nature and the unprecedented fallout of September 11 have led to a protective cocoon that seems to suit his folksy but not gregarious personality. Clinton, however, needed the crowds—and drove his Secret Service bodyguards crazy.

On the campaign trail, he would order one unscheduled stop after another. He would walk every inch of long rope lines, determined to shake each and every hand stretched out to him. The spontaneity proved nerve-wracking and never ended once he was elected.

Clinton always resisted the idea that he had to live in the Secret Service "bubble." His friend Arkansas State Police Captain Buddy Young, who was Clinton's security chief for a decade in his home state, said, "I don't think he likes all this Secret Service business. It's just such a circus."

Stephen D'Andrilli, a private bodyguard for dignitaries, said: "If he [Clinton] thinks he's going to be able to jog around town . . . without a lot of protection, he will expose himself to extraordinary danger."

Until the Lewinsky scandal isolated Clinton from the public appearances he relished, his agents came to realize that they had to be ready for him veering into crowds, restaurants, and other public places anytime, anywhere. His security was always a fluid proposition for his detail. But whether the president is Bill Clinton, George Bush, or anyone else, agents are always at his side, his back, and his front.

No matter the president's personality, the agents' mission comes down to that one life-and-death goal—building a zone of safety around the protectee.

PART FOUR

# THE SECRET SERVICE
# TODAY AND TOMORROW

# CHAPTER 13

# BREAKING THE CODE OF SILENCE—
# FROM JOHN F. KENNEDY TO KEN STARR

*"We had an unwritten oath. . . . I have never discussed [protectees'] personal lives, and I wouldn't: That's the code."*
— *Former Secret Service Agent, April 2002*

The unwritten rule has always been for agents not to talk about whatever they see or hear—ideally, not *ever.* Any agent who publicly steps outside the "code of silence" earns the enmity of Secret Service brass, though not always all fellow agents. In 1985, when former agent Dennis D. V. McCarthy's memoir of protecting presidents was published with numerous and revealing anecdotes about presidents and their families, ex-Secret Service public Affairs Chief Jack Snow branded the book "an embarrassment."

Oklahoma Governor Frank A. Keating, who oversaw the Secret Service as assistant treasury secretary during the Reagan administration, observed, "Agents should not be talking about purely private matters in purely private situations."

Describing the Secret Service's unwritten law of silence, former agent Chris Von Holt says:

> We're [Secret Service agents] nonpolitical. We can't have any interest in what the protectee is doing politically with Congress, or with a certain bill or a certain stance on any issue. We don't have any interest in what the protectee does in his or her personal life, and we should be there as people fulfilling our mission. We purposely don't listen when the protectee is in the back seat of a limo. There's an agent driving and the supervisor of the

detail in the front passenger seat and they aren't listening to what's going on in back. They've got too many other things on their minds.

Besides the invasion of personal space of the protectee and their family, agents need to cultivate and maintain the delicate bond of trust with presidents and families. As agents stand silently for hours outside the bedroom or ride with the First Couple to the opera or scan a crowd while the candidate and his managers talk strategy, the Secret Service is often privy to what the candidates and image-makers and spouses would regard as political and sometimes personal secrets; often, the revelations are not so much grand strategy, but foibles, quirks, or embarrassments that no politician wants aired. If protectees are forced to regard their agents with the same trepidation as *National Enquirer* reporters or various gossip columnists, the president and his family would not want agents around them. Protectees would insist on grater distance between themselves and "snooping" agents, which would widen the Service's "perimeter" of safety, possibly placing agents too far from a president to provide split-second protective action.

Agents have always claimed that they do not listen to presidential or other protectees' private conversations, not even during the Ken Starr investigations of the Clintons. Former Agent Chris Von Holt and others from the Service point out that agents have far more on their minds than eavesdropping. Their highly trained senses are focused on protection, on the safety of the environment at all times around the protectee.

Still, as many agents acknowledge off the record, distraction or interruption of protective tunnel vision is inevitable: agents are human. If, after three hours of silence while an agent guards a hallway in the White House, a crash and a shouted expletive emerge from the First Couple's bedroom, no one believes that the agent does not hear it. In the backseat of the limo, an otherwise low-key conversation between the president and his chief-of-staff erupts into a presidential tirade about one of his political opponents, and the agents don't hear? Picking up quickly on sounds in the "bubble" is what agents do. While popping sounds are more relevant than presidential expletives, no agent can filter in one sound and block the other.

In the Clinton years, when rumors of First Family fights circulated in the media right after the inauguration, the president and First Lady suspected the Secret Service of leaking stories that would embarrass the new administration. Hillary Rodham Clinton reportedly blamed the Secret Service for spreading a rumor that she threw a lamp at the president. A former presidential advance man notes, "Then there's the rumors of them [agents] being Republican leaning. There were rumors that they leaked schedules to the Republicans. . . . No trust!"

In defense, another agent claimed, "D.C. was abuzz with all these unfounded stories about the personal lives of the Clintons. We were cited as sources for these baseless, unfounded rumors out there." The Clintons were not "watched" by agents, he insisted: "There's no way we would have been exposed to anything like that. That's why it's so ridiculous."

Agents have control over what they choose to discuss or not discuss with each other about protectees, but have no say in how much they are exposed to a First Family's private matters. The Service's unwritten code of silence dictates that agents keep their observations to themselves. Today, many agents still do not want to accept that anyone among the Clintons' protective details broke the long-understood rule: "There's no way we would have talked about it. There's an agency culture, an unwritten code. That was a pretty tough time for us."

Former agent Tony Sherman asserts, "Presidents ask agents to step aside any time they are too close when they play golf. The [security] system is difficult to overcome. I don't think a president will think, 'These guys are going to blab about whatever I say.'"

Though the scenario might hold true on a golf course, as he contends, Sherman himself came to embody the confidentiality problem. He was one of four retired agents who talked openly about President Kennedy's philandering to author Seymour Hersh in the still-controversial 1997 book *The Dark Side of Camelot.* The Service's brass and field agents remain so furious about the revelations that few agents, past or present, want to go on the record with a journalist or author for fear of being pilloried by their colleagues and superiors.

In contrast to the four agents whom Hersh interviewed about President Kennedy, the loyalty of silence can persist for decades among some agents. As journalist Anthony Summers recounts:

> As late as 1992, shown a press picture of himself with President
> Kennedy in Chicago, a former senior agent suggested ludicrously
> that the photograph might be a fabrication, in which his head had

been pasted onto another person's body. The context, in that interview, was a question about Kennedy's activity with one of his mistresses.

When, in 1997, ABC television ran a special entitled "Dangerous World: The Kennedy Years," based on the recollections of Hersh's four Secret Service "tattle-tales," it did not go unnoticed by Agency Director Lewis C. Merletti. He issued a strong letter of reminder to all current and former (living) agents that they not talk about "any aspect of the personal lives of our former protectees." He further reminded them of their swearing of the Secret Service oath "to be worthy of trust and confidence," and that this bond of confidence "should continue forever" between the agency and the president, as well as his family.

A retired agent who served on several of the "all-star teams"—presidential protection details—says:

> We had an unwritten oath. It may even have been written as well, I don't recall, but it certainly was an oath. . . . You must honor the confidentiality of the personal life of the person you're protecting. I honor that thirty years later. I have never broken it and never will. Some agents have. . . . I get memos from the chief [head of SS] reminding me not to discuss personal lives of [protectees].

The ex-agent, both amused and slightly annoyed that anyone in the Service thought he needed to be reminded of his oath, added, "I have never discussed personal lives, and I wouldn't: That's the code."

Andrew Johnson, in the late 1860s, was the first president to charge that he was being spied upon by Secret Service agents, so he disbanded the agency. As the president had surmised, agency head Lafayette Baker was looking to get Johnson impeached, neglecting the Service's anticounterfeiting mission to go after Johnson politically.

Former Secret Service Director John R. Simpson, who headed the agency from 1981–1992, recalled that one protectee demanded to know, "Are you a spy?" All Simpson could do was to say, "No."

In the real world of presidential protection, human nature guarantees that presidents and their families will always have some sense of being spied upon by the Secret Service. Much of what agents see and hear is mundane;

however, as in the matter of President Clinton and Monica Lewinsky, agents often encounter potentially incendiary scenes. In truth, most agents respect the unofficial vow of silence, fearing that the potential paranoia could end up in such a breach of trust that the worst could happen.

As agents would attest—though on grounds that their names not be used—Harry Truman, who signed a number of progressive bills on race and civil rights and directed the desegregation of the U.S. military, never completely shed the prejudices of his Missouri upbringing. Agents often heard him use the word "nigger" when there were no microphones or cameras present.

An agent who served on Nixon's detail tells Anthony Summers how Nixon and his friend Bebe Rebozo loved talking with a young woman at a Caribbean resort who would "come our of her cabana topless." According to the agent, "she would place herself at a discreet distance [on the beach] from Nixon, but close enough so he could still ogle her. He and Rebozo were out in the water, it was only waist-high . . . they couldn't admit to each other they'd been looking at her tits, at her body . . . they couldn't be real with each other."

Among agents, talk about White House drinking is a taboo subject, and most of the details who protected Betty Ford and Pat Nixon kept silent about their problems. A former Secret Service agent breached the etiquette in 1993: "Pat Nixon had a problem . . . I think at one point she was almost an alcoholic. She had to have counseling, arranged through her friends . . . It was during the second term. "

Many agents consider the first gross breach of the code to have been the "in-house" revelations about John F. Kennedy and his womanizing. *The Dark Side of Camelot* and the accompanying ABC-TV special, which featured the four agents criticizing Kennedy was a real crisis for the Service, second only to Ken Starr's subpoenas.

Though a number of agents and reporters of the day agree with Hersh's sources, who alleged scenes of debauchery by Kennedy and his friends that were one step from ancient Roman bacchanals, not all agents who worked on Kennedy's detail tell the same stories. According to one agent, "No one [previously] *ever* talked about the personal lives of presidents. . . . When you are put in a position of confidence and learn things you wouldn't ordinarily know, you have an obligation to the code, the oath: you can't breach that just because you know things." Though he allows that Kennedy was a womanizer, it was not on the sordid scale of the four agents' claims. The agent also suggests that the four who talked were, like him, very junior agents in Kennedy's time and that the juniors would be kept at a distance where they would not have likely known what was going on; if the Kennedy "orgies" happened, senior agents, who were the only ones in a position to know the real facts, would not talk, and certainly not to junior agents on the career make because they would fear losing or jeopardizing their Service pensions.

The retired agent also contests the Hersh agents' claim that Kennedy tarnished the office, and offers: "Kennedy had the most respect for the Office of any president I have seen."

Still, he is not challenging the assertion that Kennedy was a womanizer— the agent is questioning the accuracy, the scale, and the sheer venom, in his opinion, of the four accounts. More important, he takes them to task for violating the code for nothing more than commercial gain.

He adds angrily, "I've never heard any agent talk about a president that way."

No agent had spoken that way about a president in public. According to Hersh's four sources, working on Kennedy's detail meant seeing a seem-ingly never-ending parade of high-class call girls and B-movie actresses and A-list starlets alike being sneaked into the White House and virtually anywhere else the president happened to be. Hersh writes, "The sheer number of Kennedy's sexual partners, and the recklessness of his use of them, escalated throughout his presidency. The women—sometimes paid prostitutes located by Power, who was a Kennedy aide and friend— would be brought to Kennedy's office or his private quarters without any prior Secret Service knowledge or clearance."

Tony Sherman, one of the agents who talked to Hersh, contended that nearly all of the presidential protection detail loathed Kennedy's behavior because they had been brought up by upstanding families and found the president's womanizing unfathomable. Similarly—and questionably, according to another of the junior agents at the time—Larry Newman described life on the Kennedy protective detail as an assignment in which agents learned to look the other way as Kennedy aide and friend Dave Powers allegedly brought an endless stream of women to the president. Newman said, "Your security is only [as good] as its weakest link, and the weak link was Powers in bringing these girls in."

No one compelled those four agents to testify about Kennedy's sexual appetite. In the case of Bill Clinton, Independent Counsel Ken Starr subpoenaed several of the president's agents and thirty uniformed officers. The furor still simmers within the Secret Service as to whether any agent should have to take the stand against a president and reveal private issues that not only shatter the trust between a president and his detail, but may also spook future presidents into always looking over their shoulders to discern if their agents are eavesdropping.

When the Clinton/Lewinsky scandal exploded in January 1998, Starr quickly moved to interrogate Secret Service agents and uniformed officers under oath about the president's sexual relationship with the young intern. Secret Service Director Lewis Merletti battled Starr in court by asserting that the agency's "protective function privilege" was a legal check to the prosecutor's authority. But in a contretemps that reached the Supreme Court, Chief Rehnquist and the majority ruled in Starr's favor, despite Merletti's warning that if the Court ordered agents to testify, they would never have a president's full trust again.

According to *U.S. News & World Report* in June 2002, Merletti may well have been fighting on principle, but several agents suspected that he feared Starr's probing would uncover alleged sexual indiscretions by several agents who had been or were still protecting Clinton, including both Merletti and current Director Stafford, who both had served as head of Clinton's protective team. Merletti denies any sexual indiscretion on his part and maintains that he fought Starr solely on principle. "The claim of privilege," Merletti responded to the magazine, "was invoked precisely and exclusively as publicly stated and strongly supported by every living former director of the United States Secret Service as well as former President Bush."

Solomon Wisenberg, one of the Starr prosecutors who interrogated the agents and officers, still claims that "it was never a part of our mandate to look into the sexual peccadilloes of Secret Service employees."

By the time Starr's legal team finished with the Service, they had interviewed not only several agents and at least thirty Uniformed Division officers, but also Larry Cockell, the supervisor of Clinton's Presidential Protection Detail. "We wanted to be able to interview those with information, while being sensitive to and balancing the needs of the Agency," Starr later said. "We didn't want to needlessly intrude into their work."

Many agents did not—and still do not—see it Starr's way. The internal debate continues within the Service about where the code of silence ends and a prosecutor's right to know begins.

In April 1999, after the Clinton/Lewinsky scandal broke and agents were being brought before Starr's grand jury, former Agent Chris Van Holt publicly aired his feelings about the spectacle:

> My personal feeling is we should be exempt from testifying about anything. Our function is to protect the people elected to office. We're non-political. We don't have any interest in what the protectee is doing politically with Congress, or with a certain bill, or a certain stance on any issue. We don't have any interest in what the protectee does in his or her personal life, and we should be there as people fulfilling our mission. We shouldn't have to worry about being called to testify about something we don't have any interest in, or that we weren't listening to . . .

From the start of the grand jury, former and present agents speculated on how the prospect of agents testifying about the man they are sworn to protect might change the mission. Tim McCarthy opined, "If the president [Reagan] had said to me, 'Tim, I have to have a private conversation with Mike Deaver, would you just step forward a little so you won't hear?'—the round that hit me would have hit the president."

Many agents concurred with McCarthy that with agents having been forced to testify against Bill Clinton, future presidents might now try to keep a distance between themselves and their details, opening up the chances that an assassin could get closer to his or her target. Independent Counsel Kenneth W. Starr countered that agents "cannot blind themselves to evidence of possible violations of law," his argument trumping Director Merletti's warning that tossing aside the agency's unwritten code of silence would result in the death of a president suspicious of his own protectors. A Justice Department lawyer for the Service similarly cautioned Starr and the Supreme Court, "It doesn't take much before you run the risk of assassination."

Though many agents' view mirrors McCarthy's pronouncement—"I was against compelling agents to testify"—there is no shortage of former agents and current agents who argue otherwise. Not surprisingly, perhaps, Tony

Sherman, one of Hersh's notorious four, says, "That's nonsense. . . . The [security] system is difficult to overcome."

Surprisingly, the same former agent who has recently pilloried Sherman and the three who discussed John F. Kennedy's sex life in graphic detail echoes Sherman about agents called in to testify:

> I disagree with many of my Secret Service colleagues. You are sworn to uphold the law and the Constitution. If you see laws being violated, you're in an awkward position. "Is illicit sex a law violation?" he asks rhetorically. "It's a thin line. If the president ordered someone to be murdered, that's a different matter. But the president's personal life? Clinton's conduct came, in part, in his office during working hours, so, technically, it's a violation of law. Logs and what agents saw [in this context] can be required. But personal life is off limits. Performance of duties in office? Agents *should* be required to talk about it."

As several agents have pointed out, few would argue that the Secret Service should keep silent about a high crime by a president. Many, however, fear that the image of agents as potential snoops and snitches has taken shape because of the Starr grand jury. The proximity of privacy with which Secret Service protection surrounds a president and other protectees fosters a difficult relationship at best. Any dwindling of trust poses a potential opening for a determined assassin, and the precedent set by the Starr investigation has opened the way for investigators to pierce the Secret Service's code of silence. In the words of a Secret Service attorney, that silence is a privilege with "an overarching national interest that requires the most zealous protection."

CHAPTER 14

# A WHOLE NEW BALLGAME— THE SECRET SERVICE IN THE AGE OF TERRORISM

*"We always try to prepare for anything—lone gunman or an organization."*
—*Secret Service Agent, Counter Terror Assault, March 2002*

Visitors sense the difference the moment they visit the Secret Service field office in Boston. Outside and inside the Thomas P. O'Neill Jr. Federal Building, across from the Fleet Center, the effects of September 11, 2001, appear everywhere. Concrete anti-vehicle barricades between Causeway Street and the sidewalk aim to prevent car or truck bombings. As anyone enters the building, he or she passes through a metal detector, and security officers X-ray all bags and packages. Uniformed guards are all around.

On the seventh floor of the O'Neill Building, the offices are arrayed in several large, mazelike corridors, with the doors to the main corridor closed. As visitors sign in under giant color portraits of George W. Bush and Dick Cheney, a sign announces "Audio and visual surveillance at all times—anything you say or do can be heard or seen by persons outside this room." A row of black and white photos of modern presidents lines one of the corridors. They are not seated portraits, but presidents in motion, probably on visits to Boston.

Striding around the offices and corridors are neat, trim, well-built agents in tailored clothes. The personnel sport a near-cinematic look of silent resolve and purpose.

In a special agent's office, an oversized Secret Service star rests on a wall, emblazoned with the agency's motto "Worthy of Trust and Confidence."

314

The office of the protective squad's head agent—a woman in her late thirties or early forties—contains a huge wall whose every inch is covered with the names of each agent in the field office, their color-coded assigned duties, and the number of days on an assignment; the assignments are written on various colored strips. The office gives off a war room feel, and although the agency's computers contain all of the information on the wall, the head agent prefers the complex visual on the wall. "When someone calls and asks to borrow agents," she says, "I can glance at the board and immediately determine who is available."

Yellow strips signify protective work—the wall is a seeming blaze of the color. According to the strips, six or eight agents assigned to the 2002 Salt Lake City had returned; another had been sent off to Kuwait to help protect Homeland Security Chief Tom Ridge, a second to work on Senator Hillary Clinton's detail, and a third to guard Vice President Cheney. Since September 11, 2002, yellow has dominated the board. The scene is also typical of other Secret Service field offices.

The Boston office is supposed to have forty-five agents, but since September 11 the figure is only "on paper" because of all the borrowing of agents to cover such new protectees as Ridge, whose position did not even exist before the attacks. As a Boston agent points put, the agency's protective mission has been "drastically expanded since 9/11. First it was the [Bush's] national security advisor; now it's the assistant national security advisor, the Homeland Security Director and *his* assistant."

In this new age of terrorism, the Service's Washington headquarters sent "senior managers" to field offices for long-term missions such as the Olympics. There, security was headed by Salt Lake City agents early on. However, as the mission grew and time got closer, the senior managers from back in Washington were "inserted" a full two years prior to the Olympics. The Service now has a "Major Events Division" that handles such events as the Super Bowl. The office has a SAIC (Special Agent in Charge), one assistant SAIC (him), and four assistants to the SAIC. Then there are "supervisors" and people at "assistant management" level, along with the "line personnel."

Even before September 11, threats to the president and other protectees dramatically escalated in sophistication. The Service does not have the resources to defend against all possible threats with equal vigor: It must, in a real sense, place its bets according to the most likely sources of an attack.

Nerve gas, biological weapons, "dirty bombs," chemical weapons, shoulder-held missiles—all of these have joined the face in the crowd and the sniper on the rooftop as threats that the Service must consider.

Because the Service believes that only one attack on a protectee was the result of a conspiracy (the Puerto Rican nationalists' attack on Blair House and President Truman in 1950), the agency used to focus on what it perceived as the primary threat—the deranged assassin. As far back as the early 1980s, however, the Service began attaching much higher priority to the possibility of assassination conspiracies involving foreign terrorists. The Service still regards lone assassins as the primary domestic threat, but in the post–September 11 world, the agency is watching for foreign-bred assassination conspiracies as never before in history.

For would-be assailants, whether they are loners, part of Al Qaeda, or other terrorist groups, there exists an extensive proliferation of weapons and weapons technology, stimulated by a flourishing black market. For the right price, arms vendors can provide everything from bazookas to heat-seeking antiaircraft missiles. Although silencers are outlawed in the United States, imports from the several European nations that allow their sale can be purchased, as well as automatic and semiautomatic weapons of all sizes and killing capacities

California Deputy Attorney General Charles O'Brien, testifying before a Senate subcommittee on international security years before Osama Bin Laden's operatives turned commercial jets into missiles, alleged that terrorist groups operating in the United States (many of them domestic in origin) were stockpiling weapons: "We have reported a large number of M-16 rifles and M-3 submachine guns that have disappeared into the radical underground. They have light machine guns and thousand of rounds of stolen ammunition too." One pamphlet titled "Improved Weapons of the American Underground," while warning the reader that the actual construction of weapons as described in the pamphlet may be dangerous and/or illegal, proceeds to offer detailed instruction concerning the materials and steps needed to craft nitroglycerin explosives, plastic explosives, detonators, fuses, silencers, and submachine guns. Similarly, during Timothy McVeigh's trial for the Oklahoma City Bombing, in 1995, *The Turner Diaries* was revealed to be a veritable terrorism handbook; this novel, a hate-soaked work that is wildly popular in white supremacist circles, relates a number of methods to make crude but effective bombs.

In the late 1970s and early 1980s, several terrorist strikes forced the Secret Service to take notice of foreign threats: the wounding of Pope John Paul II, the assassination of Egyptian President Anwar Sadat, the Irish Republican Army's assassination of Britain's Lord Louis Mountbatten, the kidnapping and execution of former Italian Prime Minister Aldo Moro, the kidnapping of U.S. General James Dozier by Italian terrorists, and the bombings of several American embassies and of the U.S. Capitol building in 1983. All serve as grim reminders of the specter of violence on the rise across the globe.

As the agency realizes, perhaps as never before because of September 11, the Service's job in dealing with international hit men and terrorist groups is even tougher because the United States is in so many ways an open society. People can travel easily within its borders, and the fact that terrorists can so easily come to the nation and remain inconspicuous until ready to strike creates dire problems for the Service's protective mission and for law-enforcement agencies. The nation has tragically learned that terrorists can easily enter and blend into the country because of its porous borders and lax passport and immigration controls. Also, the United States is a mobile society where interstate travel is extensive and does not raise any suspicions. As Al Qaeda's operatives knew, America's polyglot population allows terrorists of almost any nationality to find an immigrant community or a subculture in which to hide. The proposal for national IDs for all American citizens is in direct response to this problem.

A controversial article written all the way back in 1981 takes on new meaning since September 11. The piece's authors—N. C. Livingstone, a private security consultant whose clients have included several heads of state, and James P. Kelly, former assistant director of the Secret Service, titled the article "Could the President Survive a Real-Life James Bond Movie?" Their conclusion was *no,* because the Secret Service's existing methods were too archaic to deal with threats posed by terrorists using the most sophisticated assassination techniques.

In the assassination scenarios put forth by Livingstone and Kelly, the nightly news of 2002 emerges. The pair wrote about terrorists injecting deadly nerve gas into the ventilation system of the Kennedy Center for the Performing Arts, killing the president along with the rest of the audience; firing a heat-seeking missile (such as the Soviet SAM-7), destroying Air Force One; using a device powered by compressed gas to shoot a tiny poison pellet into the president's hand as he greets a crowd—the dart feels like a slight pin prick, and the president dies moments later.

Though the White House is equipped with sophisticated air and water filtration systems that might foil a nerve-gas attack, most public locations visited by a president lack such defenses. Several terrorist groups possess the capability to produce GB or VX type nerve gas .02 of a drop—a tiny amount—killed a dog in less than a minute during an experiment at Fort Detrick, Maryland. A tiny canister of the gas could take out a president and a lot of people around him.

Another threat is heat-seeking missiles that can weigh as little as twenty-five pounds, cost only a few thousand dollars to produce, and have a range of two miles. Assassins could launch such a missile at Air Force One as it takes off or lands. According to Livingstone and Kelly, the gas-powered poison pellet was actually used in assassination plots against Charles de Gaulle and the Shah of Iran. As early as the mid-1970s, the CIA developed a poison dart that was shot from a silent device and was accurate up to 250 feet. The dart penetrated the victim's clothing and skin without being felt and injected a lethal dose of a poison that left no trace; then the dart itself dissolved, also leaving no trace.

Whether the 1981 case of the Libyan hit squad (five terrorists allegedly dispatched by Libya's Kaddafi to assassinate President Reagan) was real or not, it was a watershed event for the Secret Service, which took extraordinary protective measures for a period of several weeks. For the first time in history, the president lit the Christmas tree from inside the White House. It was the first publicly acknowledged terrorist threat. Also for the first time, officials in Washington worried openly about missile attacks on the presidential plane and about rocket-propelled grenade launchers being used against the presidential limousine. Though the threat never materialized, the prolonged and publicly acknowledged massive increase in security—which included new security on the White House roof, providing Secret Service protection to key members of the White House staff, augmenting presidential and vice presidential protective details, and altering the president's agenda to reduce exposure—clearly indicated that the terrorist age had indeed arrived, in the perception of the agency and the Reagan White House.

CIA and law-enforcement officials, in a chilling example of the dawn of the terrorist age, foiled a 1974 plot to assassinate President Ford.

Authorities arrested Muharem Kerbegovic, a Yugoslavian native known as the "Alphabet Bomber," so named because he would telephone or mail bomb threats to authorities and would designate the bomb's location by using a single letter of the alphabet. At his trial, which was not for a presidential assassination attempt but for allegedly killing three persons with a bomb planted at the Los Angeles airport, Kerbegovic claimed to be the messiah. Historically, this would seem to give him much in common with other disturbed persons who were would-be-assassins. Richard Lawrence, who tried to shoot President Andrew Jackson in 1835, imagined himself to be King Richard III of England; John Schrank, who wounded Theodore Roosevelt in 1912, claimed to have been directed by the ghost of assassinated President William McKinley.

A significant difference in means set Kerbegovic apart from the others. Lawrence and Shrank wielded pistols, but when the Alphabet Bomber was arrested, police found in his home all but one of the ingredients needed to construct a nerve-gas bomb composed of a "highly lethal" agent. The missing ingredient had been ordered and only awaited pickup by Kerbegovic. "He was that close," said a police official. The Secret Service began to pay closer scrutiny to threats from abroad.

In 1983 Kerbegovic wrote to author Philip Melanson from San Quentin Prison because of an article Melanson had written on assassination threats to presidents. Slighted that he had not been given more prominence in the discussion, he sought to enlighten the author, "I read your crap. . . . Here I am sending you some good stuff. Just keep it. You won't be able to understand it before the Secret Service does. I am their number one case."

He then enclosed a six-page document with handwritten notations to "explain" his version of political assassinations:

> Seffeerians believe that visible possession of political and/or spiritual power is a mortal sin, as power is a narcotic; no Seffeerian can become a saint unless he assassinates at least one power junkie . . . the assassinations are tied together with an alphabetic code named 'Chinese Letter.'

The Oklahoma City bombing by homegrown terrorist Timothy McVeigh and the 1993 bombing of the World Trade Center by Islamic extremists showed that the age of terrorism had truly reached America. After eight months of study following the Oklahoma City tragedy, a congressional panel recommended that the section of Pennsylvania Avenue that ran directly in front of the White House should be closed to all vehicular traffic and made into a pedestrian zone, because the president and Executive Mansion could not otherwise be protected from a large truck bomb explosion. The recommendation of the panel, after consultations with the White House, was approved by Treasury Secretary Robert Rubin and went into effect on May 19, 1995. On the northwest and northeast intersections of Pennsylvania Avenue and 15th and 17th Streets, barriers were set up to protect the White House and would eventually be replaced with guard houses, automatic gates, underground metal barriers, which could be raised and lowered, and large concrete planters.

Initially, the White House rejected the commission's findings, fearing they would send an undesirable symbolic message of governmental fear and create a perception of separation of the president from the people. Upon closer examination, however, the explosion at the Murragh Building has less relevance to the threat of a truck bomb attack directed against the White House than is commonly assumed. In the first place, the vehicle containing the estimated twelve-hundred-pound bomb had been parked in an indented passenger loading zone only about nine feet away from the Center of the north side of the Murragh Building when the blast occurred. By comparison, the White House is set some 350 feet back from the south curb of Pennsylvania Avenue: a distance more than thirty-five times greater from where the Oklahoma City bomb was detonated.

By sheer chance, the explosion itself occurred close to one of the Murragh Building's four main support columns. The blast's impact set off a chain reaction that toppled a pair of two-story story columns, collapsing the entire north façade of the office building and causing each of its nine floors to pancake downward onto one another. The White House, however, is built on only three levels and has a low-set, "box-type" geometrical configuration built around a framed steel structure. These two characteristics not only minimize the danger of successive floor collapse but also help ensure that if any bomb goes off near the mansion, the explosion will be localized, not catastrophic.

The Murragh Building blast served to refocus President Clinton's attention on Secret Service assessments that the only way to protect the White House from an attack of this kind was simply to eliminate all vehicular traffic from the street facing the Executive Mansion. Had the Oklahoma City bombing not occurred, it is by no means clear whether President Clinton would in fact have acceded to the recommendation to close Pennsylvania Avenue, which was an option that he had previously rejected. Clinton's May 1995 decision to close Pennsylvania Avenue was unprecedented and a step heartily recommended by the Secret Service.

The decision sparked a furor in the press, especially among the ranks of unabashed Clinton foes. The closing of Pennsylvania Avenue radiated problems that were practical as well as symbolic: Pennsylvania Avenue is a key urban artery that connects eastern and western parts of the District. The Rand Corporation concluded in its 2000 report on the measure that the closure created great inconvenience, disrupting traffic and commuting patterns. Additionally, said the think tank, the closing had an adverse economic impact on local businesses by hampering access to the newly revitalized center of the downtown.

Rand estimated that reduced parking meter revenue was three quarters of a million dollars annually and that modification to the urban transit system necessitated by the closing cost another $1.5 million. Productivity declined because of circuitous commuting routes forced on federal employees, with several businesses forced to relocate.

Notwithstanding the practical issues, it was the symbolism that worried or enraged many observers and analysts. Suddenly, at the very doorstep of the "People's House," a new and disturbing image materialized—what Rand described as "an image of fortification and security that is at once both undesirable and inappropriate given the open and democratic society that is the defining characteristic of our nation." Rand noted that this was a "highly sensitive, if not emotionally charged, subject." Clinton-haters denounced the president as "chicken" and worse.

Whatever various Secret Service agents might think about Clinton's personal conduct, the word "chicken" did not have much credence to them. In fact, the president's penchant for risk taking was a constant headache for the agency.

In March 2000, President Clinton was determined to visit Pakistan for crucial diplomatic and national security purposes. The Service advised against it: the area was politically unstable, terrorists abounded, and Bin Laden and Al Qaeda were there or near there with motive, means, and opportunity. Clinton still went.

On the tarmac in Pakistan the Service rolled out no fewer than six presidential limousines, all of the vehicles big and black but of different vintages and styles. Although the scene looked something like a U.S. presidential car show put on in Pakistan by the Service, terrorists would now have only a one-in-six chance of hitting the car containing the president. Of course, it would have depended on their ordnance to reveal how effective this ploy would be. Clinton and his agents knew that Bin Laden's men had weapons that could easily destroy a city block or a fairly long stretch of road; still, he chose to go.

Clinton similarly gave the agency a tough mission with his decision to visit Botswana in 1999. The White House staff was committed to the political imagery of President Clinton riding through a game preserve in an open Jeep, looking relaxed, confident, and in touch with nature. The Secret Service brought over their heavily armored Chevy Suburbans, all to be driven by agents. On a run-through of the proposed route, the agents encountered a group of elephants. One mother, protecting her young calf, became agitated at the motorcade, and in a fit of maternal protectiveness, reared up on her hind legs and then charged. As agents gaped, a local park ranger rushed up to the elephant and somehow placated her until she eventually left without inflicting any damage. White House staffers quickly proposed that the local ranger serve as Clinton's driver—in an open vehicle. With visions—or nightmares—of rampaging elephants as well as terrorist snipers, the Service was adamant that the president's vehicle be an agent-driven Suburban. They never want a president in a vehicle that is not a Service vehicle, let alone one driven by an outsider. Eileen Parise, who did advance work for the Clintons and the Gores and now does the same for the Bush administration, recalls that there was a lot of back and forth between the Clinton team and the Service, but she knew that the outcome was a foregone conclusion: "The president wants to be in an open vehicle and he'll bite your head off. It *had* to be an open vehicle." And it was.

Retired Agent Robert Snow adds, "The Secret Service would love to put him [any president] in a Sherman tank."

Despite Clinton's frequent disdain for too much security, the Rand report charged that his agreement to close off part of Pennsylvania Avenue was a troubling reaction, perhaps overreaction, to one event, the Oklahoma City Bombing, and was a fait acompli. It was allegedly imposed without any discussion or subsequent evaluation of its wisdom or necessity. The seventy-three-page report analyzed security, concluded that the measure should be reassessed as unnecessary, and suggested alternative measures, such as redesigning the avenue outside to make it impossible for trucks, busses, or large vehicles. Also, in a democracy, the report contended, security could never be 100 percent foolproof, and the closing failed to address other threats, such as an attack from the air.

Many other critics branded the decision as reeking of a knee-jerk, bunker mentality that impinged upon the national image of openness and freedom. Defenders point out that it is not really an essential component of our national self-image to drive an SUV in front of the president's mansion or view a stream of passing traffic while walking on the sidewalk or looking out from a White House window.

In March 2000, Congress decided to hold a hearing on this controversial policy that had been in place, for better or for worse by then, for six years. There was some congressional sentiment for reopening the avenue. Though most security analysts, including the Secret Service, were opposed, the Republican Party platform for the 2000 presidential election pledged to reopen the street. President George W. Bush had stated during the South Carolina primary that he favored its reopening. After taking office, however, Bush obviously had a change of heart. After a meeting with Washington, D.C., Mayor Anthony Williams, who pleaded for reopening, the president did nothing. Perhaps he was listening to Secret Service Director Brian L. Stafford, who told Congress: "Any plan that would permit vehicles within the currently established security perimeter [800 feet] will not protect the president and the White House complex."

Pennsylvania Avenue between 15th and 17th Streets remained closed. A little over five months after Stafford's speech, all debate about the measure fell mute as the World Trade Center crumbled to the ground.

Even as the Service grapples with unprecedented terrorist threats, the specter of the "lone assassin" breaching security and getting close to a president remains a constant. A reminder came during the inauguration of George W. Bush, in January 2000.

The episode actually began at Bill Clinton's second inauguration, in January 1997, when a man talked and slipped his way past police and Secret Service at Statutory Hall, in the Capitol Building, walked right up to Clinton, and shook his hand. As a Washington, D.C., security expert says, "The Capitol Police caught some flack, but the Secret Service really looked bad. Nothing happened but that is hardly the point. For any uncleared person to get that close to the president is indeed scary. There was no protection at that point if the individual was armed and willing to give up his life."

Four years later, the Secret Service and the Capitol Police had the intruder's picture and circulated it in advance in case he tried a similar stunt; the picture was given to local police as well. Incredibly, and far less excusably than the first time, the same man walked up to Bush on the East Front of the Capitol and "passed off a coin" to the president. As the security expert says, the coin could have been a lethal James-Bondian, CIA-type toxic killing device (they do exist and the Secret Service has been warned by the CIA about such "handshake-kills"). The Service put the man on a plane back to California; no charges were filed.

A private security consultant created a digital video that tracked the intruder's route through Capitol and Secret Service security to get to the president, re-creating the gate-crasher's movements from the known record. He has given the tape to the Secret Service.

"This didn't look good for them [the Secret Service]," the analyst observes.

Who is the man who has twice embarrassed the Secret Service? The "handshake man" is the Rev. Richard C. "Rich" Weaver, a fifty-five-year-old, nondenominational Christian minister. He says, "The guards let me in like nobody's business. It happens all the time. It's so funny it's almost eerie. But this stuff is no big deal to God. God can close people's eyes so they don't see you."

For the Secret Service, there is nothing "funny" about Weaver's ability to pierce security. If he can do it, the agency has to wonder if a cunning, innocuous-looking "lone nut" or a terrorist could do the same.

Former Secret Service director Eljay Bowron said that Weaver's casual demeanor when he walked up to Bush may have prevented alarms from going off among agents. "Obviously, in an ideal world for the Secret Service, this wouldn't have happened," said Bowron, who saw a video clip of the incident. "I'm sure that they feel embarrassed."

Bowron, director from 1993 to 1997, knew the embarrassment firsthand: he had been in charge of Clinton's second inauguration, the occasion of Weaver's first presidential handshake, and described him as a "nuisance approacher" rather than a bona fide physical threat.

"If they were going to worry about each one of those individually, they'd have to put a fence around the whole city," said Bowron.

Jim Mackin, a spokesman for the Secret Service, stated, "I certainly understand the questions being raised. . . . In answering some of these questions, we would lend assistance to this happening again."

A retired Secret Service agent from Ronald Reagan's detail commented, "That man [Weaver] with President Bush looked like he belonged there."

The point was—and is—that Weaver did not belong there.

The chances of a Weaver or any other stranger actually slipping into the White House after September 11 appear remote at best. Officials from the Secret Service contend that White House security has been strengthened, but would not, of course, say how. Now, in addition to Pennsylvania Avenue, E Street has also been closed to all vehicular traffic.

From the moment shortly before 9:30 A.M. when President George W. Bush was told of the first plane crash into the World Trade Center, the Secret Service reportedly swung into action to protect the president. By day's end on September 11, many reporters and others were questioning Bush's movements to stay "out of harm's way" and would openly contest the administration's assertion that both Air Force One and the White House were terrorist targets that day. In response, the president's spokesperson Ari Fleisher said that the president had been following the Secret Service's advice all day.

When the first crash occurred, Bush was in a Sarasota, Florida, school, chatting with the children. At 9:45 A.M. the White House was evacuated, and Bush was taking off from from Florida aboard Air Force One by 9:57 A.M. He remained aloft—reportedly on the insistence of his agents—as the World Trade Center collapsed, the Pentagon was hit by a passenger jet, and another hijacked airliner crashed in a remote site in Pennsylvania before it reached Washington, D.C. At 10:08 A.M., Secret Service agents toting automatic rifles were deployed in Lafayette Park across from the White House.

Americans learned at 1:04 P.M. that Bush had landed at Barksdale Air Force Base, in Louisiana, and briefly addressed the nation to say that he had put the U.S. military on highest alert worldwide. He also asked for prayers for those killed or wounded in the attacks, concluding with the words, "Make no mistake, the United States will hunt down and punish those responsible for these cowardly acts."

At 1:48 P.M.: Bush left Barksdale Air Force Base aboard Air Force One and flew to an Air Force base in Nebraska. Neither the press nor the nation were apprised of his route because of the Service's security concerns. As anxious Americans deluged news organizations with worries about the president's safety and his whereabouts, Bush aide Karen Hughes went on the air near 4:00 P.M. to say that the president was at an undisclosed location, later revealed to be Offutt Air Force Base in Nebraska, and was conducting a National Security Council meeting by phone. Guarded by Secret Service agents, Vice President Dick Cheney and National Security Adviser Condoleezza Rice were in a secure facility at the White House.

Finally, at 4:30 P.M., the president left Offutt Air Force Base in Nebraska aboard Air Force One to return to Washington, landed at Andrews Air Force Base, in Maryland, with a three-fighter jet escort, and arrived back at the White House near 7:00 P.M. aboard Marine One (the presidential helicopter). Earlier, a motorcade had taken Laura Bush from an undisclosed secure location to the mansion.

According to a number of accounts, Bush's father, former President George H. W. Bush, was fuming at the Secret Service for making his son look like he had been "hiding out" all day. The administration took the stance that George W. Bush had followed the agency's advice throughout the morning and afternoon of September 11, but in the late afternoon had ordered them to take him to Washington, D.C. Much later, during his June 2002 political trip to Europe, the president was asked by a German reporter why it had taken him so long to get to Washington on September 11, 2001. Bush responded that he had been trying "to get out of harm's way" that day. He did not say that he was following the advice of the Secret Service. Whether it was the Secret Service or the Bush staff that kept him in the air and at secure military bases for much of September 11 depends on the source, remaining a sore issue with the White House. If the president appeared less than resolute at any point during the tragic chain of events that day, it was the fault of agents who were overzealous in their desire to protect him, administration sources have offered. The Service, whose first duty that day or any other day is to protect the president, has never publicly pointed out that Bush could have overruled them at any time and ordered Air Force One to Washington, D.C.

On the advice of the Secret Service, the administration announced that

White House tours were canceled indefinitely, and for Christmas 2001, there was no public access to the lighting of the giant Christmas tree. The Bushes did host a traditional Christmas party in the White House, but the guests were a complete departure from tradition. Laura Bush invited the Washington press corps and a large contingent of foreign journalists for food and eggnog in the state dining room. Until December 2001, reporters from Tass News Agency (Russia), Ethiopian Cultural TV, and a Polish newspaper were among the many foreign journalists who had never set foot in the White House. For the occasion, the mansion's foyer was adorned with twelve Christmas trees, a U.S. Marine played Christmas carols on a Steinway piano, an eighteen-foot fir tree stood in the Blue Room, and a 130-pound gingerbread house modeled after John Adams's White House graced a side table.

Paivi Sinsalo of the Finnish News Agency observed, "Maybe it's because the public won't be let in this year, so they want the whole world to see [the White House Christmas]."

The First Lady said, "You [the press] can really help us by letting people who can't come to the White House this year see what the decorations are like." Of course, amid those decorations stood a beefed-up Secret Service detail.

The Secret Service has been an integral player in the "bunker government" that has taken shape since the September 11 attacks, with agents assigned to guard Vice President Cheney and other government and senior federal agency officials at secure locations outside Washington as a precaution against a catastrophic strike on the nation's capital. Based in part upon old Cold War measures, agents have accompanied Cheney at "a secure and undisclosed" location several times since the terrorist strikes on New York and the Pentagon. A bunker government of "several dozen, roughly 100" senior government workers remains in place at a pair of secure ex–Cold War locations in the eastern United States.

Because President George W. Bush has chosen to continue the bunker government, the Secret Service is among the agencies compelled to constantly rotate personnel to handle a ever-expanding protective mission. Since September 11, assignments of Secret Service have been more of a fire drill. The list of the agency's protectees has expanded to include Bush's National Security Advisor Condoleeza Rice, Senate Majority Leader Tom Dashell, and other congressional leaders. With the Service having been responsible for security at the 2002 Superbowl and the Winter Olympics, agents are on call "twelve hours a day," according to Eileen Parise who sees the Service as constantly scrambling for people and resources much more so than before September 11. "Any staffer from any administration has nothing but high regard for the Secret Service." Parise has "the utmost respect" for agents, viewing them as a "very elite group of people, well-read, articulate, having political sense—all smart." Despite all that, they are men and women being stretched by the War on Terrorism to their physical and emotional limits.

Former Agent Tim McCarthy sees the necessity for the Service's new post-September 11 protective missions such as the Super Bowl, Olympics, and, more government protectees, and says that the agency is stepping up its recruiting. Yet he cautions that the new missions need to be reviewed and not just assumed to be permanent. "What is necessary now [after September 11] may not be necessary in the future," he offers. "There needs to be a review of what's going on: Is there enough intelligence to say that the Secret Service should do this? In ten years with control of the terrorist problem, there must be a review. They [the Secret Service] can't do it [the Super Bowl] every year."

"No agency is better prepared to provide such protection. They are the right agency but should not be out to protect every major event."

McCarthy notes that a look at the mission of the Service at the 2002 Salt Lake City Winter Olympics proves his point that it is too much to expect the agency to handle security for each and every major event to come. At the Olympics, according to Secret Service Director Brian Stafford, security for the Games's fifteen venues and nine hundred square miles was so thorough that he would have been comfortable with the president visiting any site, any time.

There was a "war room" to coordinate the extraordinary security plan, and the thirty-five athletes and coaches resided in a village cordoned off by a "smart fence" that asked for help electronically if it sensed it was being breached or assaulted in any way. Everything, every burger and soft drink, which came into the village was screened with the same intensity that prevails at the White House, as was screening of people. Security was at the highest level of antiterrorist alert twenty-four hours a day, no matter how calm and routine things seemed. After background checks, the Secret Service deputized and equipped a large number (the exact number is secret) of law officers from other agencies such as the National Park Service to fan out and protect the nine-hundred-acre Olympic site.

Motion sensors monitored virtually every foot of the mountainous terrain, and hand-held heat sensors could detect a 98-degree human traversing a 20-degree snowfield. For anyone thinking they could drive right up to the venues, the Service had a surprise: cars had to be parked ten miles away. The agency closed the Salt Lake City airport for certain periods and set up a no-fly zone over much of Utah with fighter-jet patrols and a warning that intruders would be dealt with "swiftly and decisively."

Throughout the Olympic Village, the Service deployed its supersecret, superelite CAT squads (Counter Terror Assault Team), rarely seen even though one always travels with the president. Their job is to repel a coordinated terrorist attack, and they were placed throughout the mountains along with "thousands" of other security personnel. The CAT team's motto is "speed, surprise, and violence of action."

Also present were the Secret Service Counter Sniper Team(s). Trained not to repel a potentially massive assault but to take out individual terrorists with precise marksmanship, the sharpshooters were hidden throughout the secured area. CBS cameras were allowed to see them practicing although the Service would not reveal how far away were the pop-up silhouettes that the agents were shooting at. When a correspondent asked an agent how many shots he would fire to bring down a terrorist, the slightly indignant reply came: *"One."* Spotters on the target range yelled out where the target was hit: "Good hit! Left lung." The precision is required so that an agent may hit a target in the middle of an innocent crowd of bystanders.

The agency brought its dogs, which are touted as "the best way to find a bomb," to the Olympics. The brown Belgian canines sniffed cars all around to detect any hint of plastic or other possible bomb-related substances. If the dogs sense something, they calmly sit down at the spot of detection to alert their agent.

There are a number of mission improvements the Secret Service is already making or likely to make in the post–September 11 world. With every federal agency straining to cover expanded duties with limited personnel, the practice of using "loaners"—other federal agents to help out the Secret Service or vice versa—should be discontinued. The Service's past practice of using loaners from the ATF, the IRS, and Customs to help fill protective details would prove too risky in the Age of Terrorism: as well-trained, patriotic, and professional as these loaners might be, they are not Secret Service agents, lacking the training and experience to fully protect a dignitary if a terrorist strike happens.

The threat of terrorists firing shoulder-held missiles at the White House have compelled the Secret Service to pay even more attention to private buildings commanding any possible view of the Executive Mansion. Though the agency has always done so, the hard fact that Al Qaeda and other terrorist groups are known to have large stockpiles of the highly portable missiles creates an unprecedented urgency to "button down" other buildings in Washington, D.C.

Despite the increased vigilance by the Service and other agencies, several private planes wandered into restricted Washington airspace near the White House in June 2002 before the Secret Service or the Air Force could react. The incursions, though innocent, indicate that there is room for improvement in protecting the presidential residence from genuine attack.

As the agency grapples with its expanding protective duties, the Service's other mission—anticounterfeiting—has also taken on new impetus since September 11. With fears that terrorists might seek to destabilize the United States by flooding the world with counterfeit green-backs, the Treasury Department is considering drastic changes in the way money is printed. Multihued bills, three dimensional surfaces, different inks—all these measures are receiving careful scrutiny by the Treasury, which hopes that the high-tech changes might thwart counterfeiters.

One aspect of the Secret Service's mission has not changed in the War on Terrorism. The Presidential Protection Detail remains the agency's all-star team, and for the men and women protecting George W. Bush, the stakes have never been higher. In March 2002, an agent serving on the president's Counter Terror Assault Team related, "We [the Secret Service] think of ourselves as the Marine Corps of federal law enforcement. Small but effective, we always try to prepare for anything—lone gunman or an organization."

The elite agent points out that, like the CIA, Americans only hear about the Secret Service's failures and not their numerous successes: "Unfortunately, the public never knows how many times we've been successful. They get to see our failures, mostly because of events outside our control.

"Many [threats] are thwarted, I assure you. Nearly every day, most of the time. We operate under the radar screen, and we prefer it that way. . . . We have to keep low and have as many successes as we can."

He likens the post–September 11 world for the Secret Service as a "sea change," similar in some respects to the time immediately following the assassination of John F. Kennedy. But the true mark of a savvy presidential protector, he asserts, remains the same: "A good agent is a good thinker on his feet."

The challenges of the post–September 11 world will test those agents in new and, as yet, undefined ways as the Secret Service works to ensure that they remain "Worthy of Trust and Confidence."

At Secret Service headquarters in Washington, D.C., *secrecy* is the operative mode. While citizens may still tour FBI headquarters and read released Bureau documents in a reading room, the Secret Service's building on H Street resembles a fortress. Uniformed guards protect the front entrance. The agency shield and motto are displayed, but public access is practically nonexistent. The visitor is informed, in a less than friendly tone, that there are no tours, no reading room, no access to the agency archive. The exclusionary procedures apply unless you are an employee or know someone there. Only the agency's extended family is welcomed. One of the government's most secret organizations has turned its public face toward the shadows.

# CONCLUSION

Since September 11, 2001, the U.S. Secret Service has not only had to contend with new protective challenges, but also an "identity crisis." President George W. Bush, the very man the agency is protecting, has called for the Secret Service to be yanked from the Department of the Treasury and placed under the aegis of the still undefined Department of Homeland Security. In a case of history repeating itself, some in Congress are contending that the Service be rolled into the Justice Department, perhaps under the purview, or at least political influence of the FBI, as J. Edgar Hoover long wanted. Because the Service still carries out its dual mission—protection and anticounterfeiting—questions arise immediately of how they could protect the nation's money supply if they are pulled from the Treasury Department. Neither the president nor politicians have addressed the dilemma.

The agency's investigative mission of pursuing counterfeiters and forgers is performed in as close to apolitical fashion as it is possible within a federal agency, but the mission for which the Service is most renowned, protection, is performed in the cauldron of presidential politics. Today, more than ever, protection has taken on an urgent tone because of terrorism and the array of weapons at the disposal of prospective assassins. Even as the Service struggles with personnel shortages because of an expanded list of protectees, and questions about which federal department it will serve under, Director Brian Stafford and his men and women must try to expand and improve its procedures.

Though few can argue that the effectiveness of Secret Service protection has increased markedly since the assassination of John F. Kennedy, the threats they face are escalating almost daily in technological sophistication— nerve gas, dirty bombs, biological agents, and shoulder-held missiles, to name only a few. No one yet knows whether the Secret Service's improvements in protective methods—which they cannot, of course, reveal—have kept pace with the increased severity of threats. Put another way, has the Service made innovative changes in its methods that are designed to meet the threats of the terrorist age or has it drifted along with a "more-of-the-same" response— the use of more resources to beef up the size of protective details rather than focusing upon improved technology of their own.

Words written all the way back in 1981 are even more apt following September 11, 2001. Former Assistant Secret Service Director James P. Kelly, writing with N. C. Livingstone, asserted that even then, the Service was losing the race to modernize its methods fast enough to keep pace with newer, more-deadly threats:

> It is true that nearly all attempts on the lives of U.S. presidents have been by single gunmen, but the Secret Service's orientation is nonetheless is reminiscent of the French General Staff in 1939: prepared to fight the previous war rather than the next one.
>
> The whole orientation of the Secret Service must be changed to anticipate the threat posed by terrorists. This will require novel strategies comparable to those developed by the crash program launched after President Kennedy's assassination.

In addition to methods and procedures, there is one suggestion that emerges. The Service's status as a dual-mission organization with personnel and resources shared between the protective mission and mission of chasing counterfeiters and forgers should be thoroughly evaluated by outside consultants, in order to determine its impact upon the effectiveness of protection. Though the Secret Service claims that the dual training of its agents and the rotating duty assignments between investigative and protective work produce more effective agents who are well rounded in their skills, this impression needs to be systematically analyzed. The Secret Service claims that it would be "impractical" to have personnel trained exclusively in protective work, but this assumes a dual-mission organization with existing limitations of money and personnel. The effects of September 11, 2001, might well mean that this maxim must be examined and perhaps changed in some way—perhaps agents training exclusively for protection.

Priorities and the allocation of resources could be changed: The "impractical" might become practical if it were discovered that protection would be much better served by a single-mission organizational structure. The notion that the quality of protection is enhanced by having well-rounded agents (with both anticounterfeiting and protection experience) is easily rebutted by the notion that effectiveness is reduced because organizational resources are spread too thinly. If ever a bureaucratic entity had a single, salient characteristic whose impact upon performance was in need of thorough and detached analysis, it is the Secret Service's status as a dual-mission agency. Such analysis may or may not confirm the Service's impression that the quality of protection is enhanced by its present structure.

As with family difficulties, sometimes the perspective of an outsider can be very valuable. One does not have to work within the agency to recognize some of the most glaring needs and problems that have come to light. If it turns out that some of the following suggestions are somehow off the mark or already adopted, so be it.

The long-standing practice of borrowing other federal agents to do protective work should be discontinued. This elevates congressional fiscal stinginess above maximum protection.

There has always been a latent hypocrisy to this practice. Whose lives merit the full contingent of the agency's front-line personnel: front-runners, candidates who emerge from inside the beltway? As with most of the recommendations here, this is purely a question of additional resources.

An increase in the number of women agents in high visibility roles is also needed. Even though the numbers have increased dramatically over the last two decades, there is still an image problem: female agents are not seen consistently and in appropriate numbers guarding high-visibility protectees. The media and the public need a more gender-balanced image. It is important that the agency culture not appear to have two subcultures based on gender. Female agents need more visible role models; female protectees, especially younger ones, would benefit at a number of levels.

In the crucial problem of politics versus protection, much more is needed. Agents training at Beltsville have included at least one seminar given by people with White House staff experience or presidential campaign managers. Call it political sensitivity training: understanding the eternal conflict between politics and protection from the "other side." Though agents gradually pick up the political tensions and negotiation tactics when they get their first protective assignment, a systematic head start would surely be helpful.

Similarly, a more generalized psychological orientation for agents would help. Before they seek individual counseling for job-related problems and pressures, basic training should include a general overview of the known psychological pitfalls. It is clear from recent events—from airline hassles to bar-room brawls—that agents need to be better grounded in a job where there is tremendous power and prestige but effective performance demands enormous self control and public anonymity.

There is also a need for more in house psychological expertise. As the protective mission has grown, more agents are making more judgment calls about whether a suspect is dangerous only to himself, to the president, or not at all. The general training of *how to judge* must be augmented by increased expertise. Obviously, a trained psychologist cannot accompany agents during every visit or interview, but the Sarah Jane Moore problem still exists and must be addressed with additional psychological expertise that is made available for this expanding task.

Though the agency resists outside reviews of organizational structure, it is time to do it again. For a relatively small organization, the Service's bureaucracy is an intricate, sprawling maze of units and functions that have grown rapidly: the Major Events Division, National Threat Assessment Center, and Technical Services Division. It is not simply that the agency's organizational chart—if there is one, it was not made available to the authors of this book—is probably bewildering; it is that the flow of information and effective functioning can be impeded by bureaucratic compartmentalization and proliferation. An outside management team should take a fresh look.

In the agency's public affairs, it is time to put the "public" back into the mix. In a democracy, key government agencies have a public face that accommodates the public's right to know while protecting privileged information. The resources should be allocated to get public affairs up and running so that it can answer questions and process requests for brochures. The failure to communicate with the public is bad for the agency's public image and bad for the goal of an informed citizenry. Public Affairs should not continue to be an emergency backup force for an overextended protective mission, with the public kept at a distance. Similarly, some thought might be given to affording greater public access to the agency's archive at its headquarters. Why should the public be banned from viewing exhibits created with tax dollars, unless they include top-secret artifacts?

There is agency need for improvement in liaison capacity. Likewise, the liaison function of the Office of Public Affairs and Governmental Liaison must be increased. The Service is understaffed for its increased missions and depends on other agencies—federal, state and local—for assistance with its protective mission and for intelligence data concerning threats. Thus the liaison function is not a nicety but an essential component of the Service's effectiveness. Liaison functions and networks with other agencies should be extensive, permanent, and given the highest priority. The office's head agent, James Mackin, responded that liaison duties "are with other law-enforcement and government agencies. Also [with] embassies of foreign countries whom our Uniformed Division protects or countries where we have an office oversees." That is a lot of liaison work. Again, if the agents responsible are out in the field filling personnel gaps, the vital networks could be neglected and weakened.

The U.S. Secret Service has largely avoided the major scandals that have plagued other agencies. The dismal failures and embarrassments that recently tarnished the CIA, FBI, and Immigration and Naturalization Service have been avoided. Still, for all of its professionalism, the agency seems to get too little respect from the executive and legislative branches of government. Some presidents find agents to be a political annoyance; some congressmen think the agency is an overpriced executive perk. Always scrambling for resources, the Service has seen a post–September 11 expansion of its mission that is Herculean. While billions of additional dollars are funneled to the military, the CIA, and Homeland Security, for a vastly expanded War on Terrorism, the Service's portion of these vast allocations has so far seemed inadequate for its mission. If this political system decided to treat it as a key national-security resource, and to resource it accordingly, its organizational performance would be far more effective in the myriad protective tasks we heap upon it.

When President John F. Kennedy was assassinated, there were approximately 300 special agents; in 1984, approximately 1,800. As of this writing, there are approximately 2,700. If this seems at all high, remember that the 1,800 agents did not protect Olympics or Super Bowls, did not interview high school killers, had nothing to do with ATM machines and credit card fraud, and did not protect congressional leadership, key White House advisors, or the secretary of state.

In ordinary times, divesting the Secret Service of its counterfeiting mission would seem a radical piece of organizational surgery that conflicts with the incremental pace of change that has typified the evolution of the federal bureaucracy. But all of this changed in June 2002 when President Bush proposed the most drastic and extensive reorganization of the federal government in the last half-century.

A cabinet-level department of Homeland Security would serve as an organizational umbrella for the fight against terrorism: A mega-agency the likes of which the U.S. bureaucracy has seen only once before—the Department of Defense. The new entity would incorporate a staggering twenty-two existing organizations and at least as many missions under one roof. These are not marginal, programmatic adjustments: It is a bold sweeping reconfiguration of the federal government. Immigration and Naturalizations Service, Customs Service, and the Coast Guard would all have a new home and supervisory structure, as would the U.S. Secret Service, plucked from its birthplace in the Treasury Department.

At this revolutionary juncture when proposals call for billions of dollars and hundreds of thousands of federal employees being uprooted and reassigned, this is the perfect opportunity to jettison the counterfeiting mission from the Secret Service: leave it in the Treasury Department where it logically belongs, as the protective mission shifts to Homeland Security. Even with this chaotic, uncharted new bureaucratic frontier, such a change will be undeniably painful for the Service. It would directly confront agency culture. It was the original mission in 1865, the only function that has remained consistent from inception to the present. It is clear from agents themselves that they relish this work: several even preferred it to protective work. Yet in terms of organizational theory, it does not make sense nor does it afford maximally effective protection. The indisputable fact is that this function should be performed by a separate agency.

Would we assign Green Berets to function as military police at various bases for years, before being assigned to combat duty? Would we assign FBI agents to do border patrol work for years before being assigned to fight organized crime or terrorism? The Service's insistence, to a person, that the skills are transferable between the two missions and that one enhances the other rings hollow, except in the most superficial sense. Treasury bills, credit cards and forged documents are simply not artifacts of the world of terrorism, political murder, and lone-nut assassins. The fact that those agents spend years protecting the currency with sporadic protective assignments before pulling full-time protective duty speaks for itself. This sea change—the potential change to the protective mission only—makes sense from virtually every frame of reference, save agency culture.

To avoid boredom and burnout—the alleged benefits of rotating between the two missions—agents could rotate among varying kinds of protective duties. A stint in protective intelligence work keeps an agent from eight-hour days of scanning crowds, listening for gunshots, and being on split-second alert, while keep him or her firmly, and broadly, within the protective mission. Even in the field, protecting Vice President Cheney is more taxing than protecting Nancy Reagan.

In the 1860s, Lafayette Baker and William P. Woods's operatives in their broad-brimmed hats, frock coats, and holstered Colt .45 revolvers could never have envisioned the challenges that now face today's agency as it devises new ways to protect President George W. Bush and other dignitaries from potential terrorist assassination plots. In a very real sense, the uneven, complex evolution of this colorful organization, from the Civil War to the Super Bowl, is a window into the tranformation undergone by the U.S. political system during the last 137 years. How the Secret Service meets its unprecedented challenges will tell the nation much about the course of the war against terrorism and about its continuing struggle to balance politics and protection in a democratic society.

# ENDNOTES

## Chapter 1: "Death to Traitors"

3      Philip H. Melanson, *The Politics of Protection,* New York: Praeger Publishers, 1984, p. 1.

3      The basic events of the Secret Service's evolution are described in "Excerpts from the History of the U.S. Secret Service, 1865-1975," Treasury Dept., U.S. Secret Service.

5      Jacob Mogelever, *Death to Traitors: The Story of General Lafayette C. Baker, Lincoln's Forgotten Secret Service Chief,,* Garden City: Doubleday & Company, 1960, Introduction.

7      Peter F. Stevens, "King of the Coney Men—Pete McCartney," *Traces Magazine,* Spring 1996, p. 38.

7      Ibid.

9      Ibid.

9      Ibid., p. 39.

10     Ibid., p. 41.

10     Ibid.

10     Ibid.

10     "Excerpts from Hist. of U.S. Secret Service, 1865-1975."

11     David R. Johnson, *Illegal Tender: Counteerfeiting and the Secret Service in Nineteenth-Century America, Washington and London:* Smithsonian Institution Press, 1995, p. 69.

11-12   Walter S. Bowen and Harry Edward Neal, *The United States Secret Service, Phil. & N.Y:* Chilton Company, 1960, p. 12.

14     Bowen and Neal, p. 147.

14     Ibid

14      Ibid., p. 149.

15      Ibid., p. 147.

17      Ibid, p. 149.

17      Ibid., p. 152.

18      Johnson, p. 81.

18      Ibid.

18-19   Ibid.

19      "Secret Service Excerpts, 1865–1975."

19      Johnson, p. 82.

19-20   Ibid., p. 135.

21      Bowen and Neal, p. 151.

22      Ibid.

23      Johnson, p. 177.

24      *The New York Times,* May 27, 1894, p. 2

**Chapter 2: "The Work of Protecting Me Has At Last Become Legal"**

27      Philip H. Melanson, *The Politics of Protection,* p. 6

27      *Moments in History,* U.S. Secret Service, published by the Dept. of the Tresury, 2001, p. 73.

28      Jeffrey-Jones Rhodri, *American Intelligence,* NY: The Free Press, 1977, p. 18.

30      *Public Report of the White House Security Review,* Secret Service, 1995, p. 28.

30      *Congressional Record,* 1st Session, 1902, 35, pt. 3: 3049.

30-31   House Committee on the Judiciary, "Protection of the President and the Suppression of Crime Against Government," 57th Congress, 1st Session, 1422, 13, 1902.

31      Ibid.

31      Warren Commission document, File 22, "Records Relating to the Protection of the President, 1954 and 1963-64."

32      "Excerpts from Hist. of Secret Service 1865-1975," p. 17.

32      Ibid.

32      Johnson, p. 178.

33      "Excerpts," p. 18.

34      *Moments in History—The U.S. Secret Service,* p. 17.

40      *Wall Street Journal,* April 14, 1922, p. 1.

40      *Moments in History,* p. 75.

44      Frank Donner, *The Age of Surveillance,* NY: Vintage Books, 1981, pp. 56-57.

44      Ibid.

# ENDNOTES

45      Ibid.

48      *Moments in History,* p. 22.

49      *Buffalo (NY) Times,* "Counterfeit Ring Believed Smashed by Secret Agents," July 2, 1935, p. 1.

49      Ibid.

51      Anthony Summers, *Official and Confidential: The Secret Life of J. Edgar Hoover,* NY: G.P. Putnam & Sons, 1993, p. 165.

52      Ibid.

53      David McCullough, *Truman,* NY: Simon & Schuster, 1992, p. 813.

55      *Moments in History,* p. 23.

57      Ibid., p. 47.

## Chapter 3: Losing Lancer—The JFK Assassination

59      Warren Commission, "Memorandum of Conference," March 13, 1964, 3 pages.

60      Warren Commission Hearings, V. 18, pp. 707-708.

61      *Final Report,* NY: Bantam Books, 1979, p. 290.

64      Warren Commission Report, p. 31.

64      Anthony Summers, *Conspiracy,* NY: McGraw-Hill, 1980, p.1.

65      U.S. Congress, "Report of the Select Committee on Assassination, pp. 35-36.

65      Interview of Retired Agent Winston Lawson by Philip H. Melanson, March 6, 2002.

65      *Report of the Warren Commission on the Assassination of President Kennedy,* NY: Bantam, 1964, p. 29.

65      Warren Commission Report, p. 41

67-68   Warren Commission Hearings, v. 4, "Testimony of Winston G. Lawson, p. 351.

68      Warren Commission Document No. 3, Exhibit 12 to Report of the U.S. Secret Service on the Assassination of President Kennedy, " Dillon Memorandum."

70      Warren Commission Report, pp. 426-427.

70      Vincent Palamara, *The Third Alternative,* 1993, p. 167.

70      Melanson, *The Politics of Protection,* pp. 167-168.

70      "Inside the Secret Service," Discovery Channel documentary, Sept. 1995.

71      Warren Commission, Document No. 3, B 1 a.

71      *The New York Times, The Witnesses: Highlights of the Hearings Before the Warren Commission on the Assassination of President Kennedy,* NY: Bantam, 1964, p. 534.

72      U.S. House of Representatives, Select Committee on Assassinations, Washington, D.C.: U.S. Gov. Printing Officee, 1979, v. 11, pp. 527-528.

72      Warren Commission Hearings, v. 3, p. 244.

72      House Assassination Committee, v. 11, p. 528.

72      Ibid.

73      *The Witnesses,* "Testimony of Clinton J. Hill," p. 40.

73      Warren Commission File No. 22, "Records Relating to the Protection of the President."

73      Warren Commission Report, p. 29.

74      Ibid.

74      *Newsweek,* Dec. 2, 1963, p. 2; Vincent Palamara; *The Third Alternative,* self-published, p. 2.

75      Ibid.

75      William Manchester, *The Death of a President,* NY: Harper & Row, 1967, p. 160.

75      Warren Commission Report, pp. 64-65.

76      *The Witness,* p. 39.

76      "Secret Service Report of Agent Clint Hill," Nov. 30, 1963; Warren Commission, v. 18, pp. 138-144.

77      Palamara, p. 2 ("Presidential Limoousine").

78      Manchester p. 290.

78      Warren Commission Report, 1964, p. 641.

78      Ibid.

78-79   Ibid.

79      Mary Gallagher, *My Life With Jacqueline Kennedy,* NY: McKay, 1969, pp. 343, 351.

79      Warren Commission Hearings, v. 4, p. 352.

79      Peter Dale Scott, *Deep Politics and the Death of JFK,* Berkeley, CA: Univ. of Cal. Press, 1993, pp. 277-278.

80      Anthony Summers, *Conspiracy,* NY: Paragon House, 1989, p. 8.

80      Ibid.

81      Warren Commission Report, p. 429.

81      Warren Commission Report, p. 430.

81      Melanson, *The Politics of Protection,* p. 173.

82      Warren Commission File No. 22, "Criminal Intelligence Section Preparation for the Visit of John F. Kennedy to Dallas on November 22, 1963," p. 1.

82      Ibid., "Report of Detective W.W. Biggis.

82      U.S. House of Representatives, "Report of the Select Committee on Assassinations, p. 135.

# ENDNOTES

82     Warren Commission Document 853, a, p. 2, "Protective Research Section Assessment of Manuel Rodriguez, Jan. 14-17, 1964.

82     Summers, *Conspiracy,* pp. 427-428.

83     "Criminal Intelligence Section Preparation" Document.

86     Melanson, p. 177-178.

87     "Inside the Secret Service," Discovery Channel Documentary, Sept. 1995.

88     Interview of Retired Agent Winston Lawson by Philip H. Melanson, March 20, 2002.

88     Warren Commission Hearings, v. 18, pp. 707-708.

88     Robert Groden and Harrison E. Livingston, *High Treason,* NY: Conseervatory Press, 1989, p. 147.

89     George Rush, Marty Venker, *Confessions of an Ex-Secret Service Agent: The Marty Venker Story,* NY: Donald I. Fine, 1988, p. 38.

## Chapter 4: Agents in Action

92     "Appointment in Laurel," *Newsweek,* May 29, 1972, p. 18; "George Wallace's Appointment in Laurel," *Time,* May 29, 1972, p. 18.

93     Ibid.

93-94  Ibid.

94     Ibid.

94     Ibid.

94     Ibid.

95     "Appointment in Laurel," *Newsweek,* p. 22.

95     Ibid.

95     *U.S. News & World Report,* May 29, 1972, p. 16.

96     James W. Clarke, *American Assassins,* Princeton, NJ; Princeton Univ. Press, 1982, p. 184.

97     "Appointment in Laurel," *Newsweek,* p. 22.

97     Ibid.

97     Laurens Pierce, "He Carried a Camera and a .38," *TV Guide,* May 1, 1982, pp. 22-23.

98     Ibid.

99     Clarke, p. 191.

99     Robert D. McFadden, "Suspect Was Defender of Manson," *The New York Times,* Sept. 6, 1975, p. 1.

100   Clarke, p. 153.

100   Ibid., p. 153.

101   Gerald R. Ford, *A Time To Heal,* NY: Harper & Row, pp. 311-312.

102   Clarke, p. 160.

103 "Can the Risk Be Cut?" *Newsweek,* p. 321.
103 "Interview with Sara Jane Moore," *Los Angeles Times,* Sept. 25, 1975, pp. 1-3.
104 "Ford's Second Close Call," *Time,* Oct. 6, 1975, p. 13.
104 "Can the Risk Be Cut?" *Newsweek,* p. 21.
105 "The New Orleans Plots," *Time,* Sept. 23, 1973, pp. 11-12.
105 Ibid.
105 Ibid.
106 *The New York Times,* August 21, 1973, p. 20.
107-108 Quoted material from Clarke, pp. 127-142.
109 Ibid.
110 *Moments in History,* p. 26.

**Chapter 5: "Go to George Washington Hospital—Fast!"**

113 Norman Black, "Agent Talks About Reagan Shooting," Bryan, Texas, *Eagle,* April 30, 1983, p. 1.
116 U.S. Dept. of the Treasury, "Management Review of the Performance of the U.S. Dept. of the Treasury in Connection with the March 30, 1981, Assassination Attempt on President Ronald Reagan," 1981, pp. 7-12, 43-49.
116 Ibid., p. 47.
116 Ibid., p. 49.
116 Ibid.
119 "Minute by Minute," Documentary on the Assassination Attempt Against President Reagan, Arts & Entertainment Channel, June 27, 2002.
120 *Time,* April 13, 1981, p. 38.
120 Ibid.
120 Ibid.
120 "Minute by Minute."
121 Philip Taubman, "Explosive Bullet Struck Reagan, FBI Discovers," *New York Times,* April 13, 1981, p. A 1.
121 "Minute by Minute."
122 Richard D. Lyons, "Witnesses to Shooting Recall Suspect Acting 'Fidgety' and 'Hostile,' *New York Times,* March 31, 1981, p. 1.
124 U.S. Dept. of Treasury Performance Report, p. 1.
125 Ibid., p. 22.
127 Ibid., p. 73.
127 "Can the Risk Be Cut?" *Newsweek,* Oct. 6, 1975, p. 19.
128 Interview of Retired Agent Timothy J. McCarthy by Philip H. Melanson, Feb. 1, 2002.

# ENDNOTES

128-129 Interview of former Agent Chris Van Holt, April 8, 1999.

129     "Minute by Minute."

## Chapter 6: Fortress White House?

130     *White House Security Review, Secret Service,* Chap. 4: Creation of the White House Complex, p. 20.

131     Ibid., p. 22.

132     Ibid., p. 24

135     *Congressional Globe,* 27th Congress, 2nd Session, p. 854, (1842).

136     *Congressional Record,* Statute 511, August 23, 1842.

139     "Echoes from the White House," PBS Documentary, Washington, D.C., 2001.

139     Secret Service Memo, December 1941, National Archives.

140     David McCullough, *Truman,* pp. 880-881.

141     *Security Review,* p. 27.

142     Ibid., pp. 13-14.

145     *Rand Report,* Spring 1995, p. 2.

147     Ibid.

## Chapter 7: A Few Good Men and a Very Few Good Women

152     Interview of Secret Service Public Affairs Director Robert Snow by Philip Melanson.

153     Interview of Former Agent Tim McCarthy by Philip H. Melanson, Feb. 1, 2002.

153     Interview of Ex-Agent by Melanson, Feb. 8, 2002.

154     Declassified CIA Documents, 1973.

157     Treasury Dept. Management Review, August 1981, p. 68.

160     Ibid., p. 38.

163     Jack W. Germand and Jules Witcover, "Nixon's Wise Decision to Drop Secret Service Protection," *Boston Globe,* March 16, 1985, p. 19.

166     Interview of Retired ATF Agent Thomas O' Reilly, Feb. 20, 2002.

166     Ibid.

166     Ibid.

168     U.S. Secret Service, "Special Agent," Washington, D.C. (pamphlet).

170     A.O. Sulzberger, Jr., "Secret Service Uniformed Division Stays Close to Capitol Diplomats," *New York Times,* June 10, 1980.

172     Howard Kurtz, "Executive Protection Racket," *The Washington Monthly,* Oct. 1978, p. 49.

173 Tim McCarthy Interview.
173 Tim McCarthy Interview.
173 "Special Agent" (pamphlet).
173 Ibid.
174 Ibid.
174 Ibid.
174 Ibid.
176 Interview of Current Agent, 2002.
177 Ibid.
177-178 Interview of Agent Mary Ann Gordon by Philip H. Melanson.
178 "The Secret Service's Dirty Little Secret," Jessica Reeves," *Time.* com, Feb. 24, 2000.
178 Ibid.
180 "Inside the Secret Service" (documentary, 1995).
180-181 Tim McCarthy Interview.
181 Ibid.
181 Ibid.
181 Interview of Robert Snow by Philip H. Melanson.
181 Ibid.
182 Ibid.
183-184 "Inside the Secret Service," documentary, Discovery Channel, 1995.
185 "Inside the Secret Service."
187 Loretta Tofani, "A Totally Up Front White House," *Boston Globe,* April 8, 1982, pp. 1 and 10.
187 Ibid.
192 *Moments in History,* The Secret Service, p. 25.
193 Ibid., p. 28.

**Chapter 8: The Politics of Protection**

196-197 Treasury Dept. Report on Attempted Assassination of President Reagan, August 1981.
197 *Newsweek,* May 29, 1972, p. 19.
197 Robert Blair Kaiser, "Presidential Candidates Disagree on Value of Secret Service Watch," *New York Times,* Feb. 10, 1980, p. 1.
198 *Newsweek,* Oct. 6, 1975, p. 19.
199 Ibid.
199 Ibid.
200 Kaiser, p. 1.
200 Ibid.

# ENDNOTES

200    Ibid.

201    *Time,* Oct. 6, 1975, p. 12.

201    "Did the Secret Service Drop Its Guard?" *U.S. News & World Report,* April 13, 1981, pp. 27-29.

201    Interview of Melody Miller by Philip H. Melanson, Jan. 27, 2002.

202-203 Interview of Eileen Parise by Philip H. Melanson, Jan. 27, 2002.

203    Interview of Former Democratic Presidential Aide by Philip H. Melanson, Jan. 24, 2002.

203    Ibid.

204    Interview with former Democratic National Committee Liason by Philiip H. Melanson, Jan. 19, 2002.

205    Interview of Former Secret Service Agent by Philip H. Melanson, Feb. 8, 2002.

205    Interview of Ex-Agent Chris Von Holt, April 18, 1999.

206    Fred P. Graham, "Tighter Security Rules Stir Friction in Capitol," *New York Times,* June 26, 1972, p. 24.

207    "Secret Service Settles Suit for False Arrest," *New York Times,* June 26, 1980, p. B 7.

207    Ibid.

208    Graham, "Tighter Security Rules," p. 24.

208    Ibid.

208    "Could the Secret Service Predict Violent Behavior?" National Academy of Sciences *News Report,* June 1982, p. 16.

208    *Newsweek,* Oct. 6, 1975, p. 19.

209    James B. Kirkham *et al* (eds.), *Associations and Political Violence,* NY: Bantam, 1970, p. 120.

210    Kaiser, p. 1.

210    Ibid.

212-213 Frank Donner, *The Age of Surveillance,* p. 227.

216    N.C. Livingstone, "From JFK to Reagan: What the Secret Service Thinks of the Presidents They Protect," *Washingtonian,* Sept. 1981, pp. 170-171.

217    Loretta Tofani, "A Totally Up Front White House," *Boston Globe,* April 8, 1982, p. 10.

217    N.C. Livingstone and James Kelly, "Could the President Survive a Real-Life James Bond Movie?" *Washingtonian,* Sept. 1981, p. 177.

217    *New York Times,* July 26, 1974, p. 29; Nov. 3, 1974, p. 23.

217    Ibid., July 3, 1974, p. 23.

218    Treasury Dept. Report, August 1981.

218-219 "Danger for Presidents Seen in Political Moves," *New York Times,* Sept. 23, 1981, p. 17.

219     Dan Rather and Paul Gates, *The Palace Guard,* NY: Harper & Row, 1974, p. 23.

219     "Can the Risk Be Cut?" *Newsweek,* April 13, 1981, p. 51.

220     Interview of Former Secret Service Agent by Philip H. Melanson, Feb. 2002.

222     Joel Allenback, "Inside the Secret Service," *Washington Post,*July 9, 1993.

222     Ibid.

223     Ibid.

**Chapter 9: "The Sixth Sense"**

227     *Secret Service Training Manual.*

228     *Treasury Dept. Review of the Assassination of President Reagan,* 1981, p. 41.

230-231 *Training Manual.*

234     John Burns, "Security Men Still Keep Nixon Under Close Guard," *New York Times,* Feb. 25, 1972, p. 14.

234     V.N. McCarthy, with Philip W. Smith, *Protecting the President: The Inside Story of a Secret Service Agent,* NY: William Morrow and Co., 1985, p. 43.

234-236 Interview of Ex-Agent Chris Von Holt, April 8, 1999.

237     Dennis V.N. McCarthy, p. 143.

237     Tim McCarthy Interview.

237     Robert Blair Kaiser, "Presidential Candidates Disagree on Value of Secret Service Watch, *New York Times,* Feb. 10, 1980, p. 1.

237     "Can the Risk Be Cut?" *Newsweek,* April 13, 1981, p. 51.

239     *Secret Service Training Manual.*

239     *Newsweek,* April 13, 1981, p. 51.

240     *Secret Service Training Manual;*   National Archives Record Group 22, Warren Commission Documents, p. 98.

241     *Training Manual.*

242-243 Treasury Dept. Review, 1981, p. 28.

244     Ibid.

246     "The New Profile," Protective Intelligence and Threat Investigations," U.S. Dept. of Justice, Robert A. Fein and Bryan Vossekuil, July 1998.

247     Ibid.

247     Ibid.

250-251 CNN, Washington Bureau, Jean Meserve: "Witnesses—Secret Service Agent Didn't Act Angry," Jan. 4, 2002; "Pilot, Secret Service Agent Trade

Charges," Jan. 4, 2002; Douglas Kiker, "Bush has Sharp Warning on Case of Agent Removed from Flight," *Boston Globe,* Dec. 29, 2001, p. 10; Connie Cass, "Airline Defends Barring Agent," *Boston Globe,* Jan. 4, 2002, p. 23.

253    Kevin A. O'Reilly, Interview with Special Agent Charles Collins, December 1981.

254    "Inside the Secret Service," documentary, Discovery Channel, 1995.

254    John Weisman, "Why American TV Is So Vulnerable to Foreign Propaganda," *TV Guide,* June 12, 1982, p. 12.

## Chapter 10: Booze, Burnout, Demands, and Depression

259    "Mike Wallace Interview of Agent Clint Hill," Dec. 1975. Grolier Educational Corporation: Vital History Casettes, Encyclopedia Tape #2, Side A.

261    Marty Venker, with George Rush, *Confessions of an Ex-Secret Service Agent,* p. 154.

261    Howard Kurtz, "The Executive Protection Racket," *Washington Monthly,* Oct. 1978, pp. 47-49.

262    "Service-wide E-mail from Director Stafford," provided to *U.S. News & World Report,* May 24, 2002.

262    *Confessions,* p. 154.

262    "Guarding the President—A Rugged Job," *U.S. News & World Report,* Dec. 10, 1979, p. 63.

262    *Confessions,* p. 154.

262    Interview of Current Special Agent by Philip H. Melanson, March 13, 2002.

262-263 Ibid.

263-264 *Confessions,* pp. 157-163.

264-265 Ibid.

266    Ibid., p. 224.

266    Ibid.

266    Ibid.

267    Ibid., pp. 224-225.

267    Ibid.

268    Ibid., 225-226.

268    Ibid.

268    Ibid.

268-269 "Guarding the President," p. 63.

269    *Confessions,* p. 227.

269-270 *Confessions,* p. 224.

270    *Confessions,* p. 224.

271    "Secret Service"—Cover Story—*U.S. News & World Report,* June 17, 20022.

271    Ibid.

272    Interview with Current Special Agent, March 2002.

### Chapter 11: Family Matters—Protecting First Ladies and First Kids

273-274  "Inside the Secret Service," documentary, Discovery Channel, 1995.

274    Dennis V.N. McCarthy, *Protecting the President,* pp. 172-173.

274    Ibid.

275    Ibid.

275    Andrea Stone, "Spontaneity, Security Odds for Clinton," *USA Today* (website), Nov. 20, 1992.

276    Dennis V.N. McCarthy, pp. 173-178.

276-277  Anthony Summers, *Arrogance of Power: The Secret World of Richard Nixon,* NY: Viking, 2000, p. 326.

277    McCarthy, pp. 174-175.

278    Ibid., p. 175.

278    Ibid., p. 181.

278    McCarthy, pp. 173-178.

279    Ibid.

279-280  Ibid., pp. 176-177.

281    "The Special Rules of Bushworld," *The Hightower Lowdown,* August 2001, p. 3.

281    Ibid.

281    Josh Tyrangiel, "This Is What You Call Protection?" *Time,* June 11, 2001, p. 18.

282    McCarthy, pp. 173-178.

### Chapter 12: Getting To Know You—Presidential Psychology

283    Peter Baker, "Proximity,: Personal Space," *Washington Post,* 1998.

284    John Davis, *The Kennedies: Dynasty and Ddisaster,* NY: McGraw Hill, 1984, p. 303.

284    Arthur Schlesinger, *A Thousand Days: John F. Kennedy iin the White House,* Boston: Houghton Miffin, 1965, p. 1024.

284    Interview of Former Special Agent by Philip H. Melanson, Feb. 2002.

285    Ibid.

285    Ibid.

# ENDNOTES

285     Ibid.

285     Ibid.

285     Ibid.

285     Ibid.

286     Dennis McCarthy, *Protecting the President,* p. 140.

286     James Roosevelt and Bill Libby, *My Parents: A Differing View,* Chicago: Playboy Press, 1976, pp. 200-201.

286     *U.S. News & World Report,* April 13, 1981, p. 28.

286     Sherman Adams, *Firsthand Report,* NY: Harper, 1961, p. 84.

287     "Guarding the President," p. 74.

287     Elizabeth Drew, *Behind the Scenes in American Government,* Boston: Little Brown, 1983, p. 21.

287     Ibid.

288     "Promimity," 1998.

289     Jimmy Carter, *Keeping the Faith: Memoirs of a Former President,* NY: Bantam Books, 1982, p. 27.

289     Dennis McCarthy, *Protecting the President,* pp. 135-136.

289     Ibid.

290     Ibid., p. 132.

291     N.C. Livingstone, "JFK to Reagan," p. 170.

291     Betty Ford, with Chris Chase, *Time of My Life,* NY: Harper & Row, 1978, p. 177.

291     Jack Valenti, *A Very Human President,* NY: W.W. Norton, 1975, pp. 175–176.

291     Dwight L. Tays, "Presidential Reaction to Security," *Presidential Studies Quarterly,* Fall, 1980, pp. 600-609.

292     Dennis V.N. McCarthy, pp. 134-134.

292     Frank Cormier, *LBJ: The Way He Was,* Garden City, NY: Doubleday, 1977, p. 136.

293     Tays, p. 603.

294     "Can the Risk Be Cut?" *Newsweek,* April 13, 1981, p. 18.

296     Tays, p. 601.

297     Dwight D. Eisenhower, *Mandate for Change, 1953-1956,* Garden City: Doubleday, 1963, p. 75.

297     Ibid, pp. 267-270.

297     "Can the Risk Be Cut?" p. 18.

298     Ibid.

299     Margaret Truman, *Harry S. Truman,* NY: William Morrow, 1973, pp. 200–202.

299     "Mike Wallace Interview with Clint Hill," Dec. 1975.

299    "Ford Won't Capitulate to Would-Be Killers," *New York Times,* Sept. 23, 1975, p. 26.
300    "Spontaneity, Security at Odds for Clinton, Nov. 20, 1992.
300    Ibid.

**Chapter 13: Breaking the Code of Silence—From John F. Kennedy to Ken Starr**

305    "Inside the Secret Service," documentary, Discovery Channel, 1995.
305    Joel Allenback, "Inside the Secret Service," *Washington Post,* July 9, 1993, p. 11.
305-306 Interview of Former Agent Chris Von Holt, April 8, 1999.
307    Peter Baker, "Starr vs. Secret Service," *Washington Post,* May 15, 1998, p. AO 1.
307    Ibid.
307    Ibid.
307    Ibid.
307-308 Anthony Summers, *Arrogance of Power,* p. 104.
308    Interview with Former Special Agent, January 9, 2002.
308    Ibid.
308    Baker, p. 1.
309    Anthony Summers, *Arrogance of Power,* p. 247.
309    Ibid., p. 38.
309    Interview with Former Special Agent, Jan. 9, 2002.
310    Ibid.
310    Seymour M. Hersh, *The Dark Side of Camelot,* Boston: Little Brown, 1997, pp. 226-229.
310    "Secrets of the Service—Pressures and Problems Confront the Police Agency That Protects the President," *U.S. News & World Report,* June 17, 2002, cover story.
311    Ibid.
311    Ibid.
312    Interview of Former Agent Chris Von Holt, April 8, 1999.
312    Tim McCarthy Interview, Feb. 1, 2002.
312    "Secrets of the Service."
312    Tim McCarthy, Feb. 1, 2002.
313    "Secrets of the Service."
313    Interview with Former Special Agent, Jan. 9, 200w.
313    "Secrets of the Service."

# ENDNOTES

## Chapter 14: A Whole New Ballgame—The Secret Service in the Age of Terrorism

315    Interview with Special Agent, March 13, 2002.

316    John Minnery, *How To Kill,* v. 4, Boulder, Col.: the Paladin Press, 1979, p. 23.

319    Letter from Muharem Kerbegovic to Philip H. Melanson, 1983 (The Alphabet Bomber").

321    Rand Report, 2000.

322    Interview of Eileen Parise by Philip H. Melanson, Jan. 27, 2002.

322    Interview of Retired Agent Robert Snow by Philip H. Melanson.

323    Rand Report 2000.

323-324 Interview of Washington Security Expert, Jan. 27, 2002.

324    Ibid.

324    David Montgomery and Arthur Santana, "Inaugural Intruder Credits God," *Washington Post,* Jan. 26, 2001, p. B1.

324    Ibid.

325    Ibid.

325    Ibid.

325    Ibid.

325    President Bush's Address to the Nation," Sept. 11, 2001, 1:or p.m.

327    Anne E. Kornblut, "White House Off Limits to Most, Tries To Spread Cheer," *Boston Globe,* Dec. 4, 2001, p. 23.

327    Ibid.

328    Interview of Eileen Parise, Jan. 27, 2002.

328    Tim McCarthy Interview, Feb. 2002.

330    Interview of current Special Agent, March 2002.

330    Ibid.

330-331 Ibid.

## Conclusion

334    N.C. Livingstone and James P. Kelly, "Could the President Survive a Real-Life James Bond Movie?" *Washingtonian,* Sept. 1981, p. 177.

# BIBLIOGRAPHY

Among the hundreds of written sources culled by the authors, the following proved especially useful.

Anson, Sam, *They've Killed the President.* New York: Bantam, 1975.

Baughman, U. E. and Leonard Wallace Robinson. *Secret Service Chief.* New York: Harper & Brothers, 1962.

Bloom, Murray Teigh. *Money of Their Own.* New York: Charles Scribner's Sons, 1957.

Bowen, Walter S. *U.S. Secret Service: A Chronicle.* Unpublished manuscript, 1955.

Bowen, Walter S. and Harry Edward Neal. *The United States Secret Service.* Philadelphia: Chilton Company-Book Division Publishers, 1960.

Burnham, George P. *American Counterfeits: How Detected, And How Avoided.* Springfield, Massachusetts: W. J. Holland, 1875.

Clarke, James W. *American Assassins: The Darker Side of Politics.* Princeton, N.J.: Princeton University Press, 1982.

Collins, Herbert Ridgeway. *Presidents on Wheels.* Washington: Acropolis Books, 1971.

Crotty, William J. (ed.) *Assassins and the Political Order,* New York: Harper & Row, 1971.

Davis, John. *The Kennedys: Dynasty and Disaster.* New York: McGraw-Hill, 1984.

Department of the Treasury. *Annual Report of the Chief of the Secret Service Division for the Fiscal Year Ended June 30, 1904.* Washington: 1904.

Department of the Treasury. *Excerpts from the History of the United States Secret Service 1865–1975.* Washington: 1975.

# THE SECRET SERVICE

Department of the Treasury. *United States Secret Service Moments in History 1865–1990*. Washington 1990.

Donner, Frank. *The Age of Surveillance*. New York: Vintage Books, 1981.

Donovan, Robert J. *The Assassins*. New York: Harper & Brothers, 1952.

Dorman, Michael. *The Secret Service Story*. New York: Delacourt Press, 1967.

Hersh, Seymour M. *The Dark Side of Camelot*. Boston: Little, Brown and Company, 1997.

Janke, Peter. *Guerrilla and Terrorist Organizations: A World Directory and Bibliography*. New York: Macmillan, 1983.

Johnson, David R. *Illegal Tender: Counterfeiting and the Secret Service in Nineteenth Century America*. Washington: Smithsonian Institute Press, 1995.

Kirkham, James B. *et al.* (eds.). *Assassination and Political Violence*. New York: Bantam, 1970.

Lesberg, Sandy. *Assassination in Our Time,* London: Peebles Press and Bobbs-Merrill, 1976.

McCarthy, Dennis V. N. and Phillip W. Smith. *Protecting the President*. New York: William Morrow and Company, Inc. 1985.

McCullough, David. *Truman*. New York: Simon & Schuster, 1992.

McKinley, James. *Assassinations in America*. New York: Harper & Row, 1977.

Montana, Patrick J. and George S. Roukis, *Managing Terrorism: Strategies for the Corporate Executive*. Westport, Conn: Quorum Books, 1983.

Neal, Harry E. *The Story of the Secret Service*. New York: Grosset & Dunlap, 1971.

Neal, Harry. *The Secret Service in Action*. New York: The Free Press, 1977.

Palamara, Vincent. *The Third Alternative: Survivor's Guilt, The Secret Service and the JFK Murder*. 1998.

Posner Gerald. *Case Closed: Lee Harvey Oswald and the Assassination of JFK*. New York: Random House, 1993.

Reilly, Michael R. *Reilly of the White House*. New York: Simon & Schuster, 1946.

Rhodri, Jeffeys-Jones. *American Intelligence*. New York: The Free Press, 1977.

Roberts, Marcia. *Looking Back and Seeing the Future: The United States Secret Service 1865–1990*. Dallas: Taylor Publishing Company, 1991.

Sheafe, Larry B. *The United States Secret Service: An Administrative History*. Unpublished manuscript, 1983.

Sifakis, Carl. *The Encyclopedia of American Crime*. New York: Facts on File, Incorporated, 1982.

Smith, Laurence D. *Counterfeiting*. New York: W. W. Norton & Company, 1944.

Starling, Edmund W., and T. Sagrue. *Starling of the White House*. New York: Simon & Schuster, 1946.

Summers, Anthony, *Arrogance of Power—The Secret World of Richard Nixon*. New York: Viking Books, 2000.

# BIBLIOGRAPHY

Venker, Marty, with George Rush. *Confessions of an Ex-Secret Service Agent.* New York: Donald I. Fine, 1988.

Wilkie, Don. *American Secret Service Agent.* New York: A. L. Burt Company, 1934.

Wise, David. *The Espionage Establishment.* New York: Random House, 1967.

Youngblood, Rufus. *20 Years in the Secret Service: My Life With Five Presidents.* New York: Simon & Schuster, 1973.

## Articles

Baker, Peter. "Starr Versus the Secret Service," *Washington Post,* May 15, 1998, p. 1.

"Can the Risk Be Cut?" *Newsweek,* April 13, 1981, pp. 18–21.

Chapman, Stephen. "The Secret Service's Biggest Secret." *New Republic,* Jan. 24, 1981, pp. 18–21.

Clines, Francis X. "Culling the Secret Service's 400 List." *New York Times,* May 8, 1981, p. 51.

"Did the Secret Service Drop Its Guard?" *U.S. News & World Report,* April 13, 1981, pp. 27–29.

Freedman, Lawrence Z. "The Assassination Syndrome." *Saturday Evening Post,* July/August 1981, pp. 66–68.

"Guarding the President: The Job Gets Tougher." *U.S. News & World Report,* Dec. 10, 1979, p. 63.

Hassel. Conrad V. "The Political Assassin." *Journal of Police Science and Administrations,* 4 (Dec. 1974) pp. 399–402.

Hightower, Jim. "The Special Rules of Bushworld." *The Hightower Lowdown.* August 2001, p. 3.

Kaiser, Robert Blair. "Presidential Candidates Disagree on Value of Secret Service Watch," *New York Times,* Feb. 10, 1980, p. 1.

Kaplan, John. "The Assassins." *Stanford Law Review,* 59 (May 1967) 1110–51.

Kurtz, Howard. "Executive Protection Racket." *Washington Monthly,* October 1978, pp. 47–50.

Leeper, E. M. "Could the Secret Service Predict Violent Behavior?" *News Report,* National Academy of Sciences, Jan. 1982, pp. 14–19.

Livingstone, N. C. "From JFK to Reagan: What the Secret Service Thinks of Presidents They Protect." *The Washingtonian,* Sept. 1981, pp. 170–71.

—"Taming Terrorism: In Search of a New U.S. Policy." *International Security Review,* Spring 1982, pp. 17–34, with and James Kelly: "Could the President Survive a Real-Life James Bond Movie?" *Washingtonian,* Sept. 1981, pp. 168–76.

Melanson, Philip. "Secret Service Survives on a Prayer." San Antonio *Express News,* Aug. 14, 1983, p. 7H.

Mohr, Charles, "For the Secret Service, a Hail of Bullets Disrupts 'Routine Duty' With President." *New York Times,* March 31, 1981, p. A2.

Robinson, Wilse G. "A Study of Political Assassinations," *American Journal of Psychiartry,* 121 (May 1965) 1060–64.

"Secrets of the Service—Pressures and Problems Confront the Police Agency That Protects the President," *U.S. News & World Report,* June 17, 2002.

Slomich, Sidney J. and Robert E. Kantor. "Social Psychopathology of Political Assassination." *Bulletin of Atomic Scientists,* 25 (March 1969), p. 9–12.

Stone, Andre. "Spontaneity, Security at Odds for Clinton." *USA Today* (website), November 20, 1992.

Sullivan, Joseph E. "Security Forces Prepare for Ford Visit to Newark." *New York Times,* Oct 2., 1975, p. 83.

Tays, Dwight L. "Presidential Reaction to Security: A Longitudinal Analysis." *Presidential Studies Quarterly,* Fall 1980, pp. 600–9.

Tyrangiel, Josh. *"This* Is What You Call Security?" *Time,* June 11, 2001, p. 18.

**Public Documents**

Central Intelligence Agency. *International Terrorism in 1979,* Springfield, Va. National Technical Information Services, 1979.

Department of the Treasury. *Management Review on the Performance of the U.S. Department of the Treasury in a Connection with the March 30, 1981, Assassination Attempt on President Ronald Reagan.* Washington, D.C., 1981.

*Report of the Warren Commission on the Assassination of President Kennedy.* Washington, D.C.: U.S. Gov't. Printing Office, 1964.

U.S. Congress House. *Report of the Select Committee on Assassinations.* Washington, D.C.: U.S. Gov't. Printing Office, 1979.

U.S. Congress, Senate, Select Committee on Government Operations with Respect to Intelligence. Alleged Assassination Plots Involving Foreign Leaders. Washington, D.C.: U.S. Gov't Printing Office, 1975.

Select Committee on Government Operations with Report to Intelligence. *The Investigation of the Assassination of President John F. Kennedy: Performance of Intelligence Agencies.* Washington, D.C.: U.S. Gov't. Printing Office, 1976.

U.S. Secret Service. *A Brief History of Presidential Protection.* National Archives, Warren Commissions files, Record Group #22, Records Relating to the Protection of the President. Washington, D.C., U.S. Secret Service, 1964.

*Election Year 1980.* Washington, D.C.: U.S. Secret Service, 1980.

*Excerpts From the History of the United States Secret Service.* Washington, D.C.: U.S. Treasury Dept.

# BIBLIOGRAPHY

*Rowley Report.* National Archives, Warren Commission file #22, Records Relating to the Protection of the President. Washington, D.C: 1964.

*The Secret Service Story.* Washington, D.C.

*Special Agent.* Washington, D.C.

*Training Manual,* National Archives, Warren Commission files, Record Group #22, Records Relating to the Protection of the President. Washington D.C., 1954.

# ACKNOWLEDGMENTS

Without the skill and support provided by the extensive involvement of my wife Judith, this project could not have been completed. For that I am extremely grateful. My research assistants Jessica Crandall, Siobahan Costello, and Rachel Lapointe provided a rich array of data. The help of Scott Lang, Don Howard, Lisa Porto, John Judge, and Bill Kelly is greatly appreciated. Much thanks to my agent Frank Weimann for his faith in my work, and to Philip Turner at Carroll & Graf for his guidance and support.

Philip H. Melanson
August, 2002

# INDEX

# INDEX

# ABOUT THE AUTHORS

**PHILIP H. MELANSON, PH.D.,** is Chancellor Professor of Political Science, University of Massachusetts Dartmouth. He is an expert on political violence and governmental secrecy, and has done original research into the JFK, RFK, and Martin Luther King assassinations, prompting appearances on the CBS Evening News, BBC, History Channel, and Discovery Channel. He has served as a consultant to the (JFK) Assassinations-Records Review Board, and is Coordinator of the RFK Assassination Archives at the University of Massachusetts Dartmouth. Using the Freedom of Information Act and the Privacy Act he has obtained the release of approximately 200,000 pages of previously classified government documents. He serves as chair of the executive board and senior research fellow at the Center for Policy Analysis, and lectures widely to colleges and universities, law enforcement agencies and at military installations. He has published articles in such publications as *The Nation, Politics and Society, Comparative Political Studies and Library Journal.* Prior to *The Secret Service,* his most recent book was *Secrecy Wars.*

The News and Features Editor of the *Boston Irish Reporter,* **PETER F. STEVENS** is a journalist and author whose books include *The Voyage of the Catalpa: A Perilous Journey and Six Irish Rebels' Escape to Freedom; The Rogue's March: John Riley and the St. Patrick's Battalion, 1846–1848; The Mayflower Murderer and Other Forgotten Firsts in American History; Notorious and Notable New Englanders;* and *Links Lore: Dramatic Moments and Neglected Milestones from Golf History.*